D0722512

10-26-8 96₹ F.

MUSIC:
A View from Delft

Edward T. Cone

Music:
A View from Delft

Selected Essays

Edited by

Robert P. Morgan

The University of Chicago Press
Chicago and London

Edward T. Cone, composer and theorist, is professor
emeritus of music at Princeton University. Robert P.
Morgan is chairman of the Department of Music at the
University of Chicago.

The University of Chicago Press, Chicago 60637
The University of Chicago Press, Ltd., London

98 97 96 95 94 93 92 91 90 89 54321

Library of Congress Cataloging-in-Publication Data

Cone, Edward T.
   Music, a view from Delft.

   Bibliography: p.
   Includes index.
   1. Music—History and criticism.   I. Morgan,
Robert P.   II. Title.
ML60.C773M9 1989   780'.9   88-20659
ISBN 0-226-11469-4
ISBN 0-226-11470-8 (pbk.)

Contents

Preface

During the past few decades Edward T. Cone has written some of the most perceptive commentary on music that has appeared in our time. In a period in which serious musical scholarship has been largely confined to specialized studies focused on isolated topics, couched in a language seemingly designed to discourage all but a tiny group of initiates, Cone has viewed the field from an unusually comprehensive perspective, writing in a style notable for its literacy and clarity. His essays have encompassed theoretical as well as historical issues and have addressed both the formal and expressive aspects of music. Not content with technical analysis alone, Cone has grappled with the more elusive questions of aesthetic meaning and critical interpretation. His sensitive and detailed readings of individual compositions, always undertaken with a view toward larger and more general concerns, possess a humanistic dimension all too rare in recent musical discourse.

The breadth of Cone's writings reflects his diverse background and wide range of interests. Having pursued musical studies at Princeton University within a comprehensive liberal-arts framework, he has continued to cultivate a deep interest in the other arts and humanities that profoundly colors all of his work. Trained as both composer and pianist, Cone has maintained all three sides of his musical personality—composer, performer, and writer—with remarkable balance. One consequently senses the "complete musician" in everything he writes. His is not the work of someone interested in abstraction and obfuscation, but of a musician concerned with the flesh and blood of a living art.

Anyone making a selection of essays from Cone's output is faced with difficult decisions. Despite a body of material of such consistent quality that any selection would produce an interesting and valuable result, hard choices had to be made to produce a book that would be both satisfying as a collection and reflective of the particular emphases in content and approach evident in Cone's writing. In general, the essays were chosen according to two essentially contradictory criteria. Some are included because they are so well known and so frequently cited as to be immediately associated with the author (e.g., "Analysis Today" and "Stravinsky: The Progress of a Method"); while others, originally published in smaller journals or in non-musical ones (it is typical of Cone that some of his finest work has appeared in literary and general humanistic publications), are here because they have achieved less visibility in musical circles (e.g., "Inside the Saint's Head" and "Three Ways of Reading a Detective Story"). In addition, an attempt has been made to represent to the degree possible the various stages of Cone's writing career. (The chronology ranges from "The Old Man's Toys: Verdi's Last Operas," published in 1954, to "The World of Opera," which appears for the first time in this volume.)

Due to the scope of material, much has had to be omitted that one would have liked to include. Those familiar with Cone's work will no doubt be disappointed to find some of their favorite essays missing; to them the editor can offer only sympathy and apology. For those desiring a more comprehensive view of Cone's work, however, a complete bibliography of the published writings is included as an appendix to the present volume.

The essays have been grouped into three sections corresponding to the three areas on which Cone has especially concentrated as a writer: 1) the methodology of musical analysis, aesthetics, and criticism; 2) the relationships between music and the literary texts with which it is associated; and 3) the history of compositional practice during the past two centuries. Within each section the essays are arranged to produce a logical progression, without regard for the original order of publication.

Although the last two headings require no explanation, the first may need some comment. It is characteristic of Cone's thinking that the seemingly disparate disciplines of musical analysis, aesthetics, and criticism are viewed as different aspects of a single activity. Matters of musical structure are inevitably tied to those of musical meaning and interpretation; and meaning and interpretation, more than mere subjective effusions, are intimately connected with matters of structure and technique. Indeed, this could perhaps be said to form, in brief, the core of Cone's "analytic method" (although I suspect he would deny having such a thing). The reader progressing sequentially through the first section of the book will thus be struck by the degree to which the articles interconnect with and mutually reinforce one another, often despite marked differences in topic, and by the way the final article ties together various strands previously initiated.

Since all of the articles included are reflections of a single, integral conception of music, there are numerous additional interrelationships that cut across the three categories provided for their organization. The essays in the second and third sections, for example, illustrate the more general philosophical and methodological issues developed in the first part. Questions of text setting, properly the focus of the second section, are touched upon in both of the outer ones (see especially the essays on Verdi and Schoenberg in the final section). Similarly, the article on Brahms in the first part, and those on Berlioz and Verdi in the second, would be equally at home in the third part. All ultimately connect with and reinforce one another.

Some years ago, in one of his earliest published articles, Cone argued for a central position for the teacher-artist in the academic community, proposing in lieu of an educational approach dedicated to "the accumulation of facts for their own sake" one "based on the primary role of creative thinking."[1] I know of no one who has lived up to this challenge more fully than Mr. Cone himself. Both as Professor of Music at Princeton University, from which he recently retired, and as writer, composer, and pianist, he has provided a remarkably individual, and unmistakably creative, voice.

Mr. Cone's own contribution to the editing of this volume has been considerable, ranging from advice on the choice of particular essays to help with countless details. For that, and even more for the many years I have enjoyed a personal association with him, first (and in all important senses still) as his student, and then as his friend and colleague, I feel extremely fortunate and grateful.

Robert P. Morgan

1. Edward T. Cone, "The Creative Artist in the University," *American Scholar* 16, no. 2 (1947): 193.

Introduction

Almost ten years ago I had the honor of selecting and editing the essays of Roger Sessions for publication in book form. Naturally I had no idea then that today I should find myself indebted to my friend and former student Robert Morgan for a similar service; but because of my own experience I can fully appreciate the discrimination, the judgment, and the sympathy that have informed every phase of his work. I am deeply grateful to him for accomplishing for me what I should probably never have undertaken for myself.

I have other debts to acknowledge as well, debts that become increasingly evident to me as I reread the present selection. For I daresay that none of these essays would have been written had it not been for a remarkable trio of teachers who supervised my undergraduate and graduate education in music: Roy Dickinson Welch, Roger Sessions, and Oliver Strunk.

Welch, who founded the Department of Music at Princeton University, was preeminent neither as a musician nor as a scholar; but he believed passionately in the educational value of music, and it was as an educator that he made his invaluable contribution to American musical life. He was, as it were, a musical humanist; and he convinced his students that music was not just a craft but, as a fine art, one of the humanities as well. He was the first to encourage me to consider teaching and writing, alongside composition and performance, as important components of my calling. Moreover, he was not like those academic administrators who, realizing their own inadequacies as creators or scholars, surround themselves with mediocrities in order to ensure their own superiority. He insisted on building the strongest possible music faculty, and in pursuit of this aim he called both Sessions and Strunk to Princeton.

If Welch expounded the masterpieces of musical literature as works of art, Sessions, imparting the theory and practice of that art, never let one forget that what he was teaching was first of all a craft. "Whatever you do in music," he counseled me when I graduated, "don't forget that you are equipped to be a dirt musician." The metaphor was ugly but it was a term of praise. Thanks to him I need not be afraid of getting my hands dirty playing with the real stuff of music, whether as composer, performer, or teacher, for I had learned the craft. That craft included not only the writing but also the analysis of music. Sessions, unlike many composers of his day, believed in the value of analysis; but unlike many analysts, he used it as a practical tool, not as the support of a theoretical superstructure nor as the exemplification of one. For him analysis, like composition and performance, was a way of grubbing around in the actual musical soil. That is why he lost interest in it when he saw it tending to become abstract and speculative (see "In Defense of Song").

For Welch and Sessions alike, a study of the repertoire was an essential aspect of musical education, but it was Strunk who insisted that the relevant repertoire was not confined to music composed since 1700—or even 1500. Not that he was merely a specialist in old music: on the contrary, his vision of musical education as ideally encompassing our entire tradition showed up most of his colleagues and students as the narrow specialists we were—in modern music. (Strunk's emphasis on our Near Eastern and Western roots may seem parochial to today's advocates of exposure to the "musics" of the entire world. His response would probably have been, "I haven't learned all of our own music yet.") His insistence on historical evidence as a prerequisite to valid criticism was salutary. His use of documents demonstrated the virtue of the true polymath who not only accumulates a vast store of knowledge but also keeps it constantly at his disposal—in Strunk's case, to clarify the subject at hand by significant connections or suggestive comparisons. When he contrasted Gothic structure with Romanesque decoration in polyphony, or when he traced the expansion of the tonally dual exposition from a binary prelude of Bach to the disintegrating sonata form of a Tchaikovsky symphony, he showed how scholarship could be put to work in the service of style analysis to yield aesthetic illumination.

Music as craft, music as art, music as documentation: that is the threefold subject presented by my mentors. It is actualized in the three-sided object of music criticism: the composition, with its three aspects of structure (or form), expression (or content), and historical significance.

For all serious criticism of music, as of any art, must deal, explicitly or implicitly, with the fundamental question: What is the relation of content to form in this particular work in its historical context? Or more simply: What, if anything, does *this* work communicate?

I stress the particularity because the question has no one type of answer applicable to all compositions in all times in all places. No generalization will do, whether negative, as in Stravinsky's notorious dictum, or positive, as in appeals to emotional expression, or neutral, as in the tempting but probably meaningless formulation that the form of music *is* its content. The problem of musical meaning is of course only one aspect of the problem of meaning in the fine arts, and for this more general question a universal answer is even more obviously impossible. Unlike science, which seeks ever more general laws, art remains stubbornly specific. The locus of value is the individual work of art, and the really important questions must be answered anew for each artist, for each work—sometimes for each new viewing or reading or performance of each work. That is why the study of music, and of art in general, affords me more genuine intellectual stimulation than any other activity: I can almost endlessly study one set of data (a composition, a picture, a poem) with the profit and delight of a constantly renewed sense of discovery. (I am sure there is a comparable pleasure to be gained from the natural sciences, but I am insufficiently trained to be able to enjoy it. Hence the latest explanation of the mystery surrounding the origins of the universe soon bores me, and I turn gratefully to the investigation of Verdi's mysterious way with the six-four chord.)

It follows that no critical formulation can ever be final. For that reason I am not ashamed of the inconsistencies and even outright contradictions that one may occasionally find among the essays reprinted here. On the contrary: I should consider total consistency a sign of obstinate self-assurance. On the other hand, I might have saved myself some embarrassment if I had taken the principle of specificity more seriously. I should have accepted the truth of one hackneyed but nonetheless useful principle: that categorical generalizations, whether of fact or opinion, are always false. Or, since that itself is a categorical generalization, the obvious modification: most categorical generalizations are false.

Keeping that in mind, I could have avoided some blatant errors of fact, such as a remark I made (in "Inside the Saint's Head") concerning the extra brass choirs in Berlioz's Requiem. "After the 'Lacrymosa,'" said I, sweepingly but falsely, "only the trombones are called on again."[1] This and other gross mistakes are quietly corrected in the present volume.

1. Edward T. Cone, "Inside the Saint's Head," *Musical Newsletter* 1, no. 4 (1971): 17.

Statements of opinion—often masquerading as statements of fact—are not so easy to alter. Besides, I feel that I should stand by them as representative of my views at the time of writing. So you will find Saint-Saëns still excoriated for his "amazing lack of style" ("Musical Theory as a Humanistic Discipline") and Debussy for the "impoverishment" of his rhythm and melody ("A View from Delft"); and you will read that Wagner gives us arias "by the orchestra, not the singer" ("The Old Man's Toys").

Even more difficult to root out, because of their protective coloration, would have been the concealed generalizations that often underlie discussions of specific instances. Such a case is my choice of Stravinsky's *Movements* as representative of his twelve-tone methods ("The Uses of Convention"). That composition turns out to have constituted, in Stravinsky's own mind, a challenge to analysts;[2] and even those well versed in the master's technique of rotation have only recently begun to unravel the knots embedded here.[3] By singling out such a problematic work I implied, incorrectly, that it is a typical example of Stravinsky's twelve-tone writing. Actually, the case I was making, that "Stravinsky's concern with the twelve-tone system is more with its vocabulary and texture than with its structure," could have been made equally well with one of the "pieces in which he had dealt with twelve-tone materials in a much more, if you wish, traditional way," to use Babbitt's phrase.[4]

My most egregious generalization, "An introduction is an expanded upbeat," is enshrined in the pages of a book.[5] Fortunately I was later given—or I took—the rare opportunity of reviewing my own work. At that time I offered a much more discriminative characterization of the role of the introduction, accusing myself of having been caught in "the snare of generalization."[6] Yet a colleague expressed great disappointment on reading my recantation, for he found the new version less forceful. Such is the power of—not just the printed word, but the *bound* printed word.

That is why periodicals serve such a valuable purpose. They encourage the essay format that I, along with many others, find congenial precisely because every critical pronouncement should be considered tentative—a condition symbolized by the soft, yielding covers of most journals. The

2. See Igor Stravinsky and Robert Craft, *Memories and Commentaries* (Garden City, N.J., 1960), 100.
3. See Milton Babbitt, *Words about Music* (Madison, 1987), 107–16.
4. Ibid., 109.
5. Edward T. Cone, *Musical Form and Musical Performance* (New York, 1966), 24.
6. Edward T. Cone, "*Musical Form and Musical Performance* Reconsidered," *Music Theory Spectrum* 7 (1985): 158.

very word "essay" implies an attempt to report on a stage of an ongoing investigation from which further bulletins can be issued from time to time. Thus "Inside the Saint's Head" contains passages on Berlioz's *Requiem* that are expanded and complemented in "Berlioz's Divine Comedy"; and "Schubert's Unfinished Business" generalizes an argument initiated in the discussion of a technical detail in my earlier "Schubert's Promissory Note."[7]

The inception and temporary outcome of another investigation—one still continuing—are exhibited by "Words into Music" and "The World of Opera" respectively. Here there is a middle term: *The Composer's Voice,*[8] a book that elaborates the conclusions of the original essay into an aesthetic of song, expanded to include opera. A modified and, I hope, improved version of that operatic theory furnishes the basis for "The World of Opera." But my work in that direction has suggested in turn a fresh perspective on non-operatic song. As a result, one task on which I am currently engaged consists in applying the relevant new concepts to song composition in general. The essay that will no doubt eventuate will thus be a great-grandchild, as it were, of the old "Words into Music."

Especially satisfying is the conversation with oneself that occasionally arises when one article criticizes another. When I wrote an autobiographical piece on my encounters with Matisse's *Blue Nude*[9] I quoted a passage from "A View from Delft" discussing the relation of representation and design in pictures: "The two structures, abstract and representational, must be more than parallel. They must fuse by analogy, so that they become two ways of looking at one single, basic structure—two points of view, either of which can be interpreted as an analogue of the other." In the *Blue Nude,* however, I found tension rather than fusion, "tension which reflects the struggle of the artist with his material: his insistence on forcing the human body into a position controlled by a powerful design, and the body's counter-struggle to retain its independence." And so in order to do justice to Matisse's picture, the author of "A View from Delft" came up with an alternative version of the passage quoted from that essay. As a substitute for the second sentence he offered: "On the one hand, they may fuse by mutual analogy; on the other, they may remain in dynamic tension—locked, as it were, in a perpetual struggle." (I would, as a matter of fact, accept that as a permanent emendation; but

7. Edward T. Cone, "Schubert's Promissory Note," *19th-Century Music* 5, no. 3 (1982): 233–41; reprinted in Walter Frisch, ed., *Schubert: Critical and Analytical Studies* (Lincoln and London, 1986), 13–30.
8. Edward T. Cone, *The Composer's Voice* (Berkeley and Los Angeles, 1974).
9. Edward T. Cone, "Aunt Claribel's 'Blue Nude' wasn't easy to like," *Art News* 79, no. 7 (1980): 162–63.

in accordance with the principle enunciated above, the essay as reprinted here retains the original version.)[10]

Another privilege that accrues to the author of an article published in a periodical is the right of responding to criticism. Strictly speaking, the authors of books reserve a similar right; yet they exercise it much more cautiously. Unless a reviewer has been guilty of glaring misstatement or hopeless misinterpretation, it is considered somehow beneath the dignity of a book writer to defend himself. (Even in an obviously justified case he may prefer to enlist a friend to do the job.) Not so the writer of an essay in a journal, for whom replying to letters of criticism is not only a privilege but a duty toward the editors, who usually welcome the controversy (unless the magazine is *The New Yorker*). When "Beyond Analysis" appeared in *Perspectives of New Music*,[11] it provoked a spirited response, partially in agreement, partially in attack, from David Lewin. Entitled "Behind the Beyond: a Response to Edward T. Cone," it was published, along with my counter-reply, in a subsequent issue.[12] I wish there were space to reprint them here, for the colloquy raised and, I hope, clarified important issues concerning the relations among theory, analysis, and criticism.

Another article, "Analysis Today," elicited two somewhat negative reactions when it originally appeared in *The Musical Quarterly*.[13] Neither was addressed to the *Quarterly*; hence I had no chance of immediate reply. Nor would any have been appropriate; for one article was a review of the entire issue, and the other was an independent essay taking off from some of my observations. Both of them raised points relevant to my present concerns, however, so I should like to offer here a belated defense.

Mel Powell, in reviewing the *Quarterly* issue as a whole,[14] correctly pointed out that although my article was entitled "Analysis Today," it focused on compositions written twenty or thirty years before, while dismissing certain classes of more recent music as unanalyzable. Calling for new methods to meet new problems, he offered two alternative titles for my own attempt: "Analysis Yesterday" and "No Analysis Today." Quite so. The point that I did not make explicit in the essay—probably

10. The slight expansion of this essay over the previously published version is due, not to the incorporation of new material, but to the restoration of passages that had to be sacrificed to the exigencies of magazine space.

11. Edward T. Cone, "Beyond Analysis," *Perspectives of New Music* 6, no. 1 (1967): 33–51.

12. David Lewin, "Behind the Beyond: a Response to Edward T. Cone," *Perspectives of New Music* 7, no. 2 (1969): 59–72.

13. Edward T. Cone, "Analysis Today," *The Musical Quarterly* 46, no. 2 (1960): 172–88. Entitled "Problems of Modern Music," this issue was based on the 1959 Princeton Seminar in Advanced Musical Studies; hence the special attention it elicited.

14. Mel Powell, review in *Journal of Music Theory* 4, no. 2 (1960): 259–69.

because it was not clear even to me at the time—is that analysis must accept the necessity of a time lag. Although for practical purposes it cannot ignore compositions of the recent past, its pronouncements must be considered preliminary. Analysis today should ideally concern itself with works of no less than a decade ago. Works of art need that much time to begin taking their place in history and tradition; analysts need it in order to be secure from both the shock and the seductiveness of novelty. After all, we are just starting to come to terms with the works of the early "atonal" period. And what many took for adequate treatments of the twelve-tone classics were simply note counts. Only much later were the really interesting analytical jobs undertaken. (As for those works that I found unanalyzable, I submit that they did and still do resist analysis— as I have defined it. I grant that the new approaches Powell was hoping for may yet be developed, but over twenty years have passed and I am still waiting.)

The other critique, by Robert Smith, dealt with the illustrative examples I had drawn from the traditional repertoire.[15] He took me to task for what he considered a farfetched explanation of the entrance of the recapitulation in the Prestissimo of Beethoven's Sonata Op. 109. Rejecting my attempt to bind the entire passage by means of an overarching II$^\sharp$-V$^\sharp$-I, he found the source of the puzzling II$^\sharp$-I of mm. 104–5 in the similar V$^\sharp$-IV of mm. 4–5. But can't both analyses tell us something of value? Must we reject one in order to accept another? For my part, I welcome Smith's suggestion. To use the terminology of "Sound and Syntax," Smith concentrated on "succession," whereas I was concerned with "progression." Naturally I still see my own account as presenting a wider perspective on the passage, encompassing a view that Smith's derivation of detail serves to confirm rather than invalidate.

Even if two analyses are at odds, so that both cannot simultaneously be heard as applicable, we are still not required to make a final choice between them. Each may contribute something to the understanding of a passage that may have a multiple meaning, like the duck-rabbit of the psychologists. So I disagree on more than purely personal grounds with Smith's pronouncement that anyone analyzing the opening of *Tristan und Isolde* as I do, making A rather than G$\sharp$ a chordal tone in m. 2, "is in a position to qualify for a hearing aid."[16] The situation is ironic, for I chose that bit of illustrative analysis precisely because I thought it was well known and widely accepted. After all, it had behind it the weight of considerable authority: apparently Kurth, Schenker, Sessions, and Tovey

15. Robert Smith, "This Sorry Scheme of Things . . . ," *The Music Review* 22, no. 1 (1961): 212–19.
16. Ibid., 218.

all needed hearing aids.[17] To be sure, Smith could equally well summon support for his choice of G♯ over A as the principal tone—Hindemith and, proleptically, Mitchell.[18] But the superiority of an analysis is not determined by the number or the eminence of its champions. Rather, it is probable that when a question like this one remains moot for so many years, very likely it will never be settled for the simple reason that there is no one solution.

I myself have modified my views on the *Tristan* Prelude, even to the extent of entertaining one hypothesis—the putative imitation of the opening A-F by the E-G♯ of mm. 1–2—that I had dismissed in my essay as "what I call prescription: the insistence upon the validity of relationships not supported by the text." In a contribution to the celebration of Milton Babbitt's sixtieth birthday[19] I revealed him as the source of that "wrong-headedness," as I had called it, for now I was prepared to discuss it more sympathetically. To my surprise I found that a derivation which I had originally refused to accept as valid—and which I still find difficult to hear in its initial context—could be construed as underlying a number of important later developments in the opera. Moreover, by taking seriously the linear connection that it implied, I arrived at a more flexible interpretation of the disputed opening. I could now perceive a gradual transformation of role from the appoggiatura G♯ of m. 2 (yes, I still hear A as its resolution), through an ambiguous B in m. 5, to an overtly chordal D in m. 10—three corresponding points in the sequence, but with three different functions.

My point is not that all analyses are valid—far from it. But no single analysis can ever be *the* correct analysis of any work that is even moderately complex. It may even be an indication of quality for a work to elicit many analyses. (I recall an examination in which each of three candidates posited a different Schenkerian *Urlinie* for the same short piece—whose identity I unfortunately forget. Thus it was variously claimed that the composition embodied the descent of a third, of a fifth, and of an octave. All the papers received passing grades, for each of them made acute observations about the structure of the work.) So I try not to dismiss any

17. Ernst Kurth, *Romantische Harmonik und ihre Krise in Wagners "Tristan"* (Berne and Leipzig, 1920), 44; Heinrich Schenker, *Harmonielehre* (Stuttgart and Berlin, 1906), 374, 408; Roger Sessions, *Roger Sessions on Music,* ed. Edward T. Cone (Princeton, 1979), 14; Donald Francis Tovey, *The Forms of Music* (New York, 1956), 68.
18. Paul Hindemith, *The Craft of Musical Composition* (New York, 1945), 1:210; William J. Mitchell, "The Tristan Prelude: Techniques and Structure," in *The Music Forum* (New York and London, 1967), 1: 174–76.
19. Edward T. Cone, "Yet Once More, O Ye Laurels," *Perspectives of New Music* 14, no. 2; 15, no. 1 (1976): 294–306.

analysis so long as it can engage my interest. (To be sure, some that seem striking at first glance cannot survive scrutiny: what is novel often turns out to be purely arbitrary. A student who insisted that Schumann's Novellette No. 1 was in D minor captured my attention until I found out that his only reason for thinking so was that the first sonority is a D-minor triad.)

The reason there can be no single definitive analysis is that true analysis, as distinct from mere description on the one hand and prescription on the other, involves evaluation. Indeed, an analysis *is* an evaluation, for it weighs the comparative significance of each event, or phase, or aspect of a work. The discipline is thus not a science but a branch of criticism.[20]

I concluded my reply to David Lewin by insisting that "we should call upon all modes of knowledge, including the theoretical, the analytical, and the intuitive, to help us achieve a proper critical response to a piece of music."[21] I have already pointed out that "all modes" must also include the historical, and one can easily think of others that should be added to complete a fuller listing: the biographical, the sociological, perhaps the psychoanalytic. Nobody can really "call upon all" of them, but one can at least maintain a balance among the approaches suggested by those modes one does control. That is what I have tried to do, not in each essay I have written, but in their totality, and in such a way that they can fruitfully interact with one another. And here once again I must express my gratitude to Robert Morgan, for I believe that his selection, a balanced choice, permits that interaction.

20. In this connection see Christopher Lewis, "Mirrors and Metaphors: Reflections on Schoenberg and Nineteenth-Century Tonality," *19th-Century Music* 11, no. 1 (1987): 26–42. His analysis of Schoenberg's *Traumleben* is somewhat at odds with mine (in "Sound and Syntax") precisely because of our different evaluations of the role of an F-major complex within an E-major tonality.
21. Edward T. Cone, "Mr. Cone Replies," *Perspectives of New Music* 7, no. 2 (1969): 72.

1

Aesthetics, Criticism, and Analysis

Music: A View from Delft

Although this discussion is to be concerned primarily with music, it received its impetus from the puzzled delight long afforded me by the contemplation of Vermeer's *View of Delft*. The picture has been a perennial joy—first in anticipation through reproductions; then in actuality at the Mauritshuis; now in retrospect, again through reproductions, but supported by the memory of the original. The puzzlement arose because I was unable to account for my reaction to this apparently objective, realistically detailed representation that, without obvious sentimental or personal associations, was nevertheless deeply moving. Of course, to have dismissed the problem would in no way have interfered with my continued enjoyment; yet it seemed to me worthwhile to try to uncover the reasons for the picture's great attraction, in the hope that in so doing I might reveal some principle of wider application to painting in general, and to the other arts.

The method by which I arrived at a preliminary solution was to compare actual scenes with hypothetical Vermeer views. What did my own eyes fail to catch that the painter's depiction would have revealed? Some kind of unity, perhaps; for on this much all traditional aesthetics seems to be agreed. In the case of the *View of Delft* it is true that on whatever aspect one concentrates, one finds visual coherence—in its surface texture, in its unobtrusive composition, in its subtle harmony of color, in its pattern of light and shade. Whether the painter found these designs in the scene before him and emphasized them, or whether he imposed them upon a formless visual matrix, the high degree of relation they exhibit is perhaps the most obvious difference between the painted landscape and the actual one. But it is not the sole difference, for the casual observer misses not only the unity in the scene before him but its bewildering multiplicity as well. It is the endless complexity of every visual event that furnishes the painter with his apparently inexhaustible store of motifs, and the most complete view is the one that does greatest justice to the variety of these forms.

The Vermeer view, then, embraces the complexities of the scene and relates them in an all-pervading unity. The artistic value of the representation is the result of the tension between these two poles. To enjoy the *View of Delft* because of its unity of design, or because of its complexity of motif, or even because of both, is to miss the point. Perception comes at the breath-catching moment of realization that the tension between the two has been brought into balance by the vision of the artist. The test of the balance is whether the unity seems to grow out of the complexity on the one hand, and to engender it on the other. The two aspects are not merely realized simultaneously; they are organically united. What is more, the unity is immediately perceptible within the medium of the art itself—it is primarily visual, not intellectual.

Further investigation led to the conclusion that the poles of unity and complexity are only the first and most important of numerous possible tensions, and that on a higher level the artist's job is to create a perceptible unity out of the complexity resulting from just this multiplicity of tensions. This complexity I call textural complexity, each of its components being a dimension of the texture. Such dimensions in a picture might consist of the following sets of poles: detail vs. whole, brushstroke vs. area, color in turn vs. form, light, and line (as the demands of the design in color might compete in turn with those of three-dimensionality, of patterned chiaroscuro, and of linear arabesque). The completed picture must not only resolve each of these polar tensions, but also combine the resolutions in such a way that they appear to be the multiple aspects of a single all-inclusive structure.

Crucial for painting is the tension between abstract and representational form, for the moment the element of representation enters a picture every motif must respond equally to the demands of the abstract design and of the depicted subject. It is not enough that the demands of a polar couple be satisfied simultaneously; they must be satisfied together organically, so that each member of the pair grows out of the other. This is the basic problem of representation, whose successful solution produces the glories of Vermeer, whose misunderstanding results in the academicism of Bouguereau, and whose avoidance permits the non-art of popular illustration. Thus the two structures, abstract and representational, must be more than parallel. They must be fused by mutual analogy, so that they become two ways of looking at one single, basic structure—two points of view, either of which can be interpreted as an analogue of the other. The position demanded by a figure's dramatic action must contribute to the movement required by the design. The arrangement of a composition must be achieved by the figures of their own accord. It should be impossible to look at the successful picture as either representation or design alone; each should imply the other.

If the apparently multiple structures comprised in the complete work are united in this way, none can lead away from the others, that is, out of the picture. The narrative element of the story-telling picture too often does just that; hence it is no accident that most of the great paintings of this kind have been based on subjects so familiar that each scene can be accepted as a self-contained visual unit, as in the well-known stages of the Passion story. At the same time, pictures suggest that the added dimension of dramatic action, properly handled, makes possible exciting complexities otherwise impossible of achievement in the art; so perhaps Sir Joshua was not far wrong in putting the historical painter at the head of his list. What this implies is that for fullest enjoyment we want the medium of art to be saturated: to be used to the fullest extent in every possible dimension. If this is so, then non-objective painting should prove ultimately less satisfying than painting that successfully exploits the tension between subject and design. For many observers that is in fact the case.

For the same reason, the richest novel or drama is the one whose metaphorical elements are integrally and indissolubly bound up with the manifest subject—as opposed to conventional allegory on the one hand, in which the two strands run parallel without cogent connection, and to pure narrative on the other, in which the symbolic dimension is completely lacking.

II

These principles—of polar tension, of fusion by mutual analogy, and of saturation—I now propose to apply to music. Two points must be stressed at the outset, both so obvious that they may otherwise be forgotten. The first is that the unity of the musical composition must be perceptible within the medium: it must be heard. The second point is that the apparently simple surface of some music may in fact conceal great richness. The unfortunate result of Gounod's attempt to add a melody to Bach's prelude suggests that the latter, in spite of its superficial transparency, is in fact a highly saturated composition of considerable textural complexity.

Since music is a temporal art, certain possibilities are open to it that are unavailable to painting. Time, of course, yields the dimension of rhythm, which will be discussed in some detail later. It also makes possible a kind of suspended saturation: the development of an idea which on first presentation may seem of insufficient moment, but which through its treatment grows in interest, its true purport being revealed only gradually. Beethoven's Diabelli Variations is a triumphant example of a completely saturated form arising from an unpromising hypothesis.

Time also permits the development of the tension between the detail and the whole in a new and important way. In painting, the relevance of the detail to the entire composition is ideally immediately comprehensible. In music, the appearance of each new detail is an occasion for suspense: how will it be related to its context, and how will the context fit into the whole? One could write a history of music—at least of the last two hundred years—in terms of varying solutions (and dissolutions) of the problems arising from this particular polar couple.

The detail/whole tension is of course not the only source of suspense, which is such an important characteristic of all time-arts that without some form of it the medium inevitably seems insufficiently saturated. Traditional tonality was fortunate in having at its command a built-in technique, so to speak, for producing and controlling suspense; and one of the fundamental tasks of the atonal idiom has been to find substitutes or analogues for its powerful effects.

Time, then, is the source not only of opportunities and advantages but of problems and responsibilities as well. Other difficulties, equally fundamental, arise from another characteristic of the musical medium: its abstractness. These have to do with the question of expressive content, and with the role of so-called extra-musical elements—verbal, programmatic, or purely emotional. Are these just extraneous adjuncts, at best useless and at worst dangerous? Are they optional embellishments? Or are they properly speaking not extra-musical at all but intrinsic to the art? Perhaps the argument from Delft can throw some light here.

I shall not try to decide whether or not music can express or communicate or embody emotions or moods or types of activity, nor shall I try to explain how such expression or communication or embodiment might be possible. I propose a simpler investigation. Assuming that music can express emotion (and you may substitute whatever verb and object you prefer), I shall try to determine a few of the consequences.

If such expression is possible, its presence will open another dimension much as the representational subject does in painting. But just as the

16

mere presence of the subject in a painting is far from being a guarantee of quality and may even be a detriment if clumsily handled, so with the expressive content in music. To say of a composition that it conveys sorrow or embodies agility or induces contemplation is to make a statement of only preliminary aesthetic importance. The artistic value arises from the coalescence of the abstract form and the expressive design in such a way that each can be interpreted as a consequence of the other. Every event demanded by the purely musical pattern must correspond to an event demanded at that point by the psychical pattern. If the composition is completely successful, the two streams, musical and psychical, of the mingled flow are felt as analogically fused—in effect as one. Our realization of the unity thus created produces an excitement like that occasioned by the breathtaking moment of perception we experience before the Vermeer.

It follows that if such enrichment of the medium is possible, failure to take advantage of it is a violation of the principle of saturation. I think this is rarely a danger. If expression of this type is possible at all, in a medium apparently so unrepresentational, it is probably because its vehicle is as deeply embedded within the medium as the meaning of words in a language. It would be as hard to write music without significant expressive pattern as to write literature independent of verbal connotations.

The question next arises whether the use of a specific extra-musical program would not offer similar, and even greater, enrichment. If so, then the principle of saturation would suggest that Liszt and Strauss were on the right track after all. But I shall try to show that the desirability of a program does not necessarily follow from the preceding argument, and that the use of one exposes a work to real danger.

Expression of the type so far expounded neither requires nor invites non-musical formulation. It is based on largely preconscious and subconscious attitudes that are uncovered only by the action of the music itself and hence defy every effort at verbalization. It is no wonder that most composers are unable or reluctant to give an account of this aspect of their work, since it depends on processes of which they are at most only partly aware. For convenience, I shall call expression of this kind, characteristic of what is usually called absolute music, inherent expression.

The program, on the other hand, by definition a non-musical formulation of content, suggests expression of quite a different kind—literal, specific, descriptive—the appropriateness of which cannot be deduced from that of inherent expression. Assuming as before its possibility, we see that content of the second kind can hardly appear in a composition except as the result of deliberate effort on the part of the composer. Its nature and origin always encourage suspicions that it is wholly or partly adventitious—doubts that have no occasion to arise with respect to the inherent expression of absolute music. It is possible, of course, and frequent in the case of the best program music, for the composer to ignore the more literal aspects of his subject and to use it purely as a suggestive source of musical thought. The results then fall into the first category and can be judged quite apart from their ostensible program.

If, however, the composer insists on employing a program in the fullest sense of the word, and if he actually needs such a stimulus to his musical imagination, what is the positive danger? Let us assume that a non-musical subject can be adequately communicated through music, by imitation, movement, and mood, and further, that a composition has grown naturally out of this subject: why should we not find in the music the same kind of added textural dimension as that afforded by a subject in painting? The comparison falls down at first examination. A painting does not move in time; the entire scene and the entire design are equally before our eyes as we look at it. The relationships of part to part and the analogical connections binding its various dimensions are constantly open to view. Music, as it moves through time, must make its formal relationships clear from moment to moment; and for most listeners it is task enough to assimilate these as they flow by. The program insists that the listener follow it as well, an independent verbal structure, and at the same time try to relate it to the musical form. What happens in fact is that the hearer concentrates on the music, in which case the program is superfluous; or he concentrates on the program, in which case he is taken out of the music (just as one is led out of a picture by bad story-telling); or he compromises and spends an uneasy time trying to direct his attention now here, now there, now somewhere in between.

There is good program music, to be sure. If a program is simple enough to be grasped without effort and obvious enough to make its point in music without elaborate translation, or if the music is so completely formed that the program is unnecessary, then one can listen with enjoyment. Otherwise the program, far from enriching the general texture, contributes to the weakening and even the disintegration of the musical fabric. And so it is that Strauss must answer for *Also sprach Zarathustra* alongside *Don Juan* and *Till Eulenspiegel*.

III

An obvious objection to the foregoing argument will have occurred to the reader. How can song exist? Isn't this the supreme example of the attempt to unite two structures of dissimilar media? And doesn't opera become quite impossible? The questions are proper, but the answers may prove surprising.

The universality of song attests that neither musicians nor their audiences have found practical difficulties in this direction. Obviously we can and do hear words and music together as forming some sort of unity—a unity, moreover, that ideally includes the meaning as well as the sound of the words. On the other hand, it is instructive to remember the failure of the Romantic melodrama, which attempted in a thoroughgoing way to create a musical accompaniment expressively paralleling the text; it turned out to be only program music with the program read aloud. The disparity between spoken word and tone makes it impossible for the listener to attend to both—a difficulty that haunts even *Sprechstimme,* a much closer approach to true song. (The effectiveness of such rare exceptions as the melodramatic passages in *Fidelio* and *Der Freischütz* depends on careful musical and dramatic preparation.)

These difficulties indicate that it is not sufficient for the music to *accompany* the words, no matter how illustrative or expressive the accompaniment may be. Nor is it sufficient for it to *set* them—to approximate as closely as possible the pattern of the verbal rhythms; for in this case the music only emphasizes what is already evident to the sensitive reader. But both accompaniment and setting have their functions in the fulfillment of the proper task of the music: to *compose* the words—to surround and envelop them in such a way that both their sound and their meaning become part of the musical texture itself. The music assumes a form and mode of expression analogous to those of the poem itself, but to the poem as modified in turn by the music—the poem as sung, rather than as read or recited. Some poets object that the result is actually a new poem—and with some reason. For the text not only shapes the music but in turn is shaped by it, in every feature susceptible of such control: its meter, its pace, its larger and smaller rhythms, its melodic rises and falls, its climaxes. Only by this interaction can the desired resolution be effected.

What is more, this unique relation of the musical and the modified poetic forms must be revealed by the primary role of the human voice, entrusted alike with the words of the poem and the controlling line of the music. Whatever the composer may wish to do besides in the way of accompaniment, of illustration, of background, is well and good; but if he forgets that the voice is the one element through which the unity of the song is manifested, he jeopardizes all—as even Wagner magnificently did. Too often his orchestral flow usurps the primary role to such an extent that the effect is only one step away from that of melodrama. The voice still sings, it is true, but only to convey the words; it has lost its musical function.

Another danger is the one into which many Baroque arias fall. They achieve a unity, but a purely musical one. The words are treated not as a text but as a pretext for the exploitation of the vocal instrument.

The successful song, as described above, is one more example of the principle of analogical fusion. Music and words appear to be, not parallel structures, but two aspects of a single organism. For this reason the text and setting of the best songs give the illusion of being "twin-born" even when not actually so. Sometimes it is difficult or impossible to think of either element in isolation once they have been heard so joined.

Such masterpieces as these, rare though they may be, show triumphantly that words and music, properly combined, produce no conflict of attention in the listener. Nevertheless, discretion in choice of text and of musical idiom increases the chance of effectiveness. It is no accident that opera composers have resorted to recitative of comparatively simple musical content in order to put over complicated expository passages and have built sumptuous musical edifices out of arias with comparatively easy words. I do not mean to imply that relative complexity of music and text must always be in inverse ratio, but I do suggest that too much activity in both may lead to the fatal division of the listener's attention. Exceptions like Bach's highly developed choruses on important doctrinal clauses are only apparent. In the first place, he could depend on the familiarity of his audience with the text (an important consideration in most liturgical music); moreover, he treated the words relatively abstractly, building huge sections out of single clauses.

Oddly enough, it can be argued that opera needs less justification than any other type of vocal music, except possibly that associated with ritual. The action on the stage, if properly coordinated as functionally analogous to the combined form of music and text, can actually clarify the relations between these two and make them more immediately, since visually, perceptible—just as the dance can sometimes clarify the rhythmic relationships by creating visual analogies for them. This may not often happen, but it is the ideal that operatic composition, both of libretto and of music, and operatic staging, direction, and performance, should always keep in mind.

As a short, suggestive example I shall take a familiar passage from Verdi, whose operatic superiority to Wagner is indicated in some measure by his simpler, more immediately apprehensible, and hence theatrically more suitable, style. In fact, at first glance an aria like "La donna è mobile" may seem too simple, until it is remembered that in music, and especially in opera, a relatively unpromising idea may be in a state of suspended saturation, depending on future developments to make its import clear. Such is the case with this aria, whose virtue lies in the fact that it will be immediately grasped and constantly retained by the audience. Just as the figure of the Duke, gradually retiring from the visible scene, remains nevertheless constantly in the dramatic background, so his tune, now as the bassoon underlines the conspiracy against him, now as he tries to sing sleepily from his bedroom, produces an analogous musical structure. The connection could be clinched by clever staging that never lets the audience forget his presence as the focal point of the intrigue. The same kind of staging could emphasize the threefold irony of the last appearance of the same air: its carefree melody, the Duke's cynical words, and the calm after the storm—all in utter contrast to the actual situation. The simple-minded tune should break upon the audience with the full horror of Rigoletto's own realization. The material is there, in the libretto and in the score. Imaginative stage direction could use it to produce an overwhelming effect.

It is not simply the combination of elements that gives opera its peculiar fascination; it is the fusion produced by the mutual analogy of words and music—a union further enriched and clarified by the visual action. It is not impossible that vocal music, by virtue of the added complication of the text, works in a more completely saturated and hence more satisfying medium than does purely instrumental music. If this is the case, it would seem to follow that opera, with the added third dimension of the stage, must offer the most intensely satisfying experience of all. For whatever reasons, many people have certainly thought so, and many evidently still do.

IV

It is now time to look at music from a more technical and hence less controversial point of view. What pattern, if any, can Vermeer's eye discern in the developments of the past two hundred years? What advice has Delft to offer us today?

The Golden Age of functional tonality, which I take to be a rough century including Bach and Handel, Mozart and Haydn, Beethoven and Schubert, witnessed a synthesis of all musical elements into forms as self-sufficient as any that music has ever known. The tension between detail and whole was here brought into equilibrium; musical suspense was under complete control; the shapes demanded by the respective needs of melody, harmony, and rhythm were integrated into a rich, multidimensional whole. Previous Golden Ages, which had produced the masterpieces of Gregorian chant and of Renaissance polyphony, had depended to a large extent on the shaping power of the word. The eighteenth century found all the form-giving factors it needed in music alone. When it used the word it did so as another dimension, analogous to the purely musical ones.

The ways in which this coordination of the compositional elements was achieved are well known. In view of what follows, however, I must recall an obvious but important point. It is impossible, except by analysis, to separate melody, harmony, and rhythm in the masterpieces of this period. Functional harmony has a life and laws of its own, but in the actual music it is constantly and indissolubly the support of the melody. Conversely, the melody, or melodic line in a polyphonic texture, can be heard, not only for its own sake, but as an element of the harmonically controlled voice leading. Most subtle of all is the rhythmic organization, which even up to now has defied proper analysis. Rhythm, which after all exists only as a series of relations, is during this period so deeply imbedded in the other elements through which it speaks, that it seems to disappear whenever we try to search it out. But everywhere we look, whether at general proportions, at phrase structure, at harmonic rhythm, or at rhythmic motifs, we find patterns interesting not only for their own sakes but also, and especially, for the way in which they control, and are controlled by, the other elements. In no other respect is the mastery of the composers of this Golden Age displayed so clearly.

It was precisely with this most fundamental and at the same time most delicate of relationships that the dissolution began. The rhythmic breakdown was the first and one of the most unmistakable of the signs that the Golden Age was over. There were indications of what was to come even in Beethoven, whose employment of rhythmic motifs sometimes seems overemphatic to those who prefer the exquisite balance of Mozart, and in Schubert, whose sense of proportion sometimes failed him in his recapitulations. Beethoven's usage heralded a development he would have deplored: the gradual dissociation of rhythm from the other components of the synthesis, a phenomenon that, while producing interesting and varied patterns in the small, nevertheless led to the ill-proportioned forms, the monotonous phrase structure, the endless sequences, and the other excesses that blemish even some of the best music of the later nineteenth century. Schumann deliberately played with the dissociation, even though he was a victim of it. Brahms strove heroically to take advantage of the resulting ambiguities (which constituted the positive contribution of the new rhythmic techniques) by bringing them into a new synthesis, emulating that of the previous century. But the course of the evolution could not be stayed. Even a great master like Wagner failed to solve the rhythmic problem; it overwhelmed lesser ones like Bruckner.

The disintegration was proceeding in other ways as well. The Romantic conception of a "melody" was an important indication. For composers of this period, a melody was just that: independent of harmony, of accompaniment, of texture, even of rhythm (witness the thematic transformations some of them were so fond of). These other elements often seem to be regarded as mere decorative adjuncts, and one melody could appear in many garbs. Contrast with this the Classical ideal, which was hardly one of a "melody" at all, but of a unique and characteristic combination in which melody, harmony, rhythm, and texture all played their parts. The rise of orchestration as an independent skill during the nineteenth century is further evidence of the same trend, the implication being that choice of instrumentation is simply an additional means of coloring a preconceived passage.

The breakdown of harmonic cohesion in favor of the proliferation of details, especially in Wagner and Strauss, has often been noted. At the same time, the harmonic integrity was being threatened in another way: by the overelaboration of function. Bruckner, particularly in his last works, stretched chordal implications further than the ear could follow, since he failed to support them by adequate melodic and rhythmic analogies.

Now, it would be an oversimplification to call impressionism, as represented by Debussy, an attempt to solve the rhythmic problem, and expressionism, with Schoenberg, an attempt to solve the harmonic one; but I believe the value of the generalization in the present context outweighs its dangers. Debussy cut the tenuous thread still holding the musical elements together, so that rhythm and melody could develop independently of harmony. What this really meant was that they developed at the expense of harmony, which became static and coloristic, almost an aspect of the newly important dimension of timbre. In turn, melody and rhythm suffered their own impoverishment. The former, deprived of functional support, found its line broken into fragmentary motifs; and even these are often less memorable for their contours than for their rhythmic patterns. Rhythm, for its part, could no longer express itself in strong harmonic movement and thus lost one of its most powerful embodiments.

The same traits of static harmony, rhythmic independence, and fragmentary melody characterize much twentieth-century music not usually classifed as impressionistic, including, for example, much of Stravinsky and Bartók. In spite of successes that number some not inconsiderable masterpieces, the style must inevitably suffer in comparison with that of functional tonality. The forcefulness of its integration, particularly on the level of detail/whole tension, is questionable; its saturation with respect to the harmonic dimension is low.

Schoenberg's interest in solving the harmonic problem represented by the continuing decadence of traditional tonality led to his discovery and systematic use of serialism, particularly in its twelve-tone form. As opposed to the impressionistic method, Schoenberg's is a thoroughgoing attempt at reintegration; as a result it is by far the more vital of the two today. But it brought with it its own difficulties, two of which are especially relevant to this discussion. The first question is one raised by atonality in general, whether serial or not: Does this style exploit the medium as thoroughly, with as great richness and complexity, as functional tonality? In a word, is its saturation as complete? A negative answer, as in the case of impressionism, would by no means invalidate the style or the music written in it; but it would point up its limitations. The second question is related more specifically to the twelve-tone method itself: Has it adequately solved the rhythmic problem? Has it found a way to build rhythmic structures analogous to those of its other dimensions?

The answers to the first question are as varied as the composers who produce them. Schoenberg soon discovered the value of row transpositions, not simply to add variety but to fulfill a form-giving function much as did modulation in older music. These transpositions, in connection with the hexachordal makeup of his rows, produce the effect in his later works of a kind of super-tonality, perceptible even when not precisely definable.

Berg was much more explicit in his tonal references, which seem to some critics trivial and obvious. It is true that the tonal functions to which he adverts are simple and of themselves not very interesting. What he was after, I think, was a new kind of tension: that produced by the poles of tonality and atonality appearing simultaneously or successively in the same composition. It is the precarious balance between them that gives much of Berg's work its peculiar intensity and individual flavor.

The music of Webern, the most thorough of the three in its rejection of traditional references, is harmonically the simplest and texturally the most transparent. Two points should be noted, however. Webern was first of all a song writer. The added dimension of the voice, to which he was unusually sensitive, may not only compensate for the thinness of the purely musical component but at times even require it. In the second place, Webern's transparency enabled him to emphasize coloristic, polyphonic, and rhythmic aspects that were more important to him than the harmonic. The apparent simplicity conceals beneath it a web of subtle relationships, the tensions among which are held in delicate balance. Some listeners find the web too fragile, its substance too slight. None can question its exquisite workmanship.

In the best of this music, then, the medium is used with something that corresponds to, or at least substitutes for, the richness of tonality.

Indeed, this is the surest criterion of quality in twelve-tone compositions. The rhythmic situation is more problematic and is still a source of deep concern to serious composers.

The tonal references of Berg and the quasi-harmonic system of Schoenberg go hand in hand with considerable reliance on traditional rhythmic procedures. The results are well integrated in their own terms, and the resulting unity is both audible and aesthetically satisfying. But many deeply committed dodecaphonists now believe that these older masters failed to realize the full potentialities of the system itself, which should be made to yield its own rhythmic types. Complete saturation of the twelve-tone medium, they feel, implies a rhythmic structure some-how derived from the principles that govern the tone row itself. Webern, in this respect as in others, came nearest to the radical ideal. So far as I have been able to discover, he did not serialize his rhythm, but he did often try to order it in a pattern parallel to that of the pitches. Thus the palindrome, in which a stated passage immediately retrogresses in both pitch and time value, was a favorite device. At the same time he must have realized two points: the impossibility, without electronic means, of a true rhythmic retrograde involving attacks (something becoming du-biously available only now, by electronic means); and the fundamental psychological fact that whatever arbitrary direction may be assigned to events in space or on paper, we can experience them in only one direc-tion—forward. It is for these reasons, I think, that he was always careful to project his abstract designs against a strict, steady meter. Performance is difficult, since it must do justice to both aspects; but when it is suc-cessful it reveals that Webern's rhythmic sense, for all its responsiveness to the demands of the new style, was firmly rooted in the past. The patterns that appear rigid on paper sound free and flexible precisely be-cause they are supported by the composer's mastery of the traditional methods of articulation.

Today these apparent compromises fail to satisfy the demands of the radicals. More and more attempts are being made to serialize not only time values but every type of relationship: dynamics, modes of attack, tempos, proportions. Superficially, it might seem that the result would be a completely saturated structure of analogies in many dimensions. The crucial question remains: Do they coalesce in an aurally perceptible unity? In an attempt to demonstrate that they do not, I pass over such techniques as the serialization of dynamics and attacks—any application of which can, I believe, be shown to be arbitrary—in order to concen-trate on the exemplary problem of the durational row, whether applied to simple note values or to longer sections.

The great stumbling block in the way of the integration of a pitch row with a durational one is that no common measure exists. There can be none even by analogy, since we perceive time and pitch in markedly different ways. We hear time segments as durations, and we measure one against another as longer or shorter or equal—even, to a certain extent, how much longer or shorter. Pitches we hear as discrete points, ordered but not quantified. Some musicians have become excited because the theory of relativity considers time as a fourth dimension, somehow commensurable with the three spatial ones. Now, even if pitches could be spatially measured, which they cannot, the theory would be of no practical help: it takes 186,000 miles of space to correspond to one second of time. Nor is Stockhausen's plan of deriving a time scheme from the frequency ratios of the pitches much better, for we simply do not hear pitches in that way. In no sense do we hear an octave, for example, as twice as high as its fundamental.

Let us assume, though, that some common measure with a basis perceptible in each dimension has been adopted. Have we really overcome the difficulty? Suppose, for example, that we measure, as Krenek has suggested, not the pitches themselves, but the intervals between each pair, and on these proportions construct a time row. Now we could argue that the progression C-E-G (four half steps plus three) is matched by the temporal ratio 4:3. We might further insist that we hear the two types of relationship as mutually analogous. But do we? Do we not at most hear each of them as an expression, in different media, of the abstract arithmetical 4:3 (if in fact we hear tonal intervals proportionally at all!)? And if we try to argue the analogy of the pitch and time intervals from this purely numerical basis, then could we not claim equally well that a rectangle of the same proportions, or any other embodiment of the 4:3 ratio, is analogous to the major triad?

Perhaps it is unnecessary to seek a perceptible common measure. Perhaps the principle of serialization itself is sufficient to unite its own divergent exemplifications. But in that case why would one time row rather than another match a given tone row? Any criterion of choice would be essentially arbitrary or else based on musical considerations foreign to pure serialism. In the first case the resultant combination would (except by chance) produce merely the unfolding of two parallel strands, each ordered within itself, but lacking the cogent connection with the other necessary for a unitary aural impression. The relationship between the two types of series would again not be audible—only inferable from an essentially abstract, extra-musical premise. In the second case the desired connection might be heard, but that would depend on factors derived from outside the system—just as in the case of the non-serialized rhythms of the three early masters.

There are further difficulties as well. How would we apply the fundamental operations of the serial system to the time row? Retrogression is easy, but what of inversion and transposition? Babbitt's suggestion that numerical complementation is analogous to inversion is brilliant, but as a practical technique it suffers from the same kind of abstraction pointed out above. We do not actually hear complementation and inversion as similar operations; we come to this conclusion only after associating each with an arithmetical equivalent. But art is not a branch of mathematics, and quantities equal to the same quantity are not necessarily equal to each other. The same argument applies to the various analogies that have been suggested to effect temporal "transposition."

The trend toward abstraction is a dominant one today, and an unhealthy one for art. The devices criticized here, introduced in the hope of achieving a perfect unity within the twelve-tone system, have resulted in producing a unity, it is true—but outside the medium, in the realm of arithmetic. They take us out of the music as directly as any program ever did. In some of the serial compositions written today the application of the tone row itself has become so abstract and far-fetched that it is no longer felt as a form-building force. In this case, the listener perceives nothing but chaos, or else he is forced to find some new kind of order. If the former, then the composition is only nominally music. If the latter, then of what value is the supposed serial order?

By the foregoing I have not meant to imply that some kind of rhythmic structure unique and proper to the system cannot be found, but I insist that it will not be discovered by the doctrinaire application of rigid principles. Rhythm, the most fundamental of musical dimensions, is the most vital and has never submitted for long to the fetters of formulation and schematization. If the new principle finally emerges, it will be in and through the music itself. It may even turn out that the classical twelve-tone composers were on the right track after all, and that the answer lies in the evolution of traditional procedures rather than in a revolution against them. If no solution is found, the serial method will nevertheless remain a noble attempt to establish another Golden Age.

[1961]

Musical Theory as a
Humanistic Discipline

By musical theory I mean nothing very profound and nothing at all new: I refer to the familiar disciplines of harmony, counterpoint, analysis, and orchestration, leading to strict and free composition in both traditional and contemporary idioms. In other words, my consideration of theory as a humanistic study includes all theory and implies no attempt to set up one particular system—such as Schenker's, or Hindemith's—as the only one worthy of so dignified a name. If at times I treat it as a subject of instruction and at times as a field for speculative thinking, I hope it will be easy to distinguish which is meant, and that the relation between the two will remain clear.

The word "humanistic," on the other hand, must be understood in a restricted sense: I use it here as referring to "the humanities," and not to "humanism." The broader implications of the term "humanities" I prefer not to deal with just yet; for the moment an ostensive definition based on practical observation will suffice. All universities would, I believe, include the arts and letters under this category; most would add philosophy; and many would admit history, at least when it is not oriented exclusively toward the social sciences.

A comparison of this list with the medieval trivium and quadrivium reveals that music, alone among the four members of the quadrivium, is now classified among the humanities. Of the other three, astronomy has long been recognized as one of the natural sciences; and arithmetic and geometry are of course branches of mathematics—a discipline that, in one university at least, is given a unique place somewhere between philosophy and the physical sciences. It is clear that music formerly took its place among these subjects because it was investigated primarily in its theoretical mode; indeed, the practical performer hardly merited the name of musician. Like its allied disciplines it was a study of measurement, of proportion; and conversely the medieval scholars sought in mathematics and astronomy the harmonious relationships they found in music. If music is found today among the humanistic rather than the scientific disciplines, is it not properly only the study of its history and literature that belongs there? Were the schoolmen not right in placing theory, with its emphasis on number, among the mathematical sciences? And would they not today, observing to what extent theory now emphasizes technical routine, banish it from the liberal curriculum altogether?

It is true that the study of theory has its routine aspects, but drill is a prerequisite to the attainment of proficiency in any discipline. It is likewise true that the study of theory may have narrowly vocational ends: the improvement of instrumental performance, for example, or the ability to arrange popular tunes. At a higher level, it is obviously indispensable in the training of composers; and for many this is the real importance of the subject. From another point of view, however, none of these purposes would admit it into the present-day humanistic curriculum: it is there as a necessary phase in the training of students of musical history and literature, and as a tool for musical scholars. It furnishes a rigorous, technical, quasi-scientific background for further musical studies.

At this point musical theory finds analogues in many other fields commonly held to be humanistic. History, literature, the other arts—all require as background certain technical disciplines that because of the nature of their inquiries and the rigorousness of their methods should properly be referred to as sciences. Epigraphy, paleography, linguistics— subjects like these suggest that there is no sharp division between the historical sciences on the one hand and the humanities proper on the other—that any distinction, to be useful, must be made on a basis of general approach to subject matter, rather than of subject matter itself. Once such a definition has been accepted, it will then become possible to admit a humanistic approach to the natural sciences and mathematics— perhaps even to musical theory considered no longer as a tool for practical or scholarly studies, but for its own sake!

I suggest that the subject matter of the humanities embraces all human activities and all records thereof—not merely those labeled as "literary" or "intellectual" or "historical"—and that the humanistic approach is concerned with the study of these activities and records as concrete expressions of human thought and embodiments of human values. Viewed in this light, a building, a geometrical theorem, and a scientific demonstration could be as fruitful as a lyrical poem or a critical essay.

An example of the difference between the scientific and the humanistic approaches may be helpful here. When a physicist is confronted with the presentation of a new theory, together with the description of the experiments that tend to substantiate it, he naturally looks for accurate observations and measurements, logical deductions, and objective conclusions. He regards the theory as an attempt to describe the universe more accurately or to formulate its workings more precisely, and he judges accordingly. The humanist, on the other hand, facing the same mass of evidence and inference, asks rather, "What was this man trying to say and why was he trying to say it?" He is less concerned with so-called objective, scientific truth than with the truth of the concrete human situation. For him a fallacious theory is as useful as any other, provided only that it reveals the attitude that called it into being. The systems of Ptolemy, Copernicus, and Einstein are equally valuable as expressions of man's views of his own position in the universe.

The subject of mathematics might be an instructive one to investigate for a moment by way of further clarification, since it is often considered to be, of all the intellectual disciplines, the one least amenable to humanistic blandishments. Because mathematics points in one direction toward physics, engineering, and technology, and in the other, through logic, toward philosophy, it is all too seldom considered as a vehicle of expression or as a medium for the transmission of values. But a comparison of the geometrical notions and methods of Euclid, Descartes, Poncelet, and Lobatschewsky, to name only a few obvious figures, reveals that their contributions to mathematical thought, far from being cold and precise abstractions, are as various and individual as the personal characteristics of the men themselves, and that the newly emerging values of every age demand new formulations, which in turn may influence the very values that called them forth. With reference to Descartes, for example, one might well ponder the fact that his coordinate geometry made possible for the first time a complete investigation of the ellipse, during the century that saw Kepler's description of the planetary orbits and the completion of the piazza of St. Peter's.

The same point could be made with reference to the aids to scholarship grouped together as historical sciences. Linguistics, for example, can be a precise, sharp tool for research; but with a different approach, as Edmund Wilson's recent essay on Hebrew[1] has shown in a non-technical way, it can be made to reveal the essentially normative function of language structure.

It is fallacious, then, to assume in advance that any subject is barren of

1. Edmund Wilson, "On First Reading Genesis," in *Red, Black, Blond, Olive* (New York, 1956).

humanistic fruit. But before proceeding further I wish to point out the opposite danger of over-enthusiasm for what I have called the technical tools, to the point of assuming that they are sources of artistic value. The relation of geometry to architecture, already cited, is a case in point: the symmetry of the Cartesian formula for the ellipse, beautiful in its own way as it may be, must never be called upon to explain the magnificence of Bernini's piazza. And as we all know, Bach and Reger were equally adept at canon. This, I believe, is also why some of us feel vaguely disquieted at analyses of the autograph score of Mozart's Requiem purporting to show, by distinctions of handwriting, inks, and watermarks, which sections are by the master and which by the pupil. Graphology should not be allowed to usurp the prerogative of critical evaluation.

What happens all too often is a confusion between two ways of looking at works of art, each valid so long as kept distinct from the other. For a work of art is both an aesthetic and a historical document. It can never be regarded purely as either; but so long as one considers it aesthetically, historical study must be used only as a means—and conversely, aesthetic judgment becomes only a means when one's aim is primarily historical. Both ways of approach are humanistic, but whereas the one uses history to clarify the meaning of the individual work, the other uses the work to enlarge our view of history.

It is clear, then, that any humanistic discipline can be used as a tool, but that no such discipline is exclusively a tool; and now at last we must return to musical theory. In precisely what way should theory serve as an aid to the more immediately humanistic branches of musical literature and history, and to what extent can it be admitted to the curriculum of the humanities as a subject to be studied for its own sake? The latter question is the more difficult and the more crucial; but the former must not be dismissed too easily. It is obvious that a knowledge of the systematic principles governing musical composition during any historical period is necessary for a complete understanding of the music of that period—or at least, of what the musicians of the period thought of their music. Knowledge of this kind, however, can never lead to understanding unless the ear itself is directly involved. All too current nowadays is the unfortunate notion that a listener or student with a completely ignorant ear can nevertheless not only fully enjoy a composition, but also adequately comprehend it—even to the extent of writing about it for publication! I am not among those who consider it necessary to label every chord or derive every theme in order to grasp the essential flow of a piece of music; but I do not see how one so unaware of elementary harmonic language that he cannot tell tonic from dominant can fail to miss the purport of a tonal composition. He need not know their names, but his ear must know the difference; and the scattered applause that invariably accompanies the general pause following the huge half cadence near the end of Tchaikovsky's Fifth Symphony indicates that there are many ears at our concerts that cannot make this distinction. One of the prime functions of theoretical instruction is to educate the ear; and no potential critic or scholar, whether professional or amateur, can afford to risk insufficient or inadequate training of this kind. Of our professionals, naturally, we expect more. They should, indeed, be able to listen for us or before us, and lead us toward hearing, if we can, what they have heard.

Theory, then, should guide the ear; and this is perhaps its greatest service to the musical historian or aesthetician. But in return it must be guided by the ear, for the most beautiful system is musically meaningless if it is not aurally perceptible. Composers and critics alike must remember this. When proponents of advanced twelve-tone methods point by way of historical justification to the isorhythmic complications of the late fourteenth century, they often fail to ask how successful these earlier compositions really were, and whether both the earlier system and the later, if carried too far, are not in danger of outstripping human hearing. Similarly Heinrich Schenker, a penetrating and illuminating critic so long as his analysis depended on what must have been a truly remarkable ear, went astray when he tried to erect his system as a rigid abstract construction.

Theory's claim to be admitted to the humanistic curriculum would seem, then, to be fair enough even if only on the auxiliary grounds outlined above. But what of the possibility previously mentioned of a humanistic approach to the subject itself? Is it possible for the student to derive from his exercise in harmony, counterpoint, and the rest, values analogous to those gained from classics, history, and philosophy?

The easiest answer to this question would point out that most instruction in theory is at the same time instruction in some specific historical style, such as Palestrina counterpoint or Bach chorale harmonization. The student thus gains an intimate knowledge of the methods of the past at the same time that he is perfecting his own technique. Unfortunately, it is all too often the case that he finds the technique thus learned irrelevant to his own needs, and his knowledge of the past no deeper than a few convenient rules of thumb. What is wrong, I think, is the frequent failure of instruction to distinguish between the general principles of musical thought and its historical-stylistic aspect. For inculcating the general laws of melodic construction and voice leading, the music of Palestrina is no more and no less useful as a model than that of twenty other composers. It becomes less useful, however, when Palestrina's individual mannerisms are so admired that they seem to have become in some mystical way normative for all succeeding generations. The mannerisms have their value, it is true, but only insofar as they can be made to indicate how all details of a successful artistic style work together toward a unified effect. It is important to distinguish basic laws such as those governing the general shape of a melody, the placing of its climax, and the approach to the cadence, from rules that are relevant only within the restricted context of the Palestrina style, such as the so-called law of melodic gravity, which insists that larger intervals precede smaller when ascending and the reverse when descending. And while it is correct to justify the prohibition of parallel fifths and octaves so long as independence of voices is a desideratum, it is hard to explain the ban on all melodic sixths save the ascending minor one except by saying, "That is the way Palestrina did it."

A better case can be made for the pedagogical functions of Bach's chorale style, for the problem with which Bach struggled is one which is bound to arise in the experience of every musician: how to achieve, in a four-part vocal idiom, the richest tonal harmonization of a simple periodic melody. If it can be demonstrated, as I believe, that in almost all cases Bach arrived at optimum solutions, it follows that the principles governing this specific historical style can, with little essential alteration, be applied as generally valid whenever a similar problem arises. Bach's chordal vocabulary is limited from the point of view of nineteenth-century standards, it is true. There is no *a priori* reason why chords of the augmented sixth should not be used in such settings; and if students are forbidden to use them they should realize that the reasons for the prohibition are historical rather than inherent. But once we accept Bach's basic harmonic lexicon, we find that almost all his stylistic principles can be deduced therefrom. The idiosyncratic element is at a minimum; indeed, I find it hard to adduce a single mannerism analogous to those of Palestrina.

Here, I think, we are at the heart of the matter, for the more one examines the Bach harmonizations the more conscious one becomes of the fact that one is dealing, not with a style, but with style itself—style not as a congeries of easily catalogued individual characteristics, but as an organic unity to which every detail, no matter how apparently unimportant, contributes. The awareness of style is neither more nor less than the ability to think in music, whether in one's own terms or in the language established by one of the great composers of the past. Here is ground upon which composer and musicologist can meet, for this fundamental sense of style is indispensable to each.

Let me give one obvious example of what I mean by this sense of style.

In the late works of Beethoven we find, embedded in an essentially traditional idiom, details of voice leading that violate all orthodox procedure. In the Quartet Op. 131, for example, there are parallel fifths that resist every simple attempt at explanation, and in the Piano Sonata Op. 106, there are flagrant parallel octaves. Such passages can by no means be termed mannered or manneristic: they call no attention to themselves, nor are they repeated for their own sake at every opportunity. They arise only rarely, and only in response to the needs of the situation. But Beethoven, consciously or unconsciously aware of the demands of his musical logic, achieved his unique ends through unique means. By violating a particular style—the traditional one based on classical voice leading—he gained the essence of style itself: the oneness of technique and expression.

At this point it should be apparent that the real importance of theory, from a humanistic point of view, resides in its direction toward the appreciation of the meaning of style itself, rather than in its narrower historical or practical orientations. I grant that actual instruction all too often ignores this ideal aim. There should not be many subjects—harmony, counterpoint, and the rest—but one, music. The interrelationships between chordal progression and voice leading, and their ultimate interdependence, must be made clear. Form cannot be divorced from harmony, nor orchestration from form. Indeed, orchestration, rightly taught, could become the crown of the entire system, demonstrating as it then would how the choice of setting must be ultimately dictated by the unified concept of the whole work. Orchestration would be, as it ought, an integral part of the compositional process; and we should be spared the absurdity of exercises that imply that instrumentation is largely a matter of caprice or merely an attempt to achieve the maximum euphony.

Naturally, for pedagogical reasons, the familiar abstractions of strict counterpoint, four-part harmony, and the like, have their part to play; but it must always be remembered that they are only abstractions. This is why it is essential always to refer to the ear, for music as heard, not music as read on the page, should be the constant standard of evaluation. (Of course, I do not mean to exclude music heard mentally; indeed, one of the purposes of ear training is to develop the ability to auralize.) For the same reason, analysis of living music of all periods is necessary at every stage; for this is the only insurance against the erection of the pedagogical abstractions into artificial norms.

The treatment of instruction in fugue is a good case in point. We all know what happened to it at the hands of the Conservatoire; we have only to read Gédalge's well-known treatise to realize vividly how a living form can all too easily become a bloodless abstraction. The *fugue d'école* no doubt has its uses for one who wishes to study the sources of Saint-Saëns's amazing lack of style, but it has no value for one who wishes to approach actual fugal composition, either critically or creatively. Nor is the solution to be expressed simply in the cry, "Back to Bach!" The serious student of fugue will go back to Bach, of course; but accurate codification and imitation of Bach's procedures alone will lead him no nearer to his goal than faithful obedience to Gédalge or Cherubini. It is easy to learn the mechanical rules for finding the correct tonal answer for a given subject, but these can be downright misleading if we do not understand their rationale. Such statements as "Bach never modulates to keys more than two accidentals away from the tonic," even if strictly correct, would be important only as an aid to the investigation of the true nature of tonal relationships in the fugue.

No. What chiefly distinguishes the masterwork in this form from an academic imitation is the relationship between the subject and its treatment: in the great fugues of Bach the subject itself calls forth and dictates the form as a whole. It may well be that fugue as an independently creative design is now dead, and that Bach's tonal idiom is archaic; but no other body of musical literature so well demonstrates the essential and intimate connection between motif and line, between theme and development. It is through observation of this principle at work that we find the applicability of the study of fugue to other musical forms and hence the best possible justification of the retention of this apparently outmoded discipline.

As I have tried to outline it, the study of fugue exemplifies theory considered as the mastery of musical thought. Conceived of in this way, it precisely meets the first of my demands of a humanistic discipline: that it approach human activities and documents as expressions of thought. What of the second—that it consider these expressions as embodiments of values? What can musical theory have to do with value?

Here again the key is to be found in the concept of style. Style, in any art, is the repository of the values of logical cogency, of coherence, of economy. It is what makes possible unity without uniformity, and diversity without disparity. Its comprehension is the source of power in the creative artist; its appreciation is the source of the critic's taste and discrimination. In Whitehead's phrase, "Style is the ultimate morality of mind."[2]

In representational arts the choice of the specific subject matter, or the way in which it is treated, is indicative of fundamental attitudes on the

2. Alfred North Whitehead, *The Aims of Education* (New York, 1929), 19.

part of the artist—that is, it embodies value. In music this easy means of communication is either lacking or restricted to relationships between music and text or extra-musical ideas. We have to fall back on style itself to give us whatever clue we can have. Whatever one may mean by the terms "musical expression" and "musical content," one must realize that they can be communicated only through the vehicle of style. But at this point theory stops, and music itself begins.

[*1957*]

Analysis Today

The analysis of music—especially of traditional music—is one of the most respected of theoretical disciplines, but the respect in which it is held would do it a disservice if it prevented the periodic reevaluation of the subject. What is analysis, or what ought it to be? What are its purposes? To what extent are traditional concepts and methods applicable to new music? What are the relations of analysis to performance and to criticism? My title refers to a discussion, from the point of view of today, of these questions; it is in no way meant to imply that I have a new system to promulgate, or that I have made startling discoveries about new music.

I

Instead of presenting at the outset a naked definition of the term under consideration, I shall begin by looking at a familiar example. The first few measures of *Tristan* have performed many services other than their original one of opening a music drama; let them serve yet another and open the argument here.

This chordal sequence can be accurately enough described as a minor

Example 1

triad on A, a French sixth on F, and a primary seventh on E; but such a description, revealing nothing of the relationships among the three chords, involves no analysis whatsoever. If, however, the analyst refers to the passage as I_3^5-$II_3^{\#6}$-$V_\#^7$, he has performed an elementary analytical act: he has related each of the chords to a tonic, and hence to one another. He has made a discovery, or at least a preliminary hypothesis to be tested by its fruitfulness in leading to further discovery. But the analysis as such ceases with the choice of the tonic; once this has been made, the assignment of degree numbers to the chords is pure description. If, on the other hand, one points out that the second chord stands in a quasi-dominant relation to the third, he is doing more than simply assigning names or numbers: he is again discovering and explaining relationships.

Example 2

Turning now to the actual score, the analyst might begin a program note thus: "The rising leap of the cellos from A to F is succeeded by a chromatic descent, followed in turn by . . ." He need not continue; this is pure description. But when he points out that example 1 represents the chordal skeleton of example 2, he is once more on the right track. He can go still further by showing that all the appoggiaturas have half-step resolutions, and that the motif so created is augmented in the motion of the bass, and paralleled in the alto, in such a way that the chordal progression of measures 2–3 becomes an amplification of the melodic half step of measure 1.

Example 3

The fact that in the above diagram no such analogy has been pointed out in the half steps E-D♯ and A-A♯ is in itself an important though negative part of the analysis, since it implies by omission that these progressions, if relevant at all, are incidental and subordinate.

Going one step further, the analyst might claim that, from a serial point of view, the opening sixth is imitated in the third E-G♯ (see ex. 4).

Example 4

This is the point at which analysis proper passes over into what I call prescription: the insistence upon the validity of relationships not supported by the text. In the above case, for example, the orchestration implies the wrong-headedness of the suggestion, since the opening interval, played by the cellos alone, is heard as a unit, whereas the E-G♯ is divided disparately between cellos and oboe.

Analysis, then, exists precariously between description and prescription, and it is reason for concern that the latter two are not always easy to recognize. Description is current today in the form of twelve-tone counting—necessary, no doubt, as preliminary to further investigation, but involving no musical discrimination whatsoever. Prescription, on the other hand, is obvious in the absurd irrelevancies of Werker's analyses of Bach but is equally inherent in some of Schenker's more dogmatic pronouncements and in those of his followers.

It should be clear at this point that true analysis works through and for the ear. The greatest analysts (like Schenker at his best) are those with the keenest ears; their insights reveal how a piece of music should be heard, which in turn implies how it should be played. An analysis is a direction for a performance.

In order to explain how a given musical event should be heard, one must show why it occurs: what preceding events have made it necessary or appropriate, toward what later events its function is to lead. The composition must be revealed as an organic temporal unity, to be sure, but as a unity perceptible only gradually as one moment flows to the next, each contributing both to the forward motion and to the total effect. What is often referred to as musical logic comprises just these relationships of each event to its predecessors and to its successors, as well as to the whole. The job of analysis is to uncover them explicitly, but they are implicitly revealed in every good performance. Description, restricted to detailing what happens, fails to explain why. Prescription offers its own explanation, referring to an externally imposed scheme rather than to the actual course of the music.

One more familiar example may clarify this view of logical—or, as I prefer to call them, teleological—relationships.

The recapitulation of the Prestissimo from Beethoven's Sonata Op. 109 bursts in upon the development in such a way that the II♯ (V of V) is followed immediately by I. From a narrowly descriptive point of view one could call this an ellipsis, pointing out that the normally expected V has been omitted. Looking ahead, however, one will find that the first

Example 5

phrase of the recapitulation ends on V, and its consequent on I. The puzzling II♯, then, only temporarily and apparently resolved by what immediately follows it, actually points ahead in such a way that the whole passage is bound together in a cadential II-V-I. The propulsion thus generated is given an extra spurt by the compressed II-V-I at the end of the consequent, and the forward motion is renewed with fresh energy by the elision that sets the next period going.

Example 6

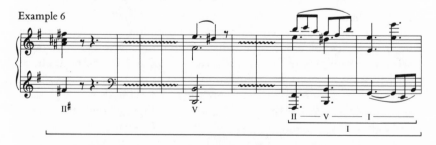

I need hardly mention the obvious effects of such an analysis on the performance of this passage. Whatever doubts one had as to the proper placing of the main accent in these phrases when they first appeared can now be resolved; the exposition can be reinterpreted, if need be, in the new light of the recapitulation.

II

It should be apparent at this point that analysis—and hence perform-ance as it has been discussed above—cannot apply to certain types of composition in vogue today. When chance plays the major role in the writing of a work, as in Cage's *Music for Piano 21–52,* logic as defined above can take only an accidental part. The same is true of music written according to a strictly predetermined constructivistic scheme, such as Boulez's *Structures.* In neither case can any musical event be linked organ-ically with those that precede and those that follow; it can be explained only by referring to an external structure—in the one case the laws of chance and in the other the predetermined plan. The connections are mechanistic rather than teleological: no event has any purpose— each is there only because it has to be there. In a word, this music is composed prescriptively, and the only possible or appropriate analytic method is to determine the original prescriptive plan. This is not analy-sis but cryptanalysis—the discovery of the key according to which a cipher or code was constructed. (If we are lucky, the composer or one of his initiates will spare us a lot of hard work by supplying us with the key.)

A third category that does not permit analysis is represented by Stock-hausen's *Klavierstück XI,* where improvisation is given such free rein that it actually creates the form of the work anew at each performance. Thus *Klavierstück XI* does not exist as a single composition and cannot fruit-fully be treated as one. Each new rendition can be discussed on its own merits, to be sure; but the relationship of all such versions to the abstract idea of the piece as a whole, and the decision as to the aesthetic value of such an experiment—these problems can be argued endlessly. At any rate they are far afield from the practical considerations that are our concern here. (It need hardly be pointed out that improvisation as traditionally applied to the framework of a Baroque concerto, for example, had pur-poses quite different. A cadenza served not only to show off the soloist's virtuosity but also to punctuate an important cadence; the soloist's elab-oration of a previously stated orchestral melody clarified the dualism inherent in the form. The quality of a given realization depended on its appropriateness to the compositional situation; the performance did not, as in many present-day examples, create the situation.)

III

The analysis of music of the periods closely preceding our own—the eighteenth and nineteenth centuries—has almost always assumed the applicability of certain familiar norms: tonally conditioned melody and harmony, periodic rhythmic structure on a regular metrical basis. Naturally such standards cannot be applied uncritically to the music of our own century, but on the other hand they should not be dismissed without examination. I contend that, in a more generalized form, they are still useful. Regardless of vocabulary, linear and chordal progressions still show striking analogies to older tonal procedures, analogies that are in turn reinforced by rhythmic structure. Only in those rare cases where the music tries to deny the principle of progression (as in the examples cited in the immediately preceding section) are such analogies completely lacking.

This point of view is more generally accepted with regard to harmony than to melody, perhaps because harmonic analysis is the more firmly entrenched discipline. After all, for many musicians theory is synonymous with harmony, melody being supposedly a free creative element, neither in its composition nor in its perception subjected to rule. (They forget, of course, that the object of the study of counterpoint is primarily the construction, and only secondarily the combination, of melodies.) Whereas Hindemith's enlargement of traditional harmony to encompass present-day vocabularies is generally known and often applauded, his attempt to find a melodic framework, actually a much less questionable procedure, is frequently ignored.

Another reason for shunning melodic analysis is that it is not always easy or even advisable to abstract the purely linear element from a progression. Wagner, in such motifs as the "wanderer" and the "magic sleep," is writing passages in which the melodic aspect is an incidental result of the chordal motion. A little later, Debussy offers examples (like the opening of *Reflets dans l'eau*) in which a linear phrase is dissolved into an atmospherically dispersed harmony that implies without actually stating the expected melodic resolution. Hyper-impressionistic pages, like parts of the "Night Music" from Bartók's "Out-of-Doors" Suite, fragmentize the melody to such an extent that the progressive element is heard to be the increase and decrease of density as the motifs follow one upon the other, rather than the specifically linear aspect, which is here reduced to a minimum. Nevertheless, wherever there are successive differentiations in pitch there is melody of some kind, and wherever there is melody the ear will try to hear it in the simplest possible way.

44

This is not meant to imply that we must expect to find behind contemporary melodic lines the simple stepwise diatonic framework that Schenker has pointed out in Classical examples. But the ear will naturally connect each tone with those nearest it in pitch. The adjacent pitches may be diatonic or they may be chromatic; they may be actually adjacent or displaced by one or more octaves; they may be present by implication only. In some cases motivic associations or peculiar scale formations may enforce the acceptance of a larger module—as in the simple case of bugle calls, the adjacent tones of which are a third or a fourth apart. (In the case of microtonal music, smaller modules may be in effect, although it is doubtful to what extent even present-day ears can accept them.) In every case the ear will do the best it can with the available intervals. It is the duty of the analyst to show the pattern of connections by which an educated ear—his own—makes sense of the total melodic flow.

Even less than in traditional melodies must one assume that there is one uniquely correct way of hearing. Rather, the best analysis is the one that recognizes various levels functioning simultaneously, as when a tone resolves once in the immediate context but turns out to have a different goal in the long run. Two very brief examples may help to clarify this point of view.

Example 7

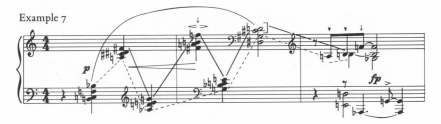

The first is the opening of Schoenberg's *Klavierstück* Op. 33a.[1] Chordal rather than melodic in conception, its linear structure is nevertheless clear. Despite the octave displacements, a line can be traced in the uppermost voice from the F♯ in the first measure to the B in the third. (Notice, however, that at one point two adjacent tones are presented simultaneously instead of successively.) At the same time, the original B♭ leads, through various voices but always at the original octave level, to the same tone of resolution. At this point the entrance of the F, repeating the cli-

1. Copyright 1947 by Universal Edition, A.G., Vienna. Reprinted by permission of Associated Music Publishers, Inc., sole agents for the United States.

mactic F of the second measure, begins a new motion that is carried forward through the succeeding phrase.

Example 8

The second passage is from the second of Sessions's piano pieces *From My Diary.*[2] Here both the F in the first measure and the G♭ in the third are associated with upper and lower chromatic neighboring tones. But what of the cadential motif? Why is the pattern altered? And why is the linear descent from the C♭ in the second measure broken at this point? There are several possible answers, all of which are probably relevant. First of all, the most prominent bass note in each of the four measures— as indicated by its repetition and by its quarter-stem—is an F, which can be heard as a resolution, at another level, of the hanging G♭—a resolution confirmed by a direct G♭-F in the bass. But at the same time, there seems to be an implied E filling the space between the G♭ and the D in its own voice—a tone suggested by the original association of E with G♭, and by the prominent whole-step motion in the melodic descent. In this case the

Example 9

line gradually increases its pace as it descends. But if it seems far-fetched to introduce an unstated, understood element, one can hear the skip G♭-

2. Copyright 1947 by Edward B. Marks Corporation. Reprinted by permission.

D as a way of emphasizing the cadence, and point out that the motif of neighboring tones aims each time more directly towards its resolution: the first time the neighbors follow the principal; the second time they precede it; and the last time the principal takes the place of one of its own neighbors. Finally, it should be noted that the next phrase takes off from the dangling G♭ in a subtle motivic reference to the beginning.

Example 10

It is of course impossible to do justice here to the role of such details in the total melodic structure, but on examination one will find the same kind of connection at work in the large. Note, for example, how much of the first theme of the Schoenberg piano piece is controlled by the high F already mentioned—whether in its original octave or in another—and by its association with the adjacent E. It is again this F, in its highest register, that prepares for the recapitulation; and it is the E that, returning first with the tranquil second theme, later closes the motion in a lower octave in the final measure. In sum, modern melody can not get rid of stepwise motion, because that is the way we hear melody; but it can and does expand (or on occasion contract) the distance, both temporal and spatial, between successive steps. From this point of view even Webern is found to be no pointillist, but a draftsman of subtle and fragile lines.

The role of harmony in the music of our century, although more extensively explored, is perhaps more difficult, complicated as it is by many factors, such as the frequent exploitation of the static, sensuous effect of the chord in addition to or even at the expense of its progressive functions. As a result, one can no longer assume the easily defined functionality of obviously tonal music. Chords can no longer be precisely named, nor can their identity be maintained in differing contexts. But it is important to realize that, even in stubbornly non-triadic music, the concept of the chord remains, by analogy at least. The composer can set up arbitrary simultaneities that, by their commanding position or by repetition, are accepted as the controlling sonorities—the chords— against which other tones can function in the manner of traditional non-harmonic tones. Bartók's *Improvisations* Op. 20 show how by such a technique quite complicated sonorities can be used to harmonize simple modal folk tunes. In the following example from the last of Sessions's Diary pieces, the metrical position and the half-step resolutions suggest that the first chord is an appoggiatura to the second; this supposition is confirmed by the appearance of the root-like D in the bass, and by the clinching repetitions that ensue.

Example 11

In fact, only where the contrapuntal aspect becomes so strong that every element of each sonority is heard primarily as a point in a moving line, or at the other extreme, where the texture is completely pointillistic, is the chordal concept seriously challenged. In such cases, one further assumption of traditional harmony that must then be questioned is the primacy of the bass. Contrapuntally or coloristically, of course, it will have gained in importance, but at the expense of its role in defining the harmony. A beautiful example of this process already at work over a century ago is shown in the opening of Liszt's *Vallée d'Obermann,* where the melodic action of the bass clouds the harmony. Not until the return of the theme adds a new bass underneath the original one is the situation made clear. A further step in this direction is taken by Mahler, who by his polyphonically opposed chords points the way towards polytonality in the magical cowbell passage in the first movement of his Sixth Symphony. A more thoroughgoing example is Stravinsky's *Symphonies of Wind Instruments,* a more truly polytonal work than any of Milhaud's often-cited *Saudades,* which in fact present only extended and elaborated harmonies over a single real bass.

There are other forces at work undermining the primacy of the lowest voice. Impressionistic parallelism, which reduces its role to that of coloristic doubling, is too well known to require citation. Less frequent, but possibly more important in the light of later developments, is the masking of the true harmonic bass by a decorative voice below it, a technique seen clearly in the repetition of the opening of *La Fille aux cheveux de lin.* Another device, common to the impressionists and Mahler, is the ostinato. From one point of view the persistent voice is emphasized, but at the same time it is removed from the sphere of action. In Debussy, as later in Stravinsky, the ostinato results in harmonic stasis; in Mahler there is a constant tension between the harmony implied by the motionless bass and those harmonies outlined by the moving voices and chords above it. In both cases the functional role of the bass is called into question.

So far no specific reference has been made to the problem of tonality. Except in comparatively rare cases, such as passages in *Le Sacre du printemps*, where an almost completely static tone or chord of reference is set up, tonality is created not by harmony alone, nor even by harmony and melody, but by their relationship with the rhythmic structure: in a word, by the phenomenon of the cadence. A discussion of certain rhythmic aspects, then, can no longer be postponed.

IV

Much of the vitality of the music of the Classical period derives from the constant interplay of meter and rhythm, the former determined by regular beats and measures and the latter by constantly varying motifs and phrases. This tension between the abstract and the concrete begins to break down during the nineteenth century, when phrase articulation is often either slavishly tied to the meter or else so completely liberated that the sense of the meter is almost lost. The retention of the measure tends to become purely conventional, and it is no wonder that later composers have abandoned the effort to keep an abstract pattern when it would conflict with the actual rhythm. For this reason the regularity of the meter in such composers as Webern must be carefully examined. Is it to be felt as a constantly present control? Is it a pure convention? Is it, as some would have us believe, an evidence of the composer's numerological superstitions?

The answers to such questions must always be given with specific reference to the text involved. When, as in the case of example 11, the motif sets up a clear cross-rhythm, the explanation is relatively easy. Webern's Piano Variations, on the other hand, present the problem in an acute form. What has happened here, I think, is that the composer has called on a complex set of interrelationships of rhythmic, metric, dynamic, and textural factors to compensate for the tenuity of melodic and harmonic interest. In the first twelve measures of the last movement, for example, I find at least seven different time divisions simultaneously functioning. These are set up by the meter (3/2), a possible cross-meter (5/4), the rhythm of the two-note motifs, the rhythm of the phrases, the tone row, the dynamic alternations, and the linear pattern (ex. 12).[3]

3. Copyright 1937 by Universal Edition, A.G., Vienna. Reprinted by permission of Associated Music Publishers, Inc., sole agents for the United States.

Example 12

The really important question to ask in all such cases—and even in cases where the composer has deliberately tried to get rid of all traditional metrical measurement—is, can we locate the structural downbeat? If we can, then we can proceed with analytic concepts in some way analogous to those of the traditional rhythm and meter, phrase and cadence. If not, some completely new rhythmic theory must be devised. Some musicians,like Stockhausen, are trying to do this, but I have as yet seen no satisfactory one emerge.

By structural downbeat, of course, I do not mean the arbitrary accentuation of the first beat of every measure; I mean rather phenomena like the articulation by which the cadential chord of a phrase is identified, the weight by which the second phrase of a period is felt as resolving the first, the release of tension with which the tonic of a recapitulation enters. (In the Webern example, I hear the downbeat as the E♭ at the beginning of measure 12; and I consider it no accident that it occurs at the beginning of a measure, preceded by a ritardando.)

It is just here that the importance of rhythm to the establishment of tonality emerges, for the cadence is the point in the phrase at which rhythmic emphasis and harmonic function coincide. It would be partly true to say that the cadence creates tonality, but it would be equally true to say that tonality creates the cadence. Where the cadence exists, it is impossible to hear music as completely atonal, even though one may be unable to define the key in conventional terms.

We know the signs by which a cadence can be recognized in traditionally tonal music: its position at the end of a phrase, the melodic resolution, the change of harmony. The actual downbeat may not always exactly coincide with the cadential point, but such unusual cases arise most often when the phrase is rhythmically prolonged (the feminine ending) or when it points ahead so clearly that the next phrase acts as a huge cadence to the first (as when an introductory section is followed by a main theme). In any case, keys are defined by the appearances of strong, cadential downbeats—whether clearly on the tonic, as in most Classical examples, or on deceptive resolutions, as notably in the Prelude to *Tristan*.

The extent to which analogous principles govern the structure of contemporary music is surprising. A few examples will show them at work.

The opening of the second movement of Bartók's Fifth Quartet may prove puzzling until it is heard as an upbeat. The first downbeat comes on the D in measure 5, clinched by an even stronger cadence on the same tone (now supported by its fifth) in measure 10. The digression that follows suggests the key of C, but this tonality is not confirmed by the cadence, which, when it arrives in measure 20, is again clearly on D.

The first page of Session's Second Sonata for Piano is much less triadic; yet when the downbeat comes in measure 11, the harmony of B♭ is clearly established. Not only the V-I implied by the progression of fifths in the bass, but the melodic resolution to D, accented by the downward leap, point toward this tonal center, which is confirmed by what follows. In the second movement, no such clear downbeat is presented, but the two important feminine cadences of measures 177 and 190 both suggest an unstated resolution to E. The important downbeat of measure 191, coming as it then does on F, is in the nature of a neighboring harmony; and not until much later, at measure 213, does the expected E occur, its extension as a pedal for ten measures compensating for its long postponement. The last few measures of the Lento act as an upbeat released in the return of B♭ in the opening of the finale. But this in turn, after a long battle with conflicting elements, gives way at the last to the key of C, on which a downbeat is firmly established in the final chord.

Stravinsky is sometimes referred to as a "downbeat composer," by which I suppose is meant that he often emphasizes the beginnings rather than the endings of his phrases. This results in a weakening of the cadential sense, it is true, the phrases so accented being, as it were, huge feminine endings to their own opening chords. A typical example is the opening of the Serenade in A. The harmonic progression would be described in traditional terms as VI$_3^6$-I$_3^5$ in A minor; actually the F of the first chord is heard as hardly more than an appoggiatura resolving to the E of the second. This would appear to be no progression at all, in which case the phrase should be a huge *diminuendo*. Yet we cannot be too sure: in a similar situation at the beginning of the third movement of the *Symphony of Psalms*, the composer, by changing the mode and the orchestration at the cadential word "Dominum," creates a clear accent even though the chord has remained essentially the same throughout the phrase.

In any event, whatever we may decide about the reading of his phrase accent in detail, Stravinsky is perfectly capable of producing a big structural downbeat at precisely the point where it is required. I need only point to the huge deceptive cadence that opens the *Symphony in Three Movements*, the dominant G of the introduction resolving finally upward to the A of the ostinato theme (rehearsal number 7); or to the way in which the Interlude acts as an upbeat to the C major of the finale.

More controversial is the attempt to find traces of tonal form in avowedly atonal compositions; yet I do not see how music like Schoenberg's, with its usually clear cadential structure, can fail to arouse certain traditional associations and responses. The previously cited *Klavierstück* Op. 33a begins with six chords, of which the second through the fifth are very easily—although not necessarily—heard as forming a progression referring to E minor. This in itself is nothing, but when the opening phrase is heard as an upbeat resolved in the third measure, and when the resolving sonority is recognized as a seventh on E, a tonal analogy is set up. The first section of the piece concludes even more unmistakably on E, with the added emphasis of a *ritardando;* and the theme that follows in measure 14 gives the effect of a sudden shift of key. In the recapitulation, the *ritardando* of measure 34 again calls attention to the following downbeat, where the E appears in the upper voice but is supported in the bass by A—in the manner of a deceptive cadence on IV. It remains for the final cadence to confirm the E, which is so strong that it is not dislodged by the dissonant tones with which it is here surrounded.

Several objections can be made to the above account: that it picks out isolated points without reference to the movement between them, that the "cadences" on E are a result of the fact that the row ends on that note, that such analysis is irrelevant to music in this style.

To the first count I plead guilty. I have indeed picked out isolated points, because these seemed to me to be the important "full cadences" of the piece. (Important "half cadences" occur at measures 9, 24, and 32.) The movement between them cannot, I grant, be explained in simple tonal terms. At some points, linear or contrapuntal motion dominates—

in which case the melodic principles suggested above will indicate the logic of the chosen cadences. At other points the sonorities themselves dominate—and these can of course be shown as derived from the opening chords. As a result, the entire piece can be heard as a development of its original cadential progression—that is, as analogous to a traditional structure.

I agree that the cadences are partially due to the use of the row. Depending on one's point of view, this effect is a virtue or a vice of Schoenberg's twelve-tone technique. It may even have been one of the points persuading him to turn toward the system, away from freer atonal methods. In no case can the argument invalidate the actual musical result.

To the charge of irrelevancy, I answer that one who cannot indeed hear such cadential phenomena in this music must judge the analysis to be prescriptive and inapplicable. But one who does hear them must admit to that extent the validity of the approach. He may counter that one ought not to hear the music in this way; but he is then criticizing the music, not the analytical method. Unwanted cadential effects would be as great a flaw in atonal music as the chance appearance of a human figure in a non-representational painting.

V

The last point suggests that there is a relation between analysis and criticism. It is not a simple one. Analysis can often reveal flaws in a work, it is true—often but not always. If it were dependable in this regard, we should be able to decide definitively between the disputed C# and Cx in the last movement of Beethoven's Sonata Op. 109 (measure 55), or whether the famous A♮ in Schoenberg's Op. 33a is indeed an A♭ (measure 22). But unfortunately, such cases all too often work both ways: the Cx that from one point of view prepares for the advent of D two measures later might have been avoided in order not to anticipate it; by the same token, although the A♭ seems more logical in the row structure (in spite of the A♮ lacking in the left hand), it may somewhat spoil the freshness of the A♭-E♭ fifth that comes soon after. The ear must be the ultimate judge of such subtleties, but insofar as analysis trains and sharpens the ear it makes its contribution to the final decision.

It would be tempting to go further and state that analysis can demonstrate the quality of a work, but this requires a faith in rationality that I am unable to summon. Judgment of final excellence must be fundamentally intuitive. If analysis leads someone to condemn a work he nevertheless continues to hear as good, he must conclude that there is something wrong either with his ear or with his method. Since he cannot dispense with the only pair of ears he has, upon whose evidence the examination should have been based in the first place, he must blame his method. He must then find a new one based on his own hearing, one that will substantiate, not contradict, his musical judgment. He may then claim that analysis has established the excellence of the work in question, but he will be wrong; his own judgment will have established the analysis.

One positive point emerges here, and it is a crucial one. The good composition will always reveal, on close study, the methods of analysis needed for its own comprehension. This means that a good composition manifests its own structural principles, but it means more than that. In a wider context, it is an example of the proposition that a work of art ought to imply the standards by which it demands to be judged. Most criticism today tacitly accepts the truth of this statement and sets about discovering the standards implied by a given work and testing how well it lives up to them. For investigation of this kind, analysis is naturally of primary importance.

Criticism should take a further step, however, and the best criticism does. It should question the value of the standards. A work that sets no clear standard denies or defies the possibility of evaluation; one that does set its standard fails or succeeds insofar as it measures up to it; one that measures up completely is at least flawless—but its value cannot exceed the value of its own standard. It is this final step that is completely beyond the confines of analysis.

The music of Webern is a prominent case in point. No serious critic denies the perfection of his forms and the complete consistency of his style. Its paucity of normal melodic and harmonic interests has been mentioned above, but in connection with other values that, replacing these, uniquely characterize his manner. What is seldom questioned is the significance of the style itself—of the restrictive standard (for it is a restrictive one) that Webern set for his own music. Are the limits too narrow to permit accomplishment at the very highest level? Only a decision of this point can determine one's final evaluation of the composer. It is a decision that depends on one's beliefs about the limits and aims of art in general and is thus not exclusively musical, although it must at the same time be peculiarly musical. It must be made on faith, and it must be accepted or rejected in the same spirit.

[*1960*]

Beyond Analysis

Examples 1–3 present the beginnings of three hypothetical compositions. If they sound both oddly familiar and familiarly odd, that is because they were derived by the simple application of a mirror to three
well-known sources: Schoenberg's *Klavierstück* Op. 33a, and the first and
third movements of Webern's Piano Variations Op. 27. Hence if the
reader wishes to complete these constructions, he will find it a straightforward and even mechanical task.

Example 1

Example 2

Example 3

The possibility of such derived compositions was suggested to me by a famous passage from Schoenberg's essay "Composition with Twelve Tones":

> *The unity of musical space demands an absolute and unitary perception.* In this space . . . there is no absolute down, no right or left, forward or backward. Every musical configuration, every movement of tones has to be comprehended primarily as a mutual relation of sounds, of oscillatory vibrations, appearing at different places and times. To the imaginative and creative faculty, relations in the material sphere are as independent from directions or planes as material objects are, in their sphere, to our perceptive faculties.[1]

No doubt I have taken this passage more literally than its author intended. So far as I know, Schoenberg never tried to demonstrate that the strict mirror inversion of a twelve-tone composition must be as valid as the original—but this might indeed be one conclusion that could be drawn from the quoted passage. It is also—and this is my real starting point—a conclusion that might be drawn from reading much, and perhaps most, accepted twelve-tone analysis today.

My research into this question has been by no means exhaustive; furthermore, although I feel confident that the analytic essays I have studied constitute a representative sample, I have no way of proving this. The only fair way of presenting my case, then, is to list the actual examples I have used and the results I have obtained.

To begin with, the master's analyses of his own works in the essay just

1. Arnold Schoenberg, *Style and Idea* (New York, 1975), 223.

56

cited would apply equally well if the compositions in question were replaced by mirror inversions of themselves. One need only make the obvious adjustments: substitute for the original form of the set its inversion, for any transposition its complement, and so on, and the analysis
can easily be made to read accurately. Only the references to instrumentation (which appear by way of description rather than analysis) might
cease to be relevant.

One may immediately counter that what Schoenberg was presenting
was not analysis but an explanation of a method—and a very primitive
explanation at that. One could not expect him to have developed the
sophisticated and powerful tools of analysis at our disposal today. Very
well, then, look at as varied a compilation as the following: Milton
Babbitt's three classic statements, "Some Aspects of Twelve-Tone Composition,"[2] "Set Structure as a Compositional Determinant,"[3] and
"Twelve-Tone Invariants as Compositional Determinants";[4] Ernst Krenek's analysis of his own *Lamentatio* and *Sestina* in "Extents and Limits
of Serial Technique";[5] the entire second issue of *Die Reihe,* devoted to
Webern; and, despite their promising titles, George Rochberg's "The
Harmonic Tendency of the Hexachord"[6] and his "Webern's Search for
Harmonic Identity."[7] In none of the foregoing would the line of argument have to be changed if the entire body of twelve-tone composition
were magically transformed into its exact inversion, for in every case the
only pitch relationships discussed are those that remain invariant under
inversion. Even such extended monographs as Joseph Rufer's *Composition
with Twelve Tones*[8] and George Perle's *Serial Composition and Atonality*[9]
exhibit only a few unsystematic exceptions to this general principle. One
further example that is especially indicative is Allen Forte's analysis of
the Schoenberg Phantasy Op. 47 in his *Contemporary Tone-Structures,*[10]

2. Milton Babbitt, "Some Aspects of Twelve-Tone Composition," *The Score* 12 (1955): 53–61.

3. Milton Babbitt, "Set Structure as a Compositional Determinant," *Journal of Music Theory* 5, no. 2 (1961): 72–94.

4. Milton Babbitt, "Twelve-Tone Invariants as Compositional Determinants," in *Problems of Modern Music,* ed. Paul Henry Lang (New York, 1960), 108–21.

5. Ernst Krenek, "Extents and Limits of Serial Technique," in Lang, *Problems of Modern Music,* 72–94.

6. George Rochberg, "The Harmonic Tendency of the Hexachord," *Journal of Music Theory* 3, no. 2 (1959): 208–30.

7. George Rochberg, "Webern's Search for Harmonic Identity," *Journal of Music Theory* 6, no. 1 (1962): 109–22.

8. Joseph Rufer, *Composition with Twelve Tones,* trans. Humphrey Searle (New York, 1954).

9. George Perle, *Serial Composition and Atonality* (Berkeley, 1962).

10. Allen Forte, *Contemporary Tone-Structures* (New York, 1955), 110–27.

for it is the only analysis in the book that foregoes some sort of Schenker-like linear reduction. In demonstrating the continuity of the Phantasy it relies entirely on connections between row statements, all of which would work equally well for the mirror inversion of the composition.

As might be expected, *Perspectives of New Music* offers an unusually rich harvest of apposite examples. These include David Lewin's "A Theory of Segmental Association in Twelve-Tone Music";[11] John M. Perkins's "Dallapiccola's Art of Canon";[12] Babbitt's "Remarks on the Recent Stravinsky";[13] Perle's "An Approach to Simultaneity in Twelve-Tone Music";[14] Peter Westergaard's "Toward a Twelve-Tone Polyphony";[15] and about a half dozen of the "Younger Composers" series.

Especially interesting is another essay of Babbitt's, "Twelve-Tone Rhythmic Structure and the Electronic Medium,"[16] which develops a method of deriving a rhythmic row from the intervals of the basic set. Perhaps here one can find a criterion for distinguishing the original composition from its inversion. But no: since the direction we choose for counting notes or for calculating intervals is a matter of pure convention, an inverted set can always be made to yield the same rhythmic row as its original (i.e., by counting intervals *down* rather than up from the origin).

Allen Forte's "Context and Continuity in an Atonal Work"[17] shows, by its treatment of Schoenberg's Op. 19, that my suggested transformation need not be limited to twelve-tone works. From this essay (as well as from appropriate sections of Perle's book) one might go much further and conclude that, barring purely instrumental difficulties, a new composition can always be constructed to fit any purely contextual analysis merely by inverting the original—regardless of its style and technique.

(It should perhaps be pointed out here that the aforementioned instru-

11. David Lewin, "A Theory of Segmental Association in Twelve-Tone Music," *Perspectives of New Music* 1, no. 1 (1962): 89–116.
12. John M. Perkins, "Dallapiccola's Art of Canon," *Perspectives of New Music* 1, no. 2 (1963): 95–106.
13. Milton Babbitt, "Remarks on the Recent Stravinsky," *Perspectives of New Music* 2, no. 2 (1964): 35–55.
14. George Perle, "An Approach to Simultaneity in Twelve-Tone Music," *Perspectives of New Music* 3, no. 1 (1964): 91–101.
15. Peter Westergaard, "Toward a Twelve-tone Polyphony," *Perspectives of New Music* 4, no. 2 (1966): 90–112.
16. Milton Babbitt, "Twelve-Tone Rhythmic Structure and the Electronic Medium," *Perspectives of New Music* 1, no. 1 (1962): 49–79.
17. Allen Forte, "Context and Continuity in an Atonal Work," *Perspectives of New Music* 1, no. 2 (1963): 72–82.

mental obstacles to literal inversion are not so formidable as one might think. Much twelve-tone music is conceived in a texture that, even when not strictly polyphonic, nevertheless depends on an equalization of voices and registers. When the analyses refer to instrumentation, they usually do so to point out identities and contrasts that can easily be maintained under inversion.)

So far I have said nothing about the possibility of another kind of systematic transformation, namely, complete retrogression, which, if accepted, would in turn imply the availability of retrograde inversion as well. Although Schoenberg insists that, just as there is theoretically no "absolute down," there is no absolute "forward or backward," there are nevertheless occasions (as often when a row is divided among two or more voices) when an exact reversal would fail to produce a correct set form. The reversion of a twelve-tone piece, then, cannot always be depended on to produce another "correct" twelve-tone piece. On the other hand, there are certainly many examples that can be reversed with impunity, especially if one is not doctrinaire and allows the reversal of approximate attack points as an alternative method to the reversal of time values. And slight modifications of the rules governing note counting (such as the option of counting a note on its *last* appearance in a given context) would open the door to universal retrogression.

To be sure, the distinction between forward and backward ought to be made from a wider point of view than that of pure note counting. Schoenberg himself, later in the above-quoted essay, implies that, regardless of theory, practice may require such a distinction. His statement that "one could perhaps tolerate a slight digression from this order [of the basic set] . . . in the later part of a work, when the set had already become familiar to the ear,"[18] suggests that a composer must, sometimes at least, take into account the order in which musical events take place. But this rule is vague and by no means self-evident; besides, there are many compositions to which it does not apply, since they never depart from the original set except in canonical ways. And when these methodical departures are used, Schoenberg's rule is frequently disregarded. We have his own example, in the Phantasy Op. 47, of a composition that begins by developing a single hexachord, stating the definitive set only when the piece is well under way. And Milton Babbitt's *Composition for Four Instruments* reserves its definitive statement for the end, after a systematic treatment of derived sets.

One may nevertheless feel intuitively that something is wrong: that retrogression in music, whatever its technique, should have as little gen-

18. Schoenberg, *Style and Idea,* 117.

eral validity as in literature or in cinema. And certainly compositions planned according to traditional rhetoric—e.g., introduction, statement, development, climax, restatement, peroration—hardly admit of intelligible reversal. Yet it is just these elements of form in the music of those composers, such as Schoenberg and Berg, who relied on older models, that a later generation has found old-fashioned and is trying to purge from its own music. Accordingly, it is just these elements that are ignored in many analyses today.

If we search the above-cited essays, we find very little help in deciding just why those compositions lacking a text move in the direction that they do, or—a related question—why they end just when they do. The analyses, with few exceptions, demonstrate connections—how one section is related to another—rather than progressions—how one section follows from another. Such relationships as repetition, similarity, contrast, common-tone linkage, and the like, are as independent of temporal as of pitch direction. Similarly, discussions of harmony concern themselves with the derivation of simultaneities, but hardly with the justification of the motion from one to another; criteria for melodic construction are never mentioned. Thus, for purely instrumental compositions lacking passages where the exigencies of strict note counting determine the direction of events, forward and backward indeed seem to be indistinguishable. Webern's fondness for the palindrome, which celebrates musical reversibility, may be an indication that his own thought was moving in this direction.

(In this paper I have not considered the systematic transformations effected by equating the chromatic scale with the circle of fifths. I leave to others the exercise of determining to what extent the cited analyses would remain applicable to versions so derived.)

So far, none of the transformations I have discussed has affected the internal structure of the compositions in question. Now, however, I should like to suggest the possibility of operations of this kind. One of the points that emerges from a recent colloquy among Babbitt, Perle, and Lewin on the Schoenberg Violin Concerto[19] is that, although it may be imprecise to treat transposition as analogous to tonal modulation (as Perle at one point seems to try to do), transpositions can nevertheless create the effect of a more or less wide departure from an originally stated quasi-harmonic area—not just by differences in register, but also and especially by common-tone relationships among segments of two or

19. Lewin, "Theory of Segmental Association"; George Perle, "Babbitt, Lewin, and Schoenberg: A Critique," *Perspectives of New Music* 2, no. 1 (1963): 120–27; followed by Milton Babbitt's reply, 127–32.

more forms of the set. The number of such common tones, e.g., between the first hexachord of the original statement and that of a given transposition, might be a measure of the "harmonic" distance of the transposition; and measures of this kind might then form a basis for "harmonic" progression through a piece. To return now to a composition to which I have already done violence, and which I intend to manhandle still further, let us see how this concept applies to Schoenberg's Op. 33a, and how it can be used to compose an alternative development to Schoenberg's—an alternative that, according to the accepted principles, should be an adequate substitute for the original. Here are the set forms Schoenberg uses (with P and I reading left to right, R and RI right to left; transposition level O has been used for the first appearance of both P and I):

P_0:	Bb	F	C	B ¦	A	F#	C#	D#	G	Ab	D	E	: R_0
I_0 :	Eb	Ab	Db	D ¦	E	G	C	Bb	Gb	F	B	A	: RI_0
P_2:	C	G	D	C# ¦	B	G#	D#	F	A	Bb	E	F#	: R_2
I_2 :	F	Bb	Eb	E ¦	F#	A	D	C	Ab	G	C#	B	: RI_2
P_7:	F	C	G	F# ¦	E	C#	G#	A#	D	Eb	A	B	: R_7
I_7 :	Bb	Eb	Ab	A ¦	B	D	G	F	Db	C	F#	E	: RI_7

First trichords arranged in fifths:

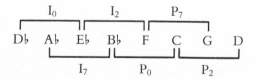

$$\begin{array}{ccccccc} & I_0 & & I_2 & & P_7 & \\ Db & Ab & Eb & Bb & F & C & G & D \\ & & I_7 & & P_0 & & P_2 & \end{array}$$

Common tones in first hexachords of P_0 and I_2: Bb F A F#
Common tones between end of development and beginning of recapitulation: C F Bb Eb Ab

Of the above forms, the exposition employs only the T_0; the development uses the T_2 and T_7; the recapitulation returns to the original forms.

Now, it can be shown that, in making his first transposition (T_2), the composer has exploited two relationships, both indicated in the above chart: the common tones of the first hexachords of P_0 and I_2, and the series of fifths implied by the first trichords of P_0 and I_0 and explicitly stated in m. 25. These fifths, extended, then help to make the connection between T_2 and T_7. But in this piece every statement of a P-form (or R) is complemented by its combinatorial I-form (or RI). The same common-tone and fifth relationships, then, could equally well have been exploited by the composer in the reverse direction by using T_{-2} (i.e., T_{10}, followed by T_{-7} (i.e., T_5). Thus:

P_{10}: A♭ E♭ B♭ A ┊ G E │ B C♯ F G♭ C D : R_{10}

I_{10} : D♭ G♭ C♭ C ┊ D F │ B♭ A♭ E D♯ A G : RI_{10}

P_5 : E♭ B♭ F E ┊ D B │ F♯ G♯ C D♭ G A : R_5

I_5 : A♭ D♭ G♭ G ┊ A C │ F E♭ B B♭ E D : RI_5

First trichords arranged in fifths:

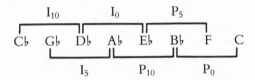

Common tones in first hexachords of I_0 and P_{10}: A♭ E♭ G E
Common tones between end of development and beginning of recapitulation: F B♭ E♭ A♭ D♭

I have written out a hypothetical new development section along these lines (ex. 4).

Schoenberg's development initially exploits the E♭-B♭-F fifths; mine, the A♭-E♭-B♭. For his common tones between R_0 and I_2, I have substituted those between RI_0 and P_{10}. The rest of my development can easily be followed by comparison with the original. At the recapitulation, Schoenberg makes a connection from the last tetrachords of R_7 and RI_7 to the first of P_0 and I_0. My version, leading from R_5 and RI_5, preserves the same number of common tones between the tetrachords of the development and those of the recapitulation—five; four of them, including the important connectives B♭ and E♭ (the first notes of the recapitulation) are the same as in the original. (In fact, of the eight tones constituting the end of my development, all but one are the same as those of the original.)

Example 4

Before going further, I must insist that my attempt in none of these rewritings has been to improve on, or even to equal, the original. I am merely trying to show that the analytical methods used by the essays cited offer no criteria for deciding in each case between the two versions.

It is now time for a brief look at those analyses that do try to offer criteria for distinguishing up from down, forward from backward. My admittedly incomplete survey disclosed several worth noting for their efforts in this regard. Claudio Spies's discussion of Stravinsky's *Abraham and Isaac*,[20] like Edward Laufer's account of Sessions's *Montezuma*,[21] can call on the demands of text setting and on other associations between music and words; but deprived of these, Spies's analysis of the "Huxley" Variations[22] has to fall back on such concepts as those of antecedent and consequent phrases—usefully evocative, perhaps, but undefined in this context. In the same spirit, René Leibowitz, in his *Qu'est-ce que la Musique*

20. Claudio Spies, "Notes on Stravinsky's *Abraham and Isaac*," *Perspectives of New Music* 3, no. 2 (1965): 104–26.

21. Edward C. Laufer, "Roger Sessions: *Montezuma*," *Perspectives of New Music* 4, no. 1 (1965): 95–108.

22. Claudio Spies, "Notes on Stravinsky's Variations," in ibid., 62–74.

de Douze Sons?,[23] makes vague analogies between Webern's phrase construction and Beethoven's. His *Introduction à la Musique de Douze Sons*,[24]
in its long analysis of Schoenberg's Variations for Orchestra Op. 31,
points out the traditional models the composer used to give shape and
temporal direction to his large-scale designs but evokes no further criteria of the kind we are seeking—save the quotation of the BACH motif.
Even the discussions of orchestration emphasize symmetries, parallelisms, similarities, and contrasts that, as I have already suggested, can
easily be retained under inversion.

Peter Westergaard gives us a glimmer of hope in his attempt to justify
the meter of the second movement of Webern's Piano Variations Op. 27.[25]
He suggests that here the invariable appearance of the lower of each pair
of three-note chords at the beginning of the measures in which they appear emphasizes the 2/4 meter. But even if one decides that Boulez is
wrong in maintaining that Webern's meters are purely conventional and
not meant to be observed in performance,[26] one must point out that the
placement of low chords in the other two movements gives us no indication whatsoever of their meters. One would also question whether the
regular appearance of the *higher* of each pair of chords on strong beats
might not equally well establish the meter. In fact, this movement, the
inversion of which is such a trivial operation that it can almost be performed at sight, offers a simple and complete demonstration of the problem I am raising. (It should be noted that Westergaard, in his mention of
"the Haydnesque wit" of the two-quarter rest just before the end, does
give us one reason for preferring the original direction of this movement
to its reversal. But one might wonder why, if such a gesture so clearly—
and so wittily—marks the end, the entire section is then repeated. And
might not the same gesture wittily serve as an introduction?)

Of the remaining critiques that I have considered, most of those that
make a structural distinction between soprano and bass—to put the
problem of total inversion in its simplest form—and concern themselves
with progression—to do the same with reversal—do so by means of
linear and harmonic outlines vaguely derived from Schenker's methods.
Attempts of this kind may be seen in two articles on Sessions: one by
Andrew Imbrie[27] and the other by Edward Laufer.[28] Richard Swift also

23. René Leibowitz, *Qu'est-ce que la Musique de Douze Sons?* (Liege, 1948).
24. René Leibowitz, *Introduction à la Musique de Douze Sons* (Paris, 1949).
25. Peter Westergaard, "Webern and 'Total Organization,'" *Perspectives of New Music* 1, no. 2 (1963): 107–20.
26. Pierre Boulez, "Propositions," *Polyphonie* 2 (1948): 67.
27. Andrew Imbrie, "Roger Sessions: In Honor of His Sixty-Fifth Birthday," *Perspectives of New Music* 1, no. 1 (1962): 117–47.
28. Laufer, "Roger Sessions: *Montezuma*," 95–108.

moves in this direction in his account of J. K. Randall's *Demonstrations*.[29] But what right has one to call on such devices in this context? In tonal music, the motion of the bass can be derived from some expansion[30] of the tonic chord; that of the soprano, by passing motion within the scale. But what does either tonic or passing tone mean when there are no previously or permanently defined chords, and no functionally operative scales? Can this music really be approached through attitudes and habits derived from listening to tonal music? And would a tentative and qualified assent to that question commit us to an acceptance of the tonal analogies Spies finds in the late Stravinsky,[31] or to approval of Martin Boykan's still bolder tonal approach to the same composer[32]—not to speak of Hindemith's rigid application of his own tonal principles in his well-known analysis (or mis-analysis) of a passage from our old friend Op. 33a?[33] Or should we put all such interpretations in the same category as the explanation of the French word sequence *Pas de lieu Rhône que nous* as making sense in spoken English?

Again, should even the presence of clear triadic references be taken at tonal face value? Leibowitz recognizes the possibility of their creating a "tonalité *vague, incertaine*," especially in the works of Berg, although ultimately it is the "logique du maniement sériel" that must provide justification for all that happens.[34] Rufer, on the other hand, seems to believe that such tonal impressions are more illusory than real, and at any rate are useless for our purposes:

> Thus triads of tonal structure can appear too, as, for instance, the "Ode to Napoleon" shows. But these, like *all* chord-structures in twelve-note music, are of purely local importance and do not produce harmonic progressions which have the effect of creating form, as happens in tonal music; for the relationship to the key-note is missing.[35]

Who is right?

The fact that one can raise such questions shows that we have arrived at a crucial point in the history of Western music. Up until now there has been no ambiguity between up and down—at least not since the fourth

---

29. Richard Swift, "The *Demonstrations* of J. K. Randall," *Perspectives of New Music* 2, no. 2 (1964): 77–86.

30. I.e., by the elaboration of the interval between root and fifth.

31. Claudio Spies, "Some Notes on Stravinsky's Requiem Settings," *Perspectives of New Music* 4, no. 2 (1967): 98–123.

32. Martin Boykan, "'Neoclassicism' and Late Stravinsky," *Perspectives of New Music* 1, no. 2 (1963): 155–69.

33. Paul Hindemith, *The Craft of Musical Composition* (New York, 1937), 1:217–19.

34. Leibowitz, *Introduction*, 283–85 (emphasis original).

35. Rufer, *Composition with Twelve Tones*, 126 (emphasis original).

was distinguished in effect from the fifth; there has been no question of choice between forward and backward since the appearance of the melodic cadence—and, later and *a fortiori,* the harmonic cadence; there has been no transpositional relationship that could not be explained by reference to some sort of tonic. But these aspects of composition, hitherto accepted as basic, are apparently unaccounted for by twelve-tone theory.

If one accepts this conclusion, one can adopt one of three attitudes toward it. One can welcome it wholeheartedly, agreeing that there really is no basis for choice among my hypothetical versions beyond the convenience of accepting what is already given and the comfort of familiarity. But that only throws the problem back where it really belongs in the first place: on the shoulders of the composer. How did he make his decisions in these matters?

This leads us to a second point of view: that twelve-tone theory is as yet incomplete, and that the superiority of one version of a composition over another depends on purely formal factors as yet unanalyzed but nevertheless eventually analyzable, analogous to the laws of linear and harmonic progression in tonal music, possibly similar to those but not necessarily so. A composition is successful insofar as its composer has made his implied choices among conceivable alternatives in accordance with his intuitive, or, better, his partly rational understanding of these presumed laws.

Finally, one can accept the primacy of the composer's concrete choices but insist that, far from being made in obedience to laws known or unknown, they are so fundamental to the composer's conception of his work as to belong, so to speak, among its basic assumptions. They are determined by what may be called *absolute decisions,* i.e., decisions for which no adequate analytical reasons can ever be adduced.

If many of us at first glance opt for the second point of view, it is because the success of theorists of tonality, notably Schenker and his followers, has given us hope that all the secrets of contemporary composition await analogous types of explication. But a more sophisticated generation of theorists—as exemplified by Milton Babbitt and Michael Kassler—has been pointing out what a flimsy systematic basis even Schenker's splendid construction rests on.[36] In trying to establish tonal theory more firmly, they dismiss Schenker's appeals to Nature, the Human Spirit, and the Overtone Series, in favor of a strictly logical system

36. See Milton Babbitt, "The Structure and Function of Musical Theory," *College Music Symposium* 5 (1965): 49–60; Michael Kassler, "A Trinity of Essays," Ph.D. dissertation, Princeton University, 1967. The essay dealing with the twelve-tone system was published in *Perspectives of New Music* 5, no. 2 (1967): 1–80, as "Toward a Theory That is the Twelve-Note-Class System."

derived from a limited number of axioms and rules of inference. For these axioms they offer—naturally—no proof whatsoever. But if we accept this approach, we must admit the possibility of equally consistent systems that we might call anti-tonal. By regular and easily definable modifications of the axioms and rules of inference, such systems could lead to compositions that are the total inversions, retrogressions, or inverted retrogressions of conventional tonal compositions. Other transformations, too, are possible. Deprived of all natural bases, what appeals could the conventional system make against such rivals save those of convenience, tradition, custom, and familiarity? (It is instructive here to note that in the earlier case we could perform the hypothetical operations on individual works, for the operations themselves constitute "rules of inference" of the system. Since this is not true of tonal music, the operations must be applied to the system as a whole, not to individual works—a possibility adumbrated in the case of inversion by proponents of harmonic dualism from Zarlino to Riemann.)

We can perhaps recognize here one motive that has driven so many theorists to find some kind of support in the existence of the overtone series, and we can sympathize with them even though we cannot follow them. They seem to consider the role of the series as somehow analogous to that of gravity in architecture: a raw fact of physics that must be taken into account in creating viable structures. But the analogy can be turned against them: every building is a success insofar as it defeats gravity. Moreover, the Gothic vault and the cantilever attest the futility of arguing that good design is necessarily based on the *visual* exploitation of physical principles. True, the overtone series does indeed make a distinction between up and down within the individual tone, since overtones are, after all, above the fundamental. Furthermore, one must take account of the series in the physical construction and practical use of instruments. Neither of these facts, however, justifies the claim that the *auditive* structure of music, whether tonal or not, necessarily depends on the composition of the series. In fact, only today, through electronic means, is it becoming possible to integrate, in a systematic and thoroughgoing way, overtone spectra, whether natural or artificial, into musical structures.[37] Ironically, the same media now offer for the first time the theoretical possibility of inverting the audible spectra. Such complete tone-color inversion would at last deprive the individual tone itself of the possibility of distinguishing up from down!

---

37. See, for example, J. K. Randall, "Three Lectures to Scientists," *Perspectives of New Music* 5, no. 2 (1967): 124–40. The third of these, "Operations on Waveforms," deals with this possibility.

If now, in spite of the discouraging example of the tonal system, we still insist on seeking some basis for making distinctions that we feel to be somehow essential, let us turn to the third alternative: that there is, and can be, no analytical ground for concrete musical choices, i.e., no ground within the internal structure of the music itself; yet that these choices are crucial in determining musical values, i.e., salient characteristics that afford a basis for distinction, comparison, and judgment. (Critical listeners, as well as composers, must also make such choices, although in a slightly different sense; for all judgments are based on implicit comparisons between actual and possible compositions, and hence on a choice among concrete values. Indeed, it was from this point of view that we initially approached the problem.) To put the position succinctly: *Concrete musical values depend on absolute decisions.* Remember that by absolute I do not mean arbitrary: there may be, as we shall see, good reasons for making one choice and not another. By absolute I mean independent of purely analytical considerations and unsusceptible of purely analytical justification.

Let me try to clarify this point by referring to another art, this time painting. Suppose an artist is painting a monochromatic picture, or simply making a drawing. Every formal element of the pictorial structure will then depend on line and light value, not on color relationships. But how does the painter decide what color to use? He might rule out certain colors as incapable of sustaining his design—yellow might be too light, for instance; but he would still have a wide range of choice. If the decision is not a purely capricious one, it must be based on reasons; but these reasons cannot be analytical, since the internal structure of the picture will be the same in any case. The reasons must therefore be external to the structure. The picture may be intended for a room with a given color scheme. The artist may feel that a warm or a cool color might be more appropriate to the subject of the picture. He may even feel that one color has a vague expressive value consonant with the subject. Or he may simply revel in the sensuous quality of one color.

Let us take another example, one somewhat analogous to the problem with which our discussion began. How does an artist (or an observer) decide which way a picture should hang—which way is right side up? Good design seems often to be independent of whether or not it is inverted—an assumption supported by the habit, common among painters, of testing their compositions by viewing them upside down, as well as by the frequency of mistakes in the hanging of abstractions. (We seem to measure balance with reference to a vertical axis, possibly because of our own physiological orientation, so that ninety-degree rotation is seldom a live option—although Carl Pickhardt has experimented with free-form abstractions that can be hung at *any* angle.) In the case of a representational picture the answer to our question is obvious—unless the artist is Chagall (or, apparently, sometimes Matisse, whose *Le Bateau* hung upside down in the Museum of Modern Art in New York City from Oct. 18 to Dec. 4, 1961).[38] But we arrive at this answer by a reference outside the picture—to the depicted subject. Indeed, from the point of view of pure design, the orientation of a picture must often be based on an absolute decision—one made with reference to representational rather than to structural values. Apparent arguments from design will in such cases merely conceal external references. For example, to the claim that a landscape must hang as it does because the lighter area looks better at the top, one can counter that the only justification for this preference is that this is the way landscapes look in nature, and one can point to many abstractions in which the lighter areas are below. How, in fact, does one determine the orientation of an abstraction? How does the artist himself make that decision? In the absence of any clear indication from the design, the decision must be absolute. The reasons on which it is based will be external to the pictorial structure, whether the artist says simply, "This is the way I like it," or more specifically, "The expressive effect of the picture would be harmed if it were inverted."

We have arrived here at an important point. Expressive values in any art—if they exist at all—depend on concrete values. They cannot arise from analytical values alone. How could they? Unless one wishes to explain what it could possibly mean for a work of art to "express itself," then one must agree that expression, by its very definition, implies a relationship between the work of art and something else; while analytical values are derivable purely from internal structure. This is in no way meant to suggest that structure has nothing to do with expression. Just as communication in a verbal language depends on both semantics and syntax, so artistic expression must involve both concrete and analytical values. Without the former, the structure could convey no message; without the latter, the message would be limited to the equivalent of primitive substantives and exclamations. Thus the expressive power of an abstract canvas cannot stem from its design alone; it must depend in part on some covert representational or other associative element (as, for example, the illusion of "mass" or "movement").

The foregoing suggests that for those who wish to make special claims for the role of the overtone series in tonal music, or for what can be much more easily defended, the primacy of the fifth, a more fruitful analogy

38. Norris and Ross McWhirter, *Guinness Book of World Records,* rev. and enlarged ed. (New York, 1966), 157.

than that of gravity in architecture might be that of representation in painting. For whereas gravity is a law of nature that controls all construction even though it may be apparently refuted to the eye, representation is merely a reference to nature that can be utilized or not according to the purposes of the artist. Similarly, even if one holds that the supremacy of the fifth in tonal harmony derives from a natural law, one must admit that a great deal of music ignores it; hence it must be a law in a different sense of the word than the law of gravity. Yet it could still be a law to this extent: that in all music that exploits the fifth in a tonal sense, the special relation of fifth to fundamental, whether due to definite though ill-defined roots in physical and anatomical nature, or simply to the growing force of conventional habit over several centuries, inevitably determines the orientation of the music, i.e., its direction both in pitch and in time—just as representation determines the orientation of a picture.

Such a view of tonality is by no means inconsistent with the recent attempts to explain the system axiomatically. It merely insists that such explanations can never adequately deal with the problem of orientation. If tonal music carries with it its built-in orientation, then it is built in absolutely, not analytically. It rests, not on the internal consistency of the system, but on some connection between the axioms and rules of inference on the one hand, and the external world on the other—whether that world is represented by acoustics, psychology, physiology, or history. The orientation is, so to speak, semantic rather than syntactic.

One who accepts the analogy implied in the last sentence may be willing to go further and admit the relevance of tonal orientation to the problem of musical expression. If the effect of the fifth in tonal music is, to some extent at least, independent of context and external to pure design, then elements of musical form inferable from the role of the fifth (e.g., tonal cadences) could serve as vehicles of some of the associative elements necessary to expression (e.g., the association of a perfect cadence with fulfillment or satisfaction). It is tempting to say of such instances that the structure alone is the vehicle of the expression; and from this error it becomes easy to generalize to the extent of basing all musical expression on pure syntax. That is because tonal music marries the semantic and syntactic aspects so closely that it is difficult to conceive of the semantic element in isolation. One should really speak here, not of syntactic and semantic, or of analytic and concrete, but of *fused* values; for in the best tonal music the two aspects of tonality are indeed indissoluble. But recent music has suggested new possibilities. Just as representational implications (such as those of mass and motion) can impart some meaning to a pictorial abstraction, so tonal references can function in non-tonal music, not so much syntactically as associatively, bringing with them implications of the orientational and expressive values inhering in tonal contexts. At the same time these references, arising as they do from syntactical origins in tonal music, must, if they are to be successfully employed, satisfy whatever syntactical expectations of this nature they arouse. Such references may vary from, say, a bald statement of consonant triads to a generalized adaptation of melodic-harmonic relationships and phrase structure.

Thus music whose syntax is primarily twelve-tone may nevertheless legitimately call upon implicit tonal functions to clarify its concrete values—so long as the functions, once summoned, are permitted, so to speak, to fulfill their tonal responsibilities. A complete explication of this music must then take these tonal allusions into account—whether they are overt, as is often the case with Berg, or concealed, as in much of Schoenberg. (Note, for example, in Op. 33a, the V-I effect created by the bass connection B♭-E♭ from the development into the recapitulation—an effect signally, and perhaps disastrously, lacking in my version.)

Today composers can choose for themselves whether or not to utilize tonal references. For centuries, of course, the individual composer had no such option. The decision was already made for him, just as the decision as to the use of representation was already made for the painter. Nations and historical periods, as well as individuals, choose concrete values through absolute decisions; hence we can speak of national and historical as well as individual styles. That is what style is: the totality of the concrete values characterizing a given body of work as a whole. The stylistic decision of a group may seem to be so completely determined by evolution, environment, or culture, that it should not properly be called a decision at all; yet it functions in the same way as an individual decision, for it results in one mode of action that rules out all alternative modes. Perhaps because of their deterministic origin, these decisions are even more binding on the individual than his personal choices, which may vary from work to work. Thus if tonality carries with it certain associations, then these associations are bound to leave their mark on all music of the tonal period just as inevitably as the presence of the realistically depicted human figure is bound to affect the content of painting from the Renaissance up to the end of the nineteenth century.

Tonal functions are, to be sure, not the only source of associative values. Once one admits the relevance of these values at all, one finds them involved in almost every area of concrete musical choice. And once we leave the specific problems of tonality, we find that many concrete values have been equally at the disposal of composers in many styles, using diverse techniques. But all these values presuppose absolute decisions;

so, although the tonal composer may never have had to wonder whether or not his composition was running in the right direction, even he, like his present-day successor, was constantly confronted by choices that could never be made on analytical grounds alone. How did he determine tempo? The internal structure of most compositions imposes certain limits within which a tempo must be sought, but these limits are often very broad indeed. We can all think of compositions that would still make perfect musical sense if taken at a tempo twice as fast or twice as slow as that indicated; why then should the indicated tempo have precedence? Because the composer chose it? But why did he choose it?

Register is another example. How would the structure of the Chopin C-minor Prelude, or of his Funeral March, suffer if the piece were written a fifth higher—or even an octave higher? Yet such transpositions would manifestly alter the effect of the pieces, and hardly for the better. (Roger Sessions reports that he once succeeded in turning Scriabin's "Black Mass" Sonata [No. 9] into a White Mass by playing it an octave higher, and in turning the "White Mass" [No. 10] into a Black Mass by reversing the process.)

Even instrumentation depends to a large extent on absolute decisions. This is especially easy to demonstrate with regard to monochromatic media, where the problems of interrelationships among colors hardly arise. Beethoven, for practical purposes, was willing to transcribe his *Grosse Fuge* for piano four-hands. Brahms did the same for his two string sextets. They are fun to play that way—but it is hard to get anyone to listen. Why? What crucial analytical values, present in the string version, are lost in the transcriptions?

Decisions in these matters must be made by all composers, regardless of style and technique. Each one of them determines certain concrete values that, moreover, are associative values; and whether we like it or not, these associations are bound to inhere in the music itself. Tempo is inevitably measured by unconscious comparisons with rates of human action; register relates itself to our concepts of height, weight, and mass; tone color brings with it obvious connotations of all kinds, from our tendency to identify melody with the human voice to resemblances of the sort that so delighted the little Stravinsky in the "dubious" noises produced by the red-haired peasant.[39] Many other areas in which associative values are unavoidably implied will come to mind: absolute dynamics, melodic direction, rhythmic and metric patterns. Again, whether the associations are in some sense "natural" or whether based

39. Igor Stravinsky, *An Autobiography* (New York, 1936), 3–4.

on generations of conditioning, they cannot be escaped by anyone musically trained in the Western tradition.

To be sure, choices in these areas are influenced by structure—but they control structure as well. Insofar as they characterize even the primitive gestures of the composer's initial ideas, and hence precede the musical design itself, they are independent and necessarily defy analysis. The design must take shape in accordance with their directions.

If one accepts the possibility and the relevance of musical expression, one may indeed feel that one's decisions here are governed, consciously or unconsciously, by the expressive potentialities of the associations inherent in one's concrete choices. Or one may insist that the decisions are, in every sense of the word, absolute. What I suspect, but am unable to prove, is that any concrete choice made on the basis of pure personal preference functions in the same way as one made with expressive intent and that the two may indeed be equivalent. To put the case at its most trivial: Why is my composition superior to its inversion? Because its melody descends. Why should the melody descend rather than ascend? Because I like it that way! But why do I like it that way? Because I want it to have the effect that can be produced by descent but not by ascent. Or—because I want it to express whatever it is that descent can express and ascent cannot express.

It should now be obvious that what I have been calling concrete choices are in many cases not choices at all, in the sense of representing the exercise of a live option. The absolute decisions of a composer—for *this* melody, in *this* tempo, in *this* register, for *this* instrument—are seldom the result of the conscious dismissal of other alternatives, even though any voluntary action implies the rejection of every other action possible on that occasion. The composer decides what piece he is going to write, not all the pieces he is not going to write; what I have been calling choices are really the assumptions basic to his concept of that piece. Yet there are certain occasions, especially frequent in connection with the development of previously stated ideas, that do seem to offer several workable alternatives. As I tried to show by means of a change in the development of Op. 33a, it is often difficult to advance analytical reasons to justify one's choice at such a point; we may perhaps now be willing to admit the example as evidence that the domain of a composer's absolute decisions embraces even the internal structure of a twelve-tone piece. As a final task, I shall try to show the same principle at work in tonal composition.

For obvious reasons, it would rarely be possible to invert successfully the harmonic direction of a tonal development as I tried to do with

Schoenberg's. But one field of choice presents itself with a high degree of regularity: the opportunity of changing mode. Once the convention of the *tierce de Picardie* was overthrown, it became a matter of the composer's choice whether a piece in minor ended in major or minor; later on, in the nineteenth century, it became increasingly common for works in major to end in minor. In many cases it seems impossible to find adequate analytical reasons for the ending actually adopted. Think over Schubert's *Moment Musical* No. 3 in F minor. Can you adduce any analytical evidence for the inevitability of its conclusion? Could you not rewrite the coda so that it ended convincingly in minor? Compare the C♯-minor *Moment Musical* No. 4 with Chopin's Etude in E minor Op. 25 No. 3 and his Nocturne in C minor Op. 48 No. 1. All three of them move to the tonic major in the middle section, so that all have, so to speak, a motive for ending in major. Only the Etude does so; the Nocturne remains in minor; while the *Moment Musical,* after a short reference to the major section, returns to minor. And what of Chopin's Nocturne in B major Op. 32 No. 1? Is there any necessary reason for its conclusion? (And just what is this conclusion, by the way? Some editions end in minor, some in major. Historical evidence seems to favor one over the other. Would you be willing, on analytical grounds, to decide which?) If you deny that these romantic examples are in the front rank of tonal structures, then work on Beethoven's String Quartet in F minor Op. 95. You can perhaps justify certain aspects of the coda by analysis, but that is not the same as proving its inevitability. Can you, on internal evidence, show that just this coda, in this tempo, above all in major, is the only possible ending for this quartet?

Whether Schubert, Chopin, and Beethoven—or, to return to our original problem, Schoenberg and Webern—made their decision on expressive grounds or whether they wrote their compositions the way they did simply because they liked them that way, my point is the same: their reasons are beyond analysis. And if we as critical listeners conclude that the composers were right, it should not disturb us to find that our own reasons are often beyond analysis, and that, when we try to explain the superiority of a composition over any alternative version, sometimes all we can say is, "It sounds better."

A great deal of current writing on music seems to imply that nothing about composition, or nothing important about composition, is beyond analysis. But surely the single most important thing anyone can say about any composition is beyond analysis: namely, "I like it." It is especially disturbing to find that many young composers, who presumably write about the music of others the way they think about their own, are either insensitive to non-analytical values or—as I think more likely—

afraid to admit their importance. As a result they often seem to be writing, not about actual compositions, but about abstractions derived from compositions. Now, I recognize the great debt we all owe to increasingly rigorous methods of analysis, and I am fully awake to the dangers of impressionistic criticism; yet I find myself completely on the side of the young composer—a rather well known one—who, when asked why he wrote as he did, replied, "I like the tunes."

[*1967*]

Three Ways of Reading a Detective Story—Or a Brahms Intermezzo

One of the reasons we like to read stories is to find out what happens. It is certainly not the only reason, and for some of us it may even be a minor one; but for others it is all-important. Obviously, then, an essential element of a narrative writer's technique is his control of the reader's awareness of events. The skillful author makes sure that we learn what has happened, what is happening, and what is going to happen, exactly when he wants us to know it, and not earlier or later.

From the writer of a mystery, in particular, we expect a high degree of precision in this regard. To be sure, we must avoid traps of the kind that Dickens laid for the unwary in *Our Mutual Friend*. As he wrote in the postscript to that novel, "I foresaw the likelihood that a class of readers and commentators would suppose that I was at great pains to conceal exactly what I was at great pains to suggest" (namely, the identity of his hero). But in the typical detective story, to allow the average reader to deduce or guess the solution too early on—before the actual dénouement—would be a major flaw revealing gross technical deficiency. For most of us, indeed, the nagging suspicion that we have already solved the riddle makes it almost impossible to continue to read a mystery with much pleasure. But if that is the case, how can we ever read a mystery for a second or even a third time—unless we have almost completely forgotten it? How can *The Moonstone* and the Sherlock Holmes canon achieve the status of classics of a sort, when classical status, if it means anything, implies that the work in question rewards close and repeated scrutiny?

The usual answer that we reread the mystery classics not for story but for style, for portrayal of character, for comment on society, is insufficient. If that were all, we should be content to browse through the Sherlock Holmes tales, savoring appropriate passages here and there. We may occasionally enjoy such selective study, but it does not satisfy the aficionado. He likes to reread these stories as stories, and the reading-for-atmosphere theory adduces no motive for him to do so. Why, to cite a specific and personal example, do I take such pleasure in yet another perusal of "The Adventure of the Speckled Band"? One probable reason is that I now appreciate it, at least to a limited extent, as a work of art. This must mean, among other things, that I apprehend it as a structure; but what kind of structure?

The plot of "The Speckled Band" is comparatively simple. An English physician, Dr. Roylott, has lived for some years in India, gaining there a reputation for violence and cruelty. On his return to England, he marries a wealthy widow with twin daughters. When his wife dies, her will stipulates that he is to enjoy her estate so long as the daughters remain single; when they marry, the money is to be divided. Subsequently one of the twins becomes engaged. Not wishing to give up her share of the estate, the doctor plots to murder his stepdaughter. He contrives each night to introduce, from his own bedroom into hers, a poisonous Indian snake, a speckled swamp adder. Eventually, as he has planned, it fatally bites the young woman. The cause of her death remains a mystery; for the dying girl's only words refer wildly to a "speckled band," and the poison is one that evades normal medical analysis. Two years later the remaining sister, Helen Stoner, becomes engaged. When certain suspicious occurrences remind her of her twin's death, she is frightened, and she applies for help to Sherlock Holmes. In answer to her appeal, the detective surreptitiously visits Dr. Roylott's house, where his investigations enable him to guess the truth. Hiding at night in Helen's room, he attacks the snake when it appears and drives it away. Returning to its master, the enraged adder inflicts on him the fatal bite intended for his stepdaughter.

This version of the tale—call it Version A—does, it is true, reveal a simple and satisfying structure: a pattern of crime and detection, of villainy and retribution, of the malefactor hoist with his own petard. But Version A is not the story as we read it. The order of events as revealed by Conan Doyle (or Dr. Watson) is quite different. Watson, after promising to reveal the truth about the strange death of Dr. Roylott, begins his narrative with Helen Stoner's call upon Sherlock Holmes. She recounts her family history, dwelling on the circumstances of her sister's death, and she describes the recent events that have driven her to seek Holmes's aid. He agrees to help her and she departs. Holmes begins to speculate on the case—misguidedly, as it will turn out—but is interrupted by the abrupt appearance of Dr. Roylott himself, whose actions in trying to avert investigation merely confirm Helen's description of his violent nature. Undeterred by threats, Holmes, together with Watson, visits the doctor's house, where, as we know, he soon deduces the correct solution to the mystery. Watson, however—and therefore, presumably, the reader—is left for a time in ignorance. Although he accompanies Holmes on his nocturnal vigil and is present during his attack on the snake, Watson remains both literally and figuratively in the dark until the moment when he sees the speckled band coiled around the head of the dead doctor. Only then does Holmes reveal to his friend, and to us, the chain of inference that has led him to the truth.

That is the story as we read it—or more specifically, as we read it for the first time, without prior knowledge of its outcome. As opposed to Version A, which recounted the events in their natural chronological order, Version B, as we may call it, arranges them artfully and purposefully. In the present case the purposes are to mystify and to create mounting suspense until a dénouement simultaneously relieves the suspense and convincingly explains the mystery. The first responsibility of a detective story is to achieve success on this First-Reading level.

A First Reading need not, of course, be literally that. The phrase refers to any reading based on total or partial ignorance of the events narrated, whether one is actually reading a story for the first time, or is making a renewed attempt to "get" a story previously read but imperfectly comprehended (perhaps found impenetrable), or is returning to a story read long ago and since forgotten. In each case, one important motivation is a desire to find out what happens—or, in the case of a mystery, to understand what has already happened.

Once one has glimpsed the structure underlying a recounted series of events—the pattern of their causes, their interrelationships, their outcome—one's consciousness of that pattern is bound to inform subsequent readings of the narrative. What I call the Second Reading (whether it is actually one's second, third, . . . or tenth) is controlled by that consciousness. It is a reading, that is to say, in which one's mental reconstruction of Version A serves as a continual gloss on Version B. As each detail occurs in the narrative (essentially Version B), it is considered in the light of its position in the plot structure (essentially Version A). B is thus regarded as the vehicle for the realization of the pattern defined by A. Mystery and suspense are banished from this reading, which admits of no emotional involvement on the part of the reader—except perhaps that resulting from his admiration of the writer's technique. In one way the Second Reading is not a true reading, or certainly not just a reading; for the reader, far from concentrating on the text before him, is constantly comparing what he is being told with what he knows from his previous encounter. His mental activity can thus be more accurately described as thinking about the story while using the text as a means of ensuring accuracy. In a word, the Second Reading aims at an analysis—not necessarily a conscious analysis, formally constructed, but at least one implied by a synoptic overview. This synoptic analysis treats the story, not as a work of art that owes its effect to progress through time, but as an object abstracted or inferred from the work of art, a static art-object that can be contemplated timelessly. Paradoxically, the Second Reading achieves its goal when it ceases to be a reading at all—when it becomes the pure contemplation of structure.

The First Reading, then, is completely innocent of analysis, and the Second Reading is for the sake of analysis, explicit or implicit. That analysis is put to use in the service of yet another reading—the Third. Like the First, this one is temporally oriented: it accepts the story as narrated. Again like the First, it aims at enjoyment; but now, guided by the synoptic comprehension of the Second Reading, it can replace naive pleasure with intelligent and informed appreciation. Yet at the same time this reading requires an intentional "forgetting." For if one is really to appreciate a narrative as such, one must concentrate on each event as it comes, trying to suppress from consciousness those elements meant to be concealed until some later point in the story. The pattern of Version A revealed by the Second Reading still exerts its control, but it must do so invisibly and silently. To be sure, it can never really be forgotten, but in the Third Reading it must remain hidden—a concealed motivation behind the actual narrative structure determined by Version B.

To put the distinction somewhat differently, one can say that the First Reading is purely experiential: one knows only what one experiences (i.e., is being told). The trajectory of the reader's thought is one-dimensional, moving along the path laid out by the author. In the Second Reading one knows much more than one is being told; the trajectory of thought is zigzag, or even discontinuous, constantly shifting back and forth between the planes of memory and experience, until at last one is able to achieve a comprehensive bird's-eye view of the narrative path. In the Third Reading there is a double trajectory. Thought moves simultaneously on two levels, one fully conscious and one at least partly suppressed. The primary, open level is once more that of experience, as the reader follows the actual narration; but this time he is in a position fully to enjoy the journey, for he is now both confident of his direction and aware of the relative importance of each event along the way. He cannot fully suppress what he already knows, for he travels at the same time on the plane of memory; but he tries to ration what he knows in such a way as to make the path of experience as vivid and as exciting as possible.

To be sure, we cannot really ration what we know. Our subconscious minds contain no selective filter to strain our memories—no sieve that allows only those memories useful for a given purpose to penetrate our overt consciousness, while retaining the rest. But we often find it necessary or convenient to pretend that this is the case and to act as if it were so. When we play games, even though no prestige or money is involved, we assume that a great deal is at stake. (People who really love a game have no need of a material risk to make the contest realistic; their imaginations are sufficient for the task.) When we go to the theater, we pretend that the actors are not actors and that the stage set is not a set. Children, of course, often create imaginary lives for themselves that are almost as vivid to them as their real lives; many adults retain something of this power in their capacity for daydreaming. It is the same faculty, or a closely related one, that enables us to respond emotionally to what we know is only fiction, and especially to experience during a Third Reading something of the excitement characteristic of the First.

For the Third Reading is an ideal First Reading. Or simply: the Third Reading is the ideal reading. It is the only one that fully accepts the story as a work of temporal art and tries to appreciate it as such. And when the Third Reading, in its turn, engenders an analysis, it is an analysis, not of an abstract structure or art object, but of the concrete work of art itself. It is not a synoptic but a diachronic analysis, one that deals with the events of the tale in their narrated order. Although it cannot avoid attending to the overall pattern investigated by synoptic analysis, it will allow itself to recognize that pattern only as a gradually emerging one, and it will concentrate on the strategies of concealment and disclosure by which the author controls the process.

Let me illustrate the differences between the three readings by reference to a specific passage in "The Speckled Band": Dr. Roylott's sudden appearance at Holmes's flat, hard on the heels of his stepdaughter's visit. The incident is obviously meant to astonish a First Reader, who, like Holmes and Watson, is utterly unprepared for the intrusion. As the situation develops, the same reader, if at all sophisticated, will begin to wonder whether Dr. Roylott is being introduced as a red herring: he is so unprepossessing, so threatening and violent, that he is much too obviously a villain. The truth must be otherwise than one has been led to suspect.

That is not the case, however: Dr. Roylott is just the villain he appears to be. The Second Reading thus entails a reconsideration of the episode. From his new vantage point the Second Reader discerns a certain symmetry: at the outset, Watson promises to reveal the true circumstances surrounding Dr. Roylott's death; at the end of the story that death is described; in between Dr. Roylott himself appears in one revealing episode. The passage is not essential to the plot, but it is necessary if the doctor is to be anything other than a shadowy figure evoked by Helen's narrative and Holmes's deductions. Without such an opportunity of meeting the villain face to face, so to speak, the reader can never fully appreciate the justice of the retribution that eventually overtakes him.

The Third Reader, too, will recognize the symmetry, but he will let himself realize it—or, if you prefer, he will pretend to realize it—only gradually, as the tale unfolds. Unlike the average First Reader, who probably fails to notice or to remember Watson's initial indication of the direction the story will take, the Third Reader will not allow the significance of the opening reference to Dr. Roylott's death to escape him. He will therefore not make the mistake of assuming that he is reading a conventional mystery in which the crime is committed by the most unlikely person. He will understand, as he is meant to, that Helen Stoner's narrative is to be taken as veridical and that her description of her stepfather is, as Holmes gets her to admit, understated rather than exaggerated. He will dutifully draw the correct conclusion that Dr. Roylott engineered one death and is now plotting another. He will realize, in other words, that the mystery is not one of Who but of How. And so, when Dr. Roylott appears on the scene, the Third Reader will find in his wild behavior confirmation of this interpretation of his character. The reader, moreover, will allow himself to luxuriate in the antipathy he is obviously meant to feel, so that he will eventually enjoy all the more thoroughly the horrid spectacle of Dr. Roylott's head encompassed by the speckled adder. But unlike the Second Reader, he must not look forward to this delicious moment. He must resolutely try to keep himself in the dark about the nature of the "band"—speculating, perhaps, like Holmes himself, on the possibility that the dying sister's words referred to a band of gypsies. Later, when Holmes and Watson visit the Roylott estate, he will depend only on the information revealed by their observations. He may permit himself to be a bit more perspicacious than Watson, whose myopia, I believe, is cunningly devised by the author to give the reader a slight sense of superiority; but he will keep the actual solution of the mystery waiting in the wings of his consciousness until Holmes is ready to bring it center stage. At that point his realization of the identity of the speckled band will remind him of Watson's original promise to explain how Roylott really died, and at the same time it will enable him to grasp the extent of the doctor's wickedness. So he will rejoice in the poetic justice of the outcome, at seeing "violence . . . recoil upon the violent," to use Holmes's phrase.

This coincidence of the fulfillment of a narrative promise, the solution of a mystery, and the execution of justice is essential to the artistic effect of the dénouement. Theoretically, it could be apprehended by a First Reader; practically, its complete appreciation must await a Third Reading. That is why I have called the Third Reading an ideal First Reading. But the effect, in any event, is unavailable to the Second Reader, for it depends on the appraisal of each event in exact narrative sequence; that is why I insist that only a diachronic Third-Reading analysis treats the story as a work of art. Such an analysis, along the lines I have sketched, would, I believe, explain the endless fascination of this much-anthologized tale: it derives primarily from the power of the narrative to control the emotional reactions of the reader in such a way as to afford him maximum satisfaction at the final revelation. At that point his emotional release coincides with his discovery of the truth. The narrative structure is not an abstract, static design but a temporal progression of events carefully arranged with a view toward their effect on a willing, sensitive reader. Hence the superiority of "The Speckled Band" over such a story as "The Adventure of the Lion's Mane." There, too, a dying man's words afford a clue to his mysterious death, which turns out again to have been caused by the sting of a poisonous animal (a huge jellyfish). But that tale is dominated by detective-story clichés: rival lovers, one of whom is killed; an obvious suspect—the surviving lover—who refuses to explain his odd behavior; a detective who keeps most of his knowledge to himself; and a solution that exonerates the suspect. The narrative structure arouses no patterned sequence of emotions stronger than that of curiosity followed by satisfaction.

It would be incorrect to generalize to the point of claiming that a Second-Reading analysis never treats a story as a work of art. Joseph Frank's seminal essay "Spatial Form in Modern Literature"[1] points out the difference between traditional novels, which are properly apprehended in narrative order, and those by writers like Proust, Joyce, and Djuna Barnes, who "ideally intend the reader to apprehend their work spatially, in a moment of time, rather than as a sequence" (p. 9). In the case of a book like *Nightwood,* the distinction between art-object and work of art no longer applies. To appreciate this novel as a work of art is precisely to apprehend it as a timeless object. Here Frank's quip about *Ulysses* is apt: "Joyce cannot be read—he can only be reread" (p. 19). For novels like these, the Third Reading is not an ideal First Reading but a more efficient Second Reading. More correctly, perhaps, one should say that there is no Third Reading but only a series of ever more thorough Second Readings.

It is thus important to distinguish between narratives for which the

---

1. Joseph Frank, *The Widening Gyre* (Bloomington, 1968), 3–62. Subsequent quotations from Frank are from this edition.

Third Reading is appropriate and those for which it is not. True, the claims of most detective stories to be works of art are at best modest, and they will suffer no great harm even if never subjected to a Third Reading. But gross misinterpretations of important works of literature have resulted from a confusion between readings and the levels of analysis pertaining to them. The popular conception of *Oedipus the King* as a tragedy of fate, demonstrating the helplessness of men in the grip of an inexorable destiny, depends on a Second-Reading analysis that arranges both the events enacted and those recounted to form a pattern of prophecy and fulfillment. But this is really an analysis of the underlying mythic structure, not of Sophocles' play. The motivation of the tragedy is Oedipus's determination to do his kingly duty and discover the truth despite all warnings. Indeed, Third-Reading analysis reveals a structure something like that of a modern mystery melodrama—the kind in which the audience is privy to the solution, but not the detective.[2]

The suppression of information that I have described as essential to a successful Third Reading may not always be possible, even as a game of pretense. On the other hand, the principle involved has some general validity that extends beyond the realm of pure prose fiction. There is, in fact, a progression among the genres and media of temporal art, leading from those in which the suppression required for the Third Reading (or Watching, or Hearing) is difficult, if not impossible, to those in which it is easy or even unavoidable. For example, a story told in the first person by an attractive and sympathetic character, whom the reader can imagine as a close friend or even as himself, offers more opportunities of success in this direction than one narrated by an omniscient author; and if the information thus imparted is further restricted to the contents of letters or diaries, the reader often finds himself sharing the limited vision of the supposed writer. A well-performed play, no matter how familiar, can rivet one's attention on the fictitious present of the action. And according to some theories, at least, a good actor is an ideal Third Reader, who really experiences the succession of emotions he is supposed to be feigning. The progression thus depends on the degree to which one can imaginatively participate in the fictitiously depicted life. And here at last we come to my real subject—music; for if what I have suggested elsewhere is correct, what I call "identification" is essential to the understanding and appreciation of a work of musical art: "an active participation in the life of the music by following its progress, attentively and imaginatively, through the course of one's own thoughts, and by adapting the tempo

2. See, for example, A. E. Haigh, *The Tragic Drama of the Greeks* (Oxford, 1896), 193. For a startlingly unorthodox interpretation of the play, see Philip Vellacott, *Sophocles and Oedipus* (Ann Arbor, 1971).

and direction of one's own psychic energies to the tempo and direction of the music."[3] The listener, and even more the performer, must experience music by living through it.

Except in the case of a simple and unproblematic composition in a well-known style, satisfactory participation is hardly possible for a First Hearing—or Reading: the difference is not essential because reading music requires (or should require) intense listening, either actual or imagined. Whichever mode of approach is employed, the purpose of one's first contact with an unfamiliar composition is to find out what the music has to say—or, in other words, what happens. So long as that is one's primary motivation for listening, one receives the music as something entirely external to oneself, and is consequently engaged in the activity of First Hearing—which may in fact extend through a number of actual hearings or readings. Only when the listener is reasonably confident of what is coming, to the extent that he can expectantly follow the course of the composition, is he ready for the Second Hearing.

At this stage, identification, rare enough in the case of the First Hearing, is completely out of the question. The Second Hearing must probably be, in point of fact, a Reading; for its aim is to arrive at a spatially oriented view of the composition as a whole, and its method is atemporal study. The Second Reader examines the composition at his own speed—even in his own order, for he may have to separate adjacent ideas and juxtapose distant ones in his attempt to uncover all the relationships governing the musical structure.

It is the Third Reader for whom identification is possible and, if I am right, crucial. Like the First Hearing, the Third is temporal and experiential; but it is characterized by an enriched perception of the temporal flow, and it realizes a controlled and appreciated experience. Fortunately, to achieve this level of perception is easier in performing or listening to music than in reading fiction. One reason for the obtrusiveness of our memories during a Third Reading of literature is the natural difficulty most of us experience in trying to concentrate exclusively on a single train of verbal thought. Concepts and images of all kinds are constantly impinging on our consciousness. It is no wonder, then, that when we read a familiar story it is hard to prevent remembered ideas and images from interpenetrating those actually before us at the moment, sometimes even replacing and contradicting them. But when we listen intently to music, the immediacy of what we are hearing makes it difficult or impossible for us to entertain other *musical* ideas at the same time. Thus our

3. Edward T. Cone, *The Composer's Voice* (Berkeley, 1974), 118. The subsequent quotation from Cone is from this edition.

memories of the Second Hearing are more likely to be verbal, or dia-
grammatic, or even mathematical. These concepts can direct, or modify,
or occasionally correct what we actually hear, but they can never replace
or contradict it—not, that is, so long as we are fully participating in the
actual music itself.

For this reason it is dismaying that so much analysis—so much of the
best analysis—not only begins but remains firmly planted in Second-
Hearing ground. Synoptic and atemporal, it proceeds from an initial assumption of omniscience; it is based on the premise that comprehension
of the whole is prerequisite for appreciation of the part. In one sense, of
course, this is true. That is why a First-Hearing analysis, except perhaps
at the most superficial level, is a contradiction in terms. But the Second-
Hearing analysis, even at the hands of a master like Schenker, does scant
justice to our experience of hearing a composition in real time. It accepts
as the goal what should be only a stage—albeit an important one—of
musical comprehension. That is the thrust of Schoenberg's reported
complaint that he could not find his favorite passages in Schenker's analysis of the *Eroica:* "Oh here they are, in these tiny notes!" he is supposed
to have exclaimed. And I insist that if anyone boasts, on the basis of
synoptic analysis, that he hears the opening chord of Beethoven's First
Symphony as a tonic, and the initial tremolo of the Ninth as a dominant,
he is probably deceiving himself and is certainly missing the point of the
music. He is confusing what he is hearing with what he has learned.

Of course, from the omniscient point of view the opening harmony
of the Ninth *is* the dominant, but even from this perspective it would be
more accurate to say that it *becomes* the dominant. A single chord can
have no function. Functions emerge only during the course of a progression, and our identification of them can shift according to what the progression reveals. Composers play with the resulting ambiguities, and one
of the great joys of the Third Hearing is to become fully aware of them.
A complete account of these effects is the task of diachronic analysis, for
they lie beyond the scope of the purely synoptic.

Thus I applaud Tovey when he writes: "Half the musical miseducation
in the world comes from people who know that the Ninth Symphony
begins on the dominant of D minor, when the fact is that its opening
bare fifth may mean anything within D major, D minor, A major, A
minor, E major, E minor, C♯ minor, G major, C major, and F major,
until the bass descends to D and settles most (but not all) of the question.
A true analysis takes the standpoint of a listener who knows nothing
beforehand, but hears and remembers everything."[4] Tovey's "true anal-

4. Donald Francis Tovey, *Essays in Musical Analysis*, vol. I, *Symphonies* (London, 1935), 68.

ysis" is of course none other than my Third-Hearing analysis, and his characteristically emphatic language explains vividly what I mean when I describe a Third Hearing as an ideal First Hearing.

Tovey goes too far in his insistence on the listener's total ignorance. I should prefer to limit that to ignorance of the specific musical content of the composition in question. For the serious music lover takes advantage of all relevant information—historical, biographical, music-theoretical—that may prepare him to receive that content. His aim, after all, is to make every hearing—even the First—as rich as possible. Thus he knows that Beethoven was counting on a contemporary audience conditioned by familiarity not only with the tonal language in general, but also with the conventions of the Classical style; therefore, as a sensitive and intelligent listener today, he tries to approach the composer's work in a similar frame of mind. When hearing the First Symphony, he imaginatively sets himself to expect the tonic consonance with which the typical Classical symphony began. Only in that way can he ever experience the delight that accompanies the transformation of puzzled wonder (Is it a dominant? Can it be a tonic?) into satisfied relief. (It was both: a tonic treated as the dominant of its own subdominant.) This is the insight of the Third Hearing that should eventually replace both a naive First-Hearing reaction (It is clearly a dominant seventh) and a sly Second-Reading interpretation (It may sound like a dominant but I know better).

In his Intermezzo Op. 118 No. 1, Brahms has developed Beethoven's opening incident into a full-fledged mystery story.[5] The mystery, of course, concerns the identification of the tonic. Probably none of us can completely recapture the flavor of his first encounter with this problematic piece, but I still recall my surprise on discovering that the key is neither the F major suggested by the opening sonority, nor the C major of the first cadence and of the reprise, but—A minor! A First Hearing (or Reading) must, I think, take the opening as V^7-I^6. Even a listener sharp enough to construe the B♭ of m. 1 as a passing tone will be influenced by its color and hence construe the chord as a dominant substitute, III^6. Accordingly, the C-major cadence at the end of the first part will be accepted as the usual tonicization of V. The development then elaborates a chain of applied dominants, VII-III-VI, the last deceptively or elliptically skipping its resolution to II and moving to V. Here, at the recapitulation, occurs the first event to give the unprepared listener serious pause: the V^7 (or III^6), instead of resolving as before to the presumed

5. For much of my discussion of this piece, I am greatly indebted to Mr. Jonathan Dunsby, whose ideas about it, expounded to me in conversation, have stimulated and interpenetrated my own.

tonic F, moves to a climactic C. Like the expected F, it is only a first inversion; but its register (the highest so far, followed by a precipitous descent), its unique variation of the opening motif, its cancellation of F (by sharping it as a neighbor to G)—these factors dispose one to accept C as the tonic after all. But then the ensuing A minor must be construed as VI—an odd cadence for a reprise, but one that might lead to a new development. Instead, a literal repetition of the second half now raises the suspicion that perhaps A minor was the goal all along—a surmise that becomes a certainty on the return of the cadence in that key, expanded and fully confirmed.

If my account is approximately correct, the First Hearing turns out to be a peculiarly unsatisfactory affair. The listener is unaware of the tonal problem until late in the piece, when his perception of the key relations requires an unexpected reorientation. Only in retrospect does he realize that there was a mystery to be cleared up. If he now investigates the nature of that mystery and tries to impose some kind of unitary pattern on his fluctuating tonal impression, he will arrive at a Second Reading informed by a synoptic analysis. Schenker has shown how the entire Intermezzo can be reduced to one concise progression: III-V$^{\sharp}$-I in A minor.[6] This formulation, kept in mind as a background for following the course of the piece, certainly obviates the disconcerting shifts in perspective that punctuate the First Hearing. But it spoils the fun. Whereas a First Hearing becomes aware of the tonal problem too late, a Second Hearing of this kind is conscious of its solution too soon. Puzzlement has been replaced by confidence from the outset that the opening section prolongs neither a dominant nor a tonic but a mediant.

Perhaps that is how the piece should really be understood. Perhaps no mystery is intended, and Schenker is right when he maintains, of similar progressions, "The tones of the [subsidiary] degrees are connected only through their relation with the coming tonic; they point the way only to it" (p. 138). If that is so, it implies that the Intermezzo and pieces like it can be comprehended only spatially, like the novels discussed by Frank. This is, to be sure, a tempting position, especially with reference to certain contemporary compositions, serial or otherwise, whose organization is abstract and complex. With regard to such works it is probably the correct position. But one surrenders too much if one adopts it unnecessarily. I am convinced, for example, that standard analyses do violence to Berg's Violin Concerto in this respect. They assume the basic twelve-tone set as an independent factor, preexisting our experience of

---

6. Heinrich Schenker, *Der Freie Satz,* 2d. ed. (Vienna, 1956), 63, ex. 110, d3. The subsequent quotation from Schenker is translated from this edition.

the composition; and they tell us, accordingly, that at the outset we are hearing alternate notes of this row. From a synoptic, spatially oriented point of view that is true; but surely the effect of the introduction, considered as a temporal event, depends on the fact that the row has not yet been defined, and that it can only dimly and fragmentarily be discerned.

In the case of the Brahms Intermezzo, I find that I cannot even rehear it as Schenker's spatial interpretation would wish. In actual performance, as opposed to abstract conceptualization, the piece stubbornly resists all my efforts in that direction. Why should Brahms be so negligent in offering me clues along the way to guide my listening, and so diligent in misleading and sidetracking me? I conclude that he intends to puzzle me. I have only to glance at the Intermezzo Op. 76 No. 4 to realize that he is perfectly capable of composing a piece that postpones the arrival of the tonic until the latest possible moment, yet never permits the slightest doubt as to the identity of that tonic. There the suspense is due to uncertainty as to when and how the tonic will arrive; here, I submit, the suspense is, or ought to be, due to the more fundamental uncertainty as to what the tonic is.

A successful Third Reading of Op. 118 No. 1, then, will accept neither the deceptive shifting of the First Reading nor the structurally precise but empirically unrealistic unity of the Second. Yet the Third Reading can never totally forget the other two. To a certain extent, in the present case, it is their synthesis, translating the shifting into tonal ambiguity, and the structural unity into a process whereby that ambiguity gives way to final clarity.

A Third-Hearing analysis of the Intermezzo tries to do justice to the complexity of this synthesis. Instead of determining the tonic ahead of time, it recognizes in the opening of the piece a marshalling of three "suspects," C, A, and F. Each appears as the bass of a characteristically ambiguous chord of the sixth—ambiguous because its function wavers between those of its theoretical root and of its actual bass. Thus the opening progression, literally a succession of first inversions (ex. 1), conceals a series of abortive attempts to complete a root position by a 6–5 resolution, each one defeated at the crucial moment by the entrance of a fresh bass note that converts the fifth into a dissonance against the next chord (ex. 2). Were these harmonies allowed to complete themselves, they would stand revealed as the three candidates for the key of the piece: F, A, and C. But they are not granted completion, and we must accept the B♭, G, and E of the soprano as the lengthened passing tones that Brahms's careful phrasing (by descending thirds) suggests. This means in particular that the first chord, despite its strong flavor, is not a true dominant seventh: the opening must be heard and played as in ex. 3, not as in ex. 4. Furthermore, the D♯ of m. 5, is not a mere passing tone but at least momentarily a resolution (as Brahms indicates by writing it thus and not as E♭). The descending fourth of the opening melodic motif has here been compressed into a simultaneous interval—an augmented fourth that converts the governing harmony of the measure into a French sixth on F. Due emphasis on that chord will give an acute listener his first hint of the possibility of an ultimate resolution into A minor (ex. 5)—a hope to be dashed by the turn of the next measure toward C. And so the Third Hearing fastens neither on the F suggested by the initial pseudo-seventh, nor on the C established at the cadence, but keeps an open mind among the three options presented.

The foregoing has dealt only with the opening section of the Intermezzo, and only superficially at that: it has not touched, for example, on the interesting role of doublings. Yet I hope it has suggested how one might carry out a complete and thorough Third-Reading analysis. One point should certainly be clear: the close relationship between a Third Reading and a performance. Indeed, a performance is, or should be, the projection of a Third Reading. For the performer, as opposed to the mere sight-reader, is intimately familiar with the entire composition. Like the synoptic analyst, he puts to work his knowledge of the whole in order to shape his conception; but unlike the analyst he must then suppress that knowledge. He must relegate it to the background of his consciousness, where it continues to influence, even to determine, his interpretation; but he has internalized it to the point where he need no longer be aware of it. His attention is focused instead on the vivid reconstruction of the actual temporal flow of the music.

This view of performance may in turn help with our earlier problem concerning the successful Third Reading of a work of fiction. One who actually performs a story—i.e., reads it aloud—must concentrate on its temporal flow; in his absorption he may even "forget" what is coming next. And the more closely a silent reader, of a novel as of a musical score, approaches in imagination the simulated conditions of an actual performance, the closer he will come to an ideal Third Reading.

Just how much a performer should allow himself to draw on his store of memory varies from work to work, even from moment to moment within the work. When Mozart, in the Adagio of his Piano Sonata K. 332, states a phrase in B♭ major and immediately starts to repeat it in B♭ minor, it would be absurdly literalistic to insist that the change occurs only with the arrival of the diagnostic D♭ on the second half of the first beat of the measure (ex. 6). Clearly the contrast is between the two phrases as a whole, and it is up to the pianist, by rhythmic articulation

Example 1

Example 2

Example 3

Example 4

Example 5

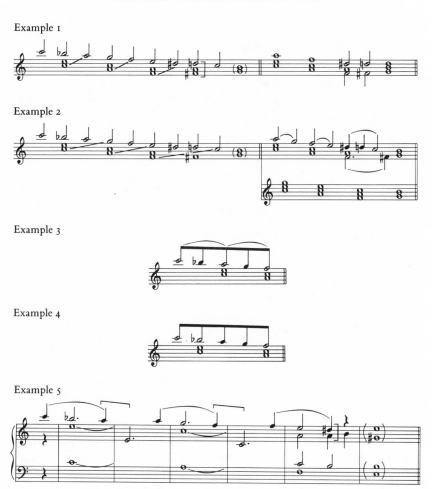

and adjustment of dynamic, to ensure that the minor coloration is already perceived at the beginning of the measure. But this reversal of mode, like the sudden return to major a few measures later (ex. 7), raises a problem of performance in wider context. Should the pianist anticipate such deceptive resolutions, or should he try so far as possible to let them take him unawares? Is his dramatic role that of a Dr. Watson, who is surprised by every new turn of events, or of a Dr. Roylott, who engineers them? Is he sharing his astonishment with his auditors or is he trying to spring a trap on them? Or is he perhaps playing a subtler part— that of a Sherlock Holmes, who deduces the course that events must take and is hence prepared for whatever happens?

Example 6

Example 7

Such distinctions are not always easy to make, but some cases, at least, ought to be obvious. When Tristan and Isolde are interrupted at the height of their passion by the return of the King and his retinue, the music is equally caught off guard; but the orchestra (like Brangäne) reacts before the lovers do, substituting an anguished dissonance for the expected resolution.

A related effect, in a purely instrumental context, can be found in the Andante Cantabile of Tchaikovsky's Fifth Symphony. When the motto theme, which once before has tried unsuccessfully to take over the course of the movement, returns for a second time (m. 158), it is obviously launching a surprise attack. The trombones and bassoons, which carry the motto, know what is coming, but not the suddenly interrupted violins.

Similarly, in Chopin's Fantasy Op. 49, when a *sforzato* diminished seventh rudely shatters the dreamy atmosphere of the central B-major section, the pianist should try to convey a sense of his own shock. The musical persona he portrays comprises at least two implicit agents, of which the one suddenly and devastatingly interrupts the other's revery. (I am using here a vocabulary developed in *The Composer's Voice*.)

On the other hand, when I wrote that "the players of Haydn's 'Surprise' Symphony must somehow surprise themselves" (p. 127), I was wrong. The players are not surprising themselves, or one another (for the strings join in the chord that interrupts their own quiet theme). They are all playing a joke on the audience, as Haydn himself is supposed to have pointed out.

The Mozart examples previously cited are typically subtle. The shifts of mode, if not actually willed by the musical persona, are at least anticipated: witness the careful textural preparation of the minor, and the asymmetrical but balancing return to major. The pianist should find ways to convey these effects in performance, leading his auditors as well to expect the shifts, or at least to accept them as appropriate. Here as elsewhere, although the version of the composition projected by the player cannot (and should not) be identical with the one realized by the listener, the power of the interpretation can be measured by the extent to which it guides that listener's First Hearing, or modifies and enriches his Third.

[1977]

The Authority of
Music Criticism

What authority can the music critic claim for his opinions? That is a
question often posed, or implied, by composers and performers, and
sometimes by critics themselves. Its relevance is not nullified by the fact
that it is usually asked by one who feels, rightly or wrongly, that he has
been misunderstood by the critic and traduced by the expression of his
opinion.

Rightly or wrongly—for some philosophers, of course, those words
are red herrings. George Boas, for example, after contrasting the instrumental values of a work of art (its usefulness for various purposes) with
its terminal values (the pleasure derived from the work itself), concludes:
"What the critic says about instrumental values is objective and binding
upon others, but terminal evaluations will in essence be purely autobiographical and will be authoritative only to men like himself."[1] Boas may
be right; yet, oddly enough, many who in theory claim to hold similar
opinions, in practice tacitly concede the existence of standards of taste
and criticism, and defer to the authority of the standard bearers. In what
follows, I shall try to avoid argument on this point by establishing premises equally valid, I hope, for a personal relativist of the Boas stripe, for
a cultural relativist, and for one who insists on the objectivity of absolute
standards.

The music critic who is to be my primary concern is one of a trium-
virate, all of whose members are engaged in some kind of critical activity: the reviewer, the teacher, and what I call the critic proper. To be sure,

---

1. George Boas, *A Primer for Critics* (Baltimore, 1937), 149.

these are not necessarily three separate persons: a single critic may, and often does, assume two or all three roles. But since the aims and activities of each are distinct, it is convenient to discuss them as three individuals rather than as three aspects of one.

For the typical member of the musical public the term "music critic" invokes the image of the reviewer whose columns he reads in the daily or weekly press. I suspect, too, that most reviewers think of themselves as practicing exemplary music criticism. In fact, however, what reviewers produce represents a genre of criticism that is narrowly delimited, even though it may preponderate in sheer bulk of output. The point becomes clear as soon as one looks at the parallel in the world of letters: "book reviewer" is by no means synonymous, or coterminous with "literary critic"; indeed, many fine literary critics review no books at all.

The reviewer writes primarily for the consumer. His reader wants to know what to buy: what concerts and operas to attend, what records to listen to, and what to think about what he hears. The reviewer's ears, then, must be fundamentally similar to those of the lay audience—although, one hopes, sharper and more focused. His essays must describe as accurately as possible how the music sounded—how it went, if it was new; how it was performed, if it was old. If he is successful his reader will say, "Yes, that is what I heard," or, "Yes, that is what I should have heard had I been more attentive," or, "So that is what I would have heard if I had been there." But the reviewer cannot stop with mere description. He must make a judgment, for what his reader is most anxious to know is: Is it worth hearing, worth attending, worth talking about, worth buying? Will I like it? (Or: Should I like it?) The reviewer's authority, then, stems from his reader's conviction that the reviewer's taste is trustworthy—which most frequently means, consonant with the reader's own. Broader and better informed, to be sure, but basically similar. Boas is certainly right about the reviewer: his opinions "will be authoritative only to men like himself."

The successful reviewer, then, must write from the layman's point of view. He is, if you will, a professional layman. The teacher-critic, by contrast, is your out-and-out professional, a professional professional. His reader, or more likely his auditor, is presumably one who is working at music seriously, either as a performer or as a composer. (I am obviously not dealing here with attempts to train recalcitrant children or apathetic adolescents—nor, at the moment, with the education of appreciative listeners.) The student of the teacher-critic is a maker, not a consumer, of music. In a word, he is a musician—whether only an aspirant, or frankly an amateur, or fully a professional. The teacher's judgment of his performance, or of his composition, is not pronounced for its own sake; rather it is directed toward helping him to improve or to perfect his work. Criticism of this kind is specific and practical. Its aim is to aid the student in achieving his own musical goals. Such a teacher's authority resides in what we call, in general, competence: the precision of his technical knowledge, the breadth of his musical experience, and the ability to apply both knowledge and experience to the solution of the student's problems.

The teacher's aim has just been defined in terms of the student's goals. But often the teacher goes beyond that limitation and tries to help the student define his goals. Indeed, at any level beyond the most elementary, the achievement of a given end merges insensibly into the reshaping of that end. It is a duty of the teacher to assist and to direct that process by constantly questioning, not only the appropriateness of the student's methods, but the value of his results as well. He interprets—a performance, a composition—and he evaluates. In so doing he becomes, to use my term, a critic proper.

The preceding discussion has excluded those who offer instruction in such subjects as music history and "appreciation." The omissions were intentional, for these teachers address a different clientele and pursue different objectives. Their students are seeking, not to produce or to reproduce music, but to understand it better or even just to enjoy it more fully. At every level, their instruction is almost bound to involve real critical activity. And when music history moves toward the understanding of style, for example, or when appreciation transcends the mere recognition of themes and patterns, the thrust toward serious criticism is evident. If such teachers often consider themselves to be true critics it is because they often are; for, as will become clear, the basic job of the critic is precisely to broaden and deepen appreciation, in the best sense of the word.

The reviewer, too, often regards himself as a critic proper, though less frequently with justification. Yet he can become one, and in much the same way. When description evolves into interpretation, when summary judgment gives way to reasoned evaluation, reviewing becomes criticism.

These activities of interpretation and evaluation correspond to the basic re-creative and judicial aspects of criticism as defined by T. M. Greene, following Asher E. Hinds.[2] (A third aspect, the historical, will be specifically considered later on.) But whereas all reviewers and all teachers (of the first type) must engage in judicial criticism, that is not necessarily true of the critic proper. On the other hand, what is essential

2. T. M. Greene, *The Arts and the Art of Criticism* (Princeton, 1940), 369–73.

97

for him, interpretation or re-creation, can hardly fail to include at least some implied evaluation, if only by his choice of works for discussion.

Here, then, is our music critic. Just as the reviewer is basically a lay-man writing for other laymen, and the teacher a practicing musician training other musicians, so the critic is an informed music lover writing for other music lovers. If the word "amateur" did not today carry with it connotations of inexperienced dabbling, I should prefer R. P. Black-mur's formulation: "Criticism, I take it, is the formal discourse of an amateur." The last word, as Blackmur immediately makes clear, must be taken in its original sense: "When there is enough love and enough knowledge represented in the discourse it is a self-sufficient but by no means an isolated art."[3] Indeed, his original reference to "formal dis-course" should have been enough to convince us that he was not using "amateur" in the sense implied by the adjective "amateurish." (If one wants additional proof one has only to look at Blackmur's own career as a professional critic.) No: for Blackmur the critic is a professional, but a professional amateur. That is a paradoxical formulation of my own, al-though it is similar to Blackmur's coinage, "master-layman," by which he characterizes the ideal scholar-critic: one whose work embodies all three of Greene's aspects—the re-creative, the judicial, and the historical. As Blackmur puts it, "He must be the master-layman of as many modes of human understanding as possible in a single act of the mind."[4]

In the case of the music critic there are at least three such "modes of understanding." First the "musicological": a recognition of the facts— ethnic, social, political, historical, biographical—that form the back-ground of the work under discussion, and above all a capacity to discrim-inate between those that are relevant and those that are not. Then the technical: a comprehension of the syntax of the musical language em-ployed, and an ability to explain, through analysis, the workings of that syntax. Finally, the experiential: the insight that can come only from personal contact with a wide range of music, familiarity with the style embodied by the work at hand, and close study of the work itself. Nat-urally, the areas defined by these modes overlap widely. When historical musicology, for example, utilizes style analysis, it enters the realm I have defined as technical. Moreover, no analysis, whether of a style or of a single work, can be trustworthy unless thoroughly grounded in the an-alysts's own experience.

What does the music lover expect of such a critic? The consumer wants to know how to buy; the musician wants to know how to play or to

3. R. P. Blackmur, *Language as Gesture* (New York, 1952), 372.
4. Ibid., 163.

compose; what does the music lover want to know? In the broadest sense, he wants to know how to listen. The critic, as I have suggested, is a teacher of appreciation at the highest level. A reader values a critic's knowledge for its usefulness as a guide toward a convincing interpretation and evaluation of a work. Interpretation: how the work can be heard in its own terms, both formal and expressive. Evaluation: how the work can be heard in relation to others, and what its ultimate significance may be. It is the critic's job to articulate these insights in such a way as to make them available to his readers: that is the purpose of his "formal discourse."

Music lovers do not constitute a well-defined class. A music lover may be a layman or a professional, a performer or a composer. A critic, accordingly, can be any or all of these. He may make his living by reviewing. He may be a first-rate musician or historian. When he points out what is wrong in a composition or a performance, and suggests how to put it right, he is a teacher. Nevertheless, the critic's knowledge, in its musicological, technical, and personal aspects, and his duties, interpretive and evaluative, ally him most closely with the performer. Every good performer is necessarily a kind of critic; it is only slightly metaphorical to say that every good critic is a kind of performer. In what follows, the term "interpreter" will refer to both. The authority of their interpretations derives from the same source: the composition. When, as they both must, critic and performer marshal to their service the facts about a work—historical, biographical, stylistic—it is essential but not sufficient that those be accurate. They must also be applied accurately, and the test of that accuracy is their relevance to the composition. Again, when analysis is invoked to clarify the course of the music, the relationships discovered must be patent in the composition.

It is by no means easy, however, to define just what the composition is. One reductive theory, popular today, identifies it with the score. Clearly the composition is at least the score (assuming that there is one); and from a purely objective point of view that may indeed be all that the composition is. But most of us do not regard music purely objectively. What interests us is not an abstraction called a composition, but a piece of music that we can actually perceive. The score is the ultimate source of all our perceptions, but it is the perceived composition that is the object of critical and interpretive thought. The interesting "facts" about such a work are not those that are simply true, but those that are relevant to our perceptions. Thus historical data may be correct, analyses may be textually demonstrable; but our opinion as to the applicability of the data, of the significance of the analysis, depends on our perception of the composition.

Perception in this context means, of course, not the physical act of hearing the work, but the *way* one hears it, in actuality or in imagination. Perception includes not only one's view of the musical structure but one's reaction to its expressive power as well. It is the basis of any re-creation, any performance, of the work. In other words: one's *perception* of the composition is the source of one's *conception* of its performance. And while the score remains one authoritative measure of the validity of all such conceptions, it can never have been so completely and perfectly notated as to permit only one re-creation as uniquely correct. (In the case of pure electronic music, perception of the composition is fused with perception of its performance—or "execution," to use David Lewin's term.[5] Re-creation is restricted to the interpretations of the critical listener.)

We should speak, then, not of *the* but of *a* correct performance, and similarly of *a* valid critique. A correct performance is one that respects the score—or more precisely, one that accurately interprets its notational code. A valid critique is one that draws correct inferences from verifiable facts. But we can still choose among such interpretations. Few of us are satisfied with correct performances and valid critiques: most of us want something more. The authoritative performance is more than correct; the authoritative critique is more than valid. Blackmur, in the passage previously cited, was not ashamed to single out and name the incremental quality as "love": "When there is enough love and enough knowledge represented in the discourse [criticism] is a self-sufficient but by no means an isolated art." Knowledge has been our subject so far; now, I fear, the discussion must turn to love. For those who find that word embarrassing, let me substitute two others, which may clarify what Blackmur had in mind: intensity and conviction. It is the intensity of the performer's involvement with a work that, coupled with his knowledge, results in conviction—conviction that manifests itself in what we call, not just a correct, but a convincing, performance. In the same way, it is the coupling of the critic's intensity with his knowledge that produces the convincing critique—that makes of criticism, like performance, "a self-sufficient but by no means isolated art."

The coupling of knowledge with intensity that informs the work of the interpreter is only a reflection of the analogous coupling that results in the convincing composition: that of the composer's craft with his enthusiasm. His craft—constructive knowledge—is basically different from the analytical understanding of the interpreter. But his enthusi-

---

5. David Lewin, "Is It Music?" *Proceedings of the First Annual Conference of the American Society of University Composers* (1966), 50–51.

asm—not just his "inspiration" but also his conviction of the significance of that inspiration—is the model for the intense appreciation that is essential to the convincing interpretation. One recognizes this intensity of appreciation when one hears a brilliant performance that illuminates a great composition, or reads a criticism that makes one long to hear an unknown work; but the principle extends even to negative critiques. Negative criticism is effective only when it is based on intensely cherished positive values.

The composer's conviction is, so to speak, an act of faith. It must precede the existence of the work that calls it forth, for it is what gives the composer the courage to undertake and complete the composition in the first place. But the interpreter's conviction should stem equally from insight, a product of the experiential mode of knowledge that, along with the historical and technical modes, is necessary to performer and critic alike. Faith without insight turns performers into fanatics, critics into propagandists.

It is musical experience, then, that leads to the conviction of both performer and critic. This includes, of course, what I have called perception: the experience gained by close study of the work at hand. One must have an accurate sense of how the work sounds—from actual hearing or from vivid auralization. One must grasp not only its formal structure but also its dramatic rhetoric. One must empathize with whatever expression of mood or emotion one may believe it to convey, with due consideration of its textual or other verbal associations. And one must try to grasp what Schumann called its spirit—*Geist*—that mysterious quality that somehow reflects the outlook of the individual, the social milieu, and the age that produced it. To be aware of these aspects is not enough: one must feel them. When musical perception is deeply felt experience it becomes the source of conviction, both of the value of a composition and of the validity of one's conception of its performance. If the work itself is the source of both the performer's and the critic's authority, it acts through a convincing conception derived from an intensely felt perception. The performer embodies that conception in actual musical sound; the critic tries to convey it indirectly, by verbal suggestion.

The projection of this conception, whether musically or verbally, is an act of re-creative criticism. To put it aphoristically: the performance criticizes the composition. But equally, although in a different sense, the composition criticizes the performance. That is a succinct way of summarizing a complex process. The criticism of a composition, as here defined, is primarily re-creative. Although it will inevitably imply certain judgments, these need never be stated explicitly. But a performance is already a re-creation; so criticism of a performance, once it moves beyond pure description, must be judicial. For the only significant way in which the critic can interpret the performance is to relate it to his own view of the composition. That inevitably means a comparison between two perceptions of the composition, the performer's and the critic's own, and hence two conceptions of its proper performance. Moreover, the comparison is bound to imply, even when it does not specifically pronounce, some sort of judgment. Thus the composition—as perceived by the critic—evaluates the performance—as conceived by the performer.

There is, to be sure, another dimension to the judicial criticism of performance. The critic evaluates not only the performer's conception but also his realization of that conception: his execution. One can, of course, concentrate on one of these aspects to the exclusion of the other—sometimes to the point of forgetting that performance is not pure execution. Hence the undue praise sometimes bestowed on sheer virtuosity; and hence the familiar disclaimer, "The composition made no sense to me, but it was well played." Nevertheless, serious criticism of any performer, as of any performance, must be related to the work performed; indeed, any serious criticism of a performance is at the same time a criticism of the work.

It should now be clear why I have called the critic a performer, and why I have claimed that his knowledge of music is most closely allied with the performer's. His re-creation of a composition is, as it were, an ideal imaginary performance, against which his evaluation of any actual performance is measured. Although he does not (as critic) realize his conception with the vividness and completeness of an actual rendition, he can, through words, enable his readers to imagine it with him. The ideal may in fact be unrealizable (the opening Allegro of Beethoven's Op. 106 can hardly be played with both optimum speed and optimum clarity); yet it is by such an ideal that the critic must measure any actual performance.

He can go one step further. He can suggest how one might profitably think about a composition in order to arrive at one's own conception of a performance—imaginary or real. A work only heard is a work apprehended through the perception of another. It is part of the critic's job to help the listener consider the work in such ways as to enable him to perceive it directly for himself, independently of any interpreter.

Perhaps, however, the performer is the wrong model for the critic. Perhaps critic and performer alike should aspire still further, to the composer's knowledge as well as to his enthusiasm. Surely the composer's perception of his own work, his conception of its performance, is the uniquely authoritative standard!

Distinctions are necessary. The composer's knowledge must be discussed under several heads, not all of which are relevant to the problem. First, there is his original conception of the composition: the idea that shaped it, and the shape that in turn it gave to the idea. There is his technical knowledge: the craft already mentioned. There is his memory of the actual inner process of composition. There is his autobiographical knowledge about the outer circumstances surrounding that process. Finally, there is his perception of the finished work, and a consequent conception of its performance.

Of these, the composer's technique is not in question. It is practical knowledge, indispensable to him in the execution of his conception. If he is a master, his craft is an object of imitation and emulation by younger composers. Like an athlete's physical power and grace, it can be an object of admiration. Nevertheless, the work itself, not the craft that it embodies, is the locus of artistic value and the source of artistic knowledge.

To be sure, it is always fascinating and often instructive to try to deduce, from sketches, drafts, and the like, a composer's way of working: how he uses his technique. Thus, although the composer's familiarity with his own creative process is necessarily unique, scholarly and critical attempts to probe that process are highly popular. Such studies can yield valuable information about the composer's methods and can help in reconstructing accurate texts; yet their relevance to the interpretation of the finished composition must remain peripheral. It is the version finally chosen, not the one rejected, by which the composition stands or falls. As Tovey has put it:

> You cannot . . . enjoy the first movement of Beethoven's Eroica Symphony if you insist on thinking the while of Beethoven's seven or eight different sketches of its exposition. They are among the most wonderful documents recording the profound workings of a creative mind; but the only way in which they can help you to enjoy the symphony is by directing your attention to what it is . . . They have helped you, not because they showed you "how it was done," but because they drew your attention to *what* was done; and on that, and that alone, your attention must remain fixed, or the whole object of all that loving and laborious sketching is lost.[6]

The composer's autobiographical knowledge about the piece is again unique and often valuable—so far as the accuracy of his memory permits. But it too is only indirectly relevant and is sometimes more puzzling than helpful. Here, for example, is what Stockhausen has to say about the genesis of his composition *Sirius:*

6. Donald Francis Tovey, "Concertos," in *Essays in Musical Analysis,* (London, 1936), 4–5.

The spirit of it is that it is music from Sirius, which is transposed on this planet and [reveals] the possibilities of this planet, because I think that the culture of this planet has been mainly formed by visitors from Sirius . . . I know . . . that I have come from Sirius, myself.[7]

More serious—or less Sirius—is the question of the composer's own perception of his finished work. Does it too occupy a uniquely privileged position? Today it is fashionable, especially in the field of literary criticism, to deny priority to any single interpretation of a text, whether by the author or anyone else. The position is a tempting one, especially with regard to arts that depend on performance. It is certainly true that a performer can discover many aspects of a composition that are unknown to its composer. After all, he has to *learn* the piece! He knows, or should know, every note, every nuance, in an intimate way. (Naturally, I refer to the conscientious performer—not the one who studies only his own part.) The composer may have known all those details once (although nowadays one cannot even be sure of that), but he may well have forgotten them. If he makes a conscious effort to learn his piece, he too is an interpreter.

When Schoenberg made his famous discovery of the derivation of the second principal theme of his *Kammersymphonie* from a skeletonized inversion of the first,[8] twenty years had passed since the composition of the piece—twenty years during which he was apparently in the dark about a relationship which he later came to think was crucial to the unity of the work. When he finally realized the thematic connection, he did so not as a composer but as an analyst, a critic—a mental performer, hearing the work in his imagination. From my own experience I can testify that a much simpler derivation in my own Violin Sonata No. 1—the reappearance in the second movement of an important motif from the first, in diminution—completely escaped my conscious attention until I had to learn the piano part for a public performance.

On the other hand, there are cases in which the composer's performance, real or imagined, of his work seems to have influenced its final shaping, his experience as a critical performer thus superseding his knowledge as a pure composer. Chopin's Prelude No. 9 in E major is characterized by the frequent use of the rhythmic pattern of a dotted eighth followed by a sixteenth. This motif, according to the manuscript, is to be coordinated with the prevailing triplet accompaniment. (The first

7. David Felder, "An Interview with Karlheinz Stockhausen," *Perspectives of New Music* 16, no. 1 (1977): 99.
8. Arnold Schoenberg, *Style and Idea* (New York, 1975) 222–23.

printed edition, which fails to assimilate the two rhythms, was apparently never proofread by Chopin.)[9] But the manuscript also shows that after completing the Prelude, Chopin altered the prevailing motif to two equal eighths at the beginning of measure 8, and used double-dotting in the remaining measures. From what we know of Chopin's rubato style of playing, we can guess how this new version might easily have arisen spontaneously during a performance. Realizing that this variation emphasized the climactic modulation to A♭ and increased the momentum toward the final cadence, Chopin might then have incorporated what was originally a nuance of performance as a definitive detail of composition.

In such cases, one must indeed accept the composer's perception of the finished composition as uniquely privileged. Other players might have adopted a similar rubato, but only Chopin could confer canonical status upon it. But there is a negative implication as well: although Chopin froze *these* details of performance, there are dozens of others that he did not write into the score. We can assume, then, that what he did not specify he intentionally left to the interpretation of those who might read or play the prelude. His work as a composer was done with the completion—or in this case the revision—of the score; beyond that point he could not seek to impose his own perceptions. As Roger Sessions has put it, "Composers have always, I believe, set down in scores everything they considered necessary for the performer's guidance."[10]

In the case just cited one might say that the composer's perception of his work has influenced, though ever so slightly, its execution—the final embodiment of its conception. The opposite also occurs: the very knowledge that is unquestionably the composer's own, that of his original conception of the work, may sometimes unduly influence his perception of it. The third piece of Sessions's suite *From My Diary*[11] is a case in point. Many attentive listeners hear this piece in E♭. Yet the signature is two sharps, and Allen Forte has manfully tried to analyze the key as D.[12] Sessions has stated that he intended B minor, although he admits the possibility of C minor. My suspicion is that Sessions's conception of the piece—the basic structural and expressive ideas that initiated and controlled its composition—prejudiced his perception; that is, it influenced him to hear the piece in ways not fully justified by the score. (For example, the opening melodic phrase in the left hand is framed by a fifth,

9. See Thomas Higgins, "Historical Background," in his edition of the *Preludes* for the Norton Critical Scores (New York, 1973), 6–7.
10. Roger Sessions, *The Musical Experience of Composer, Performer, and Listener* (Princeton, 1950), 72.
11. Roger Sessions, *From My Diary* (New York, 1947).
12. Allen Forte, *Contemporary Tone-Structures* (New York, 1955), 48–62.

E♭-B♭. That encourages one to hear the accompanying ninth, F♯-G, as the major-minor third of an E♭ chord, i.e., as G♭-G♮. But Sessions has written the first bass note as D♯, thus denying the obvious fifth connection and suggesting what seems to me a much more strained interpretation.) That the composer himself was uneasy is shown by a comparison of the first autograph with the final version. The earlier stage exhibits only a bass melody against a succession of bare ninths in the right hand. According to the composer, it was in order to clarify the tonality that he added the present middle voice—a voice that for some listeners confirms their original E♭ impression!

The composer's liability to bias of this kind is thus another reason why his perception may be suspect. We must conclude that, by and large, the composer's performances, analyses, and critiques of his own work, while of the greatest interest and value as a means of clarifying his specific intentions, are by no means uniquely authoritative. After all, suppose they were: which of Stravinsky's recordings of, say, the *Symphony of Psalms* would be the "right" one?

For all the cogency of these and other arguments, however, musicians seem unable to settle for the relativism of sheer textuality, or of what the literary world calls "deconstructionism." Today more than ever they demand "authentic" performances of accurately reconstructed scores on instruments of the period. They pore over contemporaneous theoretical treatises to discover just what certain details of notation meant. They revive obsolete methods of articulation and phrasing. These activities may seem pointless to one who insists that the composer's perception of his own work is no more valid than any other, that it possesses only historical interest. Pointless, that is, until he realizes that the aim of all this effort lies, or ought to lie, in a different direction: to present the work as nearly as possible, not as the composer *perceived* it, but as he *conceived* it. For it is his conception that constitutes his unique knowledge; whatever value his perceptions may have is connected with their usefulness in helping us to define that conception as accurately as possible. And certainly many critics, like many performers, consider it their job to project a perception of a given work that is as consonant as possible with the composer's conception, insofar as it can be ascertained. That aim, I believe, can be defended, anathema though it may be to the textualists and deconstructionists.

My position is supported by an argument both pragmatic and idealistic. The pragmatic side somewhat resembles certain apologies for religious commitment. Only by assuming the existence and the accessibility of a standard against which interpretations of a composition must be measured can we prevent performances from degenerating into displays of personal self-indulgence and critiques from becoming mere exercises in autobiography. History and recent experience alike indicate that the score alone cannot function as such a standard: the score is essential, but it is not sufficient. One must realize its stylistic implications, both historical and personal—one must penetrate, so to speak, the language in which it is written. Thus Bach's scores failed to protect us from years of what we now consider to be romantic exaggeration; it was the insistence of dedicated musicians, critics, and scholars that Bach's language was not Stokowski's or Busoni's that delivered us. Let us hope that a similar movement will succeed in driving from the stage the present spate of Freudian Dutchmen and Marxist Nibelungs.

Here the role of the historical scholar is crucial. Only through his help can critic and performer gain an understanding of the circumstances surrounding the composition of music of an earlier period, of the constraints accepted by its composers, of the range of possibilities open to them. Without such understanding the interpreter's knowledge of the composer's language is bound to be incomplete, and his attempt to establish a standard consequently suspect. In the same way, the interpreter of exotic music must depend on the researches of an ethnomusicologist—although in this case the scholar to whom he turns is often himself.

The interpreter of traditional music, too, may be his own scholar—but he certainly need not be. The historian on whom he relies, however, is, or ought to be, an interpreter. It should already be amply clear that I disagree profoundly with E. H. Gombrich when he writes: "The historian is not a critic and should not aspire to be one. All he can try to do is to tell the critic what the perspective of history has taught him."[13] Coming at the end of a lengthy historical-critical study, this remark may be ironic. If not, it is based on a narrow and mistaken conception of the nature of criticism. Surely the term "historical perspective" itself implies critical insight. Moreover, history would have nothing to teach a noncritical historian. I do not see how any true historian—as distinguished from an indiscriminate narrator or compiler of facts—can avoid functioning to some extent as a critic, if only by his choice of subjects and by the relative importance he bestows upon them.

The relation between interpreter and historian closely parallels that between interpreter and analyst. The analyst, by the very nature of his activity, is a kind of interpreter. The critic or performer, on the other hand, may not be an analyst himself, but his activity presupposes dependable analysis—just as it presupposes accurate historical orientation.

13. E. H. Gombrich, *The Sense of Order* (Ithaca, N.Y., 1979), 305. I am indebted to David Rosand for this reference.

Both "modes of understanding" (to return to Blackmur's phrase) are indispensable to the interpreter who wishes to advance beyond a purely subjective perception to a closer approximation of the composer's conception.

One who has faith in that conception will entertain none of the doubts voiced above as to the reliability of the composer's knowledge. He will insist that no composer—none worth the name, at any rate—is really ignorant, in any important sense, of his own work. Although it took Schoenberg years to discover the true connection between the two themes of his *Kammersymphonie*, although Beethoven was never aware of the complex motivic manipulation that Schoenberg found in Op. 135,[14] there must have been a sense in which each composer "knew" the relationship all along, albeit subconsciously. He conceived it, even if he never perceived it. As Schoenberg put it, such conceptions can be a "subconsciously received gift from the Supreme Commander."[15] Stockhausen, too, we trust, could, if pressed, give us a sober account of the musical structure of *Sirius*. And if Chopin did incorporate into his Prelude a variation derived from critical performance, he was not revising but clarifying his basic conception.

For the conception is broader and more flexible than any single interpretation can be. We have all heard "authentic" performances so rigid that they were quite inauthentic in effect; yet composers have rarely defined their conceptions in rigid terms. If the interpreter is justified by faith in his acceptance of a hypothetical standard as a guide, the composer on his side must match it by his own faith in the viability of his work, particularly in its powers of adaptation to changing aesthetic attitudes and social conditions. Above all, he must have faith in its ability to retain its integrity throughout the unavoidable vicissitudes of practical performance and public presentation (from which not even pure electronic music is exempt). When, like Stravinsky, he demonstrates evidence of this faith through his own example, we should rejoice, not carp. Such a composer knows that what Blackmur said of literature is equally true of music:

> So far as it is alive, [it] is made again at every instant. It is made afresh as part of the process of being known afresh; what is permanent is what is always fresh, and it can be fresh only in performance—that is, in reading and seeing and hearing what is actually in it at this place and this time . . . The critic brings to consciousness the means of performance.[16]

14. Schoenberg, *Style and Idea*, 220–22.
15. Ibid., 222.
16. R. P. Blackmur, *The Lion and the Honeycomb* (New York, 1955), 199.

Exactly so. We can know a piece of music only through its perform-ance, real or imagined. So when the discussion now turns, as at last it must, to the judicial criticism of composition, it should be accepted as axiomatic that whenever a critic praises or blames a composition, he is basing his judgment on a performance, a re-creation—either his own or another's—of that composition. In all fairness, therefore, he must try to distinguish the composer's work from the interpreter's—what is "per-manent" from what is "fresh."

Roger Sessions recounts an experience that is to the point:

> As a very young student, I for years nourished a dislike for the C minor Piano Quartet of Brahms because I had misread an important melody as two short phrases. Had I been aware of the bass-line and of the harmonic progressions, which I knew, but to which, through inexperience, I had not paid sufficient attention, I would have real-ized it was a single eight-measure phrase; I would have realized that a certain disturbing sequential repetition was only an incident in a larger design instead of, as it seemed, a rather mechanical and per-functory lapse of energy on Brahms' part.[17]

Sessions went wrong precisely because he had failed to look beyond his own performance; he had taken a limited perception of his own as au-thoritative.

Judicial criticism, then, must be informed by a faith in the conception of the composition as a standard that can be ascertained and that should be respected, for neither the technical success nor the ultimate signifi-cance of the work can be determined without reference to it. The critic can demonstrate, with comparative ease, the kinds of musical insight that arouse confidence in his evaluations of compositional technique: his sen-sitivity to sheer sound, his response to rhythm, his powers of harmonic discrimination, his sense of line and form, his analytical ingenuity. All these enable him to discuss the music in more or less objective terms, to make statements about it that can be checked against the score and the reader's own experience of the score. But such judgments can be mean-ingless or misleading without reference to a properly defined conception.

It is probably true of any non-representational form of art that concep-tion and execution are almost indistinguishable aspects of a single pro-cess; it is certainly true of music. Ready separability of the two is a sure sign of academicism, whether in the case of the traditional composer who decides to write in sonata form and thinks up themes to fill it out, or of the serialist who arranges notes purely in accordance with an ab-stract plan. For the creative composer, conception and execution are al-

---

17. Sessions, Musical Experience, 79. The passage in question is in the opening *Allegro non troppo*, mm. 70–77.

most inextricable, to the point where the conception can usually be defined only in terms of its execution. Hence the critic must be wary of trying to define the conception abstractly. He may end up in the position of his colleagues who condemned Brahms's Second Piano Concerto because it failed to display the soloist as a concerto should. But Brahms was not writing *a* concerto, he was writing *that* concerto. What he produced was not, as the critics thought, a bad example of a traditional concerto, but the prototype of a new form—as Hanslick realized when he called it a symphony with obbligato pianoforte. I once wrote that "a work of art ought to imply the standards by which it demands to be judged."[18] With respect to music I could put the same proposition this way: it is the execution of the composition that reveals its conception.

The critic's ultimate task is the judicial appraisal of that conception, and it is his most problematic. Re-creation of the composition has presumably explained what the work is trying to do; its evaluation has tried to measure how well it has succeeded. Now the judgment of its conception must assess the worthiness of that aim. Once again, it is fashionable today to deny the necessity or even the possibility of such a judgment. All media, all methods, all styles, we are told, are equally valid. Even if the critic tries to explain the composer's intention—a task that many consider irrelevant or dangerous if not impossible—he must never evaluate it. At most, he may judge the success of its realization. It is easy to understand the popularity of this position. The final step depends, not just on the critic's musical sensitivity, but on his personal values as well; and those he has no right to impose upon others. At this point, then, it seems that we must agree with Boas: the critic's "terminal evaluations will in essence be purely autobiographical and will be authoritative only to men like himself."

I refuse, however, to admit that this conclusion absolves the critic from the duty of making that final judgment. Indeed, today more than ever there is a practical urgency requiring of him such a commitment. For he can hardly claim to be a critic of music unless he is willing to define what music is; and he cannot do that without accepting, rejecting, or otherwise evaluating the bewilderingly various conceptions embodied in what is being paraded as music today. John Cage's *Imaginary Landscape* may be, for all I know, the best possible piece for twelve radios; certainly his *4'33"* is the most successful composition of utter silence yet produced. The questions remain: How "good" can a composition for twelve radios be? What is the musical (as opposed to the personal, social, or political) significance of a silent composition? Are these, in any intelligible sense, music at all?

18. See "Analysis Today," 000.

Definition means the establishment of limits. Unless one is willing to establish such limits for music, one must accept as music whatever anyone chooses to call music. Actually, the process seems to work this way: we accept as a musician anybody who calls himself one, and we then accept as music whatever any musician calls music. But then we must accept as a critic anybody who calls himself one, and accept whatever he writes as criticism. Under these circumstances the entire enterprise becomes meaningless.

To take criticism seriously, on the other hand, implies that the critic must have some standards by which he judges musical conceptions—at least to the point of deciding whether or not they can properly be called musical. And if his statements are to carry any authority at all, he must in some way make those standards clear. His definition need not be explicit; it can be implied, for example, by the traditions to which he appeals, by the comparisons he finds relevant, by the reasons he adduces for praise or blame. It is, I grant, a risky business. As I once wrote, with respect to the problem of trying to assess Webern's stature:

> It is a decision that depends on one's beliefs about the limits and aims of art in general and is thus not exclusively musical, although it must at the same time be peculiarly musical. It must be made on faith, and it must be accepted or rejected in the same spirit.[19]

In the end, the critic himself must be willing to stand judged. In a sense all of us are revealed—or shown up—by our taste.[20] Moreover, every great work of art eventually demonstrates the inadequacy of even the best critic. Mario Praz has insisted that fakes must inevitably give themselves away. They succeed for a time by capitalizing on the prevailing view of the artist they imitate:

> But let a few years pass (they need not be many), and the point of view changes insensibly but inevitably; historical and philological research alters the data of a problem; and certain aspects of the personality of an artist, not apparent before, are brought into the light, with the result that we no longer feel as our fathers did, or as we ourselves felt yesterday.[21]

For analogous reasons we constantly need new criticism of great works. The greater the work, the more partial must be any single interpretation and the more inevitable its eventual supersession.

19. See "Analysis Today," 000.
20. Graham Greene is reported to have said, "I've got no admiration for people who like Ian Fleming." (In Penelope Gilliatt's profile, "The Dangerous Edge," *The New Yorker* [March 26, 1979], 48.) We may not agree with him in this instance, but we can understand what he means.
21. Mario Praz, *Mnemosyne* (Princeton, 1970), 34.

One should not feel dispirited, however. To call an old recorded performance or critique dated is not necessarily to disparage it. What the
performer brought out, what the critic explained, may have been important news to their contemporaries, even though to a later generation the
interpretations may seem exaggerated, uninformed, or downright mis-
conceived. But yesterday's misconceptions may have contributed to today's insights; and who knows—they may one day prove not to have
been misconceptions after all. The critic succeeds, not by uncovering
eternal truths about a work, but by helping his readers to establish a
closer contact with it. If the music stands in ultimate judgment over him,
great art stands in judgment over us all.

[*1981*]

2
Music and Words

Words into Music:
The Composer's Approach
to the Text

"I am sending you a few more of my compositions, and although, except for the "Ständchen," there is nothing new among them, nevertheless none has appeared in print. They are almost all composed with respect for the meter and the verse form, and I should like to prove myself worthy of my thorough instruction in this branch of the art. The short verses, among the long, are the most difficult to set to music, if one grants in addition that the tone and spirit of a poem should likewise not be neglected."[1] So wrote Zelter to Goethe in 1800, at the beginning of their long correspondence. And the composer's "respect for the meter and the verse form" was rewarded by the poet's highest praise, for twenty years later Goethe wrote: "I feel that your compositions are, so to speak, identical with my songs; the music, like gas blown into a balloon, merely carries them into the heavens. With other composers, I must first observe how they have conceived my song, and what they have made of it."[2]

Today it is hard for us to understand Goethe's preference for Zelter's tuneful trifles over the masterpieces of Schubert, but we must remember that these men were facing a newly arisen problem—how to set to music a pre-existing poetic text not specifically written for this purpose. A short and necessarily very superficial glance over the history of text setting may help to clarify the nature of the difficulty.

1. Max Hecker, ed., *Der Briefwechsel zwischen Goethe und Zelter*, 2 vols. (Leipzig, 1913), 1:9. Translation my own.
2. Ibid., 2:59.

During the Renaissance, the forms of vocal music were to a great extent determined by the words, whether the latter were, in the case of secular song, poems written for this purpose, or, in sacred music, texts of Biblical or liturgical origin. Independent instrumental forms hardly existed before the seventeenth century, so that it was natural that the motivic shapes, the phrase structure, and the overall articulation of the music should be determined by the clearest form-giving element, namely, the text. With the rise of modern tonality in the seventeenth century, however, abstract and completely independent musical forms evolved. The freely articulated music of the sixteenth century gradually gave way to tight, logical, self-sufficient structures. Except in the recitative, which, as a compromise between speech and song, remained tied fairly strictly to the verbal declamation, songs came more and more to be based on these abstract forms, and the texts had to be written accordingly. Thus the typical Metastasian aria was designed to be fitted to the *da capo* form; and its lines were short enough and simple enough to permit the composer to fill out his musical form with the word and phrase repetitions, the melismas, and the cadenzas typical of the late Baroque Italian opera.

One result of the triumph of the musical over the poetic form was that most serious poets began to turn their attention elsewhere. The poet-musician of the Renaissance disappeared, and with few exceptions the major poets of the period gave little thought to the possibilities of musical setting. But toward the end of the eighteenth century composers began to look longingly in the direction of the great poets, and the poets themselves, inspired by the growing interest in folk song and balladry, thought once more of music. But the old days of verbal supremacy were gone forever: abstract tonal structure was now much too firm to yield to any externally imposed conditions. How then could poet and composer, each insisting on the validity of his own artistic pattern, come to terms with each other?

This is the problem for which Zelter was attempting to find a solution, and in a letter of January 10, 1824, he explains to Goethe his method of working: "Above all I respect the form of the poem and try to perceive my poet therein, since I imagine that he, in his capacity as poet, conceived a melody hovering before him. If I can enter into rapport with him, and divine his melody so well that he himself feels at home with it, then our melody will indeed be satisfying.

"That this melody should fit all strophes is a condition that is not clear even to the better composers. The objections against this are not unknown to me; you, dear friend, will at least realize at this point that I am not in favor of the *durchkomponiert* method of setting strophic poems.

Others will hold otherwise, and may act accordingly; although a melody which one doesn't enjoy hearing several times is probably not the best."³

When we look at Zelter's songs, we find that he is as good as his word: the external form of the stanza is rigidly respected, and he builds his simple melodies to conform thereto—melodies which must therefore be repeated throughout, with only such variation as a good performance can accomplish. It is the easiest solution, but one which pleased Goethe, who, as a poet, preferred to see music in a secondary role and liked to think of the composer as merely uncovering the melody already concealed in his own word-rhythms. As for the emotional and pictorial possibilities of the music, he felt that they must be limited and subordinate. "The purest and highest painting in music is the kind that you practise: it is a question of transporting the listener into the mood indicated by the poem; then the imagination, without knowing how, sees forms taking shape in accordance with the text. You have produced models of this in 'Johanna Sebus,' 'Mitternacht,' 'Über allen Gipfeln Ist Ruh,' and where indeed not? Show me who besides yourself has accomplished the like."⁴

Today we feel inclined to answer that, although Schubert may not have accomplished the like, he produced something better still—a song that when necessary sacrificed the stanza pattern for the sake of a higher dramatic or rhetorical unity, a song that was not content with vaguely indicating the mood of the poem but instead actively shaped its emotional content anew in accordance with its own interpretation.

A comparison of Schubert's setting of Goethe's familiar "Wanderers Nachtlied" ("Über allen Gipfeln Ist Ruh") with Zelter's, so highly praised in the passage just quoted, is instructive.⁵ Zelter, keeping close to the unusual stanza form (even though he has the temerity to repeat "balde" twice), produces a top-heavy musical period: it attempts to balance an antecedent of five and one-half measures with a consequent of only three and one-half. The conclusion thus arrives much too soon; and in spite of the composer's obvious effort to create the mood he has indicated as "still und nächtlich," the final impression is one of uneasiness and dissatisfaction. Schubert, on the other hand, willing to repeat words, phrases, and entire lines, produces an almost diametrically opposite musical form: he balances an antecedent of four measures with a consequent of four and one-half and produces a further extension by repeating the

3. Ibid., 2:262.
4. Ibid., 2:57. In this connection, see also Frederick W. Sternfield, "The Musical Springs of Goethe's Poetry," *The Musical Quarterly* 35, no. 4 (1949): 511–25.
5. A selection of Zelter's songs, including this one, is reprinted as one of the publications of the Paul Hirsch Music Library (Berlin, 1924). Another, edited by Ludwig Landshoff, was published by B. Schott's Söhne (Mainz, 1932).

final two and one-half measures. The musical design contradicts the stanza pattern, but the connotations of "Warte nur, balde/Ruhest du auch" are given vivid expression.

The objection would of course be raised by the Zelter school that Schubert achieves this result only through a violation of the poetic form. Such a conception of form is a very narrow one, however; form properly considered involves the organization of all the elements of a work of art and is by no means a matter of pure surface-pattern. Defined in this way, form must of necessity be multiple—ambiguous if you like—for it is impossible for an observer to see a work from all points of view at once. Architecture and sculpture furnish immediate examples, for it is obvious that buildings and statues present an infinity of visual forms, each corresponding to a different position of the beholder. "*The* form" of the building or statue is an abstraction, insofar as it can never actually be seen and can only be reconstructed mentally as the sum or resultant of the multiple visual forms.

A few examples from music will show the same principle at work. Any single performance of a composition, no matter how conscientious, can at best present a limited view of the complex whole. The phrasing of a fugue subject, for instance, must influence the shape of the entire piece; and there are few subjects for which one ideal phrasing can be found. In the Chromatic Fugue of Bach, one possible choice would be to emphasize the sequential pattern of the subject; another would be to bring out the descending structural line. The two interpretations, each valid yet to a certain extent contradicting the other, produce corresponding total musical forms in the fugue as a whole—and these are by no means the only possible ones. Nor is the multiplicity of form in a single composition limited to its varying performances. Rarely do all the form-giving elements exactly coincide, so that one can read a composition in many ways, depending on the relative weight one gives to melodic line, motivic structure, harmonic progression, and temporal proportions. If we hear the first movement of Mozart's C-major Piano Sonata (K. 545) primarily in thematic terms, we shall place the recapitulation at the return of the first theme; if we hear it tonally we shall say that the true recapitulation occurs only with the return of the second.

Like music, poetry exhibits different forms depending on the aspect the reader considers as most important. Verse form and metrical structure are often at odds with syntactic logic: I need not enlarge on the run-on lines of late Shakespeare and the failure of the Miltonic sonnet to observe the octave-sestet division. The traditional ballad by its very nature confines a progressive narrative within a static and repetitive strophic pattern. And as in music, much is determined by the interpreter, the silent or vocal reader who must constantly make decisions about speed, emphasis, tone, accent, and inflection. Indeed, poetry is much less determinate than music in these respects and offers to the interpreter what a musician would consider a bewildering infinity of choices. Not only that: in reading or listening to poetry, the mind can move backwards and forwards through the work; it can subconsciously accept or reject many possibilities of meaning and interpretation; it is constantly busy making comparisons and clarifying relationships. In a word, it is constantly trying to apprehend the poem under many of its possible forms. Not so in music, where the mind is, so to speak, chained to the vehicle of the moving sound. If it tries to struggle free of the present moment, it finds that it has lost the music in so doing. Hence it must follow the piece through from beginning to end, and it must perforce be satisfied with those relationships immediately perceptible during the one journey. But if poetry is more flexible in this regard, music is more vivid; by the very concentration it requires it presents its single aspect with greater immediacy and with the illusion of closer personal contact.

What the composer does, then, when he sets a poem to music, is to choose one among all its forms—or, more accurately, since it is impossible, except by abstraction, to isolate one single form, he delimits one subset within the complete set of all possible forms. The one so chosen may previously have been obvious to every reader, or it may have been concealed to all except the composer. At any rate, it might well be termed a latent form of the poem; and, if you will forgive the wordplays, I should say that the composer's task is to make the *latent* form *patent* by presenting it through the more specific, inflexible, and immediate medium of music. Since he is, after all, primarily a man of music, his choice will be determined not only by his conception of the poem but also by his recognition of the potentialities of realizing this conception in a valid musical structure. I do not wish to discuss here the difficult question of the extent to which the presence of a text can make up for deficiencies in purely musical logic, but it is clear from the works themselves that the great song composers of the Romantic and modern periods insisted upon musical construction that was self-sufficient, although not necessarily definable in terms of abstract instrumental patterns.

The familiar example of Schubert's setting of "Erlkönig" will show at a glance what I mean. Once he had made the decision to renounce the simple quatrains of Goethe's ballad in favor of a *durchkomponiert* design following the climactic narrative, he had still to find a way of producing a satisfactory musical unity. This he did by means of the constantly reiterated accompaniment figures, and by the translation of the child's successive outcries into three exactly parallel but tonally progressive climaxes.

It is not always so easy. Matthias Claudius's poem "Der Tod und das

Mädchen" presented a real problem in its unmediated contrast between the maiden's wild expostulation and Death's soothing reply. Schubert prevented his setting from falling into two unrelated sections by allowing the piano to precede the entrance of the voice, stating at the outset the theme to be used later by Death in his response. Thus the musical design, in contradistinction to the poetic one, is the familiar three-part *ABA* pattern. But note that Schubert, in balancing his purely musical form, at the same time clarified the dramatic structure of the poem. It is obvious that the text plunges *in medias res,* that Death has already appeared to the maiden before she speaks, and it is this situation that Schubert has made clear by his introduction. I could not wish for a more beautiful example of latent form translated into patent, and it is quite possible that Schubert had this purpose in mind rather than the strictly musical one when he composed the introduction. It makes no difference; the two results go hand in hand.

Sometimes, in his attempt to create a satisfactory musical shape, the composer resorts to a device which should apparently be condemned by anyone sensitive to poetic values: he forces the text into an arbitrary mold by the repetition of words and phrases. I grant that the motivation for so doing is usually non-poetic, but I believe that a justification can be argued in poetic terms; at any rate I think that the practice does less harm to the text than is generally assumed. If in reading poetry our consciousness (or perhaps better our subconsciousness) hovers over certain words, and ranges both forward in anticipation and backward in memory, an actual phonographic recording of our thoughts would probably involve a great deal of repetition not unlike that made explicit in certain songs. Here again is Schubert's version of Goethe's "Wanderers Nachtlied," the repetitions all being Schubert's own:

> Über allen Gipfeln
> Ist Ruh,
> In allen Wipfeln
> Spürest du
> Kaum einen Hauch;
> Die Vöglein schweigen, schweigen im Walde.
> Warte nur, warte nur, balde
> Ruhest du auch;
> Warte nur, warte nur, balde
> Ruhest du auch.

Is this an insensitive reading of the original? I can well imagine a reader pausing on "schweigen" to savor the image of the birds (the only form of animal life evoked in the poem). The suggestion of holding back implicit in "Warte nur" might cause him to dwell for a moment longer on that phrase; and lastly, on finishing the poem, he might prolong its effect by rereading the final lines.

To test this theory, I have applied it to one of the extreme examples of the literature: Schumann's version of Heine's "Ich grolle nicht." Here are the original lyric and Schumann's version, which not only repeats arbitrarily but departs sharply from the correct stanza division:

Heine: Ich grolle nicht, und wenn das Herz auch bricht,
            Ewig verlor'nes Lieb, ich grolle nicht.
            Wie du auch strahlst in Diamantenpracht,
            Es fällt kein Strahl in deines Herzens Nacht.

            Das weiss ich längst. Ich sah dich ja im Traume
            Und sah die Nacht in deines Herzens Raume,
            Und sah die Schlang', die dir am Herzen frisst,
            Ich sah, mein Lieb, wie sehr du elend bist.

Schumann: Ich grolle nicht, und wenn das Herz auch bricht,
            Ewig verlor'nes Lieb,
            Ewig verlor'nes Lieb, ich grolle nicht,
                     ich grolle nicht.
            Wie du auch strahlst in Diamantenpracht,
            Es fällt kein Strahl in deines Herzens Nacht,
            Das weiss ich längst.

            Ich grolle nicht, und wenn das Herz auch bricht,
            Ich sah dich ja im Traume,
            Und sah die Nacht in deines Herzens Raume,
            Und sah die Schlang', die dir am Herzen frisst,
            Ich sah, mein Lieb, wie sehr du elend bist.
            Ich grolle nicht,
            Ich grolle nicht.

The repetitions in the first stanza seem to me quite natural and explicable along the lines indicated in the preceding example. The linking of "Das weiss ich längst" with the first stanza is more dubious; yet logically *Das* refers backward rather than forward, and Schumann has certainly made this clear. It is still harder to justify the return to the opening lines immediately afterward, although it is easy to see that Schumann badly needed them for reasons of thematic parallelism. But another motivation was perhaps suggested by Heine himself when he returned to "Ich grolle nicht" at the end of his own second line. These words become, as it were, an ostinato motif, heard by implication underneath everything that follows, the purpose of which after all is to explain why the protagonist is not angry even though his heart is breaking. Schumann has made this ostinato explicit, and has chosen logical places to do so: after the pause suggested by the connotations of "längst" (a pause lengthened by the musical setting), and at the very end, when the listener's thoughts would naturally return to the initial paradox.

This explanation may not be convincing and I do not insist upon it, but I do insist that it is too facile to claim that every such repetition and rearrangement is an arbitrary violation of the poetic design.

Faults in prosody constitute another difficulty for critics who disagree with Mahler's reputed statement that a good song is of necessity a badly declaimed one. If Mahler actually said this, he was merely pointing out by exaggeration that musical prosody can never be a slavish imitation of verbal accentuation, for although musical and verbal meters are in many respects analogous, they by no means exactly coincide. Moreover, we tend to forget to what extent prosody is a matter of convention. "La donna è mobile" is rendered by Verdi with a strong accent on "la"—a license consecrated by centuries of tradition in Italian. In English we should not tolerate a similar accent on "the," but we allow an analogous distortion in Purcell's "Whén I am laid in earth."

Some so-called errors of this kind are errors of performance rather than of composition. Failure to recognize Handel's hemiolas leads to such absurdities as "The glory of the Lord shall be ré-veal-ed." But even outright mistakes such as Berlioz's "offerí-mus" at most distort the sound of the word and leave the sense clear. What of accentuation that, by its falsification of values, alters the meaning of a passage by throwing the emphasis on the wrong word? We must be careful here, for the composer by so doing may be revealing to us an interpretation we had not previously considered. To those who have always read, "And God said, let there be light: and there *was* light," Haydn's version "and there was *light*" must come as a shock; yet no one can hear Haydn's setting without admitting its fundamental correctness—a correctness supported incidentally by the original Hebrew.

A less familiar example is Hindemith's "La Belle Dame sans Merci," where Keats's fourth line is rendered: "And no bírds sing." On the face of it this is a bad mistake, perhaps occasioned by Hindemith's inadequate command of English. Further consideration might lead to the conclusion that Hindemith's knowledge of the language is on the contrary a subtle one and that he has chosen this way of emphasizing that not even the birds sing on this bleak hillside. In a narrow sense, Hindemith's setting is probably not correct, for it violates the prevailing metrical pattern; but it is interesting because it suggests a new way of interpreting the line.

If I have said little about content as such in the foregoing discussion of the problems of text setting, it is because I believe what I hope has already become obvious: that content and form are inseparable, and that we cannot speak about the one without implying the other. The concept of musical content is so moot that I prefer to base my arguments on the fairly concrete grounds of form, but if a musical setting is able to vitalize and vivify one among the many aspects of the total form of a poem, by so doing it presents a unique interpretation of the poem's meaning. Otherwise it would necessarily detract from our comprehension of the words, for, by emphasizing purely sensuous enjoyment on the one hand or emotional stimulation on the other, it would draw our attention away from the text. Ultimately there can be only one justification for the serious composition of a song: it must be an attempt to increase our understanding of the poem.

[1956]

The World of Opera and
Its Inhabitants

This essay developed from a wish to investigate the relation of morals to opera: adapting R. P. Blackmur, I wanted to find out "how it is that morals get into opera and what happens to them when they get there."[1] For example, what might we mean by saying that *Lulu* is a profoundly moral opera, or that *Lulu* is a profoundly immoral opera, or perhaps that it is a morally neutral opera?

Soon, however, I discovered that I could not deal with this problem until I had investigated a more fundamental cluster of questions. How does the world of opera differ from other dramatic worlds? Who are the people that inhabit it, and what sorts of lives do they lead there? That is why my subject perforce assumed a more general form.

All music lovers, I take it, have a serviceable idea of what an opera is; yet I suspect that most of us would find it hard to compose a succinct definition that would include every example we should call an opera and exclude all others. Why do we call certain works operas, even though they contain a great deal of spoken dialogue, but call other works plays, even though they contain a great deal of music? We have no doubt that *Die Zauberflöte* for all its talk, is an opera, and that Shakespeare's comedies, for all their incidental songs, are not. Why?

Instead of trying to answer the question by a rigorous definition of opera—the only advantage of which, so far as I can see, would be to exclude certain undesirable works from the canon—I find it more useful

1. R. P. Blackmur, "Between the Numen and the Moha," in *the Lion and the Honeycomb* (New York, 1955), 289: "The following remarks are meant to suggest one way of seeing how it is that morals get into literature and what happens to them when they get there."

to approach the problem indirectly, through the concept of the operatic medium. A dramatic work can then be called an opera to the extent that it exploits that medium—as it does whenever its characters express themselves and communicate with one another through song. Unlike incidental song, which occurs in situations calling for realistic singing, true operatic song replaces what in a more naturalistic medium would be ordinary speech.

Of course realistic song can occur within opera too—as when Cherubino presents his "Voi che sapete," a song he himself has written. One apprehends the character in such circumstances as "really" singing, as opposed to other occasions (such as Cherubino's first aria) when he is "operatically" singing. We may construe such operatic singing as mere convention—the stylized substitution of song for speech. Or we may hear it at the same time as expressive of the emotional or spiritual states of the characters (the point of view I shall adopt in this essay). In either case we say that the characters are not "really" singing. Indeed, we may insist that, if one properly understands the operatic medium, one realizes that the characters, as opposed to the singing actors portraying them, are not singing at all.[2]

Does the rigid distinction between realistic and operatic song hold up? By way of partial answer, let us turn to a familiar scene from a familiar opera: the colloquy between Alfredo and Violetta in Act I of *La traviata*. After having been introduced to Violetta, Alfredo is persuaded to sing a brindisi, or drinking song—one that he is probably improvising on the spot. For he at first demurs, saying "L'estro non m'arride" (Inspiration doesn't smile on me,); but after a word from Violetta, he tells us "L'ho già in cor" (It's already in my heart). So he sings the song that is in his heart, so successfully in fact that all the rest apparently catch on to the tune and join in the chorus. Then Violetta, obviously no mean poet-musician herself, contributes a second stanza. Lastly, the third stanza is the combined effort of all present. Now, no matter how improbable all this may be from a strictly naturalistic point of view, the music is clearly meant to be "real" or realistic—that is, it is experienced by the characters themselves as actual music. If you should ask them what they are doing, they would say, "We are singing the brindisi just composed by Alfredo."

At that point, to the tune of a waltz—also realistic music, played by an offstage band—the crowd departs, leaving Alfredo and Violetta alone. A short conversation follows. Here, although Alfredo and Violetta are still singing (operatically), they are no longer "singing" (realistically): their recitative is obviously meant to represent speech. Soon Alfredo em-

2. See Edward T. Cone, *The Composer's Voice* (Berkeley and Los Angeles, 1974), 29–37, where this point is developed.

barks on "Un dì felice," a cantilena that turns out to be the opening strain of a duet. The accompaniment reverts to the orchestra in the pit—a sign that, despite the continuation of the waltz meter, we are no longer hearing the "real" dance music. Nor, apparently, are we hearing a "real" song, despite the lyrical style and the formal pattern of the music. Alfredo is telling Violetta, intently and sincerely, of his feeling for her. Expressive and tuneful though the music may be, it is not realistic in the sense that the preceding brindisi and waltz were; for the duet is a continuation of the recitative conversation that preceded it. If you should ask the principals what they are now doing, they would respond, "We are talking to each other." That remains true despite the composer's eventual exploitation of two anti-naturalistic conventions: the elaborate coloratura of Violetta's response and the concluding passage of simultaneous singing. So far, then, the distinction between realistic and operatic song seems to hold good.

Let us move on a little further. The act ends with a full-fledged aria by Violetta—again, not a realistic song, but a soliloquy in which she tries to convince herself, and us, of the impossibility of true love with Alfredo. In so doing she repeats Alfredo's own striking phrase "Di quell'amor ch'è palpito dell'universo" both verbally and musically. This gesture is, of course, symbolic in the most elementary way: it tells us that she has been deeply affected by Alfredo's declaration and cannot get it out of her mind, although she certainly tries in her cabaletta "Sempre libera." But how are we to take Alfredo's own reappearance as a disembodied voice, interrupting her twice with his own reiteration of the by now familiar motif? This version cannot be purely symbolic, existing only in Violetta's imagination, for the stage direction "under the balcony" indicates Alfredo's actual presence. And Violetta's response acknowledges him: "Oh! Oh amore! Follie!" I submit that the only way we can make dramatic sense of the scene is to take it at face value: as an example of a familiar romantic situation—the serenade under the window. If a lover, under a balcony, wants his plea to be heard, what does he do? A Stanley Kowalski may shout, but the well-bred Alfredo has to rely on a more elegant tradition. Saying to himself, "Even though she has refused my love, I shall not let her forget me," he sings—realistically sings, for Violetta is too far away to hear normal speech. But his serenade depends on a crucial transformation: the musical motif that we assumed originally to be not realistic but conventional song (representing normal speech) now reappears in such a way that it must be taken as "really" sung. But in that case, it must have been "really" sung—in some sense—the first time, else there would be no actual music for Alfredo to recall and for Violetta to hear.

The scene thus strongly suggests that the rigid distinction between realistic song on the one hand and conventional or operatic song on the other cannot be sustained. The same vocal motif has appeared on three occasions, functioning differently in each situation. The original statement may be termed *directly expressive* since its purpose is to reveal Alfredo's emotional state. It is conventional song, representing speech highly charged with feeling. The second statement is *symbolic,* for Violetta uses Alfredo's motif to symbolize her memory of the original statement and her reaction to it. The last is *realistic,* since it is to be construed as actually sung rather than spoken or merely thought. But the example also demonstrates that the categories cannot be hard and fast. If the third statement is realistic, then, as I have argued, so is the first. Violetta's statement is symbolic, but at the same time it is expressive insofar as Violetta accepts the motif and adapts it for her own musical use. Perhaps it might be more accurate, though more clumsy, to refer to such statements as *symbolically expressive,* in contradistinction to those that are directly expressive. Finally, Alfredo's realistic statement does not cease to be expressive of his attitude. At the same time it symbolizes his effect on Violetta all the more vividly because of its immediacy: it is Alfredo's actual voice, not just her memory of it.

Verdi must have liked this triple statement, for the same principle is at work, perhaps even more obviously, in the threefold projection of "La donna è mobile" in the last act of *Rigoletto.* Although, as we shall see, there is some ambiguity about the first presentation, it is certainly directly expressive of the Duke's character and mood. The second version displays an obvious imitation of drowsiness and sleep; but beyond that, the new context suggests lustful ardor remembered rather than anticipated—which the literally portrayed drowsiness serves to symbolize. Lastly, when Rigoletto hears the song as the Duke passes in the distance, he is of course listening to actual singing. Here again that actuality must modify the way one regards the earlier versions.

It is instructive to compare the opera with its source, Hugo's *Le Roi s'amuse.* In the play, "La donna è mobile" is exactly matched by the King's song "Souvent femme varie—Bien fol est qui s'y fie!," which could in fact be sung to the tune we all know. The song is dramatically necessary in order for Triboulet, the jester, to recognize in the last scene that the King is still alive. His response—"Quelle voix!"—is the same as Rigoletto's "Qual voce!" But there is a significant difference between the play and the opera. In the play, we necessarily assume from the outset that the song is realistic: that is the only way it can appear in a spoken drama. In the opera, as we have seen, there is an apparent inconsistency: what we take originally to be an expressive aria, sung within the operatic convention, becomes in retrospect a realistic song. Here lies the heart of the matter, for an adequate comprehension of opera as distinguished from spoken drama rests on an appreciation of this ambiguity.

There is another important point to be derived from the comparison of opera and play. In the play we have no knowledge of the authorship of the King's song. We have no reason to assume that he composed it himself: he has given us no prior evidence of musical talent, and the verse is unlike the poetry of his standard lines. We conclude that the song is one known to the King and adopted by him as appropriate to his mood. Not so in the case of "La donna è mobile." That song belongs to the Duke through and through; indeed, in popular imagination it has *become* the Duke. (Thus a recent modern-dress version of *Rigoletto* in which the Duke introduced his song by dropping a coin into a jukebox displayed a misunderstanding of the operatic medium.)

In general, the authorship of incidental song in spoken drama is irrelevant. In opera, however, a song, whether realistic or operatic, is so intimately connected with the character who sings it that he or she is usually to be accepted as its composer. Even Alfredo's conventional brindisi is his own—just as Iago's very different drinking song is *his* own (and perhaps, though less cogently, Lady Macbeth's is hers).

To clinch this argument, let us make one more comparison: Cherubino's "Voi che sapete" and its model in Beaumarchais's play. In the play we know very well that Chérubin did not compose his own music: although the words are his, they are to be sung to the tune "Malbrouck s'en va t'en guerre." Such a setting would be unimaginable in Cherubino's case, for it would be incompatible with his musical characterization. Instead, he presents music of his own composition in a song that, again, has *become* Cherubino.

To be sure, there are numerous counterexamples. Religious choirs, whether Egyptian as in *Aida* or Christian as in *Don Carlo,* do not normally compose their own rituals; and Desdemona heard her "Willow Song" in childhood. Nevertheless, she has made it very much her own; as in most such cases, the song, though not "original," is musically in character. Moreover, as Violetta has shown, one personage can appropriate the music of another. This convention governs the typical operatic situation in which a chorus comments on a song by one of the principals, symbolizing its agreement by adopting the music just heard. Thus the realistic presentation of Alfredo's brindisi is followed by a conventionally symbolic version. (The technique is put to ingenious use in *Otello.* Iago's drinking song is eagerly continued by Cassio and admiringly appropriated by the crowd; but Cassio's later interruption reveals his drunkenness.)

An inspired adaptation of the convention effects the dénouement of

Die Meistersinger. The "Prize Song," which as we well know is Walther's composition, is appropriated by those who have heard it, in a passage proclaiming the crowd's approbation, the Mastersingers' approval, and Eva's acceptance, of Walther. In the course of this development Walther's realistic song is subtly transformed, first into the symbolic repetitions of the ensemble, and then into what must be heard as a direct expression of Eva's love—a reversal of the direction observed in Verdi's triple presentations.

The chorus is symbolic, yes, but no artistically successful symbol is merely symbolic. (I remember hearing Alfred Kazin, in a lecture, giving vent to justified scorn of a critic who had said, "Of course, in Henry James money is just a symbol." No doubt money—like almost everything else—*is* a symbol in James, but it is real money for all that, as Merton Densher and Kate Croy well knew.) Thus a performance of *Die Meistersinger* can overwhelm us only if it can persuade us to accept a fantastic situation as veridical: it must convince us that the citizenry of Nuremberg, overcome by admiration, has caught Walther's tune and can express its enthusiasm by actually singing it in chorus.

If the personages discussed up to now are typical of the inhabitants of the world of opera, then a rather startling proposition suggests itself: that most operatic characters are musicians who compose songs or sing songs composed by their friends! Before dismissing this suggestion as facetious, or at any rate as based on a limited and biased choice of representatives, one should recognize that those I have adduced do conform to a long tradition. Is it mere coincidence that so much of the early history of opera is bound up with the myth of Orpheus—and one important phase of its late history too? Was it not Orpheus the musician that interested Peri and Caccini and Monteverdi and Gluck—not to speak of Offenbach? And Orpheus was but the first of many musicians who found a home in opera: not only Walther and Hans Sachs (and Beckmesser!) but also such diverse figures as Tannhäuser, Manrico, Schwanda, and the Nightingale (as well as Palestrina, Stradella, Salieri, and Mozart!). But all of these are, so to speak, "professionals" (or at least highly trained). More relevant to this investigation are those who, like Alfredo and Cherubino, may be called amateur composers, occasionally rising to the inspiration of the moment to produce a dramatically required realistic song. Numerous other instances spring to mind. As early in operatic history as *The Coronation of Poppea,* Nero exults over the death of Seneca in true song, and Arnalta sings a lullaby to Poppea. Further on, Handel's Cleopatra sings seductively for Julius Caesar. In *The Marriage of Figaro* we hear, in addition to "Voi che sapete," Figaro singing and dancing "Se vuol ballare" (necessarily a realistic song, since he hums it to himself later on). And "Non più andrai" must be a real marching song, for it con-

cludes with a miniature parade—"Partono tutti alla militare," reads the
stage direction. Elsewhere in Mozart, Pedrillo sings a romance, Don
Giovanni serenades Elvira's maid, and Papageno introduces himself in
song (the "reality" of which he confirms by accompanying himself on
his pipe). When he plays his bells, Papageno reveals himself as an instrumental virtuoso as well; and Pamino similarly distinguishes himself on
the flute. Verdi offers many examples besides those already mentioned,
notably Azucena's "Stride la vampa," Falstaff's lovemaking, and Fenton's
nocturne. Wagner, in addition to his professionals, presents a host of
amateurs: Senta and her spinning companions (whose "dummes Lied"
she hushes in favor of her own "besseres" ballad), the singing sailor and
the piping shepherd in *Tristan und Isolde,* the Rhine Maidens, the Valkyr-
ies, Siegfried at the forge. Strauss, in addition to a very professional Italian tenor in *Der Rosenkavalier,* puts amateur dancers on the stage in the
persons of Salome and Elektra.

One of the best-known examples has been saved for the last; for it
beautifully illustrates the hospitality of the operatic medium to the character who might be called a natural musician, yet at the same time demonstrates the persistence of the fundamental operatic ambiguity (Is
speech or song being represented?). Carmen's natural musicality is evident. In her first two acts she loses no opportunity for realistic singing
and dancing. Although the Habanera might at first be taken as directly
expressive, its mocking reprise at the end of the act confirms a realistic
interpretation. As for the Seguidilla in Act 1, the Gypsy Song that opens
Act 2 (with its "tra-la-la" refrain), and the vocalization that later accompanies the dance for Don José, for dramatic purposes all must be considered realistic. Yet how does Don José react to the Seguidilla? "Tais-toi! Je
t'avais dit de ne pas me parler!" To which Carmen replies, pointing up
exactly the ambivalence that interests us: "Je ne te parle pas, je chante
pour moi-même!" One of the great attractions of Carmen—who from
this point of view might be considered the ideal operatic heroine—is her
overt realization and enjoyment of the medium in which she moves, the
medium that makes it possible for the Seguidilla to function simultaneously as speech and as song. Nor is Carmen the only character in Biz-
et's opera who takes advantage of the medium in this way. Is the Torea-
dor's Song expressive or realistic? In Act 2 it is the primary vehicle by
which Escamillo reveals himself; yet its recall at the end of Act 3, as he
sings the refrain offstage, serves realistically to inform both Carmen and
Don José of his presence nearby. The choruses, too, contribute to the
ambiguity: almost every one of them, whether sung by soldiers, urchins,
smugglers, or spectators at the bullring, can be taken as real or as conventionally symbolic.

That is the richness of *Carmen,* but it is only a more obvious version of the richness inherent in all opera. What Carmen knows is what all operatic characters must know, although not always so patently: that they live in a world of music, and that they express themselves and communicate with one another in song. If it is often impossible to demarcate expressive from realistic song, that is because they interpenetrate each other. Such interpenetration occasions the apparent inconsistencies that attach not only to Carmen's song-dances, but also to much other music that is on the surface purely realistic. Thus Manrico's romance is sung troubadour fashion, accompanied on his own harp; yet it arouses the Count to a frenzy of jealousy. Senta's ballad dissolves into an expression of her own romantic aspiration. In the first act of *Tristan,* Isolde takes the sailor's song as an insult; in the last act the shepherd's piping, first in desolation and then in joy, reflects the dramatic situation.

Among more recent composers, Britten has shown a thorough understanding of the process of interpenetration. In *Peter Grimes* the action (after the prologue) is framed by a scene that at the outset establishes and at the end confirms the villagers as musicians. "Everyday work is going on," we are told by the stage direction for the opening of Act 1, "and the people sing quietly to themselves as they move about their work." Song comes so naturally to them in all circumstances that ordinary speech seems rare. For them, music is not just decorative but functional, as when they restore order in the tavern by joining in a round—a round, we should note, with which Peter's failure to harmonize symbolizes his separation from the community. Peter himself, a man one would think has no music in him, gives vent to his emotions by outbursts that border on song and are even taken as such: "His song alone would sour the beer!" exclaim the Nieces after his ranting. And Peter's last crazed monologue is full of musical quotations—of his outbreak in the tavern, of the round, of his anguished cry "God have mercy upon me!," of his dream of the harbor that "shelters peace"—is all this realistic or expressive song?

In *A Midsummer Night's Dream* it is easy to believe that when the fairies talk, they sing—because when they move, they dance. Even Puck's nonmusical speech is a kind of song.

It is interesting to find the same technique exploited—even extended—in the work of a British composer of the next generation, Peter Maxwell Davies. In the central episode of *The Lighthouse,* each of the Keepers takes his turn at producing a song, ostensibly "to cheer us up." But the songs, far from being cheerful entertainments, turn out to be autobiographical revelations of dark truths. Especially effective in indicating the extent of interpenetration is the passage where Sandy's companions dreamily comment on his song, but in Sandy's verbal and musical terms. In catch-like fashion they construct a new version in which the unintentional double entendres bring to light the concealed homosexual content of Sandy's pastoral idyll. (Davies wants the three men to "sing this inwardly," because they "are unaware of each other and of what the others sing." The music, as it were, connects their unspoken thoughts.)

The foregoing are among the more striking examples of what I have called the fundmental operatic ambiguity. To what extent can that ambiguity be resolved?

Some years ago I pointed out that "every singing persona seems to be subject to a tension between the verbal and vocal aspects of his personality. From the realistic point of view, such a character is unaware of singing, and of being accompanied. Yet on the musical levels he must in some sense be aware of both." As I suggested then, "A solution becomes possible if we conceive the contrast between the verbal and the vocal as a symbolic parallel to the contrast between the conscious and subconscious components of the personality." I urged that, "we accept the music as referring to a subconscious level underlying—and lying under—whatever thought and emotions are expressed by words."[3]

Although I still think I was on the right track, today I should be bolder. When characters subsist by virtue of the operatic medium, the musically communicable aspects of their personalities have been brought to full consciousness, so that the characters naturally express themselves in song—song of which, in the peculiar operatic world they inhabit, they are fully aware. As a result, the inner life of operatic characters, although not necessarily richer or more profound than that of their "legitimate" counterparts—or of ordinary mortals—is more openly available to themselves, to one another, and to their audiences. Joseph Kerman, in his essay on *Otello,* commented on the differences between Shakespeare's Desdemona and Verdi's: "Expanding her role meant making her more articulate . . .[Verdi's Desdemona] lives through her emotions in style."[4] He put it more disparagingly when, as I recall, he wrote in a review that we can sometimes see Tosca peeping out from behind Desdemona's skirts. To which Roger Sessions replied, "But of course; that is just the difference between opera and spoken drama." Quite simply, Shakespeare's Desdemona speaks; Verdi's Desdemona sings.

To be sure, Shakespeare's verse, too, is a powerful medium for expressing thoughts and emotions usually unspoken; as I put it earlier, "The elevated verse he employs is an expressive medium that permits the

3. Ibid., 33–35.
4. Joseph Kerman, *Opera as Drama* (New York, 1956), 160–61.

voicing of emotions and thoughts usually unverbalized at the conscious level of ordinary speech. Nevertheless, the 'level of subconsciousness' presented by an art that deals with words must lie nearer the surface than the one presented by an art of pure sound."[5] Expanding this idea, I should now suggest that what we might call the "Desdemona effect" of increased emotional intensity in the operatic character may result in part from the increased energy required to bring the more deeply buried layer of the subconscious up to the surface.

Be that as it may, the comparison with verse drama offers a useful parallel that may clarify just what it means to say that song is the natural medium of expression for operatic characters. The Elizabethan stage presents a world in which blank verse is the normal medium of speech. It may shade into prose on the one hand and into the more precise patterns of rhyme on the other: Romeo and Juliet, for example, can converse in sonnet form. In addition there are occasional quoted poems and interpolated songs. Elizabethan drama thus possesses a much wider verbal range than is afforded by the realistic convention of today. Similarly, operatic speech may be considered as moving from the extreme of the spoken word, through unaccompanied and accompanied recitative, to aria, ensemble, and realistic song. In both the play and the opera, the medium is sufficiently wide ranging and flexible to accommodate all the functions of ordinary speech, whether inwardly or outwardly voiced, informally improvised or formally delivered, composed or quoted. In the everyday world the normal medium for all such activity is spoken prose; verse is rare. Elizabethan drama reverses the relationship. In both cases, song is the exception. Now imagine a world in which singing is the norm and speaking the exception: that is the world of opera.

It is our tacit acceptance of this world that bestows dramatic credibility upon scenes such as those we have been examining. Another standard operatic situation similarly validated is the overheard soliloquy. In spoken drama, the soliloquy is a convention whereby a character can reveal his unspoken thoughts to the audience; he is, if you like, talking to himself. Normally, therefore, a soliloquy cannot be overheard; indeed, it is typically delivered when the character is alone on the stage. That convention is frequently transferred to the operatic aria, many of which are soliloquies. But these differ in one important respect: since they are sung they can be overheard. Thus Don Giovanni and Leporello comment on the revelations of Donna Elvira's opening aria before they are close enough to recognize her. And in the second-act Trio they overhear another soliloquy as she sings from her balcony. Similarly, in Fidelio

5. Cone, *Composer's Voice*, 34.

the chorus of guardsmen are aware of Pizarro's thoughts in "Ha, welch ein Augenblick": as he sings, they mutter "Er spricht von Tod und Wunde."

Suzanna, too, is overheard by Figaro in her fourth-act aria. In fact, she sings this with the specific intention of being overheard: "Diamogli la mercè de' dubbi suoi." The effect is much more poignant than in the play, where Figaro overhears only her brief colloquy with the Countess. In the opera, he can nurse his jealousy throughout Suzanna's extended recitative and aria. (Oddly enough, operatic convention also permits an effect that is the exact opposite of the overheard soliloquy. The members of an ensemble often give simultaneous voice to their private thoughts with no concern whatever for one another. In discussing the canon from *Fidelio*, I once called it a "fourfold soliloquy."[6] It is probably the most famous example of this kind.)

Recognition scenes, too, achieve added intensity if the undeceived character's ears as well as eyes are opened. When we hear a performance of *Così fan tutte*, we naturally assume that the discomfited ladies share our own recognition of Guglielmo's love song and Despina's magic spell as the men recall them to make the situation clear. And the funniest and most pathetic moments of the final unmasking in *Falstaff* occur when the protagonist is reminded of earlier musical motifs: when he turns for help to Ford, invoking his meeting with "Signor Fontana," and when he joins Mistress Quickly in her "Reverenza."

In sum, the evidence suggests that Orpheus is not the prototypical operatic hero for historical reasons only: his role as composer-singer symbolizes what it means to be an operatic character.

Before concluding, we must give some attention to the role of instrumental accompaniment according to the theory presented here. To what extent is it "heard"? Of course the *singers* hear it—or we hope they do—but what of the characters they portray?

Like song, instrumental music in opera can be realistic on the one hand, symbolic or expressive on the other. Among the former, imitatively depicted accompaniments of realistic song, like Suzanna's guitar (for Cherubino) or Manrico's harp, abound. Moreover, many crucial moments depend on the simulation of actual instrumental interpolations: the horn call in *Ernani*, the trumpet in *Fidelio*, the magical instruments in *Die Zauberflöte*, Figaro's wedding music. Naturally we understand all these as being heard by the relevant characters. But what of the usual orchestral accompaniment?

One might suppose that, unlike song, instrumental music admits of

6. Ibid., 37.

little ambiguity: either it is realistic or it is not. However, that is by no means always the case. Sometimes the orchestral role is less well defined, as when it represents sound possibly imagined by one of the characters. Thus the horns definitely heard by Isolde and Brangäne at the beginning of Act 2 gradually recede as the hunt moves into the distance. As they grow less distinct, their parts are taken over by woodwinds. Are they still real, or are they but the phantoms of Brangäne's fear, as Isolde tries to reassure her?

There is another borderline category: sounds that are programmatically suggested without being strictly imitated. Storms are probably the most frequent occasions for such music. To what extent is it heard by the characters? Siegmund hears the *storm*, of course, but what of its musical representation? And what of non-programmatic accompaniment, which can range from purely conventional strumming, through highly expressive support, to full symphonic texture? Does it inhabit, so to speak, the world of the characters?

In my earlier study I suggested that the character's awareness of the accompaniment paralleled his "unconscious" awareness of his own singing: "[He] does not realize that he is 'hearing' it. But . . . although he is not conscious of it he is 'subconscious' of it."[7] Today, again paralleling my interpretation of singing, I shall be bolder. If the characters are composers, then, like all other composers, they are constantly *thinking* music. A composer's awareness of this perpetual musical environment may vary; but whenever he stops to listen, he realizes that he is hearing it and that he has been hearing it all along. Only when it is forced from his consciousness by actual sound, or by very intense thought, does this music temporarily cease. Sometimes not even then, for his musical environment may be so vivid that his imagination will tend to transform the noises of his actual surroundings into music. That is an experience all composers share. It can explain how storms and battles and horseback rides can become music in the ears of operatic characters, for the musical environment of those who habitually express themselves in song must be vivid indeed. So the sea interludes in *Peter Grimes,* which on one level can be taken as representing the various sounds of the ocean as transformed by the creative art of one composer, namely Benjamin Britten, can on another level be interpreted as proceeding from the imagination of another composer, the collective musical consciousness of those with whom Britten has populated his village.

Thus, while the singers hear the orchestra in the pit, what the characters they enact hear is not that orchestra but the music it plays, which

7. Ibid., 36.

reproduces the music of the imaginary orchestra that they, as composers, perpetually carry around with them. I was wrong, then, when I once suggested that a singer portraying Figaro is breaking a rule "by reacting in exaggerated fashion to the mocking horns at the end of 'Aprite un po'";[8] no, the laugh he may gain thereby is perfectly legitimate.

This interpretation is by no means universally applicable. Certainly not all characters hear all the instrumental music all the time, and there may indeed be music (notably in Wagner) unheard by any of them. But when feasible, the assumption of what might be called orchestral accessibility can greatly enhance the operatic texture. The dramatic situation becomes more vivid, and the intensity is heightened, for an auditor who conceives the "sword" motif as occurring to Wotan at the same time as the image of the object itself, or Tristan and Isolde as hearing the motifs of their own fate when the magic potion opens their eyes. Indeed, I believe that is the most natural way to interpret those scenes.

There are some passages that present more specific evidence. When Carmen and Salome dance, both must have an imaginary orchestra in their ears. A quite different sort of dance, the waltz "Ohne mir," is often in Baron Ochs's mind when he is not openly singing it. "Kennt Sie das Liedel?" he asks, as we first hear the tune in the orchestra. Nor should we forget the last occurrence of the motif with which this discussion began: Alfredo's declaration of love. The violins that remind us of it while Violetta reads the letter from Germont surely correspond to what she is hearing in her own memory. Again, during the scene in *Wozzeck* that Berg calls an "Invention on a Rhythm," the rhythmic ostinato appears in innumerable guises both in the realistic stage music and in the orchestral accompaniment; it can serve its purpose of signifying Wozzeck's obsession only if, right from its terrifying inception just after the curtain falls on the murder, it reflects what Wozzeck is hearing in his crazed imagination.

It is true that much operatic vocalism assumes such prominence that we do not think of the voice as paying much attention to its accompaniment—rather, the other way around: the orchestra is following the vocal lead. But that is not always the case. When Otello completes the successive phrases of the "kiss" motif, the effect is that each time he is giving voice to the unspoken thought expressed for him by the orchestra. (Characters can also react musically to realistic accompaniments, as when Scarpia neatly fits his "Tosca, mi fai dimenticare Iddio!" between the phrases of the choral Te Deum, in the culmination of which he then participates.)

8. Ibid., 30.

The relation of voice to orchestra in the Wagnerian music drama is so complex that it deserves an entire essay—nay, a book. It would require careful analysis of a scene to reveal which orchestral music should be construed as being in the ears—i.e., in the musical consciousness—of which characters; and which music, on the other hand, is best understood as subsisting in a kind of universal world consciousness, so vividly personified in the *Ring* by the figure of Erda.

Looking back to the question that prompted this investigation, I realize that I can record no progress in the attempt to establish the role of morals and morality in opera; but I have tried to make some advance toward a preliminary understanding of the inhabitants of the operatic world. When Arnalta, the nurse, hears Poppea exulting after the death of Seneca, she remonstrates, "Pur sempre sulle nozze canzoneggiando vai,"—"You're forever going around singing songs about your wedding." But that is just what characters in opera do: they go around singing songs all the time.

[*1988*]

Berlioz's Divine Comedy:
The *Grande messe des morts*

The title is not meant to suggest that Berlioz might have had Dante's poem in mind as a model for his Requiem—there is no evidence that he did—but rather to imply that the Mass, like the poem, is the carefully constructed dramatic portrayal of an imaginary progress through this world and the next.

All too often in our discussion we over-emphasize the sensationally apocalyptic side of the Requiem. We dwell on the "Tuba mirum" but not on the "Quaerens me," on the "Hostias" but not on the "Domine Jesu Christe." We adore the convulsive turbulence of the "Lacrymosa" but deplore what we label the saccharine sentimentality of the Sanctus, failing to consider its contribution to the program of the whole. In fact, we deny that the work embodies a unified program: we look on it as a collection of picturesque movements, some from heterogeneous sources. After all, didn't the composer lift the "Tuba mirum" directly from an early Mass, and didn't he plan at one time an oratorio on *Le Dernier jour du monde?* Didn't he often work that way, appropriating the march from *Les Francs-Juges* for the Fantastic Symphony, and putting all his unconsidered trifles together for *Lélio?* Wasn't he sometimes forced to cut corners by the exigency of the limited time at his disposal? Even such a staunch defender as David Cairns suggests that "it is possible that Berlioz, with more time to fulfill his commission, might not have been content to resort to other movements in composing the final number."[1]

1. Notes for the recording by the London Symphony, Colin Davis conducting, Philips 6500 024–5.

The view I wish to defend, by contrast, is that of a unitary composition, carefully constructed both dramatically and musically in such a way that the two aspects reinforce each other. Berlioz wrote, with reference to "those enormous compositions which certain critics have designated by the name of architectural or monumental music," that

> it is above all the scale of the movements, the breadth of style and the formidably slow and deliberate pace of certain progressions, whose final goal cannot be guessed, that give these works their peculiarly "gigantic" character and "colossal" aspect.[2]

In the case of the *Grande messe des morts,* the huge-scale progressions to which he refers embrace not only the individual movements but the entire work as well.[3]

The nature of Berlioz's overall dramatic conception is revealed first of all by his departures from the liturgical text. True, some of these may have been inadvertent—such as the dropping of a "Domine" here or the inversion of a "Jesu pie" (into "pie Jesu") there. Some have apparently only (or primarily) a musical justification: for example, a line disappeared from the twelfth stanza of the "Dies irae" when, during revision, an entire phrase of the "Quaerens me" was dropped in order to tighten the musical structure. But the bulk of the additions, omissions, and rearrangements make sense if one reads through Berlioz's text not as pure liturgy but as the libretto, so to speak, of a special kind of music drama.

Like Dante's poem, this drama incorporates a series of three visions— one of Judgment Day, with its obvious threat of an imminent Hell, one of Purgatory, and one of Heaven. Unlike Dante's visions, these occur in the context of a commemorative service of the dead: they are, in fact, evoked by its imagery. They are also, to be sure, framed by its ritual— framed but not constrained, for the most extensive of Berlioz's departures from the liturgy result from his obvious desire to make the visions as vivid as possible.

What Berlioz presents, then, is not so much the celebration of a Mass as the emotional experiences of a contemplative auditor attending such a Mass—one who, allowing his imagination full play, visualizes himself as present at the wonderful and terrible scenes described, and who returns to reality at the conclusion of the service with a consequent sense of catharsis. The measure of the composer's success is the extent to which he forces each of us—members of the audience at an actual performance of the *Messe des morts*—to assume the role of that protagonist and to share, as it were, those experiences.

The chart of comparative texts (table 1) offers evidence for some such

2. *The Memoirs of Hector Berlioz,* trans. David Cairns (London, 1969), 478–79.
3. See "Inside the Saint's Head: The Music of Berlioz," in particular 231–32 and 236–37.

Table 1
Berlioz's Requiem Text Compared with its Liturgical Source

Liturgical Text	Berlioz's Version

Requiem and Kyrie

I

Requiem aeternam dona eis, Domine, et lux perpetua luceat eis.	Requiem aeternam, *etc.*
Te decet hymnus, Deus in Sion, et tibi reddetur votum in Jerusalem.	Te decet, *etc.*
Exaudi orationem meam, ad te omnis caro veniet.	Exaudi, *etc.*
Requiem aeternam dona eis, Domine, et lux perpetua luceat eis.	Requiem aeternam dona defunctis (dona eis), Domine, *etc.*
Kyrie eleison, Christe eleison, Kyrie eleison.	Kyrie eleison, *etc.*

Dies irae

II

1. Dies irae, dies illa solvet saeclum in favilla, teste David cum Sibylla.	1. Dies irae, *etc.*
2. Quantus tremor est futurus quando judex est venturus cuncta stricte discussurus.	2. Quantus tremor, *etc.*
3. Tuba mirum spargens sonum per sepulchra regionum coget omnes ante thronum.	3. Tuba mirum, *etc.*
4. Mors stupebit et natura, cum resurget creatura, judicanti responsura.	4. Mors stupebit, *etc.*
5. Liber scriptus proferetur, in quo totum continetur, unde mundus judicetur.	5. Liber scriptus, *etc.*
6. Judex ergo cum sedebit, quidquid latet apparebit, nil inultum remanebit.	6. Judex ergo, *etc.*

III

| 7. Quid sum miser tunc dicturus? quem patronum rogaturus, cum vix justus sit securus? | 7. Quid sum miser, *etc.*
9. Recordare, pie Jesu, *etc.*
17. Oro supplex, *etc.* |

Table I
Berlioz's Requiem Text Compared with its Liturgical Source

Liturgical Text	Berlioz's Version
	IV
8. Rex tremendae majestatis, qui salvandos salvas gratis, salva me, fons pietatis.	8. Rex tremendae, etc.
9. Recordare, Jesu pie, quod sum causa tuae viae, ne me perdas illa die.	9. Recordare, Jesu pie, *etc.* 16. Confutatis maledictis, (Jesu), flammis acribus addictis, voca me— et de profundo lacu. Libera me de ore leonis, ne cadam in obscurum, ne absorbeat me Tartarus.
	V
10. Quaerens me sedisti lassus, redemisti crucem passus, tantus labor non sit cassus.	10. Quaerens me, *etc.*
11. Juste judex ultionis, donum fac remissionis ante diem rationis.	11. Juste judex, *etc.*
12. Ingemisco tanquam reus, culpa rubet vultus meus, supplicanti parce, Deus.	12. Ingemisco tanquam reus, supplicanti parce, Deus.
13. Qui Mariam absolvisti, et latronem exaudisti, mihi quoque spem dedisti.	14. Preces meae, *etc.*
14. Preces meae non sunt dignae, sed tu, bonus, fac benigne, ne perenni cremer igne.	13. Qui Mariam, *etc.*
15. Inter oves locum praesta, et ab hoedis me sequestra, statuens in parte dextra.	15. Inter oves, *etc.*
16. Confutatis maledictis, flammis acribus addictis, voca me cum benedictis.	
17. Oro supplex et acclinis, cor contritum quasi cinis, gere curam mei finis.	

Table 1

Berlioz's Requiem Text Compared with its Liturgical Source

Liturgical Text	Berlioz's Version
	VI
18. Lacrymosa dies illa, qua resurget ex favilla, judicandus homo reus. Huic ergo parce, Deus, pie Jesu, Domine, dona eis requiem. Amen.	18. Lacrymosa dies illa qua resurget ex favilla judicandus homo reus. Pie Jesu, Domine, dona eis requiem aeternam.

Offertory

	VII
Domine Jesu Christe, Rex gloriae, libera animas omnium fidelium defunctorum de poenis inferni et de profundo lacu. Libera eas de ore leonis, ne absorbeat eas Tartarus, ne cadant in obscurum: sed signifer sanctus Michael repraesentet eas in lucem sanctam, quam olim Abra- hae promisisti, et semini ejus.	Domine Jesu Christe, Rex gloriae, libera animas omnium fidelium defunctorum de poenis inferni et de profundo lacu. Et sanctus Michael signifer repraesentet eas in lucem sanctam, quam olim Abrahae et semini ejus promisisti.
	VIII
Hostias et preces tibi, Domine, laudis of- ferimus. Tu suscipe pro animabus illis, quarum hodie memoriam facimus: fac eas, Domine, de morte transire ad vi- tam, quam olim Abrahae promisisti, et semini ejus.	Hostias et preces tibi laudis offerimus. Suscipe pro animabus illis, quarum hodie memoriam facimus.

Sanctus

	IX
Sanctus, sanctus, sanctus, Dominus Deus Sabaoth, pleni sunt coeli et terra gloria tua. Hosanna in excelsis. Benedictus qui venit in nomine Domini. Hosanna in excelsis.	Sanctus, *etc.* Hosanna in excelsis. Sanctus, *etc.* Hosanna in excelsis.

Agnus Dei and Communion

	X
Agnus Dei, qui tollis peccata mundi, dona eis requiem. Agnus Dei, qui tollis peccata mundi, dona eis requiem sempiternam.	Agnus Dei, qui tollis peccata mundi, dona eis requiem sempiternam.
Lux aeterna luceat eis, Domine, cum sanc- tis tuis in aeternum, quia pius es.	Te decet hymnus, Deus in Sion, et tibi red- detur votum in Jerusalem.

Table 1
Berlioz's Requiem Text Compared with its Liturgical Source

Liturgical Text	Berlioz's Version
	Exaudi orationem meam, ad te omnis caro veniet.
Requiem aeternam dona eis, Domine, et lux perpetua luceat eis, cum sanctis tuis in aeternum, quia pius es.	Requiem aeternam dona defunctis (dona eis) Domine, et lux perpetua luceat eis, cum sanctis tuis in aeternum, Domine, quia pius es.

hypothetical program. A fairly orthodox "Requiem aeternam" is succeeded by a "Dies irae" rearranged in such a way as to intensify the contrast between the public and the private, between the imagined cataclysm and a terrified personal reaction. To this end, the depiction of Hell is embellished and extended by an interpolation from the Offertory. The first movement devoted to the sequence comprises its six opening stanzas, which describe the awful event in more or less objective, third-person terms. The next is based on three stanzas in the first person (nos. 7, 9, and 17), which voice the individual's fears and hopes. Stanza 8 was postponed, probably because it combines the two modes. It is that contrast which forms the basis for a new section, "Rex tremendae," in which the omitted no. 8 and the similarly constructed no. 16 sandwich a recall of the personal appeal of no. 9. The effect is heightened when no. 16 is broken off at the crucial words "voca me," the point at which the passage from the Offertory is interpolated—slightly modified in order to maintain the vividness of the first-personal reference. The individual is again paramount in the movement that follows, encompassing nos. 10–15. Finally, the "Lacrymosa" returns to the apocalyptic mood of the "Dies—Tuba." Although the appeal that ends the hymn is retained, it is abbreviated; its effect in this context is that of one last moment of private prayer. The contrast between public and private thus prevails throughout.

In the Offertory, "Domine Jesu Christe" is interpreted (according to a subtitle Berlioz added to the second edition, but later withdrew) as a "chorus of the souls in Purgatory." Its references to Hell are consequently reduced—the omitted passages having already found a home in the preceding section. And the ending is slightly altered so as to allow a resolution on the hopeful word "promisisti."

The ritual presentation of the "Hostias" implies a return to earth; but its imagery remains in the other world, still centered on Purgatory. It is followed by the third vision, that of Paradise, in the Sanctus. The starkness of this contrast is heightened by the omission of the final words of "Hostias," with their intimation of eternal life, as well as by the extension of the period devoted to the celestial scene through the substitution of a second Sanctus for the more mundane Benedictus. The definitive return to the human sphere—an awakening from the reverie—is effected (as the music will make clear) when the Agnus Dei recalls the words of the opening "Requiem aeternam," here non-liturgically extended (to include "Te decet hymnus") in such a way as to emphasize the framing effect of the outer movements.

The chart does not show certain details of Berlioz's manipulation of the text (supported, of course, by the musical setting) for greater dramatic emphasis. Neither of the two opening stanzas of "Dies irae," for example, is stated in its complete form at the outset. Just as the various melodic strands only gradually weave themselves into a definitive polyphonic texture, just as the tempo quickens, the dynamic force increases, and the key level rises—so do the poetic stanzas only gradually complete themselves, as if mankind only slowly and unwillingly accepted the reality of the terrible event. (Note, too, the interjection of a redundant "dies illa" into the bass part each time it arrives at the motivic repetition of m. 7—a musical exigency translated into a textual urgency.)

Polytextuality, too, is occasionally put to use to support new relationships. In movt. V, stanza 10 ("Quaerens me") returns after nos. 11 and 12 in counterpoint against no. 14 ("Preces meae"), which itself has been placed ahead of no. 13, presumably for just this purpose. The image of the crucified Christ is simultaneously opposed (verbally, melodically, rhythmically) to that of the unworthy sinner; indeed, the two stanzas are interwoven at one point where Berlioz's version reads:

Quaerens me sedisti lassus,
non sum dignus,
sed tantus labor non sit cassus.

It is an extreme example of the freedom with which the composer everywhere treats his text.

The chart also fails to reflect certain repetitions and recapitulations that, often supported by parallel musical devices, modify the textual form. Thus the reminiscence of stanza 4 ("Mors stupebit") at the close of the "Dies—Tuba" effects a transition to the personal comment ("Quid sum miser") that follows; the return to the words "Rex tremendae" and "Lacrymosa," in movts. V and VI respectively, afford opportunities for musical reprises that point up the public-private contrast so basic to Berlioz's conception.

Other recapitulations are purely musical: the return of the opening melodies of the "Dies irae" in the following movement; the framing of the Sanctus by the twin "Hostias" and Agnus Dei; and perhaps most important, the recurrence of the "salva me" cadence from "Rex tremendae" to set the final "quia pius es." When these thematic relationships are considered in conjunction with the sequence of keys, so carefully controlled throughout the Mass, an overall design clearly emerges, as diagram 1 tries to make clear. Clear, perhaps, but not unambiguous—for it is one of Berlioz's prime characteristics to suggest and invite more than one way of hearing his work. From a thematic point of view, there is a major articulation at the conclusion of movt. IV, marked by an important cadence that is to return at the close of the entire work. But tonally the E major is transitional, since it functions as a dominant of the succeeding A major. The composer himself has insisted on this point by his tempo indication for movt. V: "Même mouvement que le morceau précédent."

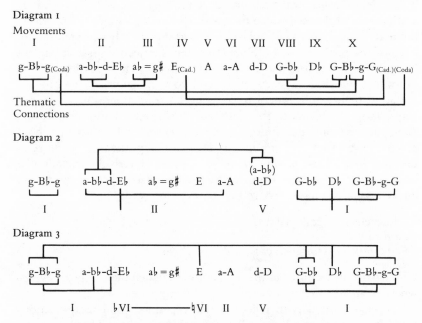

Diagram 1

Movements

I	II	III	IV	V	VI	VII	VIII	IX	X
g-B♭-g(Coda)	a-b♭-d-E♭	a♭=g♯	E(Cad.)	A	a-A	d-D	G-b♭	D♭	G-B♭-g-G(Cad.)(Coda)

Thematic
Connections

Diagram 2

g-B♭-g   a-b♭-d-E♭   a♭=g♯   E   a-A   d-D   G-b♭   D♭   G-B♭-g-G

(a-b♭)

I   II   V   I

Diagram 3

g-B♭-g   a-b♭-d-E♭   a♭=g♯   E   a-A   d-D   G-b♭   D♭   G-B♭-g-G

I   ♭VI————————♮VI   II   V   I

Nor is that the only ambiguity here. We can take the E either as a simple dominant within a predominantly A minor-major complex, or as the first of a chain of fifths leading back to the G minor-major tonic. Which we choose depends on how we hear the overall tonal structure. On the one hand we can take our clue from the rounded A minor-major of the "Dies irae," within which the E♭ of the "Tuba mirum" stands out as a passage of tritone contrast. This is balanced by a similar tritone relationship in the latter half: the D♭ of the Sanctus against its surrounding Gs. Between these two areas stands "Domine Jesu Christe." Its key, D minor-major, acts as a transitional dominant between the A of "Dies irae" and the G of the final sections. At the same time, the combination of that key with the ostinato on A-B♭ compresses into a near simultaneity the successive A-B♭-D of the second movement (diagram 2).

The alternative way of hearing the tonal organization (diagram 3) takes the E♭ of "Tuba mirum" as related to the opening G minor and its associated B♭. Indeed, the orchestral introduction of the first movement, with its rise from G, first to D, then E♭, intimates as much. In this case the A minor of movt. II is transitional, a passing area between G and B♭. The tonal goal is the same as the obvious dynamic goal: the E♭ of the "Tuba mirum." This time the A♭ or G♯ of movt. III serves as a transition to the E of movt. IV, which now initiates the sequential steps back to the tonic G. In this context it should be noted that E completes the minor-third cycle, whose other members are the G and B♭ of the opening and the close, and the D♭ of the Sanctus.

The tonal ambiguity suggests a corresponding programmatic one. Of the two patterns, the first is the simpler dramatically as well as musically. It distinctly separates the visions of the "Dies irae" stanzas and of the "Domine Jesu Christe" from each other and also from the framing earth-bound sections. Within the latter of these, the heavenly scene appears as an element of other-worldly contrast. The second pattern, on the other hand, presents the sections as interpenetrating one another. Its musico-dramatic imagery draws one only gradually into the visionary sphere, and it even seems to make Paradise less unattainable, owing to its cyclical key connection.

There is yet another perspective from which one can hear these progressions—one that offers, as it were, a timeless point of view. The two tritone-sandwiched groups are related to each other in a curiously symmetrical way. The central key of the first, E♭, is the lowered submediant of the flanking key of the second, G (which is also the tonic of the whole). At the same time, the central key of the second group, D♭ (or C♯), is the major mediant of the flanking key of the first, A. The interval in each case is a major third. The connection is made startlingly clear when the Agnus Dei, a movement that is to recapitulate the G minor of the "Hostias," opens with an A-major chord after the D♭ cadence of the Sanctus.[4] (The progression at the beginning of the Agnus is noteworthy in other respects as well. In the course of its modulation to G, it makes a

4. See the diagram in "Saint's Head," 236.

pointed reference to the A-B♭ modulation of movt. II and to the A-B♭-A
ostinato of VII. At the same time, the fluctuating bass, A-B♭-A-C-A-D,
foreshadows, in partial retrograde, the "Amens" of the final coda.)

Such long-range tonal plans occur too often in Berlioz's music to be
the result of pure chance (or of my own excessive ratiocination). I have
shown elsewhere how the added brass choirs produce their own far-flung
modulation from the E♭ of the "Tuba mirum" through the E♮ of the "Rex
tremendae" to the A of the "Lacrymosa." After firmly announcing and
reiterating the key of the "Tuba," they enter the "Rex" on a pivot chord
(E♭:♭III = E:V/V) that eventually leads to a standard cadence in E. But
here the tonic

> is prophetically converted into a dominant seventh. So, much later,
> when the brass choirs add their terrifying accents to the fugal reprise
> of the "Lacrymosa," they are fulfilling a destiny as inexorable as the
> Day of Judgment itself.[5]

As this progression shows, beneath the sensationalism of Berlioz's orchestral effects lies a tightly controlled formal substratum. It is certainly
not wrong to enjoy his instrumentation for its sensuous color and its
emotional connotations; indeed, in his *Traité* he insists on the importance
of those characteristics. But to listen to his music solely or even primarily
for the sake of that pleasure is to miss other, more profound values.
Perhaps more than any other composer, he thinks of each instrument in
terms of its role—meaning not only its dramatic characterization but also
its contribution to the total musical line. And in carrying out his "colos-
sal" projects, with their vast "progressions whose final goal cannot be
guessed," he relies heavily on those roles. Thus the brasses construct only
one of a number of instrumental lines that traverse huge areas of the
Requiem.

One of the most extraordinary of these unites the entire Mass (ex. 1).

Example 1

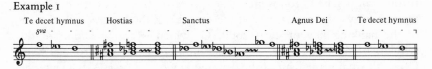

The flute-trombone combination of the "Hostias" and the Agnus has
often been cited for its unearthly sound. Rarely noticed, however, are the
way these chords weave their own progression throughout both movements, and above all how those passages connect with others in which
the flute is independently prominent (as opposed to those in which it is

5. See "Saint's Head," 235.

used primarily to double the voices or other instruments). Most obviously, the two movements frame the Sanctus, where a solo flute plays an important part in the celestial accompaniment of the tenor and chorus. Initially doubling the voices, it soon strikes out for itself. In so doing, it makes explicit the relation between that movement and the preceding: the D♭ melody, in both the vocal and the flute versions, hovers around D♭-F-B♭—the final chord of "Hostias"—before resolving to A♭. Indeed, the long-breathed flute version (mm. 5–17) is in exactly the register marked out by that final chord. Moreover, the flute solo of the second Sanctus ends with a *rallentando* on the G♭-F outlined by the first flute-trombone chords of the "Hostias." Hence, when the Agnus, after its introductory chords, settles into the material of "Hostias," the returning progression spells out the same G♭-F.

The uncanniest stroke of this reprise is its last: its transformation of the final chord, originally B♭ minor, into major, in such a way as to lead without a break into the return of "Te decet hymnus" from the opening movement. The sense here of a welcome awakening to reality[6] must have been in Berlioz's mind from the outset: "Te decet," too, had its prominent flute line—the first independent flute line of the Mass (one hears the oboe at this point as doubling the flute, not vice versa). It too was in B♭, and in the register of the "Hostias" chords. Thus the return of the G-B♭ key area toward the end of the Mass is supported by instrument, by register, by line, and finally by thematic recapitulation. No wonder "Te decet" reenters like a benediction! Although not liturgically correct, it is musically right.

A less obvious example, although within a single movement, is afforded by movt. III, "Quid sum miser." The movement is based on the fragmentation of themes from the preceding; but the continuity of the various lines, instrumental and vocal, is carefully maintained. From one point of view there are three strands: instrumental melody, vocal melody, and bass. The first two are closely related, for the entire line of the English horn is developed from the opening phrase, which it shares with the tenors.[7] (Here is a beautiful example of Berlioz's instrumental characterization: the melancholy English horn is given its only solo to accompany the prayer of the "miser.") The bass is alternately given to bassoons and strings, to the point where one wonders whether they constitute one

6. In this connection, the major chord always reminds me of Keats's "Forlorn! the very word is like a bell / To toll me back from thee to my sole self!" But the return to reality in "Ode to a Nightingale" is not a welcome one.

7. Some of the tenor line is more closely related to an earlier version of the "Dies irae" than to its final form. Compare *New Berlioz Edition,* vol. 9 (Kassel, 1978), app. 1, exx. k and l, 165.

line or two. At the outset, although their ranges are an octave apart, their material is identical. Later, however, when the contrabasses temporarily drop out, their ranges overlap and their material becomes complementary, the cellos clearly continuing the bassoon line (mm. 25–34). But the bassoons have another role: that of occasional doubling—first of the English horn and later of the tenors and basses. So the bassoons apparently play four parts: an independent bass, a bass answered by the cellos, a line that doubles the English horn, and one that doubles the voices. Each of these roles makes musical sense in itself. At the same time, the composite line can be heard as a unit: a single bassoon melody—one with a wide range, to be sure, but a range covered, extended, and resolved by the final phrase. In the same way, the entire string bass line can be construed unitarily, as a free *ABA*: cellos and basses together, then cellos alone, then a return to the combination with a reference to the original melody.

All this is within the space of a single short movement; but there is a wider reference here too. A connection both in orchestral sound (low strings, low woodwinds) and actual notes (G♯–D♯–B on the one hand and G–B on the other) exists between the final chord of this movement and the "profundo lacu" of the next (mm. 58–63). But that point leads in turn to another, again at some distance: the similarly colored cadence of "Tartarus" (mm. 73–75), which answers the G by a descent to C, this in turn to be resolved stepwise to B, the true dominant of the movement. So, within the prevailing E of "Rex tremendae," an intermittent progression can be heard as moving from mediant at the end of "Quid sum miser," through lowered mediant and submediant, to dominant—all in the somber colors and subdued dynamic level that characterize the "Quid sum miser."

That progression can be expanded by the insertion of two other steps: the obvious interpolations (textual and musical) of "Jesu" within the "Confutatis maledictis" section (mm. 43 and 47). Set off dynamically and instrumentally from their surroundings, they point up a sequence of dominant sevenths on E and F♯ that resolves deceptively on the G of "et de profundo lacu." Thus, amid the noise of "Rex tremendae," the following quiet progression is grandly making its own way: III–I♮⁷–II♯–♮III–♮VI–V, the final dominant offering at last the expected resolution of its own earlier dominant on II.

Obviously the V, in its turn, is looking forward to a tonic. And so, during the recapitulation, the clamor of the "Rex" is broken open again—four times, in fact—for the quiet appeals of "salve me" (mm. 85–105).[8] The first two of these recall the outlines of the progression previ-

8. A motif that gained immeasurably in expressivity (as well as in correctness of declamation) through revision. See *New Berlioz Edition*, vol. 9, app. 2, exx. e,f,h, and i, 169–70.

ously noted: they emphasize respectively II and V (each preceded by a diminished seventh). The third is based on another familiar detail, ♮VI–V. The fourth and last circumvents the expected tonic by converting it into a surprising ♮VII. That chord initiates a bass descent that, moving chromatically from D to B, once more touches on the C-B of "Tartarus" before turning to the tonic that is the goal not only of this intermittent progression but of the entire movement as well. But there is one further step; for the simple connection from this E-major cadence to the A major of the following "Quaerens me" constitutes a final link in the chain uniting all the sections of the "Dies irae" that I have labeled "personal" or "individual" (ex. 2).

Example 2

These long-range projects inevitably involve what seem to be interruptions of the principal musical line or interpolations within it. At the same time these can be regarded as constituting progressions of their own that may vie for primacy with the controlling one. There is no question of the correctness of one way of hearing as opposed to another; rather, one must accept them all, much as one observes the same object from different vantage points. Elsewhere I have characterized Berlioz's music as one "of multiple perspective—of contrasting points of view simultaneously presented, and of shifting points of view shown in succession."[9] As the preceding examples have shown, that multiple perspective applies to every aspect of composition: to overall thematic structure, to tonal relations, to instrumentation, to linear and chordal progressions. It is perhaps most vividly embodied in the four brass choirs

9. See "Saint's Head," 237.

which, as we have seen, impose their own instrumental and tonal viewpoint on the course of the entire "Dies irae." At the same time, physically placed as they are (or should be) so as to surround the rest of the performers, they encourage the audience to identify the musical perspective with an acoustical one, to perceive musical and actual space as analogues of each other.

A similar maneuver is equally successful in the "Hostias." The registers of the chorus and of the orchestral strings are normal, yet we hear them in the wider perspective opened up by the extremes of the flutes and trombones. We interpret the contrast between winds and voices spatially, perhaps as symbolizing the gulf between the human and the divine. The huge gap between flutes and trombones creates another space, too—between the possibility of God's grace and the peril of His condemnation, between the heavenly realm and the abyss? Even within those wind chords there is spatial play, for as the sound swells and subsides with the crescendo–diminuendo specified for each sonority, the supremacy shifts from flutes to trombones and back again. Between the two lies the chorus. Although the chant, realistically (and tonally!) considered, is a supplication from those on earth, its words, expressing the hope that the commemorated souls can still be reached and helped by prayer, refer to Purgatory. So, too, does the somber sound of its male voices, registrally framed by the stark winds. This one movement, then, encompasses in a single complex musical image the entire visionary range of the Requiem.

One of the most effective devices of shifting perspective comes into play whenever Berlioz, as he so frequently does, subjects a musical idea to successive reinterpretations. He approaches polyphony in just that way: a countersubject throws new light on its subject, or the simultaneous combination of two previously stated melodies reinterprets each of them. The opening of the "Dies irae" is a quintessential example, with its startling superposition of two independent and even harmonically opposed melodies.[10]

Reinterpretation can also affect the smallest motivic details. As previously noted, the descending whole step (G♯-F♯) of "salva me," interjected toward the end of "Rex tremendae," is given a different harmonization for each set of occurrences, resolving successively to II, V, and (after a short development) ♮VII in E major. But that is not all: the final cadence on "fons pietatis"—itself the subject of two harmonic interpretations—is in fact an expansion of the "salva me" motif (ex. 3a). When the same cadence returns in the last movement as "quia pius es," it is given yet

10. Ibid., 231–32.

another harmonization; this time it can be heard as a new version of the immediately preceding cadence of "luceat eis" (ex. 3b). A single motif is thus derived from two different sources; or, alternatively, two apparently dissimilar motifs are linked by a common variation.

Example 3

Simultaneous harmonic and rhythmic reinterpretations are displayed by the Sanctus when the reprise of the opening section (sometimes, alas, disastrously omitted in performance) magically opens two new perspectives on the original. First, it supplies a bass that was perhaps implicit from the beginning, but not completely stated. Even more arresting are the strokes of cymbals and bass drum that now quietly punctuate the movement. Ravishing in these surroundings as sheer sound, they suggest a startling new metrical organization over, under, or against the prevailing 4/4. Entering after five half measures, they continue to articulate an implied 5/2 by their persistent periodicity: *1* (2 3 4 5) / *1 2* (3 4 5). After four complete cycles of this kind, there is some variation—*1* (2 3 4) / *1* (2 3 4 5) / *1 2* (3 4 5 6) / *1 2* (3 4 5)—that still maintains the basic five as a norm (and average!). And the last cycle (if we construe the fermata as equivalent to a half note) consists of twice five groups of three: *1* (2 3).

The cymbal-drum strokes are a kind of ostinato, in this case not tonal but purely instrumental and rhythmic. Now, an ostinato, although itself relatively static or even invariable, can nevertheless throw shifting light on the texture with which it is contrasted. In turn, the ostinato itself can undergo constant reinterpretation. No doubt that is why Berlioz was so fond of the device, and why his music displays it in such variety.

The most celebrated example in the Requiem is the reiterated choral chant against the orchestral fugato of "Domine Jesu Christe." Static as the neighboring-tone pattern is, its meaning constantly changes. In the first place, the time intervals between its successive occurrences are highly irregular. At the outset, for example, the ostinato formula, which can be either single (A-B♭-A) or double (A-B♭-A-B♭-A) occurs after five measures of rest (double), two measures (double), two measures (single), one measure (single), two measures (double), three measures (double plus two singles), four measures (double), etc. All this punctuates a continuous melodic line (fugue subject, plus countersubject against answer) of twenty-seven measures. Moreover, each occurrence is harmonically differentiated: in D, major I, then minor I; in A, minor I, IV, major I, minor I; returning to D, V^7 and minor I. Thus the ostinato subjects the polyphonic lines to successive shifts in articulation, and the lines subject the ostinato to successive reharmonizations.

The choral ostinato is not the only one in this movement. The winds punctuate each entry by sounding its keynote (alternately D and A). At the fourth (and last) entry this role is taken over by a persistently throbbing pedal of alternating octaves on A in the double basses. That motif, diminshed from quarter notes to eighths, also underlines the return of the fugue subject after the contrasting middle section. Entering at this point (m. 96) as a melodically varied rhythmic ostinato evolving out of the preceding section, the undulation eventually returns to the bass to support the tonic with its now static octave reiterations. Meanwhile, as the development of the tonality has moved to III (F) and VI (B♭), the original choral motif has assumed new functions in relation to those areas.

At the same time, the choral motif has exhibited from the beginning another kind of connection with the fugato, for the neighboring-tone figure is persistently prominent in the subject as well. So when, in the wake of the gradual disintegration of that subject to a single interval (or even a single note), the chorus breaks out of its pattern, developing its motif in such a way as to build up a glowing major triad—then we hear this as a resolution of the fugue, too. Indeed, the close connection between fugue subject and ostinato is made indubitably clear in the last few measures. I once wrote, "It is almost possible to hear the piece, not as a fugue with an ostinato against it, but as a choral chant accompanied by a fugue."[11] But the conclusion of the movement opens out a vista against which each of these perspectives must seem only partial. Every level of activity in this movement must be heard as leading to, and subsumed by, the all-enveloping D major. If Berlioz meant to depict souls in Purgatory here, how better could he symbolize their ultimate beatification?

Although no other movement is based on a persistent ostinato, very few lack one or more. Movt. II is full of them. The buildup of the second stage (B♭ minor) is intensified by inverted pedals in the sopranos; when they suddenly break out of their straitjackets, as they do twice on the word "favilla" (mm. 78 and 98), the effect is terrifying. At the same time, the tenors interject an ostinato of a different kind—rhythmic (a quarter note followed by an eighth and a rest), directional (descending), and dynamic (diminuendo).[12] The climax of the "Tuba mirum" (mm. 228–37) is underlined by ten measures of a persistent triplet pattern in the bass drum.

Among later movements, one should note the reprises of "Rex Tremendae," over nine measures (mm. 76–84) of regularly reiterated dominant pedal, and of "Quaerens me," accompanied by a persistent motif of repeated eighths that functions as a rhythmic ostinato (mm. 42–67). In the "Lacrymosa," all of the contrasting sections—the second subject in exposition and recapitulation, the C-major "development" episode—despite their relative relaxation are driven onward by ostinati: the downward octave leap of horns in the exposition (mm. 44–73) and of ophicleides in the recapitulation (mm. 126–54), the throbbing basses (both choral and instrumental) in the development (mm. 74–90). (Does this section, by the way, with its plea to "pie Jesu" and with its harmonic connection of C to B (♮VI-V in E major) refer to the "Tartarus" interpolation in "Rex"? Here is yet another possible long range connection.)

The ostinato that is subjected to the most thoroughgoing treatment—reinterpretation, development, variation—in a word, evolution—is, appropriately, one that frames the entire work, appearing as it does in the opening movement and in its final reprise. I mean the chromatic motif that, as a new orchestral countersubject, accompanies the second fugato exposition of "Requiem aeternam" (mm. 57 ff). The original vocal countersubject (mm. 28ff), from which the new one stems, behaved as a normal countersubject should, shifting its tonal area to accord with each new entry. The present one, however, as an ostinato, remains stubbornly

---

11. Ibid., 238.

12. Again, a great improvement on the original version. See *New Berlioz Edition*, vol. 9, app. 1, ex. m, 165.

fixed in position (B♭ descending to G) against entries starting successively on B♭, C, D, and E♭. It is thus perforce harmonized anew each time. When, after the central section, the fugato is recommenced, further light is thrown on the ostinato; for it is now made to hold its own against an attempted revival of its parent, the original vocal countersubject (mm. 128ff). It is the ostinato that survives the encounter, assimilating its rival and remaining after the fugato for one final statement against the now homophonic chorus (mm. 142–44). Nor is this all. That statement initiates a development (mm. 144–59) that elaborates a long, slow descent until the motif at last dissolves into the luminous chords of "luceat eis."

One would expect after such events that one had heard the last of a theme. In this case one would be wrong: the ostinato, slightly expanded, yields the vocal line that presents "Christe eleison" (ex. 3c). But the "Christe" motif is at the same time a minor variation of the preceding major cadence, "luceat eis" (ex. 3b–c). Like the "fons pietatis" motif already discussed, it can be derived from either of two parent themes. By the same token, "luceat eis" can be heard as a common ancestor of both "Christe" and "fons pietatis"; that is why "quia pius es" can so appropriately replace the one by a version of the other. In so doing, it completes a musical link among the cries for mercy throughout the Requiem. It is a link forged not only motivically but also harmonically. All the cited passages, together with the Paradise to which they aspire, belong to the minor-third cycle indicated in diagram 3.

One more perspective—the grandest of all—is opened by the final cadences of the mass. Their gradual, undulating descent is surely a varied form of the orchestral conclusion of the first movement.[13] That conclusion, with its chromatic fall to a final G, was still another stage in the evolution of the ostinato countersubject. Yet the musical context suggests an alternative derivation. The descent clearly reverses an immediately preceding rise from G to D (mm. 200–01). Can it not also be heard as a reversal of the ascending scale that opened the movement (ex. 4)? If that is the case, then the concluding "quia pius es," together with the multiple "Amen," must in some sense furnish a final response to the initial questioning gesture of the entire Requiem.

I have suggested that the recapitulation embedded in the concluding movement can be interpreted as an awakening to reality. But, as the final measures reveal, that reality is not the same as the one that preceded the visions. Or rather: it is the same reality, but illumined, even transfigured, by the experience of those visions. The opening movement ended in the

13. The connection was even more explicit in an earlier version. See *New Berlioz Edition*, vol. 9, app. 1, ex. u, 167; for further analysis of the "Amens" see "Saint's Head," 226–27.

Example 4

darkness of anxiety and trepidation; that has been overcome and transformed into a glow of confident acceptance.

It is unclear just what Berlioz's religious beliefs were. In specific formulation they were certainly far from orthodox. It may well be that the faith implied by the concluding pages of the Requiem is a purely dramatic construct—an emotional state sympathetically depicted but unshared by the composer. Yet as the luminosity of those measures finally dispels the gloom of the opening, it does not seem inappropriate to recall how, centuries before, "l'amor che move il sole e l'altre stelle" at last dissipated the darkness of "una selva oscura."

[*1980*]

The Old Man's Toys:
Verdi's Last Operas

I

It is now clear that Verdi was one of the giants. Thanks to recent performances, new recordings, and reprinted scores, we can observe in detail the slow and steady growth from youthful rawness through the vigor of the middle period to the refined splendor of *Aida*—an advance predictable enough for a composer of Verdi's obvious musical gift. The final step, however—to *Otello* and *Falstaff*—could have been taken only by an imaginative intellect of the highest order. But the praise which it is now fashionable to bestow on these works is often grudgingly qualified. The critic may not go so far as Stravinsky, who for his own obvious purposes sees *Rigoletto* and *Traviata* as representing the high point of Verdi's art; but he often agrees with Shaw that in *Otello* and *Falstaff* subtlety has replaced melodic inspiration, and he considers the latter opera, for all its beauties, a meaningless puppet show, written for an old man's amusement.

Verdi himself suggested this point of view. His letters indicate that he was so afraid of making any commitments which his advanced age might not allow him to fulfill, that he protected himself by pretending that *Falstaff* was "a mere pastime." To Boito, his librettist, he writes: "Did you ever think of my huge accumulation of years? . . . I could be accused of great rashness, if I were to undertake such a task. And suppose I could not master my weariness? Suppose I could not finish the music? Then you would have your time and pains for nothing!"[1] To the Mayor of

---

1. *Verdi, The Man in His Letters,* ed. Franz Werfel and Paul Stefan (New York, 1942), 392–93.

Parma he admits: "I am writing *Falstaff,* it is true. But I am writing it in moments of absolute leisure, simply for my own amusement, and without any definite goal in view; and I do not know whether or when I shall finish it."[2] The cat is out of the bag, though, when he confesses to Gino Monaldi that "for forty years now I have been wanting to write a comic opera, and for fifty years I have known *The Merry Wives of Windsor.*"[3] The old man's toy was the consummation of a half-century's desire.

Such long-range plans are not unusual with Verdi, and they indicate from almost the earliest days a seriousness of purpose which refutes the conception of the young composer as a mere tunemonger. They suggest also that we must respect the earlier works as rougher embodiments of the same musical and dramatic conceptions which are found, refined and freed of inessentials, in the later masterpieces. Verdi himself respected them; his careful revision of *Macbeth* for the Paris performance proves it. *Macbeth* had been written in 1847—even before *Luisa Miller;* the new version was prepared in 1865—three years after *La forza del destino.* Yet his correspondence at this period reveals the liveliest interest in the new production; he was determined that it should be as musically and dramatically effective as possible. More remarkable still is the rewriting of *Simon Boccanegra* after twenty-four years. Originally the product of his first mature period, it became an important link between *Aida* and *Otello,* and marked the composer's first collaboration with the librettist of his great last works.

A real collaboration it remained, for no other composer since Mozart worked so intimately with his poets. Although he never wrote a libretto, Verdi was always a dramatist; and although he was no philosopher, his opera was from the beginning based on a sound aesthetic. If we fail to comprehend it, or even to admit its existence, we shall continue to be troubled by the apparent contrivance of *Otello* and the meaninglessness of *Falstaff.*

II

One approach to the understanding of what Verdi was trying to do is suggested by a consideration of the charge that the style of the late works is a result of waning inspiration, that artifice has replaced creativity. Shaw thought this was true already in *Aida* and attributed the richness of that opera's orchestration to the composer's attempt to make up for "the inevitable natural drying up of . . . spontaneity and fertility."[4] But in

2. Ibid., 401.
3. Ibid., 396.
4. George Bernard Shaw, "A Word More About Verdi," in the *Anglo-Saxon Review,* March 1901; reprinted in *Shaw on Music,* ed. Eric Bentley (Garden City, N.J., 1955), 135.

actuality, what we find in these works is not less invention, but more. The melody, it is true, is contented with single periods or even phrases (Falstaff's "Te lo cornifico, netto, netto," ex. 1), where the melody of *Il trovatore* would have demanded an aria; but what would have been the

Example 1

construction of such an aria? Look at "Di quella pira," at "La donna è mobile," at "Di Provenza," and you will find that one motif—a single detail—is elaborated by sequential repetition and simple modifications to fill out the entire form. Fundamentally, the pregnant vocal fragments which carry the burden of the music in the later works are equivalent to these arias, with all such obvious development suppressed. Instead, the phrases are now subjected to real development: they appear in constantly new relations and in ever more varied forms. The "cornifico" motif referred to above (*Falstaff*, Act 2, Scene 1) is not dropped after its initial presentation by Falstaff; it is kept as a constantly recurring thought beneath Ford's ensuing monologue. Two purely orchestral statements of it introduce the arioso. The first ends on a simple tonic according to Falstaff's version; but the second leads to a dissonant deceptive cadence as the import of Falstaff's words begins to affect Ford—"È sogno? o realtà." A little later, with completely altered harmonization leading into dark, abbreviated, chromatic sequences, it is reduced to only three tones, which in turn are used to form the crescendo to the outburst "O matrimonio: Inferno!" The composer returns to the device of the deceptive cadence (in a more startling form) as Ford imagines the dreaded words "Le corna," and from the original motif he derives the persistent triplet rhythm which remains throughout the rest of the passage. The fullest development is reached when, accompanying "Prima li accoppio/E poi li colgo," the little melody ascends through four octaves to break out in a newly truncated version which produces the exciting effect of simultaneous stretto and diminution. This marks the last appearance of the "cornifico"; from here on it is present only by implication in the triplets of the accompaniment.

Such is the rich orchestral treatment Verdi affords a simple cadential phrase. Other melodies, destined for purely vocal expansion, display a flexibility of line, a variety of contour, and a rhythmic subtlety unknown to his earlier style. Beautiful as "Di Provenza" is (*La traviata*, Act 2), it consists of the unvarying repetition of a single rhythmic element, broken only at the final cadence (ex. 2). Melodically, it outlines the simplest of

Example 2

stepwise motions, both in its individual phrases and in the relation of one phrase to the next. Against this, a fair example of its period, set Desdemona's opening appeal in Act 3 of *Otello* (ex. 3). Here the second

Example 3

half of the initial phrase corresponds rhythmically to the first half, it is true; but the syncopation, serving to accent the climactic F♯, adds new potential energy which is admirably discharged by the embellished cadence. Now this phrase as a whole, consisting as it does of two symmetrical halves, is answered in Otello's part by one of equal length, but indivisible. A short digression is offered by Otello's next phrase, one of only three measures in contrast to the regular four of the first two. Finally, rounding off the tiny song form, Desdemona repeats her opening melody in still another variation. Thus, although the opening motif has been heard four times, it is never rhythmically the same.

Melodically, the passage displays equal subtlety. In the opening figure the line is progressing simultaneously on two levels: from the opening G♯ up and from the high E down—both leading to the closing B. In the repetition of the figure, the sixth thus defined is expanded to an octave, widening the compass of the melody and allowing for a longer, more elaborate fall to the cadential note. The two lines continue their way throughout the second phrase, which effects a modulation to the dominant; only in the truncated middle section, contrastingly characterized by a simple scale progression, are they merged. The concluding section, again in the tonic, restores the two original levels in the expected reprise of the opening. Once more the high F♯ receives emphasis, this time by a poignant, dissonant leap which makes the closing descent to the tonic E doubly welcome. Such complex relations as these (I hardly touch on the harmonic details) indicate a concentration of expression beside which the more extended linear beauty of the earlier aria seems superficial.

Concentration—that is the clue. The aria of *La traviata* is compressed into the short arioso passage of *Otello*. Even Mozart could never have achieved this, for Mozart's arias were already highly concentrated. They are longer than Verdi's arias because they contain so much more music—so many more ideas; but they are as concentrated as possible, and so they cannot be compressed. But Verdi's diluted arias contain much less music than their own space—so he learns concentration.

III

Perhaps Wagner taught Verdi more than the latter realized: this concentration, for example, although it is sometimes hard to think of the long-winded German composer in this term. Yet his essential expression is one of highly charged detail; no one has ever packed more into a motif of two chords. Just here, though, one difference between the two musicians becomes clear: most of Wagner's expressive details are harmonic progressions; Verdi's are melodies. Even at his most nearly Wagnerian, in the "kiss" motif from *Otello* (ex. 4), Verdi remains primarily a melodist. Striking as the chromatic chords are, the fragment must be characterized as a tune, complete and rounded off with a cadence. The other

Example 4

recurrent leitmotiv in the opera, that of "jealousy" (ex. 5), although shorter and more amenable to orchestral development, is not even harmonized upon its first appearance: the orchestra merely doubles Iago's vocal line.

Example 5

Interested as he was in the expressive possibilities of harmonic color, it was natural that Wagner should come to think more and more in terms of the orchestra, and that often his vocal parts should seem to be distracting adjuncts. On the other hand, it was impossible that Verdi, recognizing that melody and song are one, should forget the primary importance of the human voice. "Opera is opera, symphony is symphony": the warning was directed toward Puccini; but in thus summing up his aesthetic, Verdi clearly showed what he must have considered the basic fallacy of his great German contemporary as well.

This is not to say that Verdi's orchestra is only an accompaniment. Already in the earlier operas, some of his most telling scenes are constructed around a primarily instrumental line: the meeting of Rigoletto and Sparafucile, the gaming scene in *La traviata*. But he carefully observes the conditions which prevent the submersion of the voice, and in the Sparafucile scene we can see what these are. The orchestration, with its single muted cello and double bass projecting an unnaturally high melodic line against a background of plucked strings and woodwinds, is striking; but it is simple and remains almost unchanged throughout the scene. Once the listener has grasped the pattern, he can continue to perceive it almost subconsciously while he devotes his attention to the voices and the action. The melody itself, based upon easily remembered figures, is developed in the most unassuming manner; true symphonic style would create a texture so interesting and self-contained that it would completely absorb the ear. The vocal parts, recitative-like, contrast with the formal melodic structure of the accompaniment; but they never conflict rhythmically, for the broken vocal phrases and the smooth instrumental ones coincide at the important cadences, such as those at Sparafucile's words "un uom di spada sta" and "La vostra donna è là." At each of these points, the conclusion of an instrumental period is marked by a similar close in Sparafucile's part, further accented by an echoing interjection from Rigoletto. The voices thus become the irregular surface of a basically simple solid.

Verdi had only to refine this particular type of writing to achieve the miracle of Otello's "Dio! mi potevi" in Act 3. In the declamatory opening, the musical burden is the orchestra's: the constantly varied reiteration of a single motif. The variations do not apply to the rhythm, however, where the rigidity sets off to advantage the free declamation of the vocal part. In the same way the subtle melodic changes of the orchestral figure contrast effectively with the voice's constant repetition of a single note. Each level—voice and orchestra—thus contains one static, monotonous element, as if to symbolize Otello's inability to free himself from his obsession. Three times Otello's part quits its reiterated A♭ for a lower note; each time coincides with a cadential point in the accompaniment. Finally, as the motif disappears in a modulation effected by an unusual deceptive cadence, the voice too surprises us by rising to a startling C♮— and the recitative is over. Here is a point at which the earlier Verdi would have introduced an aria, for the orchestra has borne the weight of the melody long enough. The late Verdi also gives us an aria here—short, asymmetrical, interrupted by dramatic exigency (the entrance of Iago), but an aria which proceeds to a satisfying conclusion at "Cielo! O gioia!"

In Wagner, as in Verdi, when we expect an aria we are given one—but by the orchestra, not the singer. Such a place is Brünnhilde's plea in the last act of Die Walküre, where the tension of the dialogue beginning with "War es so schmählich" is finally released in the passage beginning "Der diese Liebe." It is just at this point, however, that the orchestra achieves its greatest eloquence, and its transformation of the earlier tentative "pleading" motif into a definitive major form (sometimes called "the beginning of a new life") requires our total attention.

Verdi helps his voices to maintain their supremacy by orchestration which is transparent even at its most opaque; to do so he learns to produce the most startling effects by the most economical means. This tendency is already apparent in Rigoletto—in the Sparafucile scene described above, with its unearthly duet of cello and double bass, and in the last act, when the oboe interjects its solitary high tones over the empty fifths of the lower strings. Here is another aspect of the composer's desire for concentration: not of sheer mass, as in Wagner, but of what might be called orchestral attention. The entire effect of the instrumentation is focused in one salient detail, to which all others are subordinated.

Increased mastery of this technique leads to the glowing translucency of Aida. The Nile scene is famous for its coloring; yet the score reveals nothing but a single flute accompanied by muted strings in the simplest of patterns. Even this economy is carried still further in Otello, where all the evil of Iago's character can be compressed into a single unison of horns and strings, and in Falstaff, where two simple harmonics on the violins transform Nannetta's village children into the actual fairies they pretend to be.

IV

Looking at the same material in a slightly different way, I should say that Verdi at all times adheres closely to the two human sources of music: song and dance. When the voice is not predominant the body is. Such passages as those analyzed in the preceding section, in which the orchestra temporarily usurps primary interest and attention, are characterized by easily grasped rhythms suggestive of physical motion and thus referring to the human characters on the stage.

The third source of music, the nonhuman one increasingly drawn upon by Wagner as he develops from *Das Rheingold* to *Parsifal,* is pure sound. This is a new ideal which becomes increasingly important during the nineteenth century, as interest focuses more and more on the coloristic motif, which in turn points the way toward the single, highly expressive chord. Although in Wagner, a product of the German symphonic tradition, such moments of emphasis are still tightly controlled in the total flux, the intrinsic value of each is more important than its contribution to the whole. It is only a step further to Debussy, who isolates them against a colorful but static background. The detail has become disintegrative, and the musical line is lost.

Verdi, even in his last works, refused to yield to this, the great temptation of the late nineteenth century. As a writer for the stage, and therefore for human beings, he knew that the path of pure musical color, of overindividualized chord or motif, leads to dehumanization. Although the style of *Otello* and *Falstaff,* a style stripped bare of all but essentials, became at times one of expressive detail, the details remained primarily melodic and always constructive, contributing to the continuous progress of the musical line, which in turn, as context, gave meaning to the details.

It is therefore easy to see why the concept of the leitmotiv should remain foreign to Verdi, and why he should use it only rarely. For the Wagnerian leitmotiv is independent of its surroundings to the extent that it can be freely transplanted without losing its effect. Even when Verdi does invent a movable phrase, such as the "oath" in *Don Carlo,* the "kiss" motif mentioned above, and the "reverenza" figure in *Falstaff,* he introduces it sparingly. More frequently a motif will be used to characterize a single scene, never to reappear. Themes like these are meaningful in one context alone; they fit only one situation. In *Otello,* the "handkerchief" scene and the "Credo" of Iago furnish examples. Going one step further, Verdi occasionally places at a climactic point a short expressive figure which occurs once only—a detail which has found its unique place in the complete flow and which can be subject neither to repetition nor to development. A phrase like Desdemona's almost hysterical farewell to Emilia is poignant only because of its position in the complete structure of the scene (ex. 6). The instrumental introduction and the "Willow

Example 6

Song" which precede it have vacillated between major and minor, between a clearly harmonic and a modal tonality of F♯; now Desdemona's outburst resolves all doubts in a perfect major cadence. Heard in isolation, and thus unable to perform its function of discharging the tension so long sustained in the previous passage, it sounds commonplace. In contrast, a much shorter figure like "treachery by magic" (ex. 7) from *Götterdämmerung*—only two chords—can weave its spell in any context or in none. Its own sound is sufficient.

Example 7

It is Verdi's achievement of emphatic moment without sacrifice of temporal span which today attracts the attention of those composers for whom pure sound is no longer enough. Sheer sonority can neither organize a large-scale instrumental work nor present human action in terms of the human voice. The colorful detail must take its place in the complete musical phrase, and the phrase must contribute to the unfolding of the complete line. These are the principles, stated in the quartets and sonatas of the aging Beethoven, which were rediscovered two generations later, for a different medium, by the old Italian.

V

Hermann Broch, writing about Homer, suggests that one of the characteristics of the "style of old age" is an apparent preoccupation with matters of technique. This preoccupation is only apparent, he insists, even though it may deceive the artist himself. "Although the artist's problem seems to be mainly technical, his real impulse goes beyond this"; the true goal is "the reaching of a new level of expression."[5] Tech-

5. Hermann Broch, introduction to *On the Iliad* by Rachel Bespaloff (New York, 1947), 10–13.

nique and expression—these terms are more suggestive than the familiar "form" and "content." Too often the latter encourage the picture of form as a handily constructed vessel into which the content can then be poured. Technique, on the other hand, implies the living development of expressive means; and expression indicates the activity of a total organism rather than a mere "containable" substance. The compression of Verdi's last period, like that of Beethoven's, is not of formal interest only; it allows the composer to achieve an intensity—a realism, if you will— impossible in a more relaxed style. It is this intensity, transferred by association from the music to the characters on the stage, which endows them with an almost terrifying vitality. They become real in a sense unknown to the spoken drama; for a music dramatist is able to endow his creatures with a new dimension through a dual control of the temporal continuum in which they move: as a dramatist, he uses this time as a natural physical fact; as musician, he manipulates, even distorts it, to form a vehicle for psychological expression. In a word, he turns time into tempo.

I have called Verdi a music dramatist rather than an opera composer precisely because of this control of both verbal time and musical tempo. In discussing the expressive goals of his works for the stage, I might even go so far as to say that he always wrote his own libretti—not as Wagner did, completing the actual labor of versification, but as Mozart did, working constantly and intimately with a professional of the craft. The composer's early correspondence with the librettists Cammarano and Piave makes clear to what a great extent he was responsible for the choice and shaping of his own plays. *Il trovatore,* for example, seems to have been first suggested to Cammarano in a note written by Verdi early in 1850: "The subject I should like and which I suggest is *El Trovador,* a Spanish drama by Gutierrez. It seems to me very fine, rich in ideas and in strong situations. I should like to have two feminine roles. First, the gypsy, a woman of unusual character after whom I want to name the opera. The other part for a secondary singer."[6] Over a year later, after having received Cammarano's sketch for the play, he writes him again, dissatisfied: "It seems to me, if I am not deceived, that several situations no longer have the force and originality they had, and above all, that Azucena has not retained her strange and novel character. It seems to me that this woman's two great passions, *filial love* and *maternal love,* are no longer present with all their original force."[7] There ensues a detailed criticism of Cammarano's version, followed by a scene-by-scene sketch of

6. Werfel and Stefan, *Verdi,* 149–50.
7. Ibid., 164.

Verdi's own conception of the proper treatment. Equally interesting in this regard are Verdi's letters to Cammarano and later to Somma outlining his plans for an opera on *King Lear*. Here the composer indicates not only the succession of act and scene, but the exact pattern of recitative, aria, and ensemble as well, with prescriptions of the proper poetic meters at important points.

Much as we owe to Boito, then, for the specific form of *Otello* and *Falstaff*, we must not overestimate his contribution—Shaw again to the contrary; and in what follows, I attribute to Verdi the specifically dramatic content of the two works as unreservedly as their musical treatment. Nevertheless, he was fortunate in finding a librettist who, as a skillful opera composer in his own right, had first-hand experience of the problems involved. As a result, Verdi was no doubt willing to entrust to Boito details of the poetic composition which he would have felt bound to supervise in the case of men like Cammarano and Piave.

The books of the two works prove that Boito was sensitive to the difference between the problems presented by each. In *Otello* a great opera is made from a great play; in *Falstaff* an equally great opera from an obviously inferior play. The translation into the new medium must in one keep as much of the original content as possible; in the other, a new content must be provided. The libretto of *Otello* is fundamentally an abbreviated version of Shakespeare; to a certain extent *Falstaff* is a new play.

Naturally, each presents the composer with difficulties, but in some ways *Otello* lays upon him the heavier burden. Most good operas have libretti which are comparatively barren of poetry, of imagery, and of philosophical content. The music is free to add the poetry, to create its own imagery, to imply its own meanings. A play like *Otello,* still a tightly poetic drama even in Boito's denuded version, necessarily limits the possibilities of musical interpretation. Yet the boundaries are not too strict; the composer has, after all, at least as much freedom as the actor in his reading of the lines, and what Verdi has done is once and for all to fix securely his own reading of the parts. Thus his version is susceptible of much less variety in performance than Shakespeare's play, a rule generally applicable to musical as opposed to spoken drama.

A single example should make this principle clear. Act 3, Scene 2 in the opera is a condensation of Shakespeare's Act 3, Scene 4 and Act 4, Scene 2. Verdi indicates, by returning at the end of the scene to the suave opening melody, that Otello tries to conceal his fury under a veil of mock politeness. The appearance of the dissonant chord and the rise of the voice to high C on the dreaded word "cortigiana" evince his momentary loss of control; but he recovers sufficiently to finish the phrase on a note of suppressed menace, his true desperation breaking out in the immediately ensuing orchestral passage. The details of the music force this interpretation, but the corresponding lines in the play allow varying ones. (Paul Robeson, for instance, delivered them in a bellow of uncontrolled anger.) Verdi's interpretation has the added advantage that it permits him to round off the scene formally by a return to the original theme as suggested in the libretto by Otello's reference to Desdemona's hand, echoing his opening line. This repetition does not occur in the original, where the scenes are too far apart for such a device to be effective; moreover, it is a technique suited rather to musical than to purely dramatic form.

The foregoing discussion applies to passages which are essentially similar in opera and play. Sometimes, however, the poetry of the original is reduced almost to a bare skeleton—or omitted completely. One or the other is necessary if the music is to be allowed to supply its own imagery; for if the composer tried to underline and intensify Shakespeare's already heavy-laden verse, the action would be slowed down to such a degree that the opera would become impossibly long. The only alternative—merely to set the words in a purely declamatory style—would be a surrender of the musician's function. So most of the poetry has to go out of the window—only to enter again through Verdi's door. No trace of Othello's long soliloquy before the murder of Desdemona remains in the libretto. Instead, the double basses introduce an orchestral recitative, short but eloquent, and serving a similar purpose. The relation of "kiss" and "kill," put into words by Shakespeare in his last scene, is here already made apparent by Verdi in the subtle transformation of the ominous double-bass melody into the "kiss" motif from the love scene of the first act. But even Verdi would have found it an impossible task to translate into his own language the constant play on the word "light" in the original. Any attempt to reproduce this image musically, within the time allowed by his operatic economy, would have been ludicrous; the speech had to be omitted.

The problem of translation, arising in an opposite sense, also helps explain the presence of certain passages in the opera which are not found in Shakespeare at all. It is an important principle of music drama that every important motivation must at some point be translated into musical terms. It cannot merely be talked about, or acted: it must be heard as music. That is why Verdi requires a love scene in his first act. What Shakespeare tells us through his poetry, and by the action of his own first act, Verdi must have a chance to convey musically. In the case of *Otello,* a fairly long scene is required; only with *Falstaff* does the composer learn to compress the love duet into fifty short measures.

Similarly, the famous "Credo," an invention of Boito's, is necessary in order to give the music a chance to express fully the chief dramatic motivation of the play: the character of Iago. The soliloquy which concludes Shakespeare's first act will not do; it is too complicated, mixing self-revelation, self-justification, and plot development. It could be set only as a pure recitative, but the characterization would then be lost or only imperfectly translated into music. The "Credo" takes its cue from Shakespeare's last lines:

Hell and night
Must bring this monstrous birth to the world's light.

These it expands into a speech permitting a terrifying musical interpretation of Iago, one that gives him stature as one of the great operatic villains, all of whom have revealed themselves in similar monologues: the Queen of the Night, Pizarro, Kaspar, and Hagen.

In the examples just pointed out poet and composer have had to expand certain passages of the original in order to convey them adequately in musical terms. It has often been stated, on the other hand, that one technique peculiar to opera facilitates a condensation of dramatic expression: the ensemble. The concerted singing of several characters makes possible the simultaneous presentation of contrasting points of view which in a play can be made clear only successively. The septet with chorus near the end of Act 3 of *Otello* achieves an intensity unknown at the corresponding point of the original (Act 4, Scene 1), with the innocence of Desdemona soaring above the pity of her friends, the plotting of the conspirators, and the horror of the crowd. But unanimity of purpose is equally well adapted to this technique, as the oath duet of Otello and Iago testifies. *Falstaff*, even more advanced than the earlier work, presents double and triple ensembles in which the unanimity of one group of characters is contrasted with that of another. The nine-part ensemble of Act 1, Scene 2 divides itself into four (the women, rapid 6/8 meter) plus four (the men, rapid 2/2) plus one (Fenton, sustained 2/2). The finale of the second act presents Nannetta and Fenton as one unit, the three plotting women together with Falstaff as another, Ford and the other men as a third, and the chorus as a fourth. The group contrasts essential to both these passages are nicely resolved in the final fugue of the last act—probably the best formal device available to indicate general acceptance of the outcome without loss of the individuality of each character.

VI

What is this outcome, which all accept with the words "Tutto nel mondo è burla" (Everything in the world is a joke)? Is it Verdi's final judgment that all are "gabbati" (taken in)? Most critics have taken him at his word and find in *Falstaff* a trivial comedy adorned with some exquisite music. But such an interpretation is not substantiated by the libretto as a whole, differing in so many important respects from the original farce. Furthermore, such a point of view implies a misunderstanding of the nature of music drama, comprehension of which cannot be derived from a reading of the book alone. In any opera, we may find that the musical and the verbal messages seem to reinforce or to contradict each other; but whether the one or the other, we must always rely on the music as our guide toward an understanding of the composer's conception of the text. It is this conception, not the bare text itself, that is authoritative in defining the ultimate meaning of the work. And the music of *Falstaff* suggests a great deal more than "he who laughs last laughs best."

In the first place, the terrifying reality of Ford's jealousy, as portrayed in his "È sogno? o realtà," is sufficient proof that Verdi did not regard his characters as mere puppets. This is the same music that Otello sings—and this same motive reaches far into Verdi's past. *Don Carlos, Un ballo in maschera, Aida*—all turn upon sexual jealousy. Even earlier, jealousy enters into the motivations of *Ernani, La traviata,* and *Il trovatore.* But in the two late works the emotion has acquired a moral aspect: the husband's sense of right and wrong has been outraged by the supposed conduct of his wife. (To a certain extent this motive is foreshadowed in *Un ballo.*) This dimension is natural in *Otello* because it is basic to the Shakespearean original, but it is surprising to find it contributing equal intensity to Ford's emotions. In either case, it would have been easy for Verdi to create effective melodrama without this added depth, but he goes further and thus makes a tragic hero of Otello—and almost of Ford.

The comparison of Ford with Otello suggests another apparent similarity between the two situations: the guiltlessness of the woman involved. But whereas Mistress Ford is a virtuous wife, Desdemona is innocent in the complete meaning of the word. The innocent heroine is a recurring character in Verdi's dramatic mythos. Untouched by evil, her chastity is usually symbolized physically by some sort of cloister. Gilda, who is eventually betrayed by her own ignorance of the world, is shielded by Rigoletto's garden wall. Leonora in *Il trovatore* and her namesake in *La forza del destino* both find refuge in convents. Even Violetta, by no means innocent, tries to escape into a secluded village. Here I find the explanation of the scene in *Otello* during which the village children sing and dance around Desdemona. The division of Desdemona in the courtyard from Otello and Iago in the house presents a visual separation of her innocence from their guilt; the presence of the children heightens the irony of the scene.

172

In *Falstaff* it is Nannetta who is the innocent one, and on two occasions physical objects symbolize her separation from the world around her: the groves which hide the lovers in the garden scene, and the screen in the bedroom. It is noteworthy that Verdi, writing to Giulio Ricordi, makes special mention of these two details, even drawing sketches of the stage. "Lots of plants and bushes here and there, so that the people can hide themselves," he specifies; and "This screen, so to speak, takes part in the action and must be put where the action requires."[8] But the bushes and the screen differ from all the other cloisters in an important respect: they hide, not just Nannetta, but Fenton as well. For once in Verdi youthful innocence is represented by a pair of lovers rather than by a lone maiden, and for once love is pursued to a happy ending.

The identification of this series of heroines is confirmed by the music they sing. Particularly do the Leonora of *La forza,* Desdemona, and Nannetta seem to be successive incarnations of the same voice—a clear sustained soprano, rising above all the surrounding agitation. What Verdi hinted at in the earlier Leonora's counterpoint to the "Miserere," he carried out in the second Leonora's "Madre pietosa," soaring against the chanting of the monks. A more complex form of the same technique is prophesied in the *Rigoletto* quartet, to be fulfilled in the two great ensembles of *Otello,* where Desdemona detaches herself from the accompanying voices and creates her own melodic line in lonely beauty. In *Falstaff* Fenton takes this role in the first big ensemble; but in the bedroom scene he is joined by Nannetta, and through all the succeeding hurly-burly the love duet behind the screen proceeds undisturbed. In one other case Verdi contrasts united lovers with the outer world in this way—the finale of *Aida*—but here the union is achieved only in death. In *Falstaff,* the old man, gentler, permits the lovers to escape into a world of their own making.

Let me carry this one step further—into the last act, when Nannetta appears as the Queen of the Fairies (a role assigned to Mistress Quickly in the original). The music that she sings here is not unlike that which has characterized her throughout, but lighter, daintier, less solid. Her separation from the real world, already prepared in the passages previously pointed out, is now complete; contrasting, earthly counterpoint is no longer present. She has become the fairy she is pretending to be, and the elves she summons are real elves. The magical orchestration of the passage ensures the transformation.

It should be noticed in this connection that Nannetta herself takes no part in the pinching and beating of Falstaff, for she does not exist in the

8. Ibid., 416–17.

same world as the imps to whom this mission is entrusted. The latter are certainly only townspeople in disguise; and even Nannetta's band, after their leader's departure, are gradually drawn into the general fray. It is evidently in Nannetta alone that the power of transmutation inheres, and if the pretended fairies become temporarily real ones through her innocence, so too does the pretended wedding become a real one for her. Once more music reveals the truth: the gently solemn epithalamium is obviously not for Bardolfo and Cajus, but for Nannetta and Fenton. That is why it is heard again, a little later, when the young couple pleads for Ford's forgiveness. And though they may join in the fellowship of the final "Tutto nel mondo è burla," they at least have not been "gabbati."

I have said little about the character of Falstaff himself and about the broad humor which is the opera's most obvious characteristic, not because they are inessential, but because they are fully treated in most criticisms of the work. What is not usually mentioned is that the complete content involves a basic contrast. On the one hand is the world of fighting and clowning, of appetites and revulsions, of plots and counter-plots. Its depths are indicated by the darkness of Ford's jealousy; but its true representative is Falstaff himself, for "l'uom è nato burlone." Exaggerated in size and exaggerated in his actions, Falstaff is nevertheless recognized by the others as a mirror of themselves; as Alice points out to Ford and Cajus, all of them are wearing horns. For this reason they accept him wholeheartedly, even after brutally punishing him; and quite properly he becomes their leader in the final ensemble to proclaim that laughter is the only solution to his world's problems. But there is another world: that of Fenton and Nannetta, which they create for themselves. Its symbol is Nannetta's fairyland, and into its unreality the lovers are able, for a little while, to escape. But they recognize that even they must eventually come to terms with the others, that the claims of ordinary society are imperative: so they too carry their parts in the final fugue.

There is evidence that Verdi wanted to set *The Tempest*. Perhaps he did—in *Falstaff*. All that he had learned during his lifelong exploration of the darker side of human emotions and passions, he had compressed into the four concise acts of *Otello;* now at last, for the first time, he was able to give this knowledge its proper place in a larger view—much as Shakespeare had done in his own last play. But the resemblances between *The Tempest* and *Falstaff* extend even to details. The ugliness of the world opposed to the strange beauties of the fairy island, the secluded maiden united with her suitor by a kind parent, the contrasting scenes of buffoonery, the interpenetration of dream and reality: all these elements of the one Verdi was able to suggest in the other. Most important, the spirit of wise good humor is always present. The day of the premiere Verdi wrote to Bellaigue, the French critic, "I don't know whether I have hit the gay note, the true note, and above all the sincere note."[9] It is clear today that he hit all three—or rather that all three are really one.

[*1954*]

9. Ibid., 411.

3

Nineteenth- and Twentieth-Century Masters

Beethoven's Experiments in Composition: The Late Bagatelles

Although the Bagatelles Op. 119 and Op. 126 are often considered to-gether—as here—the two collections are quite different in origin. Op. 126 was apparently composed at one stretch, in 1823–24, and was published (by Schott) in 1825. The pieces were evidently planned as a unit: they were sketched on an integral group of leaves[1] where Beethoven called them a "Ciclus von Kleinigkeiten"—a term that may refer not only to their performance as movements of a single work but also, as Notte-bohm first suggested, to the major-third cycle that connects their keys.[2] The earlier set, Op. 119, was more heterogeneously conceived. No. 6 is found in a draft on sketch pages which also contain studies for the *Missa solemnis,* as Nottebohm observed; the piece would thus date from 1819–20.[3] Nos. 7–11 are sketched in a book devoted chiefly to the *Missa* and Op. 109.[4] They were published as part of a *Wiener Pianoforteschule* (by Friedrich Starke) in 1821, and had been written shortly before for this purpose.[5] In 1822 Beethoven finished five more bagatelles. These he com-

---

1. Gesellschaft der Musikfreunde, Vienna, A 50 (SV 280).

2. Gustav Nottebohm, *Zweite Beethoveniana: nachgelassene Aufsätze* (Leipzig, 1887), 195–209. Some of these pieces are also sketched on leaves now in Paris: Bibliothèque Nationale, MS 69, (SV 222) and MS 81 (SV 233).

3. Ibid., 146. The leaves in question are Bibliothèque Nationale, MS 58, no. 4 (SV 210) and MS 95 (SV 247). (This information was kindly supplied by Mr. Robert Winter.)

4. Stiftung Preussischer Kulturbesitz, Berlin, Artaria 195 (SV 11).

5. *Thayer's Life of Beethoven,* rev. and ed. Elliot Forbes, 2 vols. (Princeton, 1964), 2: 762; Georg Kinsky, *Das Werk Beethovens. Thematisch-bibliographisches Verzeichnis seiner sämtlichen vollendeten Kompositionen,* completed and ed. Hans Halm (Munich and Duisberg, 1955), pp. 244–45.

bined with the other six to create the present suite, and in that form they were published in 1823 (by Clementi in London).[6] Actually, it seems that all the "new" bagatelles were based on much older material. Nos. 2 and 4 are probably the earliest; they are sketched along with a cadenza for the Second Piano Concerto and an unfinished "Erlkönig" (WoO 131).[7] Nos. 3 and 5 are found in the "Wielhorsky" and "Kessler" Sketchbooks respectively. And since the time of Nottebohm it has been assumed that No. 1 is also of early origin, although no sketches have yet come to light.

Op. 119, then, is a collection rather than a cycle. But my present interest is not in the effect that the two sets may make, or may have been intended to make, as wholes. My concern is rather with each piece as an individual essay—as a solution to a specific compositional problem or as an experiment with an unusual technique. That, I believe, was the importance of these bagatelles to Beethoven: they gave him a chance to try new methods in a setting at once relaxing (not too much was at stake) yet realistic (they were nevertheless complete compositions). Surely it was in half-humorous recognition of this unique potentiality of smaller forms, rather than in a mood of self-disparagement, that Beethoven referred to the compositions as "Kleinigkeiten." If the composer was more adventurous in his chamber works than in his symphonies, and if his piano sonatas arrived early (Op. 26, Op. 27) at a freedom of treatment that only much later characterized his string quartets, then he might reasonably have felt, when working on a still smaller scale, willing to explore possibilities as yet untested—perhaps never to be tested—in more formal contexts. Barford believes, for example, that Nos. 7 and 8 of Op. 119 show specific relationships with some of the Diabelli Variations, a project that was still unfinished when those bagatelles were composed.[8] Whether or not the connection is direct, some of the pieces of Op. 119 certainly adumbrate techniques employed in the Variations and in the last piano sonatas, just as those of Op. 126 forecast usages of the last quartets. And although the pieces developed—often with minimal elaboration— from youthful ideas are less interesting in this regard than the others, they nevertheless display suggestive subtleties; after all, Beethoven must have found something of value in his old sketches that made them worth reworking and completing!

In this connection, one can point to evidence that Beethoven was already thinking in terms of experiment while writing at least some of his earliest set of bagatelles, Op. 33. No. 1 (E♭ major), for example, exhibits

6. Alan Tyson, "The First Edition of Beethoven's Op. 119 Bagatelles," *The Musical Quarterly* 49 (1963): 331–38.
7. Bibliothèque Nationale, MS 70 (SV 223).
8. Philip Barford, "Bagatelles or Variations?" *Musical Opinion* 76 (1953): 277–79.

an unusual dominant prolongation in the middle section of the first theme, turning a normal pattern of 8 + 8 + 8 measures (*aba*) into 8 + 16 + 8. The expansion is not particularly noteworthy in itself, but it becomes striking when heard in conjunction with the compression to which the following section then submits. That starts boldly as a trio-like contrast in the tonic minor; but hardly has its second phrase completed a modulation (to VII) than it is forced back to the tonic, only to dissolve into a dominant transition. As a result the entire section is only two measures longer than the internal contrasting portion of the first theme. In the same opus, No. 2 (C major) is called a scherzo, but its design is unique:

$$\|{:} \quad a \quad {:}\|{:} \quad b \quad {:}\| \quad a \quad \|{:} \quad c \quad {:}\|{:} \quad dc \quad {:}\| \quad aa' - coda$$
$$\quad\quad | \;(\text{Minore})\; | \quad\quad\quad | \quad (\text{Trio}) \quad\quad |$$

And the harmonic daring of No. 3 (F major) is famous.

The problems addressed and, I believe, solved in the later sets concern some of the fundamentals of musical composition. It is almost as if Beethoven were deliberately putting to the test a number of generally received ideas, raising doubts as to the universal usefulness, for instance, of clear phrase articulation, of metrical uniformity, of immediately perceptible recapitulation, of thematic contrast and harmonic balance.

Certainly the last two of these ideas are seriously questioned, although on a minuscule scale, in Op. 119 No. 10 (A major). This miniature, doubtless the shortest piece Beethoven ever completed, constitutes by virtue of its brevity an excellent introduction to the intricacies of the late bagatelles. Its interest lies not so much in the fact of its succinctness as in the nature of that succinctness. It attempts to make a complete piece out of the repetition of a single period, consisting of two four-measure phrases—two phrases, moreover, that comprise a mere V-I sequence. Beethoven had used this pattern before, in the Scherzo of the Sonata in A♭ Op. 26, and in the Allegretto of the "Moonlight" Sonata Op. 27 No. 2, but only as the first member of a song form. Those earlier examples were richer in harmony, too; the present one exhibits in detail nothing more than the same alternation of dominant and tonic that characterizes its overall form. Its design can be outlined thus:

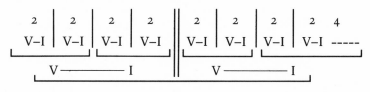

The only bow to the subdominant is a neighboring six-four in the coda. How, then, can this be a viable composition, if the similar but more complex periods of Op. 26 and Op. 27 No. 2 apparently cannot? The answer is to be found in the delicate contrast between the feminine cadence that closes the first statement and the masculine cadence that closes the repetition. This alternation transforms what appears to be the mere reiteration of a single period (*abab*) into a more highly organized double period (*abab'*), a true double period for all that the usual *harmonic* contrast of half and full cadences at the end of the even phrases has been replaced by a *rhythmic* one. The four-measure coda not only extends and clinches the masculine cadence but adds another delicate element of finality. The persistent syncopation between the two hands has produced a metric ambiguity. Hearing the piece without reference to the score, one might well wonder whether the staccato right hand or the sustained left represents the true pulse: is the meter indicated by the sharp attacks or by their harmonic supports? Only the final chord answers this question.

It may not be coincidental that No. 9 (A minor) is also one of the shortest of the bagatelles, being a compact three-part song form without coda, ‖: 8 :‖: 4 + 8 :‖. Like No. 10, it is developed from only three harmonies—tonic, dominant, and a form of supertonic (in this case the Neapolitan); and the two bagatelles are connected by key, A minor to A major. Moreover, the first phrase of No. 10 springs melodically from the end of its predecessor, a connection oddly emphasized by the sudden *pianos* modifying the cadences of No. 9. (No. 10 is devoid of dynamic markings.) And finally, the second phrase of No. 10 recalls and completes the central phrase of No. 9 (ex. 1). Did Beethoven intend the two

Example 1

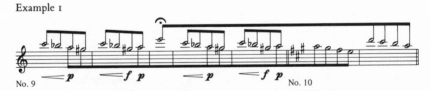

No. 9   *p*   *f p*   *p*   *f p*   No. 10

to be played together as a pair? If so, did he intend us to hear in their coupling an attempt to create a new kind of form (or to revive a very old one) linking two ostensibly independent compositions?

Two bagatelles in Op. 119, Nos. 8 and 11, appear to question the extent to which thematic reprise is essential to the effect of recapitulation. One answer was long ago established for dramatic music—by Mozart, for instance, in the duet ("Esci omai") that opens the second-act finale of *The Marriage of Figaro*. Such examples suggest that, after sufficient con-

trast, a return to the spirit or mood of the opening section, supported by
a reestablishment of its tonality (or its tonal stability) will be accepted as
a recapitulation even in the absence of strict thematic reference. That now
seems to be the case, in an absolute context, with Op. 119 No. 11 (B♭
major). Here too, despite the lack of obvious thematic return, the effect
is one of a three-part song form:

$$\|{:}\quad a\quad {:}\|\quad b\quad -\quad a'\quad a'\quad \text{coda}$$
$$\|{:}\quad 4\quad {:}\|\quad 6\qquad 4+4\quad 2+2$$

How is this result achieved? On the simplest level, the middle section
provides immediate harmonic contrast: so much is obvious by virtue of
its accidentals, of which both a and a' are singularly and completely free.
Thus an undisturbed B♭ major is contrasted with a modulatory passage
that subsequently leads to a return of the undisturbed B♭. (The coda
beautifully epitomizes this motion, for its second phrase is a summary
of mm. 6–11.) But a deeper relation between a and a' suggests that, for
Beethoven, some reference to a thematic reprise was still necessary. Play
mm. 11–14— or better, mm. 15–18—immediately after mm. 1–4, and it
becomes apparent that the two phrases join as antecedent and consequent
to form a period. The complementation is made clear not only by the
melodic line but also by motivic connections: the soprano of m. 1 is
inverted by the soprano of m. 11 and reversed by its tenor, while the half
cadence of m. 4 is recalled by the full cadence of m. 14 (ex. 2). Periodic

Example 2

balance is shown, too, in the repetition (at the lower octave) of a', matching the original (literal) repetition of a. Yet the two phrases do not quite
fit together after all, for there is a rhythmic discrepancy between them.
The antecedent divides into two-measure phrase members, of which the
second is a variation of the first. The consequent states a single measure
followed by two variations; only the last of these is completed by a second measure. It is one of the functions of b to prepare for this new phrase
rhythm. This it does by a process of rhythmic stretching. The basis of
the harmonic rhythm progresses from a quarter note to a half note to a

whole note, thereby finally expanding what might have been one measure into three (ex. 3). This triple-sized hyper-measure (mm. 8–10) is
now matched by the threefold multiplication of a single measure (mm.
11–13, also 15–17) that produces the peculiar motivic rhythm of the "recapitulation."

Example 3

Even more subtle is the treatment of the problem in Op. 119 No. 8 (C
major). The opening constitutes one of the most chromatic passages in
all the bagatelles, m. 6 in particular displaying a Tristanesque ambiguity
between chord and appoggiatura (ex. 4). Opposed to this section is a

Example 4

digression that is completely and almost statically diatonic, although in
a new key. The return to mobile chromaticism is heralded by a B♮ that
contradicts the prevailing B♭ of the middle section, thus setting into mo-

Example 5

tion a modulation back to the tonic C. Here too, the return of the tonic seems to dispense with thematic reprise. It seems, moreover, to reverse the progress of the opening statement: it begins on the dominant, reserving a definitive tonic for its second phrase. Is it then a mistake to look for a three-part form here, despite the evidence of key and texture? If one perceives a recapitulation, is one merely exaggerating the importance of an extended tonic cadence at the close of a two-part form? Affirmative answers would overlook a cleverly concealed thematic return. Measures 13–18 are a variation of mm. 3–8, hidden by their dislocated position in the eight-measure sentence (ex. 5). The original statement follows a two-measure opening; the variation leads to a two-measure cadence. The result is a unique symmetry that depends on harmony as well as proportion:

Statement: mm.   1–2   { 3–8 }
                     I–IV { V–I–V }   V–I
Reprise: mm.   { 13–18 } 19–20

Beethoven's experiment bore immediate fruit. A dislocation in the opposite sense, by which an originally initial phrase becomes part of a consequent, conceals the reprise in the Allegro molto of the Sonata in A♭ Op. 110. There the return to the tonic is effected in m. 25, but the thematic recapitulation (mm. 29–32) enters only as the last member (*b*) of an eight-measure group articulated as 2+2+4 measures (*aab*). And this phrase itself is the sequential consequent of the model just stated on the mediant (mm. 17–24). Thus the tonic return of the opening phrase is relegated to the final four measures of a sixteen-measure unit:

Statement: mm.   { 1–4 } 5–8
Reprise: mm. 17–18 19–20 21–24 25–26 27–28 {29–32}
                a   a   b   a   a   b
                ‿‿‿‿‿‿‿‿   ‿‿‿‿‿‿‿‿
                   III   I

The same principle in yet another guise governs the false reprise in C major that interrupts the development of the opening movement of the Quartet in E♭ Op. 127. Here the dislocation consists in the juxtaposition of the maestoso introduction with the cadence of the allegro period that normally follows, the main body of that period being omitted. Thus mm. 135–47 correspond to mm. 1–14, without mm. 6–11; but in compensation for those dropped measures the cadence is allowed three overlapping statements:

Opening: mm. $\left\{\begin{array}{c} 1-5 \\ 135-40 \end{array}\right\}$ 6–11 $\left\{\begin{array}{l} 12-14 \\ 141-43 \\ 143-45 \\ 145-47 \end{array}\right\}$

False reprise: mm.

Perhaps the most triumphant example of dislocation occurs at the recapitulation of the Prestissimo of the Sonata in E Op. 109. Because it follows an extended V of V rather than a simple dominant, the apparent reprise of the opening theme (m. 105), although literal (and *fortissimo*, after the suspense of a long *pianissimo*), is really an elaborate dominant upbeat to the true reprise (m. 112), which appears in the guise of a varied repetition connected with its predecessor by an elided cadence:

Statement: mm.   1–4   5–8
                                                       I–V   IV–V–I

Apparent reprise: mm. (96–104)   105–8   109–12
                            II♯   I–V   IV–V–I

True reprise: mm.   112)– 15   116–19
                                          I – V   IV–V–I

                         II♯ —   V   —   I

The passage from the sonata depends on harmonic as well as rhythmic ambiguity: on the reinterpretation of the harmonic significance of an event in accordance with a change of context. The same kind of reinterpretation on a small scale is required in our C-major bagatelle, Op. 119 No. 8, although in this case not in close connection with the phrase dislocation. Here the ambiguous event is the mysterious octave B♭ that introduces the second section (m. 9), an alteration that calls for two interpretations (at least). The first time it is heard, it follows the G-major chord that closes section *a*. Contradicting the B♮, the B♭ suggests a possible turn towards G minor. That harmony does arrive in m. 11, but within the orbit of the prominent B♭ major of m. 10. Hence the cadence in m. 12 sounds like a II–V in B♭, and the diminished seventh at the end of that measure might lead through a tonicization of II to an authentic cadence in B♭ (ex. 6). When the true situation is disclosed by the E♮ in mm. 13–14 the revelation comes as a surprise: the goal is C major after

Example 6

all. Now, however, the second half of the bagatelle is repeated, and this time the sustained B♭ is sounded in the shadow of a perfect cadence in C. Hence it is heard as a seventh, pointing to F, and the cadence of m. 12 becomes a temporary V–I. In this context the diminished seventh of that measure points directly towards C major, which comes this time as the expected completion of a large-scale I–IV–V–I (ex. 7).

Example 7

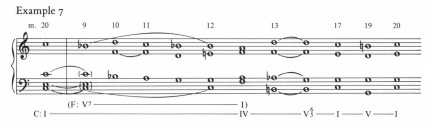

The reinterpretation of a single note, applied in the bagatelle to a detail, is developed in the F-major Quartet, Op. 135, to the point where it effects the linking of two movements. The unsullied F major of the Vivace second movement is interrupted at the end of the first section by an accented and reiterated E♭. That note is soon resolved, immediately to the E♮ of the ensuing dominant (mm. 23 ff.), subsequently to the D of a VI–II–V–I progression (mm. 44 ff.). But the Trio, with its startling tonal shifts from F to G to A, creates a new context. When the Scherzo returns, the isolated E♭, interrupting the prevailing F, suggests a similar and balancing tonal shift in the downward direction. This time the half-step resolutions to E and to D do not suffice: a further whole step down to D♭ is needed. And that is just what is supplied—in the next movement. The Lento assai is in D♭—a D♭ growing out of a single viola F that clinches the connection of this movement with the preceding Vivace.

Harmony and rhythm converge in the reinterpretation required by Op. 126 no. 5 (G major). The first time the second section, in the sub-

Example 8

dominant C major, is played, its cadence on G must be heard as a dominant, since it must lead into the repetition of that section (ex. 8a). That is to say, the root-position harmony of G must be prominent even though in an unaccented position, for it must be heard as the resolution of a feminine cadence converted into a dominant upbeat. There will thus be two harmonies, V of V leading to V, in m. 32 (ex. 8b). The entire bar should be played as metrically weak in order to lead convincingly back to the opening of the section. The repetition of the same section, however, leads through a two-measure transition to a reprise of the original theme in the tonic, G. If the return is not to sound anticlimactic, the cadence of m. 32 must not anticipate that tonic, which should definitively arrive only with the advent of the theme itself in m. 35. This effect can be achieved only if the harmony of m. 32 is now heard, not as the alteration of two harmonies, D and G, but as the prolongation of one, D—a prolongation that must extend through the next two transitional measures as well (ex. 8c). Measure 32, then, must be played this time as metrically strong; the D's of its bass must receive sufficient stress to bear the weight of three measures, underpinning the apparent tonics and converting them into second inversions. Despite such as unorthodox establishment of the dominant, despite the high tessitura of the reprise (an octave above its original statement in melody and accompaniment alike), despite the extreme brevity of this section, which results in unique proportions— ‖:16:‖:16:‖2 + 8|—the little composition nevertheless comes to a satisfying and convincing close.

The rhythmic ambiguity exploited in the above example permeates all levels of composition throughout both sets of bagatelles. At the most

188

detailed level it raises questions of phrase division. Does a given beat belong with one phrase or the next? Does it constitute a feminine ending or an upbeat? Is a certain passage to be played as one phrase or as two? Even Op. 119 no. 1 (G minor), presumably one of the earliest conceived, provides a simple but amusing example of a passage that can be read in two ways. The opening section has the superficial sound—and certainly the look—of a period consisting of two balancing phrases of eight measures each: twice 2 + 2 + 4. But the apparent continuity of the four-measure groups conceals a simpler structure of two-measure motifs. The entire section is developed through the varied repetition of the opening two measures (ex. 9).

Example 9

More problematical are those cases in which it is difficult to determine exactly where, or whether, phrase division occurs. Does the first phrase of Op. 126 No. 1 (G major) conclude with the arrival of the bass at the tonic on the first beat of m. 4, before the melody has had a chance to complete its feminine afterbeat? Or with the completion of the melody, at which point the bass has already moved away? The second phrase is clear enough, for the bass remains firmly anchored on the tonic until the melody arrives at its second-beat cadence; but the situation is oddly reversed in the recapitulation (mm. 32–39). There it is the antecedent that reaches a definite conclusion and the consequent that ends in ambivalence with a bass which, after touching the tonic on the first beat of the cadential measures, rises to the fifth. The result is again a phrase division that is no division, but rather a subtle link between the restatement and the coda.

In Op. 126 No. 6 (E♭ major), the fifteen measures (mm. 7–21) of the principal theme are similarly connected by ambiguous cadences. At m. 12 the tonic is completed only over a passing dissonance in the tenor, and in m. 15 an expected half cadence is circumvented by the addition of a seventh that calls forth a restless continuation through a deceptive resolution. This time the cadences are demarcated much more clearly in the varied (subdominant) recapitulation; m. 38 and its repetition at m. 44

confirm the new tonic, while m. 47 briefly but definitely rounds off a half cadence. An even more striking example occurs in Op. 119 No. 6 (G major). The fourth measure of "l'istesso tempo" (m. 43) completes one phrase (mm. 38–43) with a characteristic feminine cadence whose concluding tonic is simultaneously an upbeat to the next section, as the repeated motif in the next four measures insistently reveals! The technique used here was to be triumphantly exploited in the Fugue of Op. 110, where a cadential tonic becomes an upbeat to the final statement of the subject (mm. 200–201). The same principle figures in the Arietta of the Sonata in C minor Op. 111 as well: the last chord of m. 12 can work equally as cadence and as upbeat—an ambiguity to be explored by the variations.

Ambiguity at a higher level characterizes Op. 119 No. 7 (C major). Here is a short composition that gives the unmistakable effect of being a three-part form (*aba*). Yet where does the first section end? With m. 5? With m. 6? With m. 8? With m. 10? The listener's puzzlement, which only increases as he follows the piece through mm. 5–10, was no doubt one of Beethoven's primary aims. He may even have been parodying a familiar device of the composer he most admired: Handel often constructs a binary pattern in which the second section commences by a shift from V to I on the way to IV (as in the Allemande of the First Harpsichord Suite). If the model here is Handelian, the first section would end with m. 6, a conjecture supported by the repeated cadence with its square rhythm, and by the "scherzando" direction for m. 7, implying a fresh start. On the other hand, an eight-measure pattern seems to be in the building: four times a single measure, then twice a single measure, to be followed by a two-measure close. Good enough—but the conclusion demanded is not the dominant of mm. 7–8 but the tonic of mm. 9–10. So perhaps the Handelian parallel is an intentionally false scent, and the first section is really ten measures long—eight measures with an interpolated pair at mm. 7–8. On this reading the *forte* of m. 11 initiates the middle section, its subdominant representing a further harmonic step in the direction already chosen. And here there is, in fact, another sequence in the same series, extended to produce the first unmistakable four-measure group (mm. 11–14), albeit a group articulated by a hemiola in its central pair of measures. At this point—before the listener may even be aware that he is well into the second section—the move to the recapitulation begins. The exposition began with what was essentially a fourfold statement of a single measure. That measure now returns. Stated twice in a preliminary fashion (on V of II), it soon produces an extraordinary extension of eleven measures over a tonic pedal—a series of expanding var-.

iations, as it were, in which the single measure becomes now two, now four, now five, in ever faster figuration. And since the piece ends here, the recapitulation successfully refuses to comment on the problem of the proper articulation of the opening section.

At this point it may be relevant to suggest by way of comparison a movement in which Beethoven went even further in challenging the conventional three-part or rounded binary model: once again the Scherzo of Op. 110. There the double bar is obviously "misplaced," for its "normal" position in a minor movement would be after the modulation to the relative major (m. 16), not immediately after the major dominant of the opening phrases. The composer might have pointed again to Handelian precedent, but he would have had to confess again to parodistic use of his source. Handel often arrived at the dominant to conclude the first section of a binary movement in minor, but only *after* an inflection toward the mediant (as in the dances of his Third Harpsichord Suite).

The rhythmic and formal ambiguity of Op. 119 No. 7 is matched by its tonal subtlety. The arrival of the tonic pedal (a trill on C) in the recapitulation occurs under the sway of a prominent B♭ in the melody, so that the impression is that of II–V in F instead of V–I in C. This effect is all the stronger because the B♭ has been retained from the subdominant established by the preceding phrase. The note has become, so to speak, a frozen passing tone that has to work out its own responsibilities before it is allowed to revert to the true leading tone, B♮, whose own upward resolution effects the long-awaited melodic completion of the V–I progression (ex. 10). The resulting motif, B♭–A–B♮–C, is repeated in different guises at each stage of the expanding variations noted above. It is with regard to this bagatelle that Barford's claim of relationship to the Diabelli set is most tenable. Compare, for example, Variations 10, 12 and 20, in each of which the final structural tonic C enters as some form of V of IV, as in the bagatelle.

Example 10

It is interesting to find these late bagatelles, like other works of the same period (e.g., the C♯ Minor Quartet, Op. 131), evincing the composer's strong interest in taming the subdominant. In addition to the one just discussed, we remember the section of Op. 119 No. 6 introduced by the problematical B♭, and in Op. 126 No. 5 the central section with its ambivalent cadence. There are others as well: the coda of Op. 119 No. 1 takes a strong subdominant turn, and Op. 126 No. 4 has a false subdominant reprise before the true one. Op. 126 No. 6 presents what is perhaps Beethoven's most thoroughgoing subdominant recapitulation. Here the unorthodox harmony results from the expansion of a detail in the exposition, the deceptive cadence mentioned above, by which IV is substituted for the expected VI (m. 15). In the same way, the push of the development towards the submediant is thwarted and a modulation to the subdominant leads to the return in that key (mm. 25–33). Beethoven, of course, spurns the easy type of recapitulation occasionally used by the young Schubert, in which the IV-I almost literally transposes the I-V of the exposition; nevertheless the return to the tonic (mm. 48–51) is probably the weakest passage in the piece, perhaps in the entire opus. Instead of the originally straightforward melodic descent G-F-E♭-D, contributing to the dominant modulation (mm. 17–19), it offers a line that revolves lamely around a static G, relying at one point on a facile chromatic passing tone (m. 50).

Rhythmic ambiguity on the highest level, involving the form of the whole composition, is exhibited by Op. 126 No. 4 (B minor). The question that apparently interested Beethoven here—what constitutes a coda?—is one that had concerned him for a long time. From the Largo of the A-major Sonata, Op. 2 No. 2, through "Für Elise" and the Finale of the Eighth Symphony, he produced borderline examples of extensive codas which, viewed from a different perspective, could be construed as new developments-*cum*-reprises. But the bagatelle is more puzzling than any of these. So far as I know, it is a unique attempt to force the trio of a scherzo, recapitulated verbatim and in extenso, to function as a coda. For that is how the closing section is, I believe, meant to be heard. The piece, that is to say, does not consist of the mere strophic repetition of a two-part form, *AB-AB* (like the Pastorale from Liszt's Swiss *Année de Pèlerinage*), but is to be construed more organically: *A-(B as Trio)-A-(B as coda)*. If this is so, the source of the unusual effect must be found in the added measures, comprising a partial repetition of the final phrase of the Scherzo, which separate the reprise of the Scherzo from that of the Trio (mm. 157–62). These perform a double function. First, they make the Trio sound this time like a continuation of the "closing theme" of the Scherzo (ex. 11). Furthermore, the extra measures reiterate, isolate, and emphasize the melodic descent G-F♯-E-D, which has not been resolved in the Scherzo proper. In this context, the line can now be heard as moving in at least two registers from D in the Scherzo, through C♯ in the

Example 11

four *pianissimo* measures (179–82) that constitute the highly compressed digression (*b*) of the tripartite Trio (*aba*), to the B of the final measure of the piece—a moment for which resolution in the lower register has been reserved (ex. 12). The interpolated measures at the end of the second Scherzo thus have a double response, corresponding to their double function: immediately in the theme of the Trio-coda and ultimately in the motion to the final chord of the piece.

Example 12

A good performance will carry the line of the coda from the D of the interpolation (m. 160), through the C♯ of the *pianissimo* digression (m. 181), to the C♯-B resolution of the two final measures. By the same token, the player will try to prevent a sense of closure at the end of the Trio proper (the first time round). Beethoven has presented him with an obvious device for doing that. By stressing, instead of the C♯, the soprano E of the four-measure *pianissimo,* as well as its frequently unresolved recurrences, the pianist can ensure that the acute listener will await the return of the Scherzo to fulfill the demands of a note otherwise left hanging (ex. 13).

Example 13

One more rhythmic situation remains to be discussed: the occasion that demands an outright change of meter, as in Op. 126 No. 1, during the development of a unified musical thought. That qualification is important, for it distinguishes what occurs in the bagatelle from those simultaneous shifts of meter and tempo that often demarcate complete sections (as in Op. 126 No. 6). One might cite as a precedent for the bagatelle experiment such a passage as the "alla breve" towards the end of the Scherzo of the Third Symphony. But there, despite the notation, the measure itself is undisturbed; only its division is altered, from the prevailing three to a sudden two. Nor is the treatment of the bagatelle to be compared with the "tre battute" of the Scherzo of the Ninth. There again the measure is unchanged; it is merely combined in groups of three instead of four. In the bagatelle what changes is the unit itself: in the course of a single phrase the measure contracts from 3/4 to 2/4 at "l'istesso tempo" and subsequently returns to the original 3/4. What does this mean?

Underlying the overt contraction of the measure there is a fundamental expansion of the metrical harmonic unit. Each quarter-note pulse of the 3/4 has been augmented into a half note of the new 2/4. The passage might have been written more clearly in 3/2, for three measures of the new meter correspond harmonically to one of the old. The nine measures of 2/4 thus stand for three. The two measures of cadenza (mm. 30–31) then form a fourth unit to complete, as it were, a four-measure group that uniquely but convincingly balances the four normal measures that open the section. The relationship can be heard most clearly in the bass (ex. 14).

Example 14

Example 15

The stretching of each beat into one of double value is, of course, related to the similar process already observed in the development of Op. 119 No. 11. The same principle is also at work in Op. 126 No. 3, where the four measures immediately preceding the reprise (mm. 24–27) function as one (ex. 15). But both of these cases reserve the stretching for a climactic cadenza-like point; Op. 126 No. 1 works the process into the heart of the development section itself, the cadenza appearing as yet another step in the process of augmentation. The justification for such a procedure is to be found in the progression of the melody itself. A three-note motif that has already been prominent in the opening statement is now subjected to a continuous development based on a steady diminution of note values—eighths through triplets to sixteenths—which counterpoints and balances the metrical augmentation underscored by the

Example 16

bass, which itself also constantly refers to the three-note motif. The tension is at last resolved by the cadenza, in which both tendencies reach their climax: a rapid melodic filigree decorates an extreme augmentation of the motif (ex. 16).

It is suggestive to find that one of the earliest conceived of the Op. 119 set, No. 4 (A major), presents a simple version of motivic diminution contrasted with a moderate pulse (ex. 17); and even No. 2 hints at the

Example 17

same technique (ex. 18). Perhaps this feature explains Beethoven's interest in his youthful sketches. Be that as it may, the late quartets amply

Example 18

attest the composer's increasing delight in metrical contrasts. One of the simplest and most effective occurs in the Presto of Op. 131. The transition after the trio (mm. 161–68) features a fourfold expansion of the opening motif, amusingly counterpointed against the cello's anticipation of the same motif at its original speed. An example closer in spirit to Op. 126 No. 1 is found in the "scherzando vivace" of Op. 127, where during the development a meter of 2/4 twice interrupts the prevailing 3/4 (mm. 70–80). I take the divergent tempo indication here ("allegro") to refer to the shortened measure duration; the motivic connection between the two tempos at mm. 77–78 suggests that the quarter-note pulse remains the same. If so, this passage represents a further stage in the metrical complication already set in motion by the "tre battute" passage in the exposition (mm. 27–32). A similar situation obtains in the trio of the second movement of the A-minor Quartet, Op. 132, where an "alla breve" interrupts the 3/4 (mm. 218–21); again a motivic connection (mm. 221–22) suggests that Beethoven's marking of "l'istesso tempo" here refers to a uniform pulse.

Probably the most subtle of all the metrical shifts to be found in the late bagatelles is the one that occurs between the first two phrases of Op. 119 No. 6 (G major). The shift looks like no more than the differentiation of a slow introduction from the movement that follows, but the true relationship between the phases is far closer. Despite the discrepancy in meter (3/4 followed by 2/4), the change of tempo ("andante" leading into "allegretto"), and the cadenza marking the end of the "introduction," the two phrases form a period: the first (mm. 1–6) is the antecedent and the second (mm. 7–10) the consequent! A simple rewriting of the second phrase in the meter and tempo of the first makes the situation clear (ex. 19). The principle illustrated here is one that Beethoven later adapted to

Example 19

such various situations as the opening theme of Op. 127, the exposition of the first movement of Op. 109, and the magical approach to "et Homo factus est" in the *Missa solemnis*. In each case a duality of meter and tempo masks an intimate connection between phrases.

Op. 126 No. 2 (G minor) combines and summarizes most of the tendencies noted in the other bagatelles and can thus appropriately serve to bring this discussion to a close. For here is an ostensible sonata-allegro movement whose overt recapitulation is limited to the four measures of a closing phrase; here is a balanced construction broken up through motivic development and reassembled in a new and multivalent way; here is an emphatic subdominant working itself out; and here, despite metric uniformity, is a contrast of various time scales on several levels. In its most obvious form, this contrast leads to interesting motivic play—witness the interweaving that links the opening theme, the closing theme, and the melody that commences the development section (ex. 20). In a more intricate way, the contrast of time scale explains the apparent disappearance of the entire first theme from the recapitulation. Actually it is there in great part, but disguised by a series of augmentations. These are initiated by the isolation of the opening motif, a process that completes the "stretching" already begun during the exposition (mm. 16–18). There, as the "second theme" is approached, the distance between

Example 20

statements of the opening motif, which originally followed hard upon one another in a rhythm based on the quarter-note pulse, is now expanded to create a rhythm of half notes, or full measures. A passage in the development (mm. 42–49) goes one step further, separating the statements by two measures. It is the work of the ensuing extension (mm. 50–53) to push them closer together again, once more into the half-note pattern; and the next four measures (mm. 54–57) succeed in restoring the original rhythm. But the acceleration thus produced makes a normal recapitulation difficult to bring off, if not impossible. So the movement arrives instead at a climax in which the opening motif, transformed into an accompaniment of steady sixteenths but retaining its normal quarter-note harmonic motion, is simultaneously contrasted with a new figure that once more tries to stem the flow by congealing it into harmonically static two-measure—even four-measure—blocks (mm. 58–65). The two extremes are reconciled in the descent from the climax: the quarter note prevails as the pulse of the harmonic rhythm, while the two- and four-measure groups articulate the phrase structure. Thus all is calm when the closing phrase reenters (m. 78).

This activity and the consequent variation in time scale are what inhibit one's recognition of the entire section as a reprise. Motivically, of course, mm. 42–57 are derived from the opening; as progression, however, mm. 42–49 and mm. 54–57 correspond to mm. 5–6 and mm. 7–8 respectively (ex. 21), with mm. 50–53 functioning as a transition be-

Example 21

tween the phrase members. And in the same way, mm. 66–73 (with a partial repetition in mm. 74–77) present a more regularly augmented version of a hypothetical "consequent" corresponding to mm. 13–16, a "consequent" that allows the theme to cadence on the tonic instead of the mediant (ex. 22). And just as a harmonically static group (mm. 50–53) interrupted the "antecedent," now a two-fold group of the same sort

Example 22

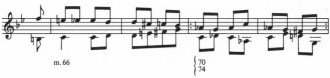

is interposed before the "consequent" (mm. 58–65), a harmonic transition between dominant and subdominant. Thus the entire passage from the first interjection of the original motif in m. 42 through the cadence in m. 77 is at once a continuous motivic and rhythmic development and a concealed reprise of a periodic statement:

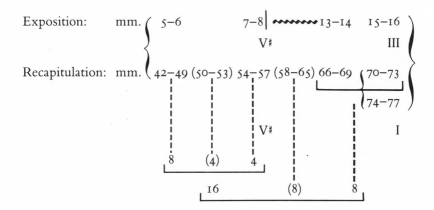

(Note the double level of the 2:(1):1 ratio.)

But there is still another element of form at work. Almost from the outset the piece makes strong representations towards the subdominant (mm. 5–7, 13–15); and that seems to be the direction in which the development is pointing (mm. 38–41)—an inference supported by the sudden interjection of the opening motif on the dominant of IV (mm. 42–43). From this point of view, it is the definitive subdominant prepared by the diminished seventh of mm. 62–65 and stated in mm. 66–67 whose arrival effects the crucial moment that must precede any satisfactory return to the tonic. And so, only as the recapitulation continues does the key reemerge—a tonic twice amplified in the closing phrase by a plagal cadence (mm. 78–85). Here, then, is a third way in which this astonishing page can be heard: as the expansion of a IV-V-I cadence it answers and completes the IV-V half cadence of the opening (mm. 7–8). Like the reprise of Op. 119 No. 11, this one too can be taken as a delayed consequent—but a consequent of thirty-six measures responding to an antecedent of eight!

[1977]

Schubert's Unfinished Business

I

In one of the Oz books—*Tik-Tok of Oz,* as I remember—the Nome King
(to use Baum's phonetic spelling) calls on the services of the Long-Eared
Hearer, a Nome with ears so large that he could listen in on any event in
the world he chose, at any distance. Composers, too, have long ears, and
they require those who wish to understand their music to grow similar
ones. These ears, however, penetrate time, not space. No doubt the composer is born with his (although he can certainly nurture them). They
work in both directions: forward into the future, backward into the past.
Those of the listener must usually be developed; they depend on a combination of attention and retention—of close concentration and long-
spanned memory. Unlike the composer's, they work in the backward
direction only. One who listens to music cannot and must not be expected to hear events before they occur—even those of a composition he
knows well.[1] (In this respect, composers are like everyone else: they must
give up their foreknowledge when they listen to their own music.)

We cannot hear forward; yet music is filled with commitments to the
future—the expectations on whose satisfaction, immediate or delayed,
its continuity depends. And although the listener is denied the power of
prediction, he is nevertheless granted the pleasure of anticipation and
also, if the ears of his memory are long enough, the joy of recognition
when a long-postponed fulfillment arrives. The final disposal of unfinished business can prove to be both formally and dramatically grateful.

1. I have discussed this point in "Three Ways of Reading a Detective Story—Or a Brahms
Intermezzo."

One type of long-range commitment is what I have dubbed the "promissory note," a specifically harmonic device involving aborted and delayed resolution.[2] Now I wish to consider a wider variety of musical gestures that, by demanding eventual formal or rhetorical completion, make effective pledges for the future.

Beethoven was of course a master of such devices. In the Fifth Symphony there is a fermata on the violins' G at the first half cadence, a dramatic pause whose significance is revealed only when it flowers into the oboe cadenza of the recapitulation. Or in the finale of the Eighth Symphony, there is the famous C♯ that obtrudes into the statement of the opening theme. Harmonically, of course, this interruption is amply explained during the course of the movement, notably by the half-step motion toward and away from the keys of the second subject—A♭ in the exposition, D♭ in the first recapitulation. But those progressions do not justify the explosive orchestration that characterizes the C♯ on each appearance. That is a rhetorical gesture, and it is at last rhetorically developed in the second recapitulation, when the C♯, ever more insistent, takes over to introduce a climactic version of the theme in F♯ minor. When the F♯ resolves to F♮, by implication completing the far-flung cycle A♭-G, D♭-C of the second-subject entries—then harmonic form, rhetoric, and drama reinforce one another in a typically Beethovenian way.

II

It was probably from Beethoven that Schubert learned how rhetoric and form can mutually support each other in situations involving subsequent attention to business temporarily left unfinished. A connection of this kind in the opening movement of the Cello Quintet Op. 163, strongly suggests the influence of Beethoven's procedures, although I doubt whether Schubert had any specific model in mind.

The Allegro ma non troppo begins quietly with two parallel ten-measure phrases, cadencing on dominant and tonic respectively. The final chord of each phrase arrives in the ninth measure and is echoed, in a contrasting register, in the tenth. But the balance is deceptive. The second echo is also a new beginning. Its overlap initiates a truncated phrase of only six measures; in these bars, over the tonic C of the bass, a chromatic line rises in a crescendo that transforms the tonic chord into a German sixth, emerging onto a *fortissimo* leading tone (together with its echo—mm. 24–25). Arriving so early in the movement, the moment is one of great tension, both dramatic and harmonic: dramatic, because of the foreshortened crescendo from *pp* to *ff*, with the latter emphasized by

2. Edward T. Cone, "Schubert's Promissory Note," *19th-Century Music* 5 (1982): 233–41.

the sudden textural change from full chords to bare octaves leaping pre-
cipitously downward; harmonic, because of those octave Bs, which,
though empty, *sound* like a major triad on VII—suggesting, in the context of the preceding augmented sixth, a turn toward III.

What follows seems to ignore both the dynamic and the tonal implications. Returning to the *pianissimo* level, it reinterprets the B as an element of a normal V^7 (ex. 1a). It proceeds almost as if the outburst of the
third phrase had never occurred. Instead, its own more measured crescendo expands the dominant, rising chromatically to a new *fortissimo*
climax: the simultaneous return of the tonic harmony and the original theme
(m. 33).

Example 1

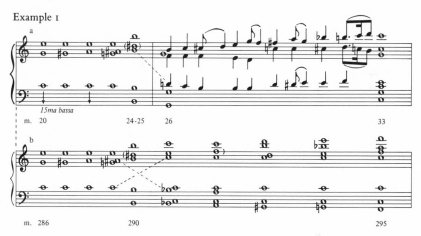

To be sure, the third phrase is not totally ignored. Its successor continues the chromatic line, and the Bb-B♮ that heralds the returning tonic can
be heard as a reinterpretation of the earlier A♯-B. But that is not enough.
Dynamically, texturally, and tonally, mm. 24–25 have been left hanging.
From the harmonic point of view they can be construed as creating an
implied promissory note. Heard as representing a V/III, the octave Bs
have implied a D♯ that, like an example cited in my earlier essay, "has
strongly suggested an obligation that it has failed to discharge—in the
present case, its function as a leading tone."[3] The V/III, even in its skeleton state, thus qualifies as a "promissory chord," one "that has been
blocked from proceeding to an indicated resolution, and whose thwarted
condition is underlined both by rhythmic emphasis and by relative isolation."[4]

That harmonic debt is repaid gradually, in several stages. Soon after

3. Ibid., 235.
4. Ibid., 236.

the second theme settles into the key of G, it makes an emphatic inflection toward VI, E minor, over a pedal on B (mm. 106–10); but once again the B-G connection wins out, now as V/VI-I. The same thing occurs twice during the closing theme (mm. 138–46). These progressions, although insufficiently isolated to create a strong promissory effect in themselves, remind us of the original problem. Perhaps that is why the goal of the long modulatory first phase of the development is a perfect cadence in E major (m. 203). Moreover, the minor continuation of that key is punctuated by persistent reminders, in cello I and violin I, of the original octave Bs (mm. 203–10). All this, however, ultimately turns out to be a preparation for the definitive tonal vindication of the unresolved dominant. That comes with the blissful E major of the Adagio.

Explicit though they are, those harmonic clarifications alone would be insufficient, for the problematic phrase was not left dangling in the harmonic sense only. None of the above resolutions answers the question implied by the sudden rise to the *fortissimo* octaves of mm. 24–25. That was a rhetorical gesture of great dramatic intensity, demanding an equally striking gesture to respond to it. The demand is satisfied when the entire phrase returns in the recapitulation (mm. 286–95). This time it is extended by four measures, thus achieving ten measures that match the dimensions of the two opening phrases. More important, the octave leap now becomes an imitative motive that pulls the sonority apart by contrary motion, driving soprano and bass alike to a new goal: F, the subdominant, a tritone away from the B. The first step in that progression, B-C in the soprano against B-B♭ in the bass, reinterprets the German sixth, inverting it and forcing it into service as V_2^4 of the new tonic to come (ex. 1b). When that F arrives to complete the phrase (m. 295), it also inaugurates the restatement of the theme. In its new version, then, the problematic phrase compresses two (mm. 20–25 and 26–33) into one (mm. 286–95), which is firmly anchored in place by elisions at both ends. Now there can be no question of bypassing it: it is the vehicle by which the first theme rises to a new registral height and to a new level of tonal contrast. Like Beethoven, Schubert indissolubly welds the formal and the rhetorical.

III

The examples examined so far are all clearly marked. Like Dido, they cry out to us "Remember me!" But unlike her, it is precisely their fate that they want us to comprehend through that memory. Schubert's music, however, is often much less outspoken. Many cases require close and imaginative attention on the part of the hearer if he is to realize that the business at hand is actually unfinished. Sometimes that awareness arrives very late—perhaps only in retrospect, at the moment of completion. The effect is subtle—the satisfaction of a subconscious longing rather than the anticipated gratification of a conscious desire.

Such delayed realization is all the more likely when the work in question is well known to us. Thus the Allegro moderato of the B-minor Symphony ("Unfinished" in quite another sense) begins with a phrase so familiar that we rarely appreciate its enigmatic character. Yet the opening melody in the low strings should raise many questions. Is it an extended introductory upbeat? Is it an independent thematic element? Is it the antecedent of an incomplete period? Does the final prolonged F♯ represent the fermata closing a six-measure phrase? Or is it a precise metrical surrogate for the missing cadence of an eight-measure phrase? At some point during the course of the movement the answer to each of these questions is probably "yes," but the definitive statement toward which the music evolves shows the melody in yet another light. That arrives only in the coda.

In retrospect we can see how carefully Schubert laid his plans. At mm. 6–8 the F♯, as an extended dominant, gives the opening phrase the feeling of an upbeat. It exerts a similar influence over the first subject proper, for that theme is twice interrupted by its recall, in mm. 20–21 and 28–30. Only on its third appearance, mm. 34–37, is the dominant integrated into the prevailing progression and allowed to proceed to a perfect cadence on the first strong downbeat of the movement. At the same time the passage introduces a 5–7♯–8 melodic formula that will play a crucial role in what is to follow. (It is most clearly heard in oboe I, mm. 35–38, ex. 2a). One could almost define the plot of the movement as the struggle of the introductory phrase to appropriate that formula.

The formula occurs prominently in the second subject as well, producing its only emphatic cadence (mm. 90–93, ex. 2b). And it is surely the source of the detail that closes both exposition and recapitulation (mm. 109–10 and 327–28, ex. 2c). But on the development section devolves the task of bringing the formula into closer association with the opening phrase.

The process takes place in two stages. At the outset cellos and basses announce a subdominant transposition of the opening. For the upward turn to the dominant fermata, however, is substituted a continuous descent from 3 (G) to 6 (C). For the moment, the interest of this move is centered on its last step, C, over which a contrapuntal buildup evolves. Only at the climactic return of the E-minor statement, now heard *fortissimo* in the full orchestra, is the 3–2–1 portion of the descent exploited as a cadence. And above it, in a first attempt at unification, rises the duly transposed melodic formula (mm. 173–76, ex. 2d).

That is an impressive moment, but it depends on a truncated version

Example 2

of the phrase; besides, it is in the wrong key. A hint of what is to come is given just before the recapitulation—which, significantly, lacks the introductory phrase. That has been rendered superfluous by the long section devoted to its development. Moreover, it is now too late for the original form (a step backward) and too early for its completion. But the future is abumbrated by what takes the place of the introduction: a ten-measure dominant pedal in the horns, over which a woodwind forecast of the coming first subject dissolves into a little flute and oboe duet based on a variation of the formula (mm. 213–18, ex. 2e).

When the coda presents an unaltered version of the introductory phrase, the first since the exposition, the cadential formula at last takes its place above the prolonged F♯ (ex. 2f). As it does so, it reveals a new and conclusive shape: the famous melody is not an eight-measure phrase ending on an extended dominant, but a nine-measure phrase resolving to the tonic. That epiphany (mm. 328–36) fully answers the question posed by the opening measures; what follows can be brief.[5] An elision produces an overlap with a variation of the same phrase, expanded now to seventeen measures through a recall of the imitative devices of the development; it rises to the same cadence (ex. 2g). Finally, only the first motif of the phrase remains, repeated to the point of exhaustion. But even this shadow still commands the cadential formula, which decisively ends the phrase and concludes the movement (ex. 2h).

IV

In the Andante con moto of the same symphony, the coda again, and even more effectively, returns to an introductory idea, not only to supply a missing resolution—one whose lack this time we may perhaps have felt—but also to expand the idea in a direction we could never have anticipated.[6] The initial motif is first heard in E major as a I-V-I progression in horns and bassoons outlining the melodic rise 1–2–3 (E-F♯-G♯), and supported by a tonic octave descent, E to E, in pizzicato basses. That octave is almost but not quite filled in: it lacks the third degree of the scale. That gap and the consequently unresolved fourth degree persistently characterize the motif. The result is a faint uneasiness associated with an otherwise calmly deliberate gesture.

The motif is, to be sure, not merely introductory. It surrounds the phrases of the principal subject, acting as a transition and codetta as well. It functions also as a source for much of that theme (e.g., for the rhythm of mm. 3–4, for the rising third of mm. 5–7, and, by inversion, for the descending third of mm. 11–13 and its chromatic continuation). Yet all attempts at integration (as at the chromatic descent of mm. 13–15) prove abortive. The motif maintains its relative isolation, through register (always in contrast to that of the subject proper) and instrumentation (winds supported by pizzicato basses or cellos). Successive statements may produce a connected progression (e.g., mm. 16–18, 22–24) or an imitation (e.g., mm. 56–60), but there is no further suggestion of expansion or completion. A promising idea remains curiously self-contained and unfulfilled.

The coda radiantly transcends all previous limitations. In mm. 268–74

5. It was even briefer—too brief—in sketch. See Martin Chusid's (revised) edition of the symphony in the Norton Critical Scores (New York, 1971), 55.

6. The sketch indicates that Schubert himself originally neither felt a need for the resolution nor foresaw the expansion (see the Norton Critical Score, 63). My own interest in the situation was aroused and my perception was sharpened by the astute questions and observations of the students in my seminar on analysis and performance at Princeton University, 1966.

(and immediately repeated in mm. 274–80) the motif, by means of over-lapping statements, expands its rising third to a fifth, then descends to complete a cadential phrase. The passage not only reveals a hidden melodic potentiality, but also fills in the incomplete bass—twice, once for each overlapping statement in the upper voices. The first time, the newly supplied third degree initiates its own octave descent. That too has a missing third, which, being identical with the dominant of the home key (III/III = V), enters naturally as part of the perfect cadence that concludes the passage. Moreover, III, functioning in this phrase as a true mediant between tonic and dominant (and not, say, as V/VI), restores in one stroke the balance imperiled by the tendency of the movement to travel in the opposite direction, toward VI and IV.

As the melody descends it incorporates a motif introduced near the end of the development section (mm. 130–33). That one, too, was isolated—a melodic fragment emerging from the final (♮VI) cadence of the development, and participating in the dissolution of that cadence. Now two overlapping statements of the same motif form the descending fifth that reverses the direction of the initial ascending overlap. The correspondence established between the two halves of the phrase discloses—or confirms—the significance of the second motif as a reversal of the first (ex. 3). The phrase thus exemplifies the satisfaction of a long-range obligation that in a sense may not really exist until it is satisfied; for the

Example 3

m. 268

m. 130

juxtaposition of elements at first widely separated often, as here, clarifies or establishes relationships of which we might otherwise have been unaware.

The passage immediately following the second statement of the completed phrase makes a more startling juxtaposition. Twice using the introductory figure of the second theme to prepare, not for its expected subject, but, surprisingly, for a return of the first theme, Schubert has altered the figure each time so as to effect an equally surprising change of key—first to A♭ major, then back to the tonic E major (mm. 280–

300). Surprising but not arbitrary: A♭ = G♯. The mediant, having just fulfilled its function as part of the I-III-V-I cadence, now assumes one of its altered forms. G♯ major, hitherto understood as V/VI, is now expanded as an independent harmony, enveloped in the glow of orchestral winds. The III♯-I connection, previously made smooth by chromatic voice leading (mm. 44–45), now stands out in high relief. More than that: the bold combination of elements from the first and second subjects reminds us—or informs us—that the two were always closely connected. The cadential figure of the second theme (e.g., mm. 90–95) was derived, through m. 30 and others like it, from the opening phrase of the first theme—the very phrase now standing in, so to speak, for the entire second subject (ex. 4).

Example 4

V

Introductory phrases are not the only ones to receive unforeseen explanatory or expansive treatment. Sometimes an apparently well-constructed and usable theme undergoes a later transformation that reveals such unexpected formal beauty and expressive power that the new version sounds like the definitive statement of which the original was only a preliminary sketch. But that can be true only in retrospect. Thus, in the opening Moderato of the C-major Piano Sonata, D.840 ("Reliquie"), not until the development section throws new and welcome light on the first subject do we become conscious of having longed for just such an illumination.

That theme, in its original form, sounds normally well balanced, but critical listening will discover that its undeniable charm is in part due to its somewhat anomalous structure. Superficially the opening eight-measure group suggests a period—or, in view of the metrically weak melodic third on which it comes to rest, the first half of a double period. But closer inspection reveals four distinct two-measure units—call them *a, b, c,* and *d*—separated by strong caesuras, and each closely hugging

Example 5

the tonic chord, stated or implied (ex. 5). They are related by oddly conflicting parallel structures. Rhythmically, *b* is a slight variation of *a*, and *d* is a development (though an idiosyncratic one) of *c*. For its part, *c* is unique in its bilateral division: a motive and its variant. Texturally, *a* and *c* are connected by their bare octaves; *b* and *d*, by their fuller sonority. Harmonically, too, *b* and *d* are related by their emphasis on the subdominant, stated as a neighboring six-four in *b*, briefly tonicized in *d*. (Interestingly enough, that chord is abumbrated in both the odd units by the note A.) Melodically, however, *a* and *b* form one unit; *c* and *d*, another. In this web, the disparate elements combine to produce an expressively indeterminate effect. Nor is that effect dispelled by the developmental repetition that follows (mm. 8–27). Expressive definition does arrive with the march-like variation of mm. 27–29 and its sequences, but the mood is now quite foreign to the tentative lyricism of the opening.

That lyricism is given full sway, however, by the thematic transformation of the development. On its first appearance the new version (mm. 104b–14) shows how *a* + *b* can be redefined as the antecedent of a true period. (Later it will go on to prove that the disparate elements of the theme are governed by a single lyrical impulse.) Heralded by a surprising modulation from G major to A major—an announcement that something momentous is about to happen—*a* and *b* return in the new key. But now the bare octaves are filled in with mellow thirds; a bass in pulsating triplets, retained from the end of the exposition, underlies the two units and spans the caesura between them. The newly unified phrase can now be heard as a real antecedent. Its consequent, although derived from the material of *a*, incorporates the subdominant tonicization of *d*.

This time the V^7/IV is given climactic prominence that intensifies its flavor and that of its brief resolution. Indeed, after the return to the tonic and the ensuing cadence—still on the melodic third, but metrically strong—the phrase is extended by two measures repeating the delicious moment. Here an octave shift registrally unifies the entire wide-ranging period. One's sheer delight in the normal resolution of the V^7/IV at this point is no doubt increased by the memory of a previous resolution of a similar chord (on A♭) as a German sixth in mm. 15–24. (As the Quintet has already shown, this particular ambiguity is a favorite of Schubert's.)

The potential of the passage, not only as a self-contained interlude of extraordinary beauty but also as a commentary on the opening, is demonstrated by its welcome return toward the end of the development (m. 150) to effect the retransition. This time the consequent appears first, in B, its extension expanded so as to initiate a series of modulations that will eventually arrive at the home key. As the tonally and thematically fluid recapitulation gets underway, the transformed theme gradually dissolves into its progenitor, now transposed to the subdominant at which it had originally only hinted. The reprise also reminds us that the transformation has after all left motives *c* and *d* fundamentally untouched. Nevertheless, the version recapitulated here is a stage on the way to a final amplification that recasts the entire theme in the new light.

The coda will take on that task, and another as well. No statement of the theme, whether original or transformed, has yet succeeded in attaining a melodic resolution on the tonic. That too is reserved for the coda. The section is initiated (m. 275) by one more statement of the transformation (in A♭), corresponding to the one that opened the development (♭VI instead of VI♯). This time the by now familiar antecedent is followed, not by its consequent, but by a development of *b*. That chordal block, the least promising among the original set of motifs, is at last given its chance. It is repeated four times, in as many keys—A♭ G, F, C—and as many registers. The sequence once more throws emphasis on the subdominant, while the last statement flowers in a cadence that confirms the return to the tonic key. It also falls melodically to the tonic note. Now *c* and *d* have their turn to demonstrate that they too can build a periodic structure. This they do in an impressive period (mm. 287–312) in which *cd* acts as antecedent; the consequent is a huge expansion of the same coupling, which reaches the melodic tonic a second time, now by an ascent, 6–7–8 (mm. 295–304). The finality of these two expansions, which between them exploit all elements of the original theme, is oddly confirmed by a concluding counterstroke. The hard-won tonic triumphantly reiterates the rhythm of the march; but it is succeeded by the delicate, *pianissimo* gesture of a six-measure reference to *b* poised melodically on 5 and 3—a touching reminder of the tentative nature of the opening.

VI

In one last example, yet another coda functions in almost every dimension—melodic completion, harmonic expansion, rhythmic balance, formal regularization, and motivic juxtaposition—to produce an expressively satisfying dénouement. This one concludes the opening Allegro of the A-major Piano Sonata, D.959.

The first subject of the movement begins so confidently that we usually fail to appreciate its uniquely one-sided structure. Yet it contains two unresolved, unappeased, antecedent phrases that demand further explanation. From the outset, the theme asserts its individuality. The melodic motion of the opening phrase is confined to lower voices—a tenor and bass rising in thirds, doubled an octave above. The soprano, however, remains fixed on a tonic pedal until its reluctant resolution to the leading tone in m. 6, as a member of a half cadence resting, not on the dominant triad, but on its seventh chord. The ensuing phrase, instead of answering the first as a consequent, develops that seventh over nine measures. Its D is retained as a new pedal in the soprano, under which continue the rising thirds of bass and tenor.

A restatement of the opening follows (m. 16). Now the soprano is more active—not, however, as the principal line, but as a countermelody to the lower voices and to the tonic pedal, here relegated to an inner part. More subdued than the opening, this phrase almost pleads for an answer. But no: although what follows does resolve the seventh harmonically, it does not act rhetorically as a consequent. It is another development, this time of the tonic. A pedal on A, now in the bass, remains steadfast until a tonicization of V (mm. 27–28) sets us off on a sequential bridge passage.

One might guess that Schubert is saving an explanation of this unique construction for the development or the recapitulation. But the development has little to say about the opening theme, and in the recapitulation the first two phrases proceed exactly as before. The less assertive third phrase, however, is no sooner stated than straightway repeated in the tonic minor, leading into a modulation to the lowered submediant, F. A fifth phrase corresponds to the original fourth; but the pedal, now on F, is even more insistent than before, for it is retained all the way to the new bridge passage (m. 231). More than ever, the theme seems to be built on unanswered antecedents.

In addition to these melodic and formal peculiarities there is a harmonic one—a characteristic the theme shares with that of the C-major Sonata. The opening phrase conceals a brief tonicization of IV in mm. 3–4, and the neighboring motion of m. 5 strongly accents the same chord. Yet neither in this statement nor in its reprise is the harmony developed further. Indeed, throughout most of the movement, that chord and its associated key are underplayed to an extent surprising in a work by a composer well known for his tendency to emphasize, even to overemphasize, the subdominant. Yet Schubert evidently wishes us to keep it in mind, for the first phrase of his second subject introduces it as an accented neighbor that strongly recalls m. 5 (ex. 6; the recapitulation is quoted for more direct comparison).

Example 6

m. 256

m. 4

The melodic, formal, and harmonic difficulties are closely linked. The coda (mm. 331–57) solves them all through a lyrical expansion that also fulfills the apparent desire of the theme to mollify its own overconfidence. Again as in the C-major Sonata, the subject in question achieves stability of phrase by allowing the subdominant to come to full flower. This it does by elaborating the brief tonicization of mm. 3–4 into a modulation; and it is just at the cadential confirmation of IV that the rising inner voice emerges into full melodic status, joining the soprano pedal as it resolves (m. 335). The two lines remain united in what follows: a second phrase, returning to the tonic through a melodically explicit cadence. Phrase is thus answered by phrase, but the result is not yet a finished period. An elision of the perfect cadence overlaps the commencement of a second pair of phrases. The modified repetition thus introduced continues to enjoy the melodic freedom achieved by its predecessor. It also roves further afield harmonically. Instead of moving to IV, its first phrase modulates to ♮VI, preceded by a brief tonicization of its dominant, ♮III. At this moment the correspondence between the two modulating cadences, on subdominant and on submediant, illuminates the entire course of the movement. The lowered mediant (of V in the exposition, of I in the recapitulation) was a prominent secondary key of the second subject. As C major-minor it controlled much of the development. F, the lowered submediant, was, as we have seen, prominent in the recapitulation. Now the two functions are brought into immediate connection and revealed as together constituting a surrogate for the subdominant.

The doubly stated period, complex though it is, unfolds serenely and naturally, exhibiting an exquisite subtlety of balance. Four five-measure phrases are converted into 5, 4, 5, 4 by elided cadences of the two even members—for the last tonic, too, undergoes elision. This time it is with a final cadential progression that introduces one more step in the C-F direction: B♭, a Neapolitan-*cum*-augmented sixth. The chord reminds us that one of the prime harmonic motivations of the movement has been half-step motion between major thirds (e.g., in the passages beginning on mm. 28, 82, etc., as well as in the development, with its alternation of C and B major). The present context confirms the origin of that motion as an alteration of the opening progression of the movement. The long-eared listener can trace the connection from A-C♯/B-D of mm. 1–2 all the way to the A-C♯/B♭-D of mm. 349–52 (ex. 7). And so this coda clarifies, completes, and summarizes the huge Allegro that precedes it. If it sounds like a quiet benediction, that effect is fully justified.

Example 7

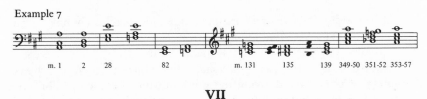

| m. 1 | 2 | 28 | | 82 | | m. 131 | 135 | 139 | 349-50 | 351-52 | 353-57 |

VII

Joseph Kerman has pointed out that many of Beethoven's codas, especially those of the middle period, effectively attend to previously unfinished business:

> Again and again there seems to be some kind of instability, discontinuity, or thrust in the first theme which is removed in the coda . . . In addition to [the coda's] harmonic function it has a thematic function that can be described or, rather, suggested by words such as

"normalization," "resolution," "expansion," "release," "completion," and "fulfillment."[7]

Certainly the same kinds of terms can be applied to the Schubert codas we have been examining. "Fulfillment" and "completion" probably apply to the first movement of the symphony; "expansion," to the second. Or perhaps that is too weak a term for a motive that burgeons into a new phrase as we listen to it: "generation" might be more accurate. "Normalisation" might cover the process of redefinition and reformulation in the C-major Sonata. But what of the A-major? All the suggested characterizations are too weak; nothing short of "transfiguration" will do.

One can look at these operations from another point of view. There is one word that covers them all, for there is one activity that subsumes them all: criticism. I have described the long ears of the listener as attentive and retentive; if those of the composer are to span the distance from exposition to coda, they must be acutely critical as well.

When a composer returns to earlier musical material in order to complete it, clarify it, reshape it, or the like, he is not merely winding up unfinished business. He is also, to a certain extent, calling attention to the fact that the original version is, for certain purposes, inadequate—incomplete, or unclear, or imprecise. He is, in a word, criticizing it. That criticism, however, should not be taken as predominantly negative. The essential act of criticism is appreciation, not judgment. The critical ear is one that fully appreciates both the object of its attention and the potentialities of that object. The critical composer is one who can actualize those potentialities.

Criticism and composition, then, are not necessarily distinct. As Edgar Wind has put it:

> These age-old enmities between artist and critic, their historical quarrels and recriminations, are perhaps but an outward reflex of a perennial dialogue within the mind of the artist himself. For however much his creative impulse may resent the critical acumen by which it is tempered, this discipline is part of the artist's own craft, and indispensible to his genius.[8]

Or more succinctly, "Criticism can be a creative force in the very making of a work of art."[9]

---

7. Joseph Kerman, "Notes on Beethoven's Codas," *Beethoven Studies,* vol. 3, ed. Alan Tyson (Cambridge, England, 1982), 149.
8. Edgar Wind, "The Critical Nature of Art," in *Music and Criticism,* ed. Richard F. French (Cambridge, Mass., 1948), 56.
9. Ibid., 57.

Richard Poirier, in discussing Eliot and Joyce, is more specific: "Critical reading . . . is simultaneously a part of the performance of writing, and to some degree it has always been."[10] He goes on to describe how, by Faulkner's own account, the entire structure of *The Sound and the Fury* took shape through the author's dissatisfaction with each successive narration, from a different character's point of view, of the same story. The result was "a novel made from Faulkner's having read what he had written as a source of what he would then write."[11] Each narrative affords a critical perspective on all the others. Can we not think of the successive variations or developments of a musical theme in much the same way?

The critic is often accused—sometimes justly—of inventing instead of discovering meaning: of claiming to find in a work of art a significance that he has in fact introduced. In similar fashion, one might argue that since composition (whether literary or musical) consists primarily of the continual creation of new values, the process by which the composer appears to criticize an idea by exposing its hitherto hidden import may be illusory. Perhaps he is really injecting additional meaning into the idea he is reshaping, while at the same time artfully suggesting that the new meaning was all along concealed in the original statement. That is probably often true of, say, Liszt and Strauss. Is it also true of a composer like Schubert?

My answer is that the cases of critic and composer are indeed similar. If the critic can convince us of the relevance of his interpretation, then it is valid. If the composer can persuade us to accept *his* suggestion—if he can impel us to hear the transformed idea as implied, or foretold, or necessitated, by its source—then that is the way it is. And so it is with Schubert.[12] When he reworks a musical idea, he convinces us—provided our ears are long enough—that he is letting us hear what was there all the time, although we could never have discovered it for ourselves.

[1984]

---

10. Richard Poirier, "The Difficulties of Modernism," *Humanities in Society* 1 (1978): 279.
11. Ibid., 280.
12. I consider the Scherzo of the "Wanderer" Fantasy an exception. There may be others, although I cannot think of any.

Inside the Saint's Head:
The Music of Berlioz

I

It may be that Berlioz is still his own best critic. References to his compositions found here and there among his prose writings almost always reveal an unusually perceptive awareness of his own expressive aims and technical methods, couched in terms of an intentionally cultivated objectivity. True, his attitude occasionally becomes archly self-conscious or ironically modest. The *Grand traité d'instrumentation,* for example, discusses the effect of violins *col legno* in an otherwise unidentified "symphonic movement that mingles the horrible with the grotesque" (the finale of the *Fantastic Symphony,* of course), and it explains the novel use of trombone pedal tones by "the composer of a Requiem." But Berlioz never adopts such a pose dishonestly, in order to garner praise. With a clear view of his own achievement, he has no need of that. Despite these lapses of tone, and with due allowance for some humorous exaggerations, his self-evaluation is to be taken seriously. More than that, I think it is basically trustworthy.

Berlioz's fullest and most general discussion of his own musical style is to be found in a letter dated May 25, 1858, to an unknown recipient, later published as a postscript to his *Memoirs.*[1] This critique is so apposite

1. The letter is headed: "Letter sent, together with the manuscript of my memoirs, to M. ——, who requested notes for writing my biography." David Cairns has tentatively identified M. —— as Eugène de Mirecourt, whose short and inaccurate life of the composer was published in 1856. If this conjecture is right, the letter must have been postdated. Furthermore, as Cairns points out, its mention of "one scene of *The Capture of Troy*" suggests some later tampering, for this opera was not separated from its sequel and given a

and suggestive that it makes one regret that it is very short, and that most of the letter is given over to polemical anecdotes, amusing though they may be. Two paragraphs must be quoted in full:

> My style is in general very daring, but it does not display the slightest tendency to destroy any of the essential elements of the art. On the contrary, I try to increase the number of these elements. I have never dreamed of creating a music "without melody," as they so foolishly allege in France. A school of this kind does now exist in Germany, and I hold it in abhorrence. One can easily ascertain that I always take care to supply my compositions with a profusion of melodic ideas, not restricting myself to the use of a short motif for the theme of a piece in the manner frequently adopted by the greatest masters. One may perfectly well dispute the worth of these melodies, their distinction, their novelty, their charm: it's not up to me to evaluate them. But to deny their existence, I insist, is dishonesty or stupidity. True, these melodies are often on such a huge scale that immature observers, at short range, cannot clearly perceive their form; or they are united with other secondary melodies that veil their outlines for these same immature observers. In short, these melodies are so unlike the little jokes called melodies by the musical rabble that it cannot agree to calling both kinds by the same name.
>
> The chief characteristics of my music are impassioned expressiveness (*l'expression passionnée*), inner intensity (*l'ardeur intérieure*), rhythmic sweep (*l'entraînement rhythmique*), and surprise (*l'imprévu*). By impassioned expressiveness I mean an expressiveness eager to convey the inmost meaning (*sens intime*) of its subject, even when that subject is the opposite of "passionate" and it's a matter of expressing sweet, tender feelings or the deepest calm. This is the kind of expression attributed to *The Childhood of Christ,* and especially to the scene in Heaven in *The Damnation of Faust* and to the Sanctus in the Requiem.

Let us look at these paragraphs in reverse order. Berlioz chooses his four "chief characteristics" carefully. The first two are concerned with expressive content; the two last are specifically related to musical technique. Of those dealing with content, the first, "impassioned expressiveness," is defined in terms of the relation of the musical content to an external subject, whose "inmost meaning" that content tries to make clear; and it should be noted that "impassioned" refers, not to the subject treated, nor to the emotional effect produced, but to the composer's im-

---

title until 1863. See *The Memoirs of Hector Berlioz,* translated by David Cairns, New York, 1969, p. 474 n. 1, and p. 612. The letter is found on pp. 474–81, but I have made my own translation of the quoted passages.

pulse toward this type of expression. The second trait, "inner intensity," obviously refers to the power of the music in and of itself, without dependence on its programmatic or dramatic significance. The one is measured by the appropriateness of the expression; the other, by its force.

It should be stressed that Berlioz always conceives of the connection between the music and its external subject in the most general terms. Far from being the champion of "descriptive" music that he is sometimes assumed to be, he insists on the limits of its usefulness[2] and resorts to it in his own compositions only rarely. The examples he adduces here clearly indicate that the aim of his "impassioned expressiveness" is a correspondence between his music and the emotional associations of its subject, not the physical accidents of that subject. His position is thus not so far from that of Schoenberg, who found art on the highest level to be concerned with the "reproduction of inner nature" (*Wiedergabe der inneren Natur*).[3] The chief difference lies in the fact that Berlioz's musical imagination almost always needs some external impetus to set it going; but once started, it is self-propelled.

One piece of corroborative evidence for the view that Berlioz's music achieves ultimate independence from its poetic inspiration has, ironically, sometimes been held as a reproach against him: his use of the "March of the Guard" from his unfinished opera *Les Francs-Juges* as the "March to the Scaffold" in the *Fantastic Symphony*. Actually, this bit of self-piracy, the fact of which now seems well established,[4] indicates precisely that the composer was more interested in the spirit than in the letter of his program, and more concerned with the musical contrast of moods and rhythms than with exact storytelling. True, the young composer, not yet sure of his expressive powers, did add the abortive return of the *idée fixe* and the depiction of the executioner's stroke. A more mature Berlioz would probably have realized that the movement was both musically and dramatically in place without these literal details, which are unique in the entire symphony (and perhaps in the composer's total *oeuvre*) for their reliance on programmatic justification.

II

The remaining terms of Berlioz's self-analysis deal with technical matters: rhythm and expectation. There is an interesting parallel between

2. E.g., in the long footnote to one of his programs for the *Fantastic Symphony,* and in his essay *De l'Imitation musicale.*
3. Arnold Schoenberg, *Harmonielehre,* 3rd ed. (Vienna, 1922) 14.
4. See Hugh Macdonald, "Hector Berlioz 1969—a centenary assessment," *Adam* 331–33 (1969): 35–47.

this pair and the first. Probably more than any other single factor, it is rhythm that determines the appropriateness of a musical movement to its extra-musical subject. (Doesn't Berlioz imply this close relationship between mood and movement by linking "tender feelings" with "deepest calm" in his examples?) Furthermore, as I hope to show, the element of unexpectedness in his music is one of the most important sources of its intensity. Thus, although the correlation is by no means exclusive, one can set up the rough coupling of impassioned expressiveness with rhythmic sweep, and of inner intensity with surprise.

Berlioz's "sweep" does not, on this view, refer solely to the vigorous drive of his fast movements. To be sure, these call upon a kind of energy, nervous but tightly controlled, that is highly characteristic of the composer. Merely to mention a few of them, almost at random, will indicate the variety they manifest: the opening of *Romeo and Juliet,* the "Queen Mab" Scherzo, the *Roman Carnival* and *Corsair* overtures, the finale of *Harold in Italy,* "Mephistopheles's Serenade" from *The Damnation of Faust,* the final duet of *Beatrice and Benedict.* Moreover, within each one of them an unflagging rhythmic inventiveness produces a complexity of pattern that makes Schumann's persistent syncopations and cross-meters seem mechanical by comparison. Yet I am sure that what Berlioz means by *entraînement* is to be found at every speed. There is no other composer who can more quickly establish and then more deftly alter the rate at which musical events are happening without ever losing sight of their goal, and without ever forgetting that their primary reason for happening lies in their drive toward that goal. Sometimes the goal is delayed, sometimes it is anticipated, sometimes it is not even fully revealed until the moment of arrival—but it is always there awaiting us. Berlioz is a master of all these variations, and it is through their manipulation that he is able to achieve the illusion that his music really does succeed in "conveying the inmost meaning of its subject."

A single example may clarify this interpretation of *entraînement.* Cellini's melody "O Teresa" in *Benvenuto Cellini,* act 1, (ex. 1) begins with a superficially regular eight-measure period. (The same melody is familiar as the English horn solo in the *Roman Carnival.*) But its harmonic rhythm is by no means regular. The first four measures, I-V-I, establish one harmony per measure, a pattern continued (with slight variation) into the second half. Now, the classical phrase often increases its rate of change as it approaches its cadence; so it would not be surprising to find, for example, two harmonies in the seventh measure leading to a cadence on a tonicized dominant (ex. 2). But that is not the way Berlioz has written it. With a sudden speedup to three chords in the seventh measure, one on each beat, he effects an almost breathless return to the tonic—a small-scale but convincing testimonial to Cellini's ardor. So far, however,

Example 1

(A♭) I   I   V   I

O Te - re - sa,   vous que j'aime___ plus que ma vi - e,   Te -

Example 1 (cont.)

II⁶₅   ⁴₃   I⁶₄   V   V⁷ of V   V⁷   I

re - sa,   ♭Te - re - sa,   Te - re - sa___ je viens___ sa - voir,___

Example 2

V(E♭): I   V   7   I

Example 1 (cont.)

I⁶ - III⁵   VII⁶ - II⁵   VI⁶ - I⁵   V⁶   ⁶₅   I   I⁶₄   V

Si loin de vous,___   Si loin de vous, triste et ban - ni - e,   Mon

Example 3

V

Triste et ban - ni - e   Mon

Example 1 (concl.)

V(E♭): I⁶   V⁴₃   I   I⁶₄   V⁷   I

â - me, mon â - me   doit___   per - dre l'es - poir.

Example 4

I⁶₄   V⁷   I

doit per - dre l'es - poir.

the four-measure balance has not been violated. That occurs in the next passage, where a descending sequence is set up, measure by measure. It would again have been easy to bring this succession to a half cadence in the fourth measure by continuing the sequence in slightly varied form (ex. 3), but no: Berlioz, having gained extra time by word repetition, arrives at the same goal by expanding the sequence to fill two measures. Thus the sentiment of the words here, "triste et bannie," is reflected in the rhythmic stretching and the consequent delay of the goal.[5] Finally, to

5. This phrase is adapted from Berlioz's early cantata *The Death of Cleopatra,* where it sets the words, "Où sur le sein des mers, comparable à Vénus," as the heroine sadly recalls how she appeared to the Romans in her days of glory.

round off the stanza, we find the long-awaited modulation to the dominant. Here, in sudden contrast to the drawn-out suspensions of the preceding phrase (which make the two harmonies per measure sound like only one), a new spurt of energy ("mon âme") changes the harmony on every beat and suggests that perhaps the phrase will end early—thus balancing the original 4 + 4 by 5 + 3 (ex. 4). Wrong again: Berlioz holds out his cadential six-four for an extra measure, allowing the hero ample time to "perdre l'espoir."

It is thus not only by general tempo and movement that Berlioz tries to make his music imitative of his poetic subject, but by every kind of rhythmic nuance as well—deviations from the expected norm which, if Leonard B. Meyer is right,[6] are a basic source of musical expressiveness. At the same time, if such deviations are to work they must make musical sense. Berlioz sees to it that they do, although—obviously—it cannot be the kind of sense one expects. But then, "surprise" is one of Berlioz's cardinal points too.

It is interesting to watch this control of rhythmic energy at the service of widely differing musical and poetic contexts. The several themes apparently associated with the mercurial hero in the "Roméo seul" section of *Romeo and Juliet* display a constantly shifting variety of symmetrical and asymmetrical balance, of discrete and elided phrases; in the love scene, on the other hand, the great horn-and-cello melody consists of a single unbroken ten-measure phrase, which later yields a similarly long-breathed seven-measure refrain.

The theme associated with the hero of *Harold in Italy* begins in a relatively straightforward, four-square manner but becomes more tentative and exploratory as it proceeds. By contrast, the *idée fixe* of the *Fantastic Symphony* starts with a period of 8 + 7 measures but continues with four-measure sequences. These become less regular, however, and their expansion leads to a concluding phrase that once more achieves a full eight measures. The consequent feeling of unpredictability is intensified by a rhythmically capricious accompaniment, by often countermetrical dynamic markings, and by variations in the basic tempo. In this way Berlioz tries to present a musical parallel to the "passionate, yet noble and shy" nature of his heroine—as we know by his admission, for the original program speaks of a "double *idée fixe*" consisting of a "model" and "its melodic reflection." (There is another level of meaning as well, for the connection between the two in the mind of the artist-hero symbolizes the relation of the actual composer's music to its poetic inspiration.)

6. Leonard B. Meyer, *Emotion and Meaning in Music* (Chicago, 1956).

III

Rhythm, however, is not just a matter of motifs, phrases, and themes: on the highest level, rhythm is musical form itself. Berlioz's approach to form in the large is just as bold as his treatment of rhythm in detail. The fact that he occasionally uses conventional patterns (e.g., sonata forms with repeated expositions, fugues) should not mislead us, since they are often only convenient frameworks or even foils for the real musical design. His elastic sense of phrase works hand in hand with his highly developed aptitude for sustaining long musical lines in order to create a special type of large-scale construction, conceived less as the development of one or more motivic or thematic ideas than as a wave-like series of motions toward a succession of proximate goals, each of which in turn initiates a further motion—and so on, until the final goal is reached. The music thus constantly pushes forward, and it can be followed only by tracing and inwardly reproducing that propulsion as it is specifically embodied in each composition. Hence this music often resists analysis in terms of standard systems, whether thematically or tonally oriented. That is why Schenker failed to appreciate Berlioz: the hierarchical structure of background, middleground, and foreground may not be entirely missing from his music, but it is often irrelevant to an understanding of what the composer is up to.

Again, this view of Berlioz's form as another aspect of his rhythmic sweep applies equally to allegros and to adagios, to movements superficially adhering to a standard pattern and to those apparently free. Let us therefore examine two examples: a "standard" allegro and a "free" adagio.

The opening Largo-Allegro of the *Fantastic Symphony* can be classified as a slow introduction followed by a sonata form. This done, one must immediately start making exceptions: the development contains a false recapitulation of the second theme in the tonic and of the first theme in the dominant; the two themes are reversed in the true recapitulation, and there is another development between them; and so on. It is hard to make any sense of this either as an academically "correct" sonata form or as the prolongation of a single controlling tonal progression. But somehow the movement always works in performance—at least for those who are willing to take it as it comes and to listen to each event in context.

Then the opening measure of the Largo, a tentative, gradually clarified upbeat, becomes a symbolic clue to the introduction as a whole; for this too is an upbeat, constantly trying to turn its tentative C minor into a firm major, and finding permanent success only with the entrance of the Allegro. Thus the exposition of the main theme (the *idée fixe*) is heard as a long-awaited resolution. So, in fact, are its two other full statements; and the almost symmetrical placement of these three well-defined units at the beginning, middle, and end of the Allegro (I, V, and I by the way) gives the movement its stability. By contrast, the second theme is introduced as a cadential inflection in a larger progression that continues through and beyond the theme itself (back to the beginning of the exposition if the repeat is taken, or else on into the development). The same is true of its second appearance early in the development, the apparently premature tonic proving to be no point of rest but the starting point of a striking chromatic passage pushing toward the central dominant. Only its third and last appearance, after a polyphonic crescendo, allows the second theme clear tonal definition—and even now it must be aided by a cadence derived earlier from the *idée fixe,* for the exposition had no true "closing theme." If there is a flaw in the movement it is here. Although the second theme has at last run its course and achieved a firm tonic cadence, the first theme has yet to return in its own tonic glory; but now the music has lost its momentum and has to be set in motion again. The passage that accomplishes this (the extra development mentioned above) is so extraordinary in sound, with its free-ranging oboe melody against tightly imitative thematic fragments and chromatically moving chords, that one is grateful for the fault that necessitated it.

The foregoing account, focusing on the rhythmic functions of the chief thematic statements as areas of emphasis or points of inflection, has, I hope, made it clear why the first movement of the *Fantastic Symphony* is only nominally in sonata form. The Adagio ("Scène d'amour") from *Romeo and Juliet* has not even a name for its unique pattern. From this point of view, then, it does not "have" a form, or it is not "in" any form. Yet, like all successful pieces, it has *form,* or it *is* a form. This movement cannot be described by any number of *A*'s and *B*'s and *C*'s; even more than the one just discussed, it must be taken as it comes.

Omitting the choral introduction, as we so often must in performance (which is a pity, for its depiction of the departing revelers, with its tender transformation of the boisterous ball theme, is one of the great delights of the symphony)—what do we hear? First of all two roughly balancing stanzas, each consisting of two huge phrases. The first phrase in each case is motivically, even isorhythmically, organized, measure by measure; the second, in contrast, is the lyrically expansive cello-horn theme already noted. Here, then, is a section of over fifty slow measures, moving from I (A) to III (C♯ minor), then from I to ♮III (C♮), consisting of only four phrases and the transitions between them! One could ask for no better example of Berlioz's *entraînement* exerting its force, even in a slow movement, over a vast segment of time. But this section, impressive as it is, never recurs as a whole; parts, only, of the lyrical phrase are to be reused in later contexts.

The succeeding section, although entirely different in effect (it is Allegro agitato and 2/4 instead of the original 6/8), oddly parallels the opening. It again comprises two stanzas, each consisting of an isorhythmically motivic passage followed by a more sustained melody—this time a recitative on the cellos. The first stanza, beginning in ♮III, moves back to the tonic; the second, shorter and more breathless, modulates toward VI. The dominant of this key heralds the last and longest of the three sections of the movement.

Returning to the tonality, the meter, and (roughly) the tempo of the opening, this section nevertheless avoids all strict recapitulation. After two tentative starts, a new lyrical melody unfolds itself, modulating in two phrases from VI back to I. The period appears to be almost exactly balanced, six measures followed by five; but the second phrase is expanded, through repetitions and extensions, first by three measures, then by ten more. Even here it does not stop but proceeds by elision into a seven-measure refrain that for the first time makes clear the connections between this section and the lyrical phrase of the opening. After a brief contrast a repetition of the refrain brings to a close this first stanza—for the third section, like the others, contains two long stanzas. This time the second stanza, while balancing the first in proportions, introduces a wealth of new ideas that it discusses with the greatest rhythmic and tonal freedom until it is time to return to another double statement of the refrain.

At this point begins a coda—or better, a peroration—exhibiting in marked degree the rhythmic stretching so characteristic of the whole movement. Achieved by postponing for as long as possible the ends of already extended phrases, it succeeds in creating a musical analogue of "Therefore stay yet; thou need'st not to be gone." Perhaps the most remarkable example is the passage by which the coda begins. Here the seven-measure refrain, by virtue of two false starts and a modulatory development, is made to cover seventeen measures, including one of silence—a gap that the rhythmic momentum is easily strong enough to bridge without difficulty. What follows again contains two stanzas. The first rises to a climax that connects the refrain more explicitly than ever with the broad phrase of the opening section; the second leads to a final drawn-out, fragmented statement of its cadence.

The movement is thus an *ABA* in spirit, though not in detail. It is further held together by the prevalance of the two-stanza pattern. Most of all, it is unified by the rhythmic impetus that makes of each stanza a single whole, and binds each to the next in wave after wave of passionate energy. So it is easy to understand why Berlioz writes, later in the post-script: "If you now ask me which of my pieces I prefer, I shall answer: my opinion agrees with that of most artists; I prefer the Adagio (the love scene) from *Romeo and Juliet*."

IV

The fourth of Berlioz's enumerated traits is "surprise." As we have already seen, it is often achieved through rhythm. But that is by no means the only method. Berlioz's harmonic processes are so persistently characterized by unexpected chordal progressions that one is almost forced to take seriously the fanciful suspicion that the composer has in-vented harmony anew for himself; that he has refused to take any previously evolved procedures for granted—not even the authentic cadence—but has worked out every chordal succession in relation to its immediate context. Berlioz's harmony sounds like nobody else's—by which I mean the way one chord follows another, for his harmonic vocabulary is not only standard but, for his day, somewhat limited. Occasional miscalculations and some downright gaucheries have elicited damning criticism from Fétis on; yet the harmony always sounds fresh and never palls as, say, Liszt's sometimes does. Berlioz's most striking moves somehow always remain breathtaking; no matter how well one knows them one never fully expects them. The result is a triple intensity—one that operates in three directions. The intensity of the composer's conception, creating each successive harmonic event, as it were, for the first time, must be matched by the closeness of the listener's attention (and, of course, the performer's!) if he is not to lose the thread of what is going on. And the listener, if he is sympathetic, interprets this twofold intensity as yet a third, inhering in the musical expression itself—Berlioz's *ardeur inté-rieure*.

The conclusion of the Requiem exhibits the composer's ability to force even the most commonplace chordal formulas to yield unexpected treasures. After the moving return of the close of the "Rex tremendae" to effect a conclusive authentic cadence in G major ("quia pius es"), the IV-I of the first "Amen" may strike the listener as a conventional plagal ending (even though the four-part chord of kettledrums is anything but conventional in sound). Actually the authentic cadence is both a close and a new beginning—of a whole series of cadences: V-I, IV-I, III-I, II-I, VI$^6_\sharp$-I, N-I, V-I. The bass of the first chord of each pair moves successively closer to the tonic (D, C, B, A, G$\sharp$ = A$\flat$), but this approach produces more and more distant harmonies—until the tension is broken by a familiar progression that has the effect of a long-awaited benediction (ex. 5). Two clichés, the plagal and authentic cadences, have thus been

Example 5

redeemed: the former by a startlingly original context that allows it to be heard afresh, and the latter by its simultaneous role as contrast and resolution. At the same time it should be noted that the unexpected harmonies are not arbitrary or isolated. They are derived from a descending bass that has previously moved chromatically down from G ("cum sanctis tuis") to D ("quia pius es"); so the descent during the sixfold "Amen" is a natural continuation. But Berlioz has something else in mind as well. The opening "Requiem aeternam" also ends with a semichromatic descent from D to G—a motif clearly derived from obvious thematic elements of the movement. The Agnus Dei includes an extended recapitulation of much of the text and music of that movement, and so the entire mass is appropriately brought to a close by a new version of its ending.

This example of thematically derived harmony is by no means unique. A more literal use of the same device produces the peculiarly archaic effect at the end of the "Te ergo quaesumus" in the Te Deum. Here the theme appears verbatim in the bass, every note (except the leading tone) functioning as the root of a triad.

Occasionally, it must be confessed, Berlioz surprises us unpleasantly and perhaps inadvertently, by the use of a flatly obvious or otherwise inappropriate progression—by the cliché misplaced rather than redeemed. Such are the two perfect V⁷-I cadences that come so early in the "Rex tremendae" of the Requiem, with the second so hard upon the first (mm. 10–11 and 15–16) that they produce a disappointingly slack effect. This is certainly a miscalculation on the part of the composer; yet I believe that it is the by-product of a well-conceived plan. A glance at the recapitulation of these measures suggests that Berlioz is aiming at a large-scale contrast. The original perfect cadences, perhaps illustrating the self-sufficiency (and the complacency?) of the "Rex tremendae majestatis," are now made deceptive, and the assertive music of the opening is persistently interrupted by the pleading "salva me." This motif is in turn expanded into the wonderful "fons pietatis" cadence—only I_4^6-V^7-I, but composed anew for the occasion. So the cliché, although originally misplaced, is redeemed after all. The flatness of the opening must be forgiven in the light of a close which so affected the composer himself that he returned to it at the end of the Requiem.

It must also be admitted that Berlioz is by no means free of his own harmonic clichés. Certain chromatic progressions show up again and again in his music—especially what might be called the reversed resolution. Normally, we expect a temporary leading tone produced by chromatically raising a diatonic note to resolve by moving a half step upward (either directly, or by a displaced resolution in another voice). The reversed resolution deceives us by moving a half step downward (with no compensatory displaced normal resolution). Classical composers usually reserved this device for major shifts of direction. Berlioz adopts it so frequently, placing it so noticeably in exposed outer voices, that we find ourselves listening out for its occurrence. Nevertheless, as in every case of successful deception, we remain surprised.

The formula is particularly characteristic of the composer's middle period, so *The Damnation of Faust* affords numerous examples. Two especially clear instances occur toward the end of Faust's aria "Merci, doux crépuscule." The approach to the climactic "Seigneur!" is supported in the bass by a G♯, which, although heard as a temporary leading tone (of III in F major) resolves, not up to A, but down to G♮ (ex. 6). The effect is echoed a little later, to underline the tenor's final cadence; this time it is a C♯ in the bass that moves down to a C♮ (ex. 7).

Example 6

Quel air pur je res - pi - re____ Sei - gneur!

Example 7

(mar)- ty - re, Que de____bon - heur!

Now, one might suspect that the composer, in reversing the conventional resolutions, is deliberately searching for the unexpected: but such a view would be far too superficial. His insistence on this mannerism suggests that it is less the result of a mere desire for novelty than the symptom of a pervasive attitude toward harmony. Berlioz, although working within the general outlines of classical tonality, never regards the functionality of a chord as sacrosanct. In his music chords often arise from the voice leading, as details in the overall movement. This practice is, to be sure, standard procedure, by no means new with Berlioz. But with him, these configurations are rarely unusual dissonances that call attention to their own special status; most often they are apparently normal chords—triads and common sevenths—that seem to demand functional analysis yet refuse to submit to it. At the same time, he frequently tends to emphasize certain chords as elements of color—of immediate contrast—within a controlling functional progression. These too are less often unusual dissonances than familiar chords in unfamiliar—e.g., chromatic—contexts. It is now easy to see that the simultaneous combination of these two tendencies may often result in the reversed-resolution formula. In the first example above (ex. 6), the G♯ is a passing tone in the descending bass A–G–F, acting as a foil to the rising chromatic progression in the melody. In the second (ex. 7), the C♯ is an accented passing note or appoggiatura, giving emphatic definition to the I⁶₄ that heralds the cadence. In each case the tightness of the voice leading keeps the interpolated chord from producing a loosely impressionistic effect. On the contrary, each coloristic element is also an element of tension.

It is a subtle use of the same technique that makes the "fons pietatis" cadence so telling, both at its first appearance and even more at its recapitulation—an ambiguous case, since its leading tone is a member of a multivalent diminished seventh. More straightforward is the fourth component of the sixfold "Amen."

In all the foregoing examples the guiding chromatic element is in the bass, but this is by no means always so. The leading tone is often in the melody, as in Marguerite's romance "D'amour l'ardente flamme" at the words "Sont pour moi le cercueil." Here C♯, as a passing tone between D and C♮, creates a coloristic leading tone that poignantly underlines the connotations of the text (ex. 8). A more complex version of the same chromatic line, D–C♯–C♮, controls and explains the puzzling third phrase (mm. 10–13) of "Roméo seul" (ex. 9). Here the first two elements, D–C♯, are in the violin melody. The C♯ seems to imply a dominant, returning to D; instead the resolution is downward to the C♮ of the pizzicato chord at the end of the phrase. The connection may appear somewhat farfetched, but it is not only clearly prepared by the D♭–C of the first phrase and the G♯–G♮ of the second, but also paralleled by the chromatic descent to the tonic in this one.

Example 8

Example 9

In general, Berlioz seems to love an ambiguity as to the functionality of a given chord, or even of a whole progression. Such an apparently innocent song as the Villanelle that opens *Nuits d'été* is full of passages of this kind. In A major, its first important move is to B♭. This sounds like a probable Neapolitan II, pointing toward the dominant. It turns out to be a factitious chord, a detail of the voice leading on the way to VI♯⁶, the dominant of the normal II (ex. 10). And to take only one more example from the same piece, the introduction to the last stanza contains what appears to be an important modulation to the minor subdominant. It turns out to be only a detail in an expanded plagal cadence that arrives at the tonic when the voice enters (ex. 11).

Example 10

Example 11

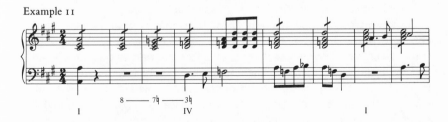

Once in a while Berlioz does produce a passage obviously designed to shock, but even so he takes care to prepare it so that it will be musically justified, and so that the alert listener will have received some clue as to what is coming. The famous juxtaposition of D♭-major and G-minor chords in the "March to the Scaffold," unusual though it is, summarizes a relationship already enlarged upon earlier in the movement.

A still more startling but subtler stroke is found in the "Dies irae" of the Requiem. It is the result of careful planning. The movement begins with the lower strings stating an unharmonized melody of twelve measures, in a severely natural A minor. It is answered by twelve measures in which the sopranos sing a melody likewise unharmonized, but clearly modulating to E minor. The event Berlioz now prepares is nothing less than the contrapuntal combination of these two lines, tonally divergent though they are. The following diagram makes his design clear:

Sopranos:		b		⎧	e		e ⎫	b
Tenors:			c	⎬	f	f	⎫	c
Basses (or lower strings):	a		a	⎩ d		d	d ⎭	a
No. of measures:	12	12	12	(4	4	4	4)	12

It will be noted that the contrasting inner section begins by copying, in short phrases, the pattern of the first three longer periods. Thus its arrival at a simultaneous statement of its own three melodic members (*d, e,* and *f*) prepares, and perhaps makes seem inevitable, the final period combining *a, b,* and *c.* What is more, when phrase *d,* which ends on Phrygian E, is combined with phrase *e,* which apparently moves to G major, there is an obvious clash of tonal goals that forecasts what is to come when *a* and *b* are at last combined. When this happens, and the bass forces the soprano cadence, formerly in E, to become part of a Dorian A, the resulting tonal wrench produces a point of instability that Berlioz is able to exploit in favor of a still more wide-reaching plan: that of moving through the successively rising tonal planes of A, B♭, and D. And these levels in turn anticipate and justify an even greater surprise, the immense E♭ burst of the "Tuba mirum," for this is reached by a half-step rise (D-E♭) that parallels the earlier one (A-B♭).

In this music, then—as in all the best music—no dénouement is completely unexpected. We appropriately react somewhat as we do to a good mystery story: not, "I could never have foreseen that!" but rather, "I should have known it all along."

V

The foregoing discussions have focused on rhythm and harmony, but they have unavoidably dealt with melody as well. In the first of the quoted paragraphs Berlioz makes four specific points about his melodic style, and all are admirably illustrated by the "Dies irae." He does not rely, he says, on the development of small motifs; in the present instance, although certain phrases contain internal motivic repetitions, it is the phrase or period as a whole that is used as a structural member of the complete form. What Berlioz claims that his music does exhibit, on the other hand, is a luxuriant abundance of melodic ideas. Certainly this is true of the "Dies irae." None of the six elements I have labeled *a* through *f* is conceived as a mere subsidiary counterpoint; each is capable of sustaining the primary melodic line and in fact each at some point does so, the "tune" of the entire segment described above being *abcdefeb*. But that is not all, for as we traverse the rest of the movement each change of key brings with it at least one new melody, strikingly different in rhythm and character from any that have preceded it.

The composer's third point concerns the scale of his themes, which is often so grand as to present difficulties to the casual listener: thus the opening A-minor section of our example is properly apprehended as a single line of sixty-four measures. Lastly, the relevance of this movement to the fourth point—that the melodies are often obscured by contrapuntal combinations—is obvious.

The same four points bear an especially interesting relationship to another passage previously discussed: the development preceding the tonic return of the *idée fixe* toward the end of the first movement of the *Fantastic Symphony*. Originally these fifty measures consisted of the imitative sequential development of a short motif derived from the *idée fixe* itself. During his revision of the movement, Berlioz apparently felt that the passage was too bare in its restriction to this rather mechanical repetition. Accordingly he added a new woodwind melody that with one stroke relieved the motivic monotony, added to the wealth of melodic ideas in the movement, united the short-winded sequences under one long-breathed curve, and increased the polyphonic complication of the development!

It is true that such melodies as this one, or those of the "Dies irae"—perhaps even those of the "Scène d'amour"—may seem austere in their refusal to rely on short, obvious themes, literally repeated or symmetrically balanced. Berlioz rightly refuses to make any claims for their superficial charm or immediate appeal. But equally rightly he insists that they deserve to be called *melodies,* though that name is usually reserved for popular tuneful trifles.

VI

One sentence of Berlioz's account remains to be explained, and it is a puzzling one. Let us return to the beginning. As I have tried to show, Berlioz is amply justified in calling his style "daring," yet also in claiming that it preserves all the "essential elements" of music. But what does he mean when he says, "I try to increase the number of these elements"? Is he merely referring to his abundant melodies, his novel chord progressions, his rhythmic and formal innovations—which, it is true, have added to the resources of his art? Or does he mean that he has tried to add a new kind of element, a new dimension as it were? Since Berlioz never overtly returns to this claim, one can only guess at his intention; but the continuation of the discussion after the two paragraphs already cited suggests that he wishes to imply that he has not only increased the number of familiar musical elements, but also, on occasion, produced a new kind of music altogether. He goes on to say:

> In connection with [the Requiem], I should call your attention to one conceptual realm which I am almost the only modern composer to have entered, a region never even glimpsed by the old masters. I mean those immense compositions that have been termed architectural or monumental music by certain critics, and have impelled the German poet Heinrich Heine to call me a "colossal nightingale, an eagle-sized lark, such as they say used to exist in primeval times" . . .
>
> These musical projects that I have tried to realize . . . are exceptional in their use of extraordinary forces. In my Requiem, for example, there are four brass bands, separated from one another and engaging in a far-flung dialogue around the main orchestra and the chorus. In the Te Deum it is the organ that, from one end of the church, engages in conversation with the combination of orchestra and double choir at the other end, and with a third choir of many voices in unison, which assumes the role of the congregation that, from time to time, takes part in this grand religious performance. But it is above all the form of the movements, the spaciousness of style, and the tremendous slowness of certain progressions whose outcome cannot be guessed, that give these works their extraordinary gigantic character, their colossal appearance. It is also the huge scale of this form that has the effect of either leaving the hearer completely unaware of what is going on or else overcoming him with

terrifying emotion. How many times at performances of my Requiem, side by side with one listener who is trembling in the throes of profound emotional perturbation, sits another who does his best to hear but can grasp nothing! He is in the position of the sightseers who climb up into the statue of St. Charles Borromeo at Como, and are greatly surprised at learning that the "room" where they were just sitting is really inside the saint's "head."[7]

Berlioz thus explains his enlargement of musical resources as twofold: the creation of forms conceived on such a large scale that they only gradually and grudgingly reveal their outlines and directions, and the use of multiple performing groups for the realization of these conceptions. I have tried to suggest the connection between these two aspects by translating *largeur de style* as "spaciousness of style," hoping thereby to imply a double meaning: not only figurative breadth, or amplitude, in the temporal dimension, but also the immanence of a new dimension, literally "spatial" rather than "spacious." For what makes these works of Berlioz really "monumental" is the way that the spatial element is controlled in order to support and clarify the temporal. All the works that he proceeds to list are of this kind:

> Those of my works characterized by the critics as architectural music are: my *Funeral and Triumphal Symphony* for two orchestras and chorus;[8] the Te Deum, the finale of which ("Judex crederis") is without any doubt the most impressive work I have produced: my *Emperor Cantata* for two choruses, performed at the concerts of the Palace of Industry in 1855; and above all my Requiem.

Above all, the Requiem. We have already found one large-scale plan at work in the "Dies irae": the triple statement of the theme on three tonal levels, leading from A minor to the E♭ opening of the "Tuba mirum"— and with it the entrance of the brass choirs. But this is only a temporary goal. From here to the "Lacrymosa," which ends the section, a huge tonal progression works itself slowly out: "Tuba mirum," E♭; "Quid sum miser," A♭ = G♯ minor; "Rex tremendae," E; "Quaerens me," A; "Lacrymosa," A minor-major. Thematically the section is unified by the recapitulation of the "Dies irae" in the "Quid sum miser"; and while the "Quaerens me" is based on a new melody, it is similar enough to these two in tempo, meter, and texture to confirm a pattern of return in each

7. The statue, known locally as "San Carlone," is not at Como but at Arona on Lago Maggiore. Erected in 1697, it is 75 feet high on a 40-foot pedestal and can be climbed like the Statue of Liberty.
8. Berlioz here refers to the revised version that adds a string orchestra and chorus to the original brass band.

alternate movement (if we consider the "Tuba mirum" as separate from the Dies irae).

The brass choirs are restricted to the even movements, precisely those that are not related in theme or mood to the opening. Here we find another of Berlioz's immense forms, at work *within* the general progression. For not only do the brass passages punctuate and clarify the movements in which they take part, but—incredibly—they also effect their own gigantic modulation from the "Tuba mirum" to the "Lacrymosa." Look at the brass parts by themselves. The opening blast of the call to judgment states and confirms E♭, the tonic that underlies the vocal statement that follows. After a period of silence, the brasses reenter on the dominant, leading to a tonic reprise. So far, then, I-V-I. The four choirs next appear in the "Rex tremendae," where they intensify the contrasting moods inherent in the recapitulation. This movement is in E♭ but the chord on which the brasses enter is not the tonic; it is a pivot between the old E♭ and the new key. This happens twice, once at the climax of the development and once at the entrance of the recapitulation. Each time, the chord is a form of F♯, or V of V, which is at the same time G♭, or ♭III in E♭. Conversely, one can equate E♭ with D♯ in the coming key. Thus when F♯ leads to the dominant, and through it—near the end of the movement—to the tonic E♮, the entire progression can be interpreted as the gradual development of the new dominant before the final cadence.

$$E♭ = \underbrace{D♯ - F♯ - B}_{V} - \underset{I}{E♮}$$

There is one more step to be taken. The brasses are to make their last appearance in the "Lacrymosa," where they are once more to point up the recapitulation. No connection could be simpler: E is the dominant of A. But Berlioz adds one clinching detail, a clue to the whole design. The last full brass sonority in the "Rex tremendae" is indeed a chord on E—but it contains a D♮. In other words, it is prophetically converted into a dominant seventh. So, much later, when the brass choirs add their terrifying accents to the fugal reprise of the "Lacrymosa," they are fulfilling a destiny as inexorable as the Day of Judgment itself (ex. 12).

Just as this section displays a form underlying and working through all its individual movements, so the entire Requiem. I need not explain in detail how the whole composition can be heard as an enormous expansion of the key of G; but I should like to point out some interesting parallelisms. The emphatic E♭ of the "Tuba mirum," a startling tritone

Example 12

away from the A-minor tonic of its own section, is much closer to the underlying tonic of the whole work: the relation is that of a major third. Similarly, the latter half of the Requiem is marked by the unique D♭ of the Sanctus, also a tritone away from its surrounding tonality. At the same time it is equivalent to C♯, and hence related by a major third to A—a connection made explicit at the opening of the Agnus Dei. There is thus a neat balance between the opening and the close of the Mass:

$$
\begin{array}{ccc}
 & \text{A} & \\
\text{G}\!-\!\!-\!\!-\!\!-\!\!-\!\text{E♭} & & \text{G} \\
\text{A}\!-\!\!-\!\!-\!\!-\!\!-\!\text{D♭} & & \\
 & \text{G} &
\end{array}
$$

The G-B♭ progression of the "Hostias," and of its recapitulation in the music of the Agnus, clearly recalls a similar progression in the opening movement: hence the reprise of that movement is natural and welcome. What could not have been foreseen, however, is the concluding master-stroke that I cannot forebear mentioning once more: the return to the cadence of the "Rex tremendae." Certainly we are inside the saint's head here! It is almost as if an enormous sonata-allegro were somehow buried within the manifold texture, rising to the surface only at occasional points of illumination.

VII

The "Dies irae" section is certainly impressive in its use of physical space at the service of a dramatic and pictorial presentation of the Last Judgment, always under the control of a careful musical design. Admirable, too, is Berlioz's restraint: he employs his extra forces sparingly and judiciously, restricting their massed use to the three movements described. Elsewhere only the trombones are given a distinctive role. Their famous combination with the flutes in the "Hostias" and the Agnus Dei creates a psychological effect of vertical space, the distance between the lowest and highest regions of the orchestra being perhaps symbolic of the separation of Heaven from Earth. But while the actual location of the trombones around the rest of the players may contribute to the remarkable acoustical effect of the sonorities, the sense of space is produced by ordinary musical means—the contrast between low trombones and high flutes.

If we look further into the Requiem, we realize that space of this kind, psychological rather than literal, is independent of the physical position of the performers. It is the result of the simultaneous use of contrastingly characterized musical materials—not just polyphonic textures, but the juxtaposition of different *kinds* of lines, of sonorities, of tone colors. We have examined one such example in the opening of the "Dies irae." The bass and soprano melodies are in tonal opposition: the one clings to its Aeolian A minor, the other modulates to the dominant. Yet they are ultimately combined, and the resulting cadence in the Dorian mode throws new light on both lines. It forces us to hear each from an unforeseen point of view. And the next stanza (B♭ minor) shows the *cantus firmus* in yet another perspective, the result of two new countermelodies, each highly individualized, that are contrasted with it. As the bass traverses the *cantus* the tenor constantly repeats a single striking rhythmic motif, while the soprano seems to look ahead with its simulated fanfares. The result is not merely three strands of counterpoint, but three planes of sound, from each of which one can obtain a different point of view of the basic movement, and hence of the significance, of the entire texture. This is a music of multiple perspective—of contrasting points of view simultaneously presented, and of shifting points of view shown in succession.

Here at last we have found an important element that Berlioz has added to the resources of his art. After all, polychoral and polyorchestral effects were not new. They were common in Renaissance Venice, where the composers of St. Mark's knew how to exploit physical space. And Berlioz himself tells of being impressed by the opening chorus of Bach's *St. Matthew Passion*.[9] But Berlioz's use of space, even when its value is clearly programmatic and theatrical, has a novel purpose: to contribute to the realization of musical structures that, like buildings, can be viewed from more than one direction. The true space of the music, however, is not physical but psychological.

The Offertorium, again from the Requiem, is an excellent illustration. It employs one of Berlioz's favorite means for achieving multiple perspective: the ostinato. The repeated element may be a note, a chord, a melody, perhaps a tone color. Sometimes one of them is transformed

---

9. Berlioz, *Memoirs*, 332–33. Oddly enough, Berlioz seems quite unaware that this movement, with its dramatic play between the two choirs, each supported by its own orchestra, and all unified by the over-arching chorale of yet another group, anticipated his own architectural constructions. Could a vague memory of it have influenced the layout of the Te Deum?

into another. But in every case a static, unchanging element is contrasted with a moving texture, each constantly throwing new light on the other. In the present instance, the voices reiterate the formula of a half-step neighboring tone at varying time intervals against an orchestral fugue. This static neighbor-formula, however, is not like most pedals, which exert an unwavering harmonic influence even when the opposing mass moves far away. In the Offertorium the meaning of the ostinato must constantly be reinterpreted in the light of the progress of the fugue, so that the static element itself appears to move. This illusion is increased by the irregular and unpredictable time intervals at which the ostinato appears. When the half step is at last converted into a whole step, and minor becomes major, the effect is that of reaching a long-approached goal. It is almost possible to hear the piece, not as a fugue with an ostinato against it, but as a choral chant accompanied by a fugue. (The mutual influence of ostinato and fugue is made even more evident in the funeral procession of *Romeo and Juliet*. It is built on a similar pattern, but halfway through the movement the parts are reversed. The voices, with some woodwind doubling, continue the fugue, while the ostinato is relegated to the strings.)

The Te Deum, like the Requiem, exploits spatial effects, but even less than in the Requiem are they at the service of pictorial ideas. From the opening chords of the first movement, which antiphonally separate the organ from the orchestra in such a way that each completes its own cadential progression, the spatial setup is used primarily to clarify and intensify the musical events and to reinforce the perspectives they suggest. Thus, as the organ completes the opening passage, it states a melody that seems at the time to have a purely cadential function. Yet later, with the counterexposition of the fugal chorus, the same melody reappears, underlining the entry of the third choir, and acting as a countersubject that throws new light on the harmonic possibilities of the fugue theme.

The "Judex crederis," which Berlioz called "the most impressive work I have produced," deals once more with the Last Day, but the depiction is symbolic rather than descriptive. Again the spatially separated forces are used primarily to define planes of musical action and to clarify the form. The organ, with its initial modulation from E♭ minor to B♭ minor, not only states a tonal ambiguity that is to permeate the movement, but also defines its own chief function, which is to bring the harmony back to the tonic from successively more distant points: IV, later VI, and finally, in major, V_2^4 of VI. The third chorus (the "congregation") enters with an independent part to contribute to the climax of the development. It reinforces the recapitulation by doubling other parts but returns to independence in the coda. The main thread of the continuity, of course, is carried by the principal choirs, supported by the orchestra: but their roles with respect to one another produce a fascinating interplay as they vary in accordance with the needs of the musical design.

The movement is again under the protection of St. Charles, for it is a complex amalgam of fugue and sonata form, interpenetrated by various kinds of ostinatos. One of them, with both a melodic and a purely rhythmic component, is derived directly from the fugue subject. Another is taken from the second theme ("Salvum fac"); its first motif is later detached and subjected to twenty-six repetitions in as many measures. More important than either of these is a third kind of ostinato, often a member of the others, but leading an interesting life of its own: the note B♭. One could summarize the plot of the movement as the successful effort to establish B♭ as the tonic. The attempt to do so results in a complex series of shifting perspectives. In the opening organ fanfare the note is heard as the fifth of E♭; and the succeeding fugato is so ambiguous in tonality that when it actually cadences in B♭ we suspect that this may be the key of the dominant—a suspicion confirmed when the second theme enters in the same key. Throughout the development the persistent reiteration of the note is unable to establish its primacy, although its intrusive efforts to do so effect a terrifying climax just before the recapitulation. Here too the outcome is in doubt. The fugato recommences in A♭, and every approach to B♭ is circumvented by a deceptive cadence. Only the eventual entry of B♭ major makes the tonal goal unmistakably clear. Now all the old ostinatos are repeated for the last time—but for the first time in the new perspective afforded by the context of a definitive B♭-major tonic. The movement ends in a blaze of glory, but Berlioz ensures it against degenerating into bombast. He breaks open the concluding cadences in order to insert an expressive phrase from the second theme— now for the first time in the tonic major—that he has saved for the last possible moment. One may perhaps be forgiven for finding here the completion of a musical analogue of the Hidden God at last revealing himself as Lord of the Universe.[10]

VIII

It should now be clear that the method of multiple perspective in no way depends on the presence of unusual musical forces. In fact, it distinguishes much of Berlioz's conventionally scaled music from the earliest

10. This interpretation is supported by the resemblance of the interpolated phrase in the theme of the "Hosanna" in the Requiem—a derivation hidden up to this point, but now revealed by the simple reversal of the order of two notes. Patrick Smith called this reference to my attention.

period on. In the *Fantastic Symphony* there are several obvious spatial effects. In the third movement the distance between the two piping shepherds, later between the lone shepherd and the far-off thunder, provides one level of contrast; the framing effect of both these sections around the main body of the movement, another. In the finale the bells, the plainchant, its parodies, and the sabbath round all define different planes of action. And throughout the entire work moves the *idée fixe,* which, as it appears in different guises, simultaneously comments on the events of each movement and is observed from varying points of view.

Somewhat more complex in this respect is *Harold in Italy*. This symphony really has two *idées fixes*—Harold's theme, and the solo viola itself. While the former undergoes little transformation (at least until the last movement) and represents a fixed point of view, so to speak, from which the varied musical events can be apprehended, the latter provides a highly flexible comment on the action—sometimes coinciding with the theme, sometimes invoking other melodic ideas, sometimes quite free. No doubt it is from the interaction of these two that the character of the hero is to be inferred.

The second movement, the "Pilgrims' March," contains in addition a unique ostinato in the form of the bells that ring on C (harp and horns) followed by B (harp and woodwinds) at the end of each phrase of the march. Here again is a static element that gives the illusion of motion, for each time the bells appear the harmonic context is different. It is a source of great delight to hear the phrases of the march aspire to successively higher goals—D♯, E, F♯, G♯, A, B—only to have each cadence (except the last) return to the tonic (E) through the intervention of the bells. Berlioz was quite right in rejecting Fétis's charge that the two tones were always non-chordal.[11] It is precisely their shifting harmonic role that enables them to exert their force on the melody of the march, and conversely to be heard from ever-changing points of view. Now, in contrast to these two planes of march and bells, enters the solo viola (doubled by woodwinds) with Harold's theme to create a third. For it is not merely a counterpoint to the march: it provides a completely new rhythmic organization. The march is in regular groups of eight measures: Harold's theme, translating its triple meter into measures, must move in groups of threes. Yet the combination sounds so natural that it is hard to hear just where the necessary adjustments take place. The viola melody, essentially unchanged from the first movement, is nevertheless strikingly altered in effect by the new orchestral, harmonic, and rhythmic context; in its turn, it affords a new vantage point from which to

---

11. Berlioz, *Memoirs,* 257. Fétis's complaint is valid only with regard to the cadence on B.

hear the march. But other combinations of levels are in store: the viola, forsaking its theme (which dies away unfinished), attaches itself directly to the march, its role now reduced to that of a mere accompanying counterpoint. It is to go one step further: as the march gives way to the *canto religioso* (except in the bass, which never ceases to remind us of the original rhythm), the viola assumes the role of pure accompaniment. It embarks on a continuous series of arpeggios that is given up only when the march makes its abbreviated return—and then regretfully, with backward glances. The character of the solo is thus subjected to a twofold transformation during the course of the movement: from independent countermelody to subsidiary counterpoint, and finally to chordal accompaniment. The opposing points of view of Harold and the pilgrims are reconciled—by purely musical means.

It is interesting to compare this outcome with that of the next movement, the "Serenade of a Mountaineer." Here again the principal action combines a new theme, the serenade, with Harold's, again given to the viola. But in the coda, which brings together three ideas—the serenade, Harold's theme, and the dance-like introduction of the movement—the second of these is now relegated to flute and harp as the viola takes over the first. Again two contrasting points of view have been united: Harold assumes the mountaineer's role, his own theme forming a dream-like background.

These examples would be enough to show Berlioz's unique method at work even among works that are not obviously "monumental." Concerning them, he continues in the paragraph last quoted:

> As for those of my compositions that are conceived on a normal scale, and without recourse to unusual means, it is precisely their inner intensity, their expressiveness, and their rhythmic originality that have done them the most harm, because of the qualities of performance they require. To do them justice, the performers, and above all their conductor, must *feel* as I do. These works demand a combination of absolute precision with irresistible energy, a controlled impetuosity, a dreamy sensitivity, a sickly melancholy, so to speak, without which the principal outlines of my ideas are altered or completely erased. It is therefore terribly painful for me to hear most of my compositions conducted by someone else.

Berlioz must be aware that his requirements, taken literally, contradict one another. Irresistible energy cannot yield completely precise results: impetuosity does not submit to control; sensitivity, melancholy, and sickliness can hardly be called for where energy and impetuosity have taken over. What he may be voicing, in paradoxical form, is the requirement that his conductors approach each composition from more than a single point of view, that they try to grasp the multiple levels on which these works move. In order to accomplish this, it may indeed be necessary to adopt attitudes that seem diverse, even contradictory; but the attempt must be made if the music is to be realized in performance.

IX

There is indeed a source—a very extensive source—of models for Berlioz's innovations: the operatic literature. Certainly, one can find multiple levels in almost every ensemble Mozart wrote—in, say, the opening scene and the first finale of *Don Giovanni,* to name one opera that Berlioz knew and admired. Moreover, all Berlioz's works, including those that do not deploy huge forces, display a dramatic, nay, theatrical side that attests the composer's love for opera and its influence on his style. The twofold *idée fixe* in *Harold*—the solo viola with its recurring theme—like an operatic character makes entrances and exits, taking part in various scenes. And this instrument and theme illustrate in obvious form what happens, perhaps more subtly, in almost every work of the composer. Perhaps, then, his contribution consists merely in the application of standard operatic procedures to compositions designed for concert or ceremonial use.

There is some truth in this conclusion. What is wrong is the word "merely." By applying dramatic methods to instrumental music, by conceiving of themes and instruments as individuals, Berlioz evolves new forms and new sounds. One reason that his orchestra seems so alive is that he treats it as if it *were* alive. So far as possible he assigns a vivid role to each instrument or to each choir—not just to the protagonist, but to the subsidiary actors as well. We have already seen how he tries to give each line of a polyphonic web its own personality.

It would be surprising if a composer with these predilections did not turn to the opera for models; it would be equally surprising if a composer of Berlioz's intelligence and originality did not transform these models in a unique way. A brief glance at the greatest of them may clarify the nature of the transformation.

Even in Mozart's most complex ensembles, there is always one musical line or plane of action clearly primary, in terms of which the others are to be understood. In the opening of *Don Giovanni,* the two duologues, first between the Don and Donna Anna, later between the Don and the dying Commendatore, function in this manner. Unified thematically or rhythmically, each of these is welded into a single leading part, upon which Leporello comments. But Leporello is always in a subsidiary role: the others never comment on him. And the accompaniment makes it clear that his rhythm is secondary, and interesting only as contrast.

The ballroom scene goes much further in the direction of multiple levels of musical action, and it must have been a great source of pleasure to Berlioz. Yet here too, in spite of the polymetric complications, there is no question of primacy. Our sympathies are with the masked intruders; so are those of the main orchestra. It is by the minuet that the other two dances are measured. Of these only the contredanse offers real rhythmic contrast (which I must confess I have always found difficult to hear). Even when Don Giovanni and Zerlina converse in 2/4 to its accompaniment, one can follow them more easily in terms of the prevailing triple meter.

As opposed to Mozart's lucidity, Berlioz cultivates a deliberate ambiguity. In his most characteristic music, a given line or plane is to be taken now as controlling others, now as under their control. Together with the frequently altered perspective, this reciprocity generates an often puzzling ambiguity. When Harold's theme enters against the pilgrims' march, it is impossible to determine which of the two is the leading part and which is to be measured against the other—where, symbolically, our sympathies are supposed to lie. It is fruitless to ask, for it is just this double significance that makes the combination here endlessly fascinating. That is why it is superior to the "Réunion des deux thèmes" in the ballroom scene of *Romeo and Juliet,* for there the dance music knuckles under as soon as Romeo's theme enters. Indeed, the former so easily assumes the role of accompaniment that one suspects it to have been devised for just this purpose.

(Were it not out of the question, it would be tempting to suggest another source for the counterpoint of individually characterized parts that result from Berlioz's dramatic approach: the polyphony of the later Middle Ages. Despite the basic differences of musical material and aesthetic purpose, the two styles show obvious, if superficial, resemblances. There is, of course, no possibility of influence or of intentional imitation; but it is interesting to find, during an age of Gothic revival in architecture, a composer who unconsciously reverts to Gothic musical effects.)

X

It would be natural to assume that Berlioz's own dramatic works (among which I include *The Damnation of Faust*) abound in complex examples of the same kind. This is not in fact the case, perhaps because the libretti do not often invite the exploitation of the full range of his musical subtleties. Nevertheless, when the dramatic situation permits, his music is ready to clarify the simultaneous and shifting points of view on the stage, and to intensify their effect. This happens in the opening of the carnival scene of *Benvenuto Cellini.* Two pairs of characters, first Balducci and his daughter Teresa, then Cellini and his friend Ascanio, are in turn allowed to hold the stage. The first two are presented in short contrasting solos: Balducci tries to placate his daughter, she meditates sadly on her decision to run away. The two friends, on the other hand, are given a rapid dialogue as they prepare for Cellini's elopement. Thus the two duos yield three vocal strands—those of father, daughter, and the two friends—all of which are now to be united polyphonically. But at the moment this combination begins, a new element is added: an orchestral pedal on the tonic, which persists until it is clarified by the entrance of the chorus of citizens. At this point it becomes obvious that the pedal note belongs to them, for their basses appropriate it, continuing it as a foundation for a choral crescendo that overwhelms the soloists.

What follows, although lively and brilliant, is less interesting for our purposes, since it relies on such standard devices as antiphonal dialogue and massed ensemble. Only during the performance on the mounte-banks' stage, when the chorus comments on the orchestral pantomime, is there again a suggestion of a double point of view, heightened by the parodistic nature of the music assigned to the orchestra. The effect might be called stylistic perspective: the effect of one style seen from the point of view of another.

The Damnation of Faust also makes use of this kind of contrast in the "Amen" fugue and in Marguerite's Lydian "Gothic Song." More impor-tant to the structure and content of the whole work is the way Berlioz has placed his multiple points of view at the service of dramatic irony. The heart of the cantata, the entire Marguerite episode, is framed by choruses of soldiers and students, each of which comments unwittingly on the dramatic situation—the soldiers with their "Si grande est la peine, / Le prix est plus grand . . . Fillettes et villes / Font les difficiles; / Bien-tôt tout se rend"; and the students with their "Gaudeamus igitur! . . . Per urbem, quaerentes puellas, eamus!" The introduction of the two groups shows Berlioz's familiar techniques at work. At the end of part 2, as the soldiers enter, the major shift of emphasis in the plot is fore-shadowed by the modulation from D to B♭. The students' song, which follows, is in D minor, and in 2/4 instead of the previous 6/8. As we have come to expect by now, the two are combined, the differences in key and meter proving to be no impediment at all. The soldiers win out tonally, but the students gain the upper hand melodically, for Faust and Mephi-stopheles take over their words and tune. A transition to part 3 is effected by the familiar trumpet call of the retreat. It is still in B♭, but the timpani reiterate a pedal on the dominant, which is to become the prevailing key of the new section—Marguerite's key, as it were. This F extends even into the beginning of part 4, as the key of Marguerite's touching Romance. Thus it is possible for all three commentaries to return—the retreat, the soldiers' chorus, and the students' song—all in their original keys, but all now over a pedal on F. That is to say, all are now observed by Marguerite, who suggests, by repeating some of the soldiers' words, that she is beginning to understand their relevance.

In *The Trojans* it is primarily the figure of Cassandra that conveys the irony of the situation. Throughout the first two acts of the opera, she presents a point of view that, because we know it is the correct one, is bound to affect the way we interpret the apparently joyful scene. At the same time, we are caught up by the sweep of the Trojans' music; so we can appreciate their antipathetic reaction to one who is continually interrupting their celebrations. Cassandra's music is usually at odds with that of the other characters. In her duet with Chorebus she rejects his cantilena with an extended dramatic recitative: when he continues to press his suit, she insists on breaking in, bringing her own orchestral accompaniment with her. The opposition is continued until their mutual love—or operatic convention—forces them to conclude with a cabaletta. Still more effective, because visually supported, is her monologue during the entry of the Wooden Horse. She alone holds the stage with her recitative as the procession advances and recedes—and the Trojan March with it. At the climax, when the chorus and the march break off at the sound of arms within the horse, there appears to be a chance that she may win her point yet. But no—"Présage heureux!": and the triumphal procession continues to what Cassandra knows is its doom. Throughout the scene her interjections, fragmentary though they are, form one continuous melodic line. Only at the climactic pause does the chorus join her in her declamatory style—and even adopt her motifs, the basses' "Qu'est-ce donc?" echoing her previous "La voici!" Here both the musical texture and the movement in real space reinforce the psychological situation. The procession has approached Cassandra from a distance; it is when the crowd appears on the stage in her vicinity that it is closest to her musically and emotionally. But the moment quickly passes; the procession moves on into the distance, leaving Cassandra to complete her soliloquy, spatially isolated and deprived of sympathy.

It is interesting to trace the fortunes of the Trojan March through the rest of the opera. It becomes almost an *idée fixe,* subject to various transformations in accordance with the vicissitudes of the nation it represents. At the end of the final act it again plays a part in a dramatic conflict, now between Carthage and the Rome of Dido's vision. This time it is the chorus of Carthaginians that attempts to overcome it, both rhythmically and tonally, by insisting on their own phrase structure and key (E♭ against the B♭ of the march). This time, however, destiny is on the side of the march, for its ultimate victory is attested both by the tableau of the Roman Capitol and by its own musical triumph.

XI

It is strange that Berlioz has almost nothing to say about orchestration in the postscript. Perhaps it is because he feels that he has already delivered himself on that subject in his *Traité;* perhaps because, as he points out at the end of the letter, his mastery is generally recognized:

> Everyone, in France and elsewhere, acknowledges my *maestria* in the art of instrumentation, especially since the publication of my didactic treatise on this subject. But I am often accused of overusing "Sax's instruments" (no doubt because I have often praised the talent of this clever inventor). As a matter of fact, up to now I have used them only in one scene of *The Capture of Troy,* an opera of which no one yet knows a page.[12] I am also accused of excessive noisiness, and of partiality for the bass drum, which I have included in a very few pieces where its use is well motivated. Besides, for twenty years I have been the only critic to protest insistently against the shocking abuse of noise and against the thoughtless use of bass drum, trombones, etc., that one finds in little theaters, in little orchestras, in little operas, in popular songs, where they're even using the snare drum now.
>
> Rossini, in *The Siege of Corinth,* was the man really responsible for introducing orchestral clatter into France; but the French critics refrain from mentioning him in this connection, and from blaming the shameful exaggeration of his system on Auber, on Halévy, on Adam, on a dozen others, in order to blame it on me . . .
>
> . . . I believe that this laughable error has arisen from the fact that I have often conducted huge orchestras at festivals. Thus Prince Metternich said to me one day in Vienna:
>
> "Are you the man who composes music for five hundred musicians?"
>
> To which I responded: "Not always, my lord; sometimes I write for four hundred and fifty."
>
> But what difference does it make? My scores are now published; it is easy to verify the accuracy of my statements. And if no one should do so, again, what's the difference!

There is probably another source of the "laughable error." At the end of the *Traité,* Berlioz muses on the possibility of "uniting all the musical forces that one can bring together in Paris." He proceeds to discuss the potentialities that might be offered by this mammoth assemblage of 465

---

12. He must have forgotten his use of saxhorns in the march that concludes the Te Deum.

instrumentalists and 360 choristers, and the problems of rehearsal involved. It is clear that he is indulging in fantasy. Nowhere does he imply that such an orchestra represents his ideal—merely that to put one together would be an interesting experiment. Berlioz, in fact, insists that the proper size of any group depends on the nature of the music it is to perform, and that the orchestra would have to have music specially composed for it. For most purposes, an orchestra of about 120 players would produce the best results. Nevertheless, one reads again and again of Berlioz as the composer for whom no existing orchestra was large enough, and who longed for the day when he could have four or five hundred instrumentalists at his command.

As for his reliance on the publication of his scores to correct misconceptions, it was premature. It has taken more than a hundred years for some of them to become available to the public, while the familiar works appear in versions that are often inaccurate when not deliberately distorted. And those who read them still find it impossible to free themselves from prejudice. Cecil Forsyth, for example, accuses Berlioz of writing "a part for the unusual orchestral instrument, 'Distant Cannon,'" in *The Fifth of May*.[13] An examination of the score reveals no such thing. The part is assigned to the bass drum; the composer has added a note to explain that it represents the sound of a distant cannon.

Nevertheless, Berlioz felt that his orchestration spoke for itself, and if not, "what's the difference!" I shall respect his feelings; yet I cannot resist citing two small examples to show how, with even the most limited instrumental means, Berlioz uses the orchestra to throw light on his musical intentions.

The first of these is the Villanelle from the *Nuits d'été*. Here a basically strophic form is given a unified shape by the development of a little refrain in the accompaniment at the end of each stanza. It invariably begins with a rising fourth, but this interval is displaced one step upward every time it reappears: B-E, C♯-F♯, D-G. The passage is marked for emphasis in the piano version, but it is very difficult for the accompanist to warn the listener from the outset that this motif is going to have a special life of its own. In the orchestral version the design is made beautifully clear. The refrain is given each time to the bassoon, which, being silent during the stanza itself, is reserved for this purpose. The new sound calls attention to the importance of the new motif. Only the last time does the bassoon continue beyond the usual resolution of the refrain, thus signaling the arrival of the coda and the end of the song.

The other example is the "Farewell of the Shepherds" from *The Child-*

13. Cecil Forsyth, *Orchestration*, 2d ed. (New York, 1935) 459.

hood of Christ. Again a strophic form is given shape by the accompaniment. The setup is simple: oboes and clarinets begin with a little introduction that recurs at the end of each stanza; the chorus is accompanied only by strings, which double the voice parts. In the third and last stanza, however, the woodwinds assume a more active role. The phrases they interject are for the most part derived from their own refrain and form a coherent though fragmented progression, but they have a more important function. They uncover and underline motivic and linear connections that lie hidden in the choral texture. By so doing they disclose a more continuous melody, a more organically unified form, than one would have suspected possible from the precisely articulated phrases of the vocal parts.

It would perhaps be an exaggeration to say that Berlioz's orchestration creates form; but it certainly reveals it. It is one of the surest guides we have to help us find our way inside the saint's head.

[*1971*]

Sound and Syntax:
An Introduction to
Schoenberg's Harmony

By *sound* and *syntax* I mean to distinguish the two aspects of harmony: chordal vocabulary and harmonic progression. Actually, there is also a third aspect to be considered, one lying somewhere between the first two. It is concerned with connections at the most detailed level: the specific chords chosen, the accessory tones decorating them, the voice leading from one to the next, and the comparative complexity of the sonorities. Let us call this aspect *succession*. Those familiar with Hindemith's theory will find parallels here: his table of chord groups is an attempt to classify all possible chordal constructions; his "harmonic fluctuation" is one of the effects of what I have called succession, and his "degree progression" links succession with harmonic progression in the larger sense. True, his method of analysis is probably even less in vogue today than his music; yet it can often be helpfully suggestive if separated from the rigid interpretations and applications that Hindemith himself often supplied.

My own interest in what I have called chordal vocabulary is not so precisely analytical as Hindemith's. For present purposes I am less concerned with the exact categorization of chords than with a determination of the types of sonorities employed by a given style, with the aim of recognizing the characteristic "sound" of that style. And I am less concerned with establishing roots for these chords—an essential for Hindemith's analysis of degree progression—than with discovering the relations between the way the chords are constructed and the way they move. How do the sound and the syntax affect each other, and what kinds of permissible chord succession result?

One of the earmarks of any well-defined style—whether of a period, or of a composer, or of a composition, or sometimes even of a specific passage—is its sheer sound. By this we recognize, instantly and almost, as it were, intuitively, that a work is by Mozart and not by Chopin, that it is the C-major Quartet (K. 465) and not the B♭ (K. 458), that it is the Adagio introduction and not the slow movement. We make this judgment spontaneously, without having to follow specific themes or to trace formal patterns. And an important criterion (though by no means the only one, or necessarily the most important) is the specific chordal vocabulary. Or perhaps better, the vocabulary of characteristic sonorities, since it might include a number of simultaneous combinations of tones that would not qualify under some theoretical rubrics as chords. Now, it is true of any music we consider as typically tonal, although not true exclusively of such music, that whatever sonorities its characteristic vocabulary may include, among these will be the major and minor triads—or at the very least, one major or minor triad or diagnostic component thereof. Moreover, triads are compositionally exploited—e.g., by preponderance, by rhythmic importance, by formal articulation—in such a way that they constitute normal sonorities for such music: sonorities with which all others are implicitly compared. Without a final statement of such a sonority no composition can sound complete—indeed, hardly even a phrase. If, then, a normal sonority is one that is normally used as a cadential chord, its definition can be restricted still further: what might be called the normal form of a normal is a triad in root position (or a diagnostic component). And there is a hierarchy of such triads, the one we call the tonic being the normal of normals.

Classical theory, from Rameau on, has tried to show that tonal syntax is based on the relations among normals: that even the most complex progressions, no matter how elaborated by dissonant chords, chromatic alterations, and non-harmonic tones, can be ultimately reduced to one that consists of connected triads in root positions. Schenker, elaborating the more practical and less abstract principles of thoroughbass, has offered a more convincing alternative. Yet it is one that builds tonal syntax even more firmly on normal ground. For Schenker, the background of every tonal composition is the single tonic triad. The fundamental harmonic progression is from tonic to fifth and back—the defining interval of the triad. Elaborations are effected by arpeggiation, by subsidiary fifth progressions, by neighboring and other apparent chords produced by voice leading; but these merely disguise the control of the normal tonic.

Even the principles of succession are subject to the control of the normal triad. Just as the composition typically consists of movement away from and back to *the* normal, so the sound of a typical tonal passage

depends on motion away from and toward *a* normal. Even a passage—
or more rarely an entire composition—that starts abnormally must, in
traditional tonal writing, push toward a normal. Indeed, it is the return
to a normal—the resolution of dissonance, as it is usually called—that
furnishes much of the local motive power of this music. The tension built
up by a series of dissonances depends on our expectation that a triad must
ultimately follow. Moreover, certain sonorities strongly imply specific
syntactic situations. The most obvious example is the primary ("dominant") seventh. Whether natural or applied, we confirm the regularity of
its resolution to its tonic by calling all other resolutions deceptive.

Classical tonality (and by classical I mean standard, without reference
to historical period) thus displays a consistency of sound, syntax, and
succession—a synthesis based on a characteristic vocabulary that includes the triad, and on a chord grammar that relates all other sonorities
to the triad as normal. But as the late Romantic style developed in the
nineteenth century, it appeared increasingly to question the assumptions
underlying this synthesis. In particular, the triad became less and less
characteristic of the sound of this music; yet at the same time it remained
the normal to which all successions of dissonances, no matter how pro-
tracted, must ultimately resolve. And a stubbornly triadic syntax often
underlay passages expressed in the most complex sonorities. Compare,
for a moment, the opening of "Fingal's Cave" with that of *Tristan und
Isolde*. Mendelssohn relies on a succession of normals, modified by
simple dissonances immediately resolved. The clarity of the sound is
matched by that of the chordal progression, which, stating successive
triads on B, D, and F♯, arpeggiates in harmonic terms the tonic that is
melodically arpeggiated by the opening motif (ex. 1). The Wagner example *sounds* as unlike as can be: a chromatic melodic line supported by

Example 1

a succession of dissonances stretched almost to the breaking point,
achieving a resolution only on a conventionally deceptive triad modified
by an appoggiatura. Yet the sequential pattern—although based on a series of sevenths, not triads—reveals, just as "Fingal's Cave" does, the
arpeggiation of a minor triad, E–G–B, each member of which, as a dominant, points to a corresponding element of the unstated triad, A–C–E,
implied as the normal of the entire deceptive progression (ex. 2). Sound
and syntax are here in a state of the gravest tension, and an extraordinary

genius like Wagner can only just hold them together. Even a great talent like Strauss occasionally fails, as when the high dissonance level of *Elektra* is suddenly relaxed for a conventional cadence.

Example 2

A younger composer like Schoenberg, coming to maturity during this critical period in the development—or the decline—of the style, could hardly hope to master at once the complexities of advanced tonal chromaticism with complete success. Indeed, the system had arrived at the point where such success was hardly possible, for the search for new harmonic resources was pushing beyond the limits of the tonal realm. It was Schoenberg's gradual realization of this situation that made of him a seminal figure in the development of twentieth-century music; and it is their reflection of this gradual realization that makes his early works so fascinating.

One would not expect the music of such a gifted composer to display obvious discrepancies of style: incompatible sonorities, inconsequent chord successions, meaningless progressions. But there are at least three kinds of inconsistency of which the early Schoenberg is guilty: inconsistency between sound and succession, between succession and syntax, and between sound and syntax. His early songs offer examples of all three.

"Schenk mir deinen goldenen Kamm," Op. 2 No. 2, presents an almost classical instance of the first. Why is the perfect cadence in mm. 5–6 almost bathetically saccharine? Not because the final chord is a triad: there have been two in the first measure. Not because it is major: if anything, a minor resolution, affording less contrast, would be even less acceptable. Not because of the descending-fifth chordal succession: that is prominent throughout the phrase, which can be heard as a clear, though highly chromatic, elaboration of the opening F♯. No: the cadence fails because even such a short passage has conditioned us to expect each member of a fifth-succession to be adorned with a dissonance, whether chordal seventh, suspension, passing tone, or neighbor. If, taking a cue from Wagner's handling of a somewhat analogous problem at the first cadence of *Tristan,* we alter the final consonance by the addition of an appoggiatura, all is saved (ex. 3). Note that the same objection does not

Example 3

apply to the V⁷-I in G minor of mm. 7–8. Although equally unadorned, the resolution here is protected by the fermata, the rest, and the consequent delay of the new tonic, which enters only as an upbeat of the next phrase. But by the time we return to the original key in m. 19, the old context has been reestablished, and once more the consonance disappoints us.

Was Schoenberg himself a bit uneasy about this letdown? Perhaps that is why his final tonic is as beautifully delayed as any in *Tristan,* again an obvious model. The last functional dominant (m. 36) is separated from the final tonic by six measures; its immediate resolution, although to a consonance, is deceptive. The tonic, when it arrives, is preceded by a seventh—but not of its own dominant, which is elliptically omitted: the bass, in a formula frequently used to end these songs, traverses a tritone. Tonal demands are met, but the flatness of a direct authentic cadence is avoided.

In Op. 3 No. 5, "Geübtes Herz," occurs another case of this kind, one that is perhaps even more striking because it mars an otherwise totally consistent texture. The song carefully avoids sudden changes in harmonic tension. It adorns all triads with appoggiaturas or else gingerly approaches them through relatively mild dissonances until the entrance of the Neapolitan sixth, *forte,* on a downbeat, after the harshest sonority in the entire composition (mm. 18–19), comes as a rude and inexplicable shock.

Succession and syntax come into conflict in Op. 3 No. 2, "Die Aufgeregten." The introduction, through its combination of rhetorical gesture (a recitative-like declamation supported by powerful chords and rhythmic motifs) and harmonic progression (basically a descending half-step sequence apparently leading to a functional dominant), appears to be preparing for a tonic G minor. But the resolution is deceptive: the body of the song begins in a tentative F minor (ex. 4). During its course

Example 4

it returns to the introductory motifs and even frankly to the dominant of G (mm. 13–14), again to resolve deceptively, this time leading to an authentic cadence in G♭ (ex. 5). When the introduction is recapitulated, almost literally, the acute listener, accepting the clue of the VI-II-V-I progression in G♭, may decide that tonal syntax will after all prevail; the

Example 5

expected tonic on G will arrive to round off the piece. But he would be wrong. What prevails is the rule of succession that dictates a deceptive resolution for the seventh on D. Schoenberg tries to achieve here a tour de force, admirable even in its failure. Presenting yet another deceptive resolution, he uses this as a passing chord to the original F, which closes the song as a normal, if not as a fully established tonic (ex. 6).

Example 6

I have described this song as one displaying unconventional successions that are inconsistent with its traditional syntax, but a more profound analysis would reverse these terms: it would find a general non-tonal syntax at odds with the local preservation of certain conventional chord successions. For even if a final resolution to G were achieved, the structure would still depend on voice leading rather than on functionality; only now it would be based on the passing chromatic motion F-G♭-G♮ instead of the neighboring F-G♭-F of the actual composition.

It is instructive to compare this song with an earlier one, Op. 2 No. 3, "Erhebung," which is troubled by a similar problem, but in a much less strenuous setting. Its syntax is frankly tonal; yet its ending is no more satisfactory than that of "Die Aufgeregten." This is because strong expectations have been aroused during the approach to the final climax (mm. 17–20), which seems to express an intention to modulate to the dominant, E. But no: a tendency to thwart the tonicization of V has been set up as early as mm. 2–3 and strengthened by the passage leading into the reprise at mm. 11–12, essentially a V of V resolving deceptively to I. And when the same situation recurs in m. 21, the pull of the succession is too strong, despite the altered context. Once again a tonic resolution rejects the demand for a dominant; this time syntax unmistakably gives in to succession.

In contradistinction to the last two examples, Op. 3 No. 3 is successful in its own idiosyncratic terms. The song sounds tonal, but it is actually so only in an inverted sense. The chordal progressions that have traditionally taken on the burden of large-scale structure are now demoted to details of succession; the harmonic motion is assigned to progressions once typically subsidiary or even decorative. For here a tonic, B♭ minor, is established by a series of plagal (descending-fourth) progressions skillfully united by a combination of diatonic and chromatic linear connections. The rare descending-fifth progressions—which never involve the tonic—are only sequential details. (See, for example, mm. 4–7.) Yet they are not obtrusively out of place, for the ambiance is superficially tonal. The song thus demonstrates that one can employ unconventional syntactic structure in a context of apparently conventional tonality. The title, "Warnung," is perhaps more appropriate than the composer realized. For, along with "Die Aufgeregten," this song can indeed be heard as a warning: that henceforth tonal syntax must not be accepted as allpowerful; that the traditional subordination of voice leading to harmonic progression may be reversed; that a functional dominant is not necessary for the establishment of a normal. The corollary that the normal need not be a tonic in traditional terms may not have occurred to Schoenberg at this point, but it was bound to sooner or later.

Tonal syntax vies with novel sound in Op. 2 No. 1, "Erwartung," which is nevertheless both an effective song and an early step in the direction that the composer was to take later. Its first characteristic dissonance is a chord created by applying half-step neighbors to the tonic (ex. 7a); but in intervallic content it is very close to another characteristic sonority consisting of an appoggiatura applied to a minor dominant ninth (ex. 7b). Yet this connection of sounds is misleading: the progress of the piece is determined, not by the characteristic chords, but by the

Example 7

m. 1   transposed   4   17 - 18   20 - 21

tonic-dominant syntax of their resolutions. The basic tonal structure is conventional: I-VI-V-I. Only in the approach to the recapitulation does the composer bring sound and syntax into a more intimate connection. By leading into the crucial I$_4^6$ first from an augmented sixth (m. 17) and then from a raised subdominant (m. 20), he surrounds B♭ harmonically by two of the half-step neighbors that characterize the opening dissonance (ex. 7c). And this chord itself is accorded the status of a true dominant when it succeeds the I$_4^6$ just before the reprise (m. 23). Its retransformation during the next few measures back to its original neighboring status is magical.

Further away from the characteristic tonal sound than any of the songs we have yet examined is Op. 6 No. 4, "Verlassen," which for long stretches forsakes ordinary tonal procedures. Hence its reversion at the climax to a traditional dominant-tonic construction is a striking instance of sound-syntax inconsistency. The ostinato motif of the opening measures, although concealing a normal tonic E♭, certainly gives more emphasis to other sonorities: first to two forms of ninth on E♭, then to two forms of a chord that is to become a great favorite of the composer—the combination of a perfect and an augmented fourth, which for convenience I shall henceforth call an *x*-chord (ex. 8). The opening melodic

Example 8

9th   9th   x   x

motif of the accompaniment is developed in the first vocal line, which expands it in such a way as to suggest yet another ninth, on D, which includes the second of the *x*-chords (ex. 9). When the harmony at last

Example 9

begins to move, the bass is controlled by this ninth, which is restated as the sonority that leads to the first important harmonic shift. Yet the resolution of the ninth is highly irregular, to a "*Tristan* chord" whose bass simultaneously completes a chromatic progression derived from the descending component of the opening motifs, and commences a diminution of its ascending component (ex. 10). This is the complicated context

Example 10

in which the rising climax gradually but ever more insistently asserts a structural dominant. It is prepared by a series of secondary dominant sevenths, all irregularly resolved yet leading clearly to an unmistakable V: B♭ (mm. 20–22). Because it is very dissonant and because its resolution to the E♭ of the opening motif is disguised and delayed, the specific succession here is appropriate and effective; but that does not alter the basic conventionality of the crucial syntactic structure.

Another large-scale departure from the tonic soon follows. This one, built on a fundamental D, returns to the tonic by way of the same ninth that originally departed from it—a beautiful example of syntax derived from, rather than opposed to, a characteristic sonority (mm. 42–43). Yet Schoenberg still feels that he must confirm the final cadence with another true dominant—one so simple in form and so directly followed by its tonic that, unlike its climactic predecessor, it introduces what can only be felt as an inappropriate detail of succession. Authentic cadences are comparatively rare in Schoenberg's music, even of this period, for what should by now be obvious reasons. It is too bad that he felt the need of one here.

Before leaving these early, tonally bound songs, I should like to pay tribute to one of the most beautiful. Superficially adhering to the conventions, ingratiating in sound, Op. 6 No. 1, "Traumleben," might be heard as a regretful, nostalgic farewell to the nineteenth century. But this interpretation would overlook the forward-pointing elements concealed beneath its calm surface. True, it develops a serene, uncontested E major; and although the first phrase begins tentatively, it comes to rest on an authentic cadence. But the dominant of that cadence is anything but typical (ex. 11). It states simultaneously the boundaries of the first vocal phrase, a minor ninth that is one of the most prominent melodic and

Example 11

harmonic intervals in the song. The melodic resolution of the dominant is by a diminished fourth (or augmented fifth) already subtly prepared by one in m. 2. What this striking interval (C♮-G♯) does is to call our attention to an association that will be important throughout the song, that of C♮ with the tonic chord of E major. It is the shift from E to a dominant seventh on C that moves into the development (mm. 12–13), and it is the return from this chord, reinterpreted as an augmented sixth, that effects the transformed reprise. Another C, this time as the bass of an altered IV$^6_5$, leads into the tonic of the coda. Most remarkable of all is the way the dominant of the first cadence, in the course of its chromatic elaboration, strikes—at perhaps its moment of greatest tension—a sonority that both sums up the course of the melody so far and forecasts all the tonic cadences to come! For this sonority consists of B, A, E♯ (F♮), and C, the first four tones of the vocal line. B is of course the root of the chord in question; a seventh on A precedes the tonic at the next cadence (mm. 8–9); the cadences involving C have already been discussed—but it should be mentioned that the second of these is introduced by a first-inversion F, yielding the bass A-C-E. Lastly, the final cadence of the song involves a root-position F (ex. 12). Thus, despite the unquestioned supremacy of the tonal normal on E, the syntax is based on a

Example 12

m. 3   4   8   9   24   25   29   30   31   34   35

characteristic sonority, one that leaves its stamp on both melodic and harmonic progressions throughout. Even in a relatively conservative idiom, Schoenberg is on the verge of the kind of unification of simultaneous and successive events that characterizes serial methods.

In the two songs of Op. 14 the role of the triad as normal is seriously questioned. No. 1, "Ich darf nicht dankend," is based on two types of fourth chord, one the *x*-chord and the other combining two perfect fourths (*y*). Both the sound of these chords and the succession from an *x* to a *y* characterize the highly consistent texture of the song. In proto-serial style, important linear motions as well are governed by these so-norities, as the introductory phrase illustrates: the bass outlines a motion from F♯ to C♯ to B, decorated by neighbors and appoggiaturas (ex. 13).

Example 13

This phrase shows something else, too: the succession *x-y*, after a slight delay, is completed triadically, as the bass of an apparent $^6_4$ moves upward to form a root-position B (minor-major). That, if we are to trust the key signature and the last chord of the piece, is to be heard as the tonic. But note what a tentative metrical position it occupies, and how it is blurred by an appoggiatura and a moving bass at its reprise in m. 18. And if, as these measures suggest, the syntactic foundation of the song is not functional harmony but the voice leading implied by the succession *x-y*-triad, then it is interesting that the triad is often either an inversion (as in mm. 11, 16, and 20) or else omitted altogether (as in m. 5). Striking, too, are the sequential chains formed from *x* and *y*, as in mm. 9–10, 13–14, and especially 24–25. The result is to raise the question whether the final chord is really "right." For the first time a triad—the B-minor "tonic"—follows *x* instead of *y*. Schoenberg has explained irregularities of this kind in his *Harmonielehre,* where he speaks of harmonic formulas that have become "so unequivocal that the initial chord, once sounded, straight-away and automatically enlists our expectation of the predetermined con-tinuation: the formula leads inevitably to a foregone conclusion. Given such a premise, the intermediate steps can even be omitted, the begin-ning and the end directly juxtaposed, and the whole progression so to speak 'abbreviated,' set down simply as premise and conclusion."[1] Schoenberg adduces in illustration of this principle cadences embodying tritone bass-motion similar to that at the close of Op. 2 No. 2; no doubt he would have argued in the present instance that the same principle would hold despite the unfamiliarity of the idiom. But the more funda-mental question would still remain: is the "tonic" chord necessary? In-

1. Arnold Schoenberg, *Harmonielehre,* 3rd ed. (Vienna, 1922), 432.

deed, is the triad a normal for this composition? Could it not—should it not—end with a repetition of the two chords with which it began? In this connection it is perhaps revealing that Op. 14 No. 2, "In diesen Wintertagen," does end with a dissonance derived from its opening measure—although newly redistributed as a triad with added sixth.

Das Buch der hängenden Gärten, Op. 15, returns to these problems and begins to provide definitive answers. Look at No. 7. Again, at the outset two dissonances, an augmented triad and an *x*-chord (the tritone at first below, later often above), lead to a consonance, now simply a minor third. This rule of succession is observed more faithfully and completely than that of Op. 14 No. 1, for much of the accompaniment consists of the two chords alternating with chains of parallel thirds. But the rhythmic structure and the dynamic pattern of the first few phrases make it clear that the characteristic dissonances have here become the normals: they are the downbeat resolutions toward which the restless thirds push (e.g., in mm. 3–4). And since this interpretation is confirmed by the rest of the song, it is only proper that the music should end as it began, with the same two characteristic sonorities.

In this respect No. 7 is a microcosm of the entire cycle, all of whose characteristic vocabularies are frankly based on dissonances. Consonant sonorities may of course be included, but they are not specially privileged. Only one, No. 6, can be construed as ending on a consonant triadic normal. In the opening phrase of this song a perfect fifth, B♭-F, comes to rest on what one might suspect to be a more characteristic interval, the tritone B♭-E. In the context, this could well be a "resolution," but during the course of the voice line there are two prominent passages where the original melodic F-E is completed by motion to D (mm. 4–5, 7–10). The second of these is heard in association with two emphatic statements by the piano of the original fifth (mm. 8–9). When the vocal line twice more refers to F-E (mm. 10–13) we expect the completion that comes—twice in fact—in the concluding phrases, each time over a B♭ bass (ex. 14). The song is tonal only insofar as it is based on a

Example 14

triadic normal. Its principles of succession and syntax come from its own characteristic sounds—notably the association of B♭ with F and E, a grouping that will be immediately recognized as a form of the *x*-chord, a sonority that is almost ubiquitous throughout the cycle.

At least one other song, No. 10, establishes a triadic normal. Even though here, as before, the opening measures state an *x*-chord—both simultaneously and melodically—the tritone D-G♯ is immediately resolved to a perfect fifth. This move, supported by the bass, initiates a progression that can be heard as unfolding a triad on D: major $^6_4$ through minor $^6_4$ to major $^5_3$ (ex. 15). The rising bass line, with its concealed arpeggiation, controls the course of the song until the concluding measures. Now the prevailing upward half step G♯-A is prominently reversed

Example 15

in the bass, leading to G (mm. 28–29). There follows the frankest possible statement of a normal D major as a resolution of the opening motif, but the song is not allowed to end here. The tritone G♯ reappears over the fundamental D and moves to a final resolution—but on A♯, supported by a return to the same dissonant chord on G that immediately preceded the cadence.

Here, then, is another important departure from tonal principles. Schoenberg no longer considers it necessary to end on the normal—even when it is a triad. Not that the step was a revolutionary one: Mozart had taken it in an obvious example, although with parodistic intent. Schumann had been willing to end on an inversion of the tonic; Chopin had added a seventh; Schoenberg himself, as we have seen, had added a sixth (in Op. 14 No. 2). And there are a few curious instances, like Chopin's second Ballade and Schoenberg's Op. 3 No. 6, "Freihold," which seem to vacillate between two tonics. But the conclusion of "Das schöne Beet" deliberately leads away from its final cadential normal. Why? Whatever expressive reasons might be adduced, the formal one depends on the old problem of consistency of sound, succession, and syntax. Throughout the song, the normal is openly sounded only during the course of a phrase; cadentially it is always sidestepped—until the end. But by then it is too late to introduce a convincingly firm tonic. The tendency of the chord to move on has already been well established, and that is the way it must behave even on its final appearance.

The distinction between normal and non-normal finals must be observed as well when, as in most of Op. 15, the normal is dissonant. Like consonant normals, dissonances may be established at the outset. No. 13, for example, develops by a series of neighboring motions from its opening sonority, to which the last measure of the song returns. But No. 2, which states and then discusses a simpler sonority with clearer tonal implications, moves away after a final return. An arpeggiation of the opening chord, D-F-A-C♯, underlies the entire bass. This moves chromatically from D to F (mm. 1–6), then emphasizes A and F (mm. 7–8). Next, falling chromatically through E (developed in terms of a subsidiary sonority already associated with E in m. 4), it passes beyond D to C♯. But the ensuing resolution back to D, which brings with it a restatement of the opening chord, yields to the prevailing chromatic motion. The bass rises to E♭—a so to speak hyper-dissonant neighbor to an already dissonant normal (see ex. 16).

Example 16

m. 1   4   6   7   8   11

More problematic are the dissonant normals that are delayed—established as late goals of harmonic motion, like those delayed tonics of which Brahms was so fond (e.g., that of his Intermezzo Op. 76 No. 4). But whereas one can be certain that Brahms's normal will be a triad, and can usually predict from the outset just which triad, the range of possibilities open to Schoenberg makes such confidence unwarranted. Still, the main thing is to be able to recognize the normal when it arrives—as I believe one can at the end of No. 5, even though the specific final sonority is unique in the song. Its conclusiveness is due partly to its intervallic makeup: it is framed by a perfect fifth, and in a texture characterized predominantly by tritones it conspicuously contains none; in fact, it is the only sonority on a downbeat that neither contains a tritone nor resolves to one in appoggiatura fashion. More than that, it effects the only cadential point not vitiated by an appoggiatura-like feminine ending. At the same time the sonority is well prepared. The falling D-G of the bass is derived from an early "cadence" (mm. 3–4) that was aborted by an immediate rise in the bass. The piano chords of that cadence return to lead to the close (mm. 15–16), but this time the G remains in place, strengthening the cadential downbeat. A second statement subtly alters the progression, providing a transitional form that enables us to hear the final chords as still another variation of the by now familiar cadence. And although the tritone has been banished from the harmony, the last melodic interval in the vocal line reminds us of its importance.

Despite these examples, it must be confessed that the decision whether a certain ending is normal or non-normal is often problematic when the normal can only be a dissonance, and especially problematic when that dissonance is one not clearly established at the outset. If we heard a traditionally tonal composition end on the dominant seventh, or on a chord neighboring the tonic, we should immediately call that ending non-normal. But it might be very difficult to make such a determination in a more complex situation. In No. 9 is the normal the quasi-dominant that begins and ends the song (except for an evanescent diminuendo)? Or is it the quasi-tonic that twice "resolves" the first sonority (mm. 3 and 9)? Questions of this sort inevitably suggest more general ones. Must the normal always be a chord of relative resolution? Must it be among the characteristic sonorities of a composition? Must it always be stated? More drastically, must every composition have a normal?

I shall not try to give general answers—even to the extent of saying that no general answers are possible, for that would be tantamount to answering No in each case. But I believe I can tell what Schoenberg's answer would have been, at least so far as his own music was concerned. Look again at No. 7. You may have wondered why, in my discussion of that song, I avoided stating which of the two opening chords is the normal. Is the first an appoggiatura to the second, or is the second an incomplete neighbor of the first? I see no way to decide the question, nor do I see the necessity for a decision; but that need not mean that the piece lacks a normal. The normal might consist of the succession of the two chords. "Am Strande," a posthumously published song apparently written during the same period as Op. 15, seems to go one step further. The opening consists of an arpeggio succeeded by a chord (c), but the arpeggio is soon divided into two components: a and b—I take the C♮ in the first measure to be a misprint for the B that later consistently replaces it (ex. 17). During the course of the song each of these components is combined with chord c (especially in mm. 12–13). The normal, then, might

Example 17

well consist not of one chord but of three, which can be stated not only successively but also in part simultaneously. The conclusion refers only to a and c, an abbreviation somewhat like the one noted at the end of Op. 14 No. 1.

We thus find Schoenberg, even at this early date (1908–09), already on the verge of serial techniques, although their thoroughgoing adaptation is still years away. For the normal that depends, not on a single chord or tone, but on a succession; the ordered components of a collection that can be stated both successively and simultaneously; the resultant identification of sound and succession: these are basic elements of serialism in general and of the twelve-tone method in particular. One achievement of that method is to be a firmer definition of syntactic principles derived from these premises. Let us therefore conclude this survey of Schoenberg's lieder with a brief look at his three twelve-tone songs, Op. 48, to see how each employs its syntax to establish a normal.

No. 2, "Tot," relies on a single form of the row and its retrograde (ex. 18). Even this distinction, at best a minimal contrast, is often blurred.

Example 18

How, then, without inversion or transposition, can one statement be established as normal at the expense of another? The structure of the song is based on the original division of its row into tetrads; the combinations of these three units, progressing from the simpler to the more complex and back, produce an obvious arch design. The song is over when the original simple disposition returns, with the third tetrad repeatedly stated as a free ostinato beneath the other two. This, then, is the normal: not a chord, not even a succession of chords, but a special way of handling the row.

The syntax of No. 3, "Mädchenlied," is more complex, since it depends on the combination of a prime (with its R) and an inversion (with its RI). The former is shaped, and the latter is chosen, in a manner typical of Schoenberg: the resulting combinations of corresponding half rows produce twelve-tone aggregates (ex. 19). Nor are such hexadic combinations restricted to the prime against the inversion; the two halves of

Example 19

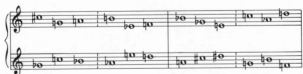

each form are similarly counterpointed against each other. Again there is a progression from simplicity to complexity and back. At the outset the hexads are divided into triads, regularly and obviously ordered. But as the song develops, dyadic division takes over and the ordering becomes much looser. Even when the triads return they are combined in fresh ways reflecting the freer ordering, and they sometimes overlap one another. The row forms, once carefully restricted to either voice or piano, now straddle the two. It is through the return of a simple R against RI, with clearly demarcated triads, that the piano coda reestablishes a normal.

No. 1, "Sommermüd," employs two transposition levels of the inversion. As we might expect, the complete pattern is rounded off by a return of the prime, which has been restricted throughout to a single tonal level. But the normal is more specific than that. The song opens with a division of the row into tetrads, of which the third is consistently given to the piano against the other two in the voice. In the piano coda the left hand states each tetrad in turn against a combination of the other two in the right hand. The song is over when the third has taken its turn in the bass. This, then, seems to be the normal: a statement of the prime with the third tetrad harmonically supporting the other two. But what of the larger syntax of the composition? How is the twelve-tone texture related to the choice of the two inversions? Not, as in No. 3, by hexadic combinatoriality. Here, where the primary division of the row is tetradic, the connections from one row form to the next are established by relations among these segments—and occasionally others, longer or shorter (ex. 20). The exploited similarities between the prime (A) and the first inversion (B) adhere to the corresponding segments, whereas some of those

Example 20

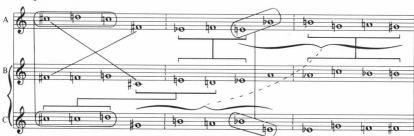

involving the second inversion (C) are more abstruse. Hence it is appropriate that this form does come second, and that the main burden of the song rests on the other two.

The above examples suggest the generalization that, for Schoenberg at least, the standard twelve-tone pattern is analogous to the standard tonal pattern: statement of normal, departure from normal, return to normal. If that generalization is valid at all, it must admit numerous exceptions. Just as many tonal compositions diverge from the standard, so do many twelve-tone compositions, including some of Schoenberg's: I need mention only his Violin Phantasy. But whether his composition begins with the normal, or ends with the normal, or both, or neither; whether the normal depends on a certain transposition of the row, or division of the row, or combination of rows—I submit that there is always a normal to be found, and to be heard.

A recent review of a performance of Schoenberg's music compared the composer to "a man who gives up a profitable life as a banker to go exploring at the South Pole."[2] It should be clear why I consider such a view entirely wrong. If we wish to retain the simile of the explorer, let us think of Schoenberg as a mountain climber who, approaching the timberline, realizes that he must give up the protective cover of the forest. But the ground beneath his feet is still the same solid earth.

[1974]

2. Donal Henahan in *The New York Times,* Oct. 8, 1974, 37.

Webern's Apprenticeship

It is impossible to listen with an unbiased ear to the juvenilia or the student works of a well-known composer. What we know of his mature production is bound to influence, favorably or unfavorably, our judgment of his early efforts. In particular, we are exposed by our prior knowledge to one of two temptations—sometimes to both at once. On the one hand, since we cannot help remembering the superior works yet to come, it is hard not to look condescendingly upon compositions that, except in the case of a young Mozart, are bound to be imperfect copies; and it is great sport to point both to their imperfections and to their obvious models. On the other hand, it is even more amusing to find intimations of a style yet to be formed—occasional phrases or devices that seem to foreshadow the works of the composer's maturity. To be sure, both games, legitimately played, can lead to valuable insights. The one is a temptation only because it is so easy; it is usually safe. The other is challenging and potentially more rewarding—but accordingly more dangerous.

The recent publication of a substantial collection of early works of Webern, from the University of Washington's Moldenhauer Archive,[1] opens a new field for sportsmen of both varieties. As always, there is opportunity for both legitimate and illegitimate plays; but in this case

1. Anton Webern: *Three Poems for Voice and Piano; Three Songs after Poems by Ferdinand Avenarius for Voice and Piano; Eight Early Songs for Voice and Piano; Langsamer Satz for String Quartet; String Quartet* (1905); *Im Sommerwind, Idyl for Large Orchestra; Five Songs after Poems by Richard Dehmel for Voice and Piano.* All published by Carl Fischer, Inc., New York, by whose kind permission the music examples are reprinted here.

attention to the clearly stated chronological sequence of the works will help the conscientious participant to avoid flagrant errors. Each composition is dated as to year, and some of the songs even more closely. Assuming the accuracy of this information, we can divide the works into three convenient groups. The first consists of three sets of songs: the *Three Poems,* the *Eight Early Songs* (both collections on heterogeneous texts), and the *Three Songs after Poems by Ferdinand Avenarius.* These all belong to the years 1899–1904; but, for reasons not explained in the published versions, they are arranged (by Webern or by the editors?) according to no clear order within that period. The second group, spanning the years 1904–06, is devoted to instrumental music: the orchestral *Im Sommerwind* and the two compositions for string quartet. Finally, from the period 1906–08, we have the *Five Songs after Poems by Richard Dehmel.* Surveyed thus, in chronological order, the compositions present a striking record of increasing technical mastery and growth towards a personal style.

The earlier songs, as one might expect, are at worst awkward and at best derivative. Indeed, they owe much of their awkwardness to insufficient assimilation of the late Romantic styles from which they naturally derive. They contain a few self-consciously simple passages that attempt to evoke either a religious or a folk-like atmosphere, but for the most part their harmonic technique is an inept combination of Wagnerian and impressionistic methods. Typical examples abound in augmented triads and Tristanesque chords connected by chromatic part writing, by stepwise sequences, and by even more frankly parallel chord successions, sometimes over a long-continued pedal, sometimes in a series of restless modulations. The results, in Webern's inexperienced hands, are a lack of harmonic direction and of clear tonality. Wagnerian in another sense is the role of the piano, which, far from being a mere accompaniment, is usually the prime vehicle of the musical line. Rarely is the voice given striking melodic material; it is conceived as declamation rather than as melody.

In sum, these lieder are, in every sense, formless. The youthful composer seemed to think that a dramatic interpretation of a text, held together musically by a few repeated motifs and momentarily arresting chord progressions, could create a song. His mistaken belief is understandable enough, for it was only echoing a common error of the late nineteenth century—an error based to a certain extent on a misapprehension of Wagnerian principles. After all, it is only recently that many of us have come to the realization that Wagner's music dramas were not conceived in primarily orchestral terms.

There would seem to be little hope, then, of detecting traces of the later Webern amid such uncongenial surroundings. Nevertheless, I believe that some can be found—but they are not the obvious ones that, tempting us at first glance, turn out to be false clues. In this connection even the earliest song, "Vorfrühling" (the first of the *Three Poems*), primitive though it may be, is instructive. At the outset one spots a most suggestive detail: the similarity of the introductory motif (ex. 1a) to the first vocal phrase (ex. 1b). And the immediate repetition of this motif in retrograde (or inversion, ex. 1c) supports one's hope that Webern's later

Example 1

etc.

methods of composition are already adumbrated here. Unfortunately, nothing further in the song confirms this hypothesis. The relation of the vocal motif to the accompaniment was no doubt deliberately contrived, since it is repeated verbatim at the close; it performs a formal function, though a limited one. The retrograde relationship, however, can only be either fortuitous or adventitious; it is certainly of no importance in the development of the piece as a whole. The same may be said of similar details to be found elsewhere in these early songs. The introduction to "Fromm" (the third of this set), for example, likewise contains a motif followed by its own transposed retrograde; and the opening of "Tief von fern" (from *Eight Early Songs*) contains a brief line that, like ex. 1b, is its own retrograde inversion. But in neither case does the discovery of the device lead to further insight into the composition; the detail remains purely a detail.

How, then, does "Vorfrühling" provide the clue we are seeking? Oddly enough, by its very awkwardness. The gaucherie of immaturity is often at least partially due to the burgeoning of new concepts, and this may well be the case here, as we shall see. Much of "Vorfrühling" is static: over half of its twenty-two measures are on a tonic pedal. What chordal motion there is proceeds mainly by neighboring tones, with few clear dominant functions. E♭ is hardly established before it is interrupted by D♭ on one side, shortly to be followed by F on the other. The resulting sense of tonality is very uneasy and gives the song a highly tentative sound. Nevertheless, these harmonic progressions elaborate melodic relationships already obvious in the opening measures (see ex. 1). The F-E♭ step is an important detail of the introduction (where it is supported by a slower C-B♭), and the E♭-D♭ step is the goal of the voice. Just as it arrives there, it is accompanied by a striking downward seventh in the bass—E♭-F—followed in turn by a descent through E♭ to D♭, the first new harmonic center. This shift is balanced a few measures further on by a modulation to F, which in turn leads back to the tonic. In the voice, too, the F-E♭ connection is constantly present, both in the small and in the large.

My conclusion that the foregoing relationships were at least partly contrived by the composer is supported by the fact that the second song in chronological order, "Tief von fern," also exploits the connections between a major tonic and major harmonies a whole step on each side of it. This one is more successful, owing to its smoother (and more conventional) use of transitional chords, but even here one is not quite convinced by the final return to the tonic.

What was perhaps trying to work itself out through these early efforts was a struggle between the traditional norms of tonal harmonic progression and Webern's as yet dimly perceived goals. The ideal of a single motivic configuration as a germinal source for both melodic and harmonic content is just perceptible here, even though Webern himself may not have been conscious of it. Even if he was, his control of his harmonic vocabulary was not yet strong enough to sustain progress in that direction.

His troubles with tonality soon became acute, as the third song, "Heimgang in der Frühe" (from Eight Early Songs), shows. In this one, the first to betray clear Wagnerian influence, the harmonic material is out of hand. Key follows key in bewildering fashion, no doubt in an attempt to reflect the course of the poem. Towards the end a sudden turn to D♭, although unprepared, nevertheless seems to promise some stability. A programmatic interpolation on the last page dashes even this hope, and the final cadence, in spite of returning to D♭, fails to reestablish the key. In other songs, too, the text plays a similarly disruptive role, notably in "Aufblick" and "Bild der Liebe" (from the same collection) and in "Freunde" (from the Avenarius set).

More interesting, because they try more explicitly to solve the problems of harmonic control, are those songs in which Webern countered his steps towards tonal freedom by dutiful gestures towards conventionality. As early as the previously mentioned "Fromm," the tendency of the piece is away from the tonic E♭, the chief motion being downward by thirds towards the subdominant. The expansion of A♭, however, is thwarted at the end by an unconvincing return to E♭, now—unfortunately for any sense of finality—heard as a dominant. Again, in "Sommerabend" (from *Eight Early Songs*), Webern evidently took the opening chord on B as representing a tonic, although the succeeding progressions strongly suggest an expanded dominant on D followed by its tonic G. At this point there is a sudden return of B, but it sounds like a mere coloristic interpolation before a modulation to the flatted VI. Accordingly, on the last page, it is a return to G as tonic that we look forward to—but no, we are disappointed by a bald V–I in B!

The same insistence on a return to the opening chord as a tonic may explain the difficulty Webern had with the ending of "Nachtgebet der Braut" (from *Three Poems*)—a difficulty of which he himself must have been aware, since he apparently tried two versions of the passage, both of which are indicated in the score. Neither is satisfactory. This time, however, the problem he had set himself was an interesting and potentially fruitful one: how to reconcile the conflicting claims of two keys. Here the original A major is a reasonable candidate for the role of tonic, but it is not the only one: soon after the beginning, tendencies towards F assert themselves, and the course of the work can be regarded as a struggle between the two. In this early example (1903), Webern's misjudgment in giving the victory to the original tonic may still have been due to a conventional bias; for in another song of the same year, "Gebet" (from the Avenarius set), a contest between the original C♯ minor and the later established E major is likewise resolved in favor of the former—this time after a final phrase of almost agonizing indecision.

A song of the next year, "Gefunden" (from the same set), is the most successful of all those written up to 1904, for it exploits tonal duality with great assurance. Here for the first time one can be confident the principle was applied with full consciousness of its implications. The conflict this time is between the opening C♯ and the ensuing A. These two areas are presented with subtlety, the C♯ appearing in the introductory measures as the dominant of an unstated F♯, and the A in the first vocal phrase as the dominant of an unstated D. Not until the climax of the phrase does A become a tonic—but even here in turn through its own dominant. There is no full cadence of any kind until, almost exactly halfway through the piece, a piano interlude brings a resolution on C♯ major. The second stanza returns to the fray, but the conclusion once more affirms the C♯ tonic.

It is indicative of the direction of Webern's thought that this, the best of the early group, should be tonally so fluid. Yet it is important to note that, within each tonal area, the harmonies move surprisingly slowly. What appears superficially like real motion can be reduced by analysis to

voice leading over a stated or implied pedal, neighboring harmonies surrounding a principal chord, or sequences disguising chromatic parallel
progressions. In "Der Tod" of the same year (from *Eight Early Songs*),
the movement of the entire composition is restricted to that of the upper
voices over a constantly reiterated tonic pedal.

At this point one begins to suspect that the young composer's predilection for static harmonies, evident from the first, may not have been
due solely to timidity. It may not have been merely the result of an awareness of tonal unsteadiness and a consequent attempt to correct it. In connection with his use of neighboring chords, stepwise sequences, and
frank parallelism, it may have been looking forward to a style in which
voice leading and harmonic motion would coalesce—when (as already
in Mahler) functional harmonic progressions could be replaced by polyphonic movement over a pedal, or by predominantly linear motion from
one important point to the next. The tonal unsteadiness, in turn, spring-
ing in all probability from a desire to reconcile traditional demands for
tonal unity with a vaguely felt need for more flexibility, might also lead
to a more expanded sense of key—even pointing towards what Schoenberg, for one, always preferred to call "pantonality." It is generally held
that, of the classical trinity of twelve-tone composers, Webern departed
furthest from the traditional concepts of harmony and key. Is it only a
coincidence that his early works should show little interest in the exploitation of functionality? (Contrast, for example, the almost excessive concern with harmonic elaboration displayed by the young Schoenberg.) Is
it too far-fetched to find in the palindromes and the symmetrically self-
inverted passages beloved of the mature Webern a successful means of
achieving an effect—of motion around an unmoving axis—towards
which his early harmonic efforts were groping?

Im Sommerwind (Idyl for Large Orchestra) belongs to the same year as
the last of the early songs. It is a tone poem, Lisztian in its squareness of
phrase and its sectional form, Straussian in its attempt to form a grand
peroration by a contrapuntal combination of themes. Orchestrally it exhibits several obvious miscalculations; harmonically it demonstrates on
a large scale the tonal insecurity that marks so many of the lieder. It is
probably the least interesting of the newly published scores, all the more
so by contrast with the works for string quartet that follow it. How does
it happen that these, composed not more than a year later, display so
much more confidence and skill? Why does the year 1905 inaugurate a
period of such rapidly increasing technical mastery that the output of
the previous years seems by comparison amateurish and even puerile?
The answer is obvious: Webern had begun his four years of study with
Schoenberg.

It is interesting to try, by studying the works in question, to reconstruct something of Schoenberg's pedagogical approach. No doubt he persuaded his pupil that it was high time for him to set himself free from his dependence on texts, but that he should try something less ambitious and more restrictive than a tone poem. The Langsamer Satz, which I take to be earlier than the harmonically and formally more complex String Quartet (1905), is certainly strict enough to serve as one of Schoenberg's own "models for beginners." The opening statement (ex. 2) is self-consciously tight in its construction from a few opening motifs. If we

Example 2

call the first three measures A, B, and C, the theme becomes: A, B, C, C, B, B inverted, A inverted, cadence. B, of course, is rhythmically almost identical with A, and its inversion is altered in such a way as to bring it close to C. The next phrase is entirely developed from C, and it is dutifully followed by a polyphonically elaborated repetition of the original statement. The following transition to the first contrasting section not only arises from the preceding cadence but also foreshadows the new theme to come. This subject is the source not only of its own countersubject (ex. 3a) but also, by a more subtle transformation, of a third subject (ex. 3b). In the recapitulation—or is it the coda?—these two themes are brought still closer together in contrapuntal combination.

It should be clear that behind Schoenberg's teaching stands the ghost of Brahms. The construction of a melody by motivic manipulation, the use of thematic material to create accompaniment figures, the transformation of one theme into another, the devices of foreshadowing and reminiscence—all these are familiar methods of the Old Master. Even the principle of octave equivalence that must be assumed in order to identify the beginning of ex. 3b with ex. 3a is not, as one might suppose, Schoenberg's personal contribution. Brahms had already pointed the

Example 3

way in his Fourth Symphony when he used the device to transform the opening of the first movement on the occasion of its return in the finale.

An important forward step in the Langsamer Satz is to be found in the way its key relationships are handled. Is the movement in C minor or in E♭ major? The opening statement, leading from the one to the other, summarizes the progression of the movement as a whole—as, indeed, the opening of the melody alone does on a still smaller scale. (The motion C–D–E♭ is also simultaneously reversed in the bass.) With even more concision, the first chord, a minor seventh on C, combines the two harmonies! It may well be that Schoenberg, recognizing the tendency of his student's earlier efforts, encouraged him in this direction, showing him how harmonic duality, properly controlled, could be organically developed throughout an extended movement.

The String Quartet (1905) is also a single movement; but, as in Schoenberg's much longer First Quartet (of the same period), its broad range of tempo and mood implies the compression of several standard movements into one. Much of it is developed from the opening motto of a descending half step plus an ascending major third (ex. 4a). The extent to which this will pervade the entire texture is forecast by the immediately following repetition, where it is accompanied by a suggested diminution and by an explicit inversion (also in diminution). At the same time the major third of the motif is reduplicated harmonically to form the augmented triad that, together with other whole-tone chords, will provide much of the characteristic sound of the Quartet. Ex. 4b shows how another important motif, that of a half step plus a tritone, is developed from the original. If we again accept octave equivalence, we can hear the new motif and its inversion arise simultaneously in first

Example 4

violin and cello—in each case by the juxtaposition of an incomplete and a complete statement of the motto. Later the motto undergoes other transformations: intervallic contraction (ex. 4c, from p. 7) and expansion (ex. 4d, from p. 11)—again in combination, in the first instance with itself, in the second with the tritone motif. This motif in turn yields both the subject of a fugato (ex. 4e, from p. 12) and, in a completely new guise, an important theme of the final quiet section (ex. 4f, from p. 21). In the continuation of this phrase a retrograde of the motif briefly appears; similarly, one can find its retrograde inversion in the bass of ex. 4d by overlapping successive measures. Like a few other details of this kind that can be detected here and there, these may be purely accidental; certainly no important developments arise from them.

Although the Quartet is clearly tonal, we are thus on the verge of the cellular construction that helps hold together many of the early atonal compositions. It is therefore no surprise to find the motto appearing simultaneously on more than one compositional level (ex. 4g, from p. 15; ex. 4h, from p. 16). Webern was here making primitive use of a technique that Schoenberg was later—from Op. 11 on—to exploit so effectively.

For all its contrapuntal elaboration, however, the Quartet remains, for long stretches, harmonically slow moving. The passages in which several themes are combined look complex, to be sure, but underlying them is always a simple pattern, usually of stepwise sequences. Compared with the dense harmonic network of superficially similar passages in Schoenberg's First Quartet, their texture seems essentially decorative. Even the fugato gives the effect of dissonant voices elaborating a very slow fundamental progression—a progression that is made explicit when the cello takes eight measures to complete the bass of a simple II-V-I cadence. On the other hand, the occasional attempts to produce rapid harmonic change indicate that the composer had not yet mastered his craft. Listen, for example, to the strange course of the E-major theme announced at the first climax (p. 9), with its startling shifts of direction, or to the equally unexpected cadences that precede the fugato (pp. 11–12).

The persistence of harmonic inconsistencies in these compositions may explain why Webern, apparently while working on the comparatively advanced *Five Songs after Poems by Richard Dehmel* of 1906–08, should at the same time produce the conventionally tonal Quintet for string quartet and piano, known to us from its recording.[2] He may have felt unwilling to take leave of the methods of the past without having

2. In Columbia album K4L-232, *Anton Webern, the Complete Music Recorded under the Direction of Robert Craft.*

mastered them. The Quintet represents a long step towards this goal, but only with the Passacaglia Op. 1 did he achieve a personal solution to the problems of traditional tonal writing. And what better form could he have chosen to discipline himself on the one hand, and to demonstrate his success on the other, than that one, which restricts the composer to the steady pace of a constantly recurring progression, and challenges him to make it interesting and convincing?

Be that as it may, Webern's personal predilection was undoubtedly leading him in a different direction, for the Dehmel songs point directly to the George songs, Opp. 3 and 4, that closely follow them, and thence to works with which we are familiar. Harmonically, they move a long way in the direction of atonality, although none completely forsakes the sense of key—indeed, all have signatures. But the methods we have already seen at work—lines moving over a pedal, the polyphonic manipulation of motifs, the free use of neighboring and passing harmonies—are combined now with a chromatically extended melodic and chordal vocabulary in such a way that for long stretches it is impossible to hear this music in terms of the older concepts of functionality. The new melodic freedom also makes it possible for the vocal parts to flourish as they never could before. In contrast to the often characterless lines of the earlier songs, uncomfortably adapting themselves to the predominant piano part, these now bear the chief—but by no means the only—melodic burden. Voice and accompaniment, now integrally related, exchange their material back and forth, using the traditional devices of imitation and double counterpoint with the flexibility now made possible by the extended use of octave equivalence.

This textural organization is reflected in the temporal dimension as well. The songs are fully formed and—again in contrast to their predecessors—can all be satisfactorily grasped as abstract musical designs. They can even be conventionally classified: the first three exhibit clear three-part patterns and the fourth can be read as a free sonata form. The last, "Helle Nacht," is of special interest, harmonically as well as formally. Although assigned a key signature of one flat, its tonic sonority can best be heard as an augmented triad (F-A-C♯). From the outset, a frequently recurring progression resolves on this triad, to which, however, a tritone (B) is always added (ex. 5). Only at the end is this tone removed, leaving the pure triad, with F doubled as the bass (although I nevertheless hear A as its real root). The text is in three stanzas, and the song is strophically organized; but an elaborate triple counterpoint involving the voice and the two hands of the piano prevents monotony. In the second stanza, the voice and the right hand exchange parts; in the third, the right and left hands exchange. What is more, the original left-

Example 5

Sehr zart, mässig

hand part follows the voice in free canon—a relationship naturally retained throughout the exchanges.

Of all the scores, then, the Dehmel songs are probably the only ones that are interesting purely on their merits. This of course does not imply that the rest are of no value and that their publication was ill-advised. At the very least they satisfy the curiosity—and the genuine interest—always aroused by the uncovering of a hitherto hidden stage of a great artist's development. But in this case the artist was also the pupil of a great teacher, and the period we are invited to study is precisely the one that enables us to gauge the teacher's influence and to deduce some of his procedures. The present publications, therefore, useful as they are for filling in our knowledge of the youthful Webern, are almost equally important as documentation of Schoenberg's teaching.

Because of the special interest of these works to scholars, it is all the more to be regretted that care was not taken to make the edition as accurate and as useful as possible. As I have already suggested, questions arise even before one looks at the musical text. By whom were the songs grouped, and according to what principle? The Avenarius and Dehmel sets are each unified by date of composition and by choice of poet, the others by neither. Two of the *Eight Early Songs,* for example, were composed after the first, but before the remaining two, of the *Three Poems.* And what determined the order of the songs in each set? No clear principles, either chronological or musical, are discernible.

Turning more specifically to the music, we find other problems. First and simplest are the obvious misprints. In *Im Sommerwind,* for example, the fifth and sixth horns are erroneously assigned a bass clef on p. 6. In the same work, on p. 15 at m. 4 the A♯ for the trumpets is surely wrong, since it is the only violation of strict octave doubling in the passage. Throughout the scores can be found similar cases where doublings, repetitions, etc., indicate that correction is required. Often dots are missing, or measures are misaligned. Unquestionable errors of this kind, when due to slips of the editors, can be corrected in later editions, or at least noted in an errata list. But if they are faithful reproductions of the composer's own mistakes (as I suspect that some of these are), an editorial note should say so.

A second category comprises presumptive misprints, which may or may not demand correction. Some of them are certainly the composer's fault—but these are just the cases where editorial guidance is most needed. Again in the orchestral idyl, at No. 2 (p. 7), should the last note of the second violin part really be G♯? In the following measure, should the second horn not move chromatically like its fellows? Is the first flute part correct in the third measure on p. 11? If so, why is it spelled so peculiarly (E♯—G)? Questions like these constantly arise.

It was evidently not a matter of principle that editorial help should be withheld. Bracketed directions occur in the orchestral score, and at one point (No. 14, p. 28) two apparently missing measures for the flutes have been filled in. But it would have been even more helpful if the editor had offered advice on when to remove mutes—a subject on which, if the edition is to be trusted, Webern was almost entirely silent. (Apparently his direction *mit Dämpfer* was meant to apply only to the immediately succeeding passage, but it is by no means always clear just how long the passage was thought of as continuing.)

Sometimes it is hard to tell how far editorial activity has gone. A footnote informs us that "Nachtgebet der Braut" (from *Three Poems*), although printed in the key of A, was originally in E. A later note on the same song refers to two autograph manuscripts. Was one of these the source of the transposition, or was this due to the editor? Was the original higher or lower than the printed version? Another transposed song, "Bild der Liebe" (from *Eight Early Songs*), raises an even knottier question. We are told that it was "composed in the key of C major"; but some readers might object that the transposed version—in spite of its signature of one sharp—is in C major! Actually the tonality of the song is so vague as to make any pronouncement dangerous. Most probably Webern's original was a fourth higher (or a fifth lower) than the present version, without signature, and the editor, transposing, dutifully added a sharp— even though other songs in the same set prove that lack of signature is unreliable as an indication of C major.

Finally, a word about the translations of the poems. With one exception, they are literal, making no attempt to follow the rhyme or meter of the original; they are intended for study, not performance, and are certainly useful. Unfortunately they are not always correct. "Corn," in contemporary English, is no longer an equivalent of the German "Korn";[3] "bis er entschwunden/ dem Zauberreich," does not mean "Till

3. From "Gebet," in *Three Songs*.

it vanishes,/ Rich in magic," but ". . . From the magic realm";[4] and so on. Even from the point of view of pure English usage there are some strange locutions: can one really write "aspires downward"?[5]

Physically, the edition is admirable. The musical typography is excellent: even the orchestral score, although reduced in size, is easily readable. The paper is strong and the outer covers are durable. Parts can be purchased for the string quartets and rented for the orchestral work. The scores, then, are intended for use and are designed to sustain it. This is a laudable aim; yet it should not be primary in the case of music whose chief value, as I have tried to show, is biographical and historical.

[*1967*]

4. From "Bild der Liebe," in *Eight Early Songs*.
5. From "Himmelfahrt," in *Five Songs*.

The Uses of Convention: Stravinsky and His Models

I

The persistent vitality of conventional patterns in music has often been noted. Whatever the reasons for their original development, one advantage of their use is clear: in an art both abstract and temporal they furnish signposts to aid the listener, who can neither turn back nor pause to look around him. The danger, of course, is that the composer will use them as a crutch; and it is true that the academic conception of the forms as molds has encouraged the production of much facile and undistinguished music. But when, as during the period of the Viennese classics, original musical thought and generally accepted procedures find not only mutual accommodation but mutual reinforcement, the results are happy for composer and audience alike.

The acceptance of conventions presents another possibility, which is my concern here. A composer may deliberately defeat the expectations aroused by the specific pattern followed; the resulting tension between the anticipated and the actual course of the music can be a source of aesthetic delight. This is the way Stravinsky has used conventions—stylistic as well as narrowly "formal"—of the past, but it is important to realize that composers of the periods of interest to him have also played with their own conventions. A look at Haydn with this in mind will, I hope, not only increase our admiration for the earlier composer's musical intelligence and wit but also throw light on what Stravinsky has been doing.

First, however, a word about one element necessarily associated with any departure from accepted norms: surprise. Certainly Haydn intended the drumbeat in the "Surprise" Symphony to shock; and no doubt Beethoven was counting on more subtle reactions of the same kind when he began a symphony on an apparent dominant seventh and a concerto with a piano solo. But can any such effect escape being greatly diminished and even nullified by successive hearings? And is it possible for audiences today, after long familiarity, to experience to any degree the sensation of violated propriety apparently calculated by the composers?

Logically the answers should be "no." But just as, in seeing a suspense-filled play for the second time, we are so caught up in the flow of events that we allow ourselves to forget that we know what is coming next, so in following a skillfully written piece of music, however familiar, we can become so intent on what we are actually hearing that we do not anticipate exactly what is to come. When shocks occur under these circumstances, they are never so violent as before, but they register their artistic effect nevertheless. (To be sure, this solution does not apply to the Beethoven examples; but listeners trained to appreciate the historical effect of the cited openings can, paradoxically, even prepare themselves here to be caught off guard.)

The element of pure surprise is, after all, of minor aesthetic interest. The considerations of real importance are that a deviation from the anticipated course should tell as a musically effective contrast, and that an apparently incongruous turn of events should prove to be integrally connected with the whole. These relations may become the clearer as the more visceral manifestations of shock subside. Their appreciation requires a high degree of musical sophistication on the part of the listener, and it is enlightening to contrast the kinds of knowledge presupposed by the cases about to be discussed. Haydn, writing for an eager audience that constantly demanded new works, could reasonably assume as his ideal hearer one familiar with every detail of the style of his own day; Stravinsky has to rely on the passive, historically oriented concertgoer of the twentieth century.

II

Haydn's liberties with patterns he himself had so notably helped to establish are of two kinds. On the one hand, they may arise apparently spontaneously from the exigencies of the musical material, as when motivic development recasts the recapitulation of the first movement of Op. 76 No. 2. But in other cases the composer seems deliberately to play with the form—to use the pattern itself as a subject for creative development. Such treatment is a closer analogue to Stravinsky's, and for this reason I have chosen for analysis the finale of the Quartet Op. 54 No. 2.

It is probable that no printed program accompanied the performance of a new Haydn quartet, and in any event the listing of movements was not at that time a general practice. The Adagio of the finale, then, must have found an alert listener totally unprepared, since he would have been expecting the usual fast romp. How would he have taken the Adagio? No doubt as a typical slow introduction; and if so, he would have been guilty of the first of a series of mistaken interpretations, all encouraged by the composer and cleverly ordered in such a way that the subsequent correction of each merely exposes the listener to the next error. The introductory character of the opening motif is immediately thrown into question by the exact balance of the eight-measure period that it initiates; and when this entire section is repeated, one reinterprets it, not as an introduction but as the first statement of a song form. Wrong again! It *is* an introduction, although of an unusual kind, and the real song form begins with the first violin's new development of the opening motif over the slowly unfolding cello arpeggio that takes shape after measure 8-bis.

The three-part song form now develops so smoothly that suspicion is allayed—until the sudden turn to minor, emphasized by a succession of three barely disguised parallel fifths. The stand on the dominant that closes this section surely heralds a return to major, and obviously to another statement of the principal theme of the song form. The major appears, it is true; but nothing can be accepted as obvious in this movement. Now, when all hope of a fast finale has been given up, a Presto begins. Was the entire Adagio, huge as it was, an introduction after all? So the course of the Presto seems to suggest as it runs through its own three-part pattern in a manner typical of the openings of many Haydn rondos. But at the point where the first theme should normally come to a full cadence, to be followed by a contrast in key or mode (see, for example, the finale of Op. 54 No. 1)—just here the cadence is made deceptive, and it is followed by a dissolution with a pause on the dominant.

What can this mean? What follows is probably the single most original stroke in the entire movement. One might have foreseen a return to the theme of the slow song form, but surely not a reprise of the opening introductory period—a reprise at once so striking and so satisfying in effect as to bring home the realization that it was more than a mere introduction after all, since it is now bearing the weight of the recapitulation. And indeed when the expansive song of the first violin does return, it is in the nature of a coda, with its characteristic bow to the sub-dominant over a tonic pedal. Thus, although the design of the whole is established as a ternary Adagio with a Presto interlude, it is nevertheless unique. The apparently introductory period of the first statement assumes full thematic stature on its return; while the melody originally developed most fully is relegated to the coda.

It is useless to ask of this movement, "What 'form' is it in?"—useless but not irrelevant. Appreciation of the points discussed above requires that the listener be familiar with the conventions of the day; for the composer is constantly arousing expectations based thereon, and then defeating them—or fulfilling them in a novel way. He may even be poking fun at a pedantic insistence on regularity.

At the same time it is important to realize that he has created a new design, valid for these specific musical materials and comprehensible without reference to violated standards. From this point of view the movement can certainly be understood and enjoyed on its own terms. But the invited comparison between the unique pattern and the normal one leads to an awareness of the tension between them that sharpens one's perception of the extent to which Haydn has here widened the boundaries of his own style.

III

Stravinsky's preoccupation with the contrast between the idioms of earlier periods and those of his own is most obvious in works like *Pulcinella,* based on frankly borrowed materials; and one can certainly learn much about his methods from the way he adroitly and often comically reworks his sources. My concern, however, being the composer's use of stylistic and formal conventions, I have chosen a work based on a Classical model but without actual thematic quotation: the Symphony in C.

Unlike Haydn, Stravinsky could expect his audience to be more familiar with the musical language of the past than with that of the present—familiar enough, at any rate, to draw certain conclusions from the information furnished by programs he could normally (again unlike Haydn) expect them to be reading. What they would find there—the announcement of a symphony openly characterized as tonal, with four movements following the traditional order—would suggest a conservative, not to say reactionary, pastiche. (What they might have read previously in popular accounts of Stravinsky's "retrogression" would only confirm this surmise.) But these signposts would prove to be misleading guides for the unwary; and Stravinsky (this time like Haydn) may well have hoped that the more alert among his listeners might gain added enjoyment from the interplay of the anticipated and the actual.

Certainly the traditional framework is emphasized here: the Classical orchestral layout, the diatonic melodies, the metric regularity, the apparent harmonic simplicity, the ostensibly typical patterns. At the same time, any expectation of a work easily comprehensible in a comfortably familiar idiom is defeated, even for the most sanguine hearer, by certain immediately perceptible features: the distinctive instrumental sound; the persistent, though mild, dissonance; the sudden harmonic shifts; the peculiar heterophonic part writing (most obvious in the second movement). Now, the simple filling-out of a Classical mold with contemporary stuffing could produce nothing more important than a parody in the manner of Prokofiev, but Stravinsky's intention is serious. He confronts the evoked historical manner at every point with his own version of contemporary language; the result is a complete reinterpretation and transformation of the earlier style.

A convincing demonstration of Stravinsky's method depends on closer analysis, for which I have chosen the opening Moderato alla breve. The traditional model here is clearly the sonata form; and as in the Fifth and Ninth Symphonies of Beethoven, an introduction abumbrates the first theme, which appears in proper form at m. 26. But the first measure, even as it (probably intentionally) recalls the opening of the Fifth, contradicts its ancestry by its reiteration, not of the dominant, but of the leading tone; and the role of this leading tone in the movement to come is one of the clearest indications of Stravinksy's intent. For the shock of this apparently incongruous detail is not produced for its own sake, or for the purpose of parody; it calls attention to the fundamental tonal ambiguity of the symphony: the tendency of B to act as a dominant rather than as a leading tone. The consequent struggle between E and C is evident throughout the introduction, and the tonic established with the appearance of the theme in m. 26 retains the E as the bass of its first inversion. The E asserts its strength later at many crucial points: at the end of the exposition; at the false recapitulation, heralded by the establishment of the leading tone of E; throughout the first half of the coda. Even the final chords of this movement and of the entire symphony retain the inverted form.

Another example of the new perspective on older procedures is the presentation of the first theme, recalling as it does the corresponding passage in Beethoven's First Symphony with its I–II–V sequence. With Beethoven the movement from each degree to the next is a clearly functional harmonic step; with Stravinsky these movements sound less like true progressions than like his characteristic harmonic shifts. There are several reasons for this effect. In the first place, the C–E ambiguity casts doubt even on the solidity of the tonic. This doubt extends to the dominant, which is also suspiciously tinged with the E coloring. Then there is the peculiar phrase structure: extended, repetitive developments over an ostinato so nearly static that harmonic inflections within each phrase sound like incidents in the part writing. Owing to the consequent absence of unambiguous harmonic cadences, clear phrase divisions must be achieved by interruption and even by interpolation, as in mm. 39–42. As a result the function of the supertonic statement thus prepared is obscured, in contrast to the corresponding harmony in the Beethoven, un-equivocally established by an applied dominant. When Stravinsky's dominant arrives (m. 48) it is heavily colored by the previously noted E. What we hear then, suggests the stepwise shift of I-II-III as an alternate and even more persuasive interpretation of an ostensibly functional I-II-V.

This typically Stravinskyan kind of harmonic motion explains much that happens later in the movement. Just as the I-II step of m. 43 is already hinted at in the inner voices of m. 30 and prophesied even more clearly in m. 35, so is it reflected on a large scale in mm. 61–93. This time the tendency of II to become a dominant is encouraged; but when the expected theme arrives, another stepwise shift takes place, silently as it were: IV replaces the long-prepared V. This substitution in turn permits another series of shifts (mm. 120–28), as a result of which V finally makes its appearance.

Perhaps the most interesting of Stravinsky's transformations is that of the sonata form itself. The Moderato adheres only superficially to the canons; its fundamental rhythm is of a different order. The clue is to be found in a striking crescendo that occurs twice. In the exposition, it is part of the bridge that heralds the second theme (mm. 74–93); in the recapitulation, now cut completely out of the accordingly reduced bridge, it recurs, suitably transposed, as a preparation for the coda (mm. 293–309). The passage is all the more noticeable for the sudden pause that follows it each time, and its displacement cannot go unremarked. This parallelism between two passages that, in the usual sonata movement, would not correspond, points to a unique structure. Accepting the pauses as important points of articulation, I suggest the following divisions, more natural for this movement than the standard ones, and startling in the close parallel of their proportions:

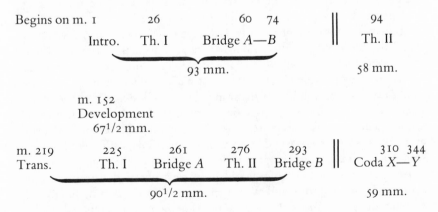

(Notes on the above:

1. I have included the transition of mm. 219–25 in the recapitulation, because it furnished an upbeat to Theme I corresponding to the introduction.

2. I have included a few measures of upbeat each time as the beginning of Theme II.

3. In spite of the empty measure at m. 148, I have regarded the next three measures as constituting the cadence of the exposition. There is a close parallel here to the end of the movement.)

The balance of the movement, then, is not of exposition against recapitulation, but rather of the exposition on the one side against the recapitulation plus coda on the other. Not only does the second theme in the exposition balance the coda, but the internal divisions of the two sections show close parallels. The second theme, beginning in IV, moves to V at m. 128, the resulting division being 34–24 measures (of which the last three are cadential chords). The coda is divided by the reappearance of Theme I in the proportions 34–25 measures (of which the last five are cadential chords).

The subdivision of Theme II in the exposition brings to light another structure, one even more at odds with the progressive development inherent in the Classical form. Embedded within the more obvious parallel balance is a completely symmetrical layout:

Intro.	Th. I	Bridge	Theme II C	—	D
25 mm.	34 mm.	34 mm.	34 mm.		24 mm.

This fails of being a perfect arch by only one measure. Nor is this all. The shortened and altered recapitulation is susceptible of less subdivision than the more relaxed exposition, and I think that the score here can be shown to justify the cluster of Transition-Theme I-Bridge *A* as one group and Theme II-Bridge *B* as another. If these are accepted, the entire movement takes on the shape of a huge arch. Such a symmetrical ordering paradoxically appears to contradict the previously outlined balance of parallel sections; yet the composer undoubtedly meant this alternative plan to be heard. The correspondence of the beginning and the end is apparent, for both Theme I in the exposition and Coda *X* are divided by pauses into twice 17 measures. An analogous pause in the recapitulation at m. 243, now the most obvious articulation in Group I, produces a division matching that of Theme II in the exposition. These subdivisions, indicated by parentheses, underline the symmetry of the following plan, in which each leg of the central arch is itself a smaller arch:

Intro.	Th. I	Br.	Th. II	Dev.	Group I	Group II	Coda	X—Y
25 mm.	34 mm.	34 mm.	58 mm.	67½ mm.	56½ mm.	34 mm.	34 mm.	25 mm.
	(2 × 17)		(34 + 24)		(24½ + 32)		(2 × 17)	

The development is, of course, virtually twice 34 measures. This is the middle of the movement, and perched square on the center (mm. 181–90) is the false recapitulation! The proportions of the movement are thus roughly:

$$5 \;-\; 7 \;-\; 7 \;-\; \underset{(7+5)}{12} \;-\; \underset{(2 \times 7)}{14} \;-\; \underset{(5+7)}{12} \;-\; 7 \;-\; 7 \;-\; 5$$

A close examination of the phrase structure will disclose, even in the details, a remarkably consistent adherence to the ratios derived from these numbers.

What is the importance of all this? It is twofold. First, a scheme of this kind affords a clue to the problem of Stravinsky's harmonic rhythm, since it offers a rationale for his choice of turning points between harmonic areas. Further, it indicates a reason for Stravinsky's interest in the eighteenth-century framework. The Classical balance of phrases and periods, so carefully adjusted to the demands of functional tonality, becomes an analogue for the organization of his own kind of diatonicism. But the typical Classical balance, even when apparently rigid, controlled contrasting events moving at varying speeds, so that the listener's experience usually belied the exact parallel of the time spans and defeated most attempts to measure one against the other. Stravinsky's sections—rhythmically persistent, harmonically static, melodically circular—not only invite the hearer to make the comparisons leading to just such measurement, but also reward him for doing so. Far from exploiting the sonata form as the traditional vehicle for realizing the musical or dramatic potentialities of tonal conflict and progression, he adapts it to his own perennial purpose: the articulated division of a uniform temporal flow.

IV

Haydn was attacking certain conventional presuppositions of the Classical style from the inside, since he had grown up within it—or rather, it had grown around him. Almost every moment in his quartet movement represents a questioning, a reexamination of these standards, and in every case the solution avoids the obvious on the one side and the arbitrary on the other. It is a narrow path, but one that Haydn maintains successfully to his goal: a broader redefinition of his own style.

Stravinsky, approaching the Classical from outside, as a historically defined manner, superficially follows its conventions more closely than Haydn. The influence of his personal idiom, however, is so strong that the resulting reinterpretation goes far beyond that of the earlier composer. The result is not an extension but a transformation of his model.

Now, it is interesting to see the same kind of force at work when Stravinsky turns to an idiom of his own day. When he uses the twelve-tone method it is again, so to speak, as an outsider adopting a historically defined mode. Since what he is now appropriating is not a generalized plan of formal organization but a detailed technique that necessarily influences the choice of every note, the analogy must not be pushed too far; still, it will be instructive to contrast briefly Stravinsky's handling of a few aspects of the new conventions with that of one who had eminently developed them.

By the time Schoenberg came to write his late works, he was manipulating his tone rows in a way that, while very free, nevertheless always respected the basic structural role of the series. In the String Trio, for example, the ordering of the notes varies greatly in detail, but the fundamental hexads are rarely violated. Again, Schoenberg feels under no compunction to state the entire row in canonical form at the outset, so long as its basic properties are clear. In the Phantasy, Opus 47, the appearance of the second hexad is delayed until m. 10, and only in mm. 32–33 is the row given its first unequivocal statement. But these apparent licenses reveal the interaction between the general method and the specific formal demands. The second hexad punctuates an important phrase division, and the entire row underlines the brief reprise that closes off the first section. Throughout these works, the important divisions of phrases, periods, and sections are emphasized in just such ways; and both the twelve-tone texture and the rhythmic shape gain clarity by this mutual reinforcement.

In the case of Stravinsky's *Movements* for piano and orchestra, it is obvious from the start that his use of the system is divergent. After an initial statement, the row is promptly obscured—obscured in such a way by orchestral doublings, note repetitions, and changes of order that its profile becomes unclear and its structural function doubtful. Doubtful it should be, for in m. 7 there emerges a series (not of twelve tones, for there are many repetitions), motivically related to but derived in no conventional way from the original, and vying with it in importance. The new series is completely stated three times during the first half of this movement, only to disappear into the tone row from which it came. At this point it is already evident that Stravinsky's concern with the twelve-tone system is more with its vocabulary and texture than with its structure. Earlier, the Classical framework was an aid in the control of a pre-ponderantly diatonic language; now the new mode offers an even closer control of chromaticism, and serves as a source of material as well.

The real structure, now as before, remains his own. What that is can be seen most clearly through his use of well-defined instrumental colors to mark important divisions: the trumpet that precedes and follows the piano's initial statement; the contrast of the three statements of the sub-sidiary series—piano virtually alone, flute, and piano together with plucked strings; the sustained cello harmonic that closes the section; the trombones that begin the second half. Stravinsky is proceeding here, as before, with clearly marked portions of time, but his former harmoni-cally static blocks of sound have given way to a more pliant, elastic, chromatic polyphony. Look, for example, at the three strokes of the harp that accentuate the pauses in the piano line of m. 42. These form a kind of instrumental ostinato by the introduction of a static, unifying tone color; at the same time they are moving in pitch—in fact, they are inau-gurating a new statement of the series. Again, the transitional passages connecting each movement with the next are sometimes clearly explic-able as twelve-tone units, sometimes not; but they are always easily per-ceptible instrumental units, set off from the main body of the work as contrasting blocks, and each orchestrally differentiated from the others.

Occasionally Stravinsky reverts even now to a true pedal or ostinato (although less frequently than in *Canticum sacrum* and *Threni*). Here again a comparison with Schoenberg may be of value. The passage beginning with m. 40 of the Phantasy shows how an ostinato accompaniment fig-ure can be logically introduced within a twelve-tone context. The mel-ody in the violin runs through one hexad; the ostinato in the piano is based entirely on its complementary inversion. The ostinato is composed of two two-note motifs, to which a third motif is soon added; in terms of the row, they are made up of elements 1–2, 3–4, and 5–6 respectively. Thus within each hexad the ordering is preserved; and because the hex-ads are mutually complementary, no casual doublings can occur in spite of the continued ostinato. When the melody moves on to another hexad, the accompaniment shifts correspondingly.

Contrast this technique, developed from the exigencies of the system itself, with that of Stravinsky in *Movements* IV, which throws the piano part into relief against a series of static four-note chords in string har-monics. Each of these chords is derived in the same way: by the sustain-ing of elements 3–4 and 7–8 of a stated row (retrograde inversion the first and third times, inversion the second). Thus the ordering is not preserved, for these four notes are not normally adjacent. Furthermore, since complete statements are sounded against each chord, fortuitous doublings are inescapable. Unlike the Schoenberg ostinato, which defines a thematic phrase by completing the twelve-tone aggregate, these act as harmonic poles to support a symmetrical division into three time blocks. It is ironic that this movement, the clearest of all in its derivation from the tone row, should depart so far in its overall structure from usually accepted twelve-tone ideals.

V

The contrast between Schoenberg and Stravinsky is roughly analogous to the one involving Haydn. Schoenberg, like Haydn, modified the conventions and extended the techniques of his musical language from within—from the vantage ground of one who had played a preeminent role in the shaping of the language in the first place. Stravinsky, approaching each from without, reinterprets and transforms it so radically to fit his own needs that it remains only superficially related to the original.

If this were all, Stravinsky would have become at most an interesting mannerist, and an inconstant one at that. But this is not all. What has been omitted—or only hinted at up to now—is of crucial importance: the relation of manner and mannerism to style. Style is the vitality that comes from the integrated and balanced interaction of all the dimensions of an art. By manner I mean a style, whether of the past or of the present, viewed reductively as rigidly defined and historically restricted. Mannerism is the result of the personal appropriation of such a manner, with the frequent concomitants of exaggeration, distortion, and fragmentation. What Stravinsky has demonstrated convincingly is the feasibility of putting manneristic elements to good use in the service of a powerful style.

This discussion has been misleading insofar as it has implied that Stravinsky's borrowings from past and present and their distortion at his hands are the chief sources of interest in his music. I now suggest that exactly the reverse is true: that the fate of these adopted elements, although a matter of legitimate aesthetic concern, is nevertheless secondary to their real value: their influence on his own highly individual musical image. With Stravinsky, as with Haydn and Schoenberg, the contrast between the expectations aroused by the accepted conventions and the actual use to which they are put produces tension—but with Stravinsky, the resultant pull is in a different direction. In listening to the Haydn and Schoenberg examples we are engrossed by the way in which the personal style is constantly reshaping the general convention. We should hear Stravinsky in just the opposite sense: what is of prime importance is how the borrowed convention extends and modifies the personal style.

We have already come to hear the neo-Classical works in this way, and that is why the Symphony in C and other compositions of its period are now, after years of attack as parodistic pastiches, being recognized as masterpieces. No doubt one day we shall be able to hear the recent works in the same way. Stravinsky's style is too strong and too individual to permit long disguise. To watch it preserve its identity through all its adventures is endlessly fascinating.

[*1962*]

Stravinsky:
The Progress of a Method

I

For many years it was fashionable to accuse Stravinsky, like Picasso, of artistic inconstancy: of embracing a series of manners instead of achieving a personal style. Today it is becoming increasingly clear that Stravinsky, like Picasso, has been remarkably consistent in his stylistic development. Each apparently divergent phase has been the superficial manifestation of an interest that has eventually led to an enlargement and a new consolidation of the artist's technical resources.

This does not mean that all questions concerning Stravinksy's methods are now settled. Some of his most persistent characteristics are still puzzling, and as a result it is hard to explain why some of his greatest successes really work. But they do work, and this essay will try to throw some light on how they work by examining one of these characteristics: the apparent discontinuities that so often interrupt the musical flow.

From *Le Sacre du printemps* onward, Stravinsky's textures have been subject to sudden breaks affecting almost every musical dimension: instrumental and registral, rhythmic and dynamic, harmonic and modal, linear and motivic. (Almost every one of these can be found, for example, in the first dozen measures of the *Symphonies of Wind Instruments*.) Such shifts would be noticeable in any context, but they are especially so because of other peculiarities of Stravinsky's style. A change of chord after a long-continued static harmony comes as a shock; so does a melodic leap interjected into a predominantly conjunct line; so too a new temporal context after a metrically persistent rhythm.

It could be argued that such points of interruption in scores like *Le*

Sacre and *Les Noces* are meant to be analogous to corresponding actions on the stage, and hence that their origin is primarily extra-musical and practical. Even so, none of the stage works exhibits so consistent and musically functional use of the device as the "abstract" *Symphonies*—which would indicate that, whatever its origin, the method was musically important to him. That he has never relinquished it suggests that it is musically necessary.

On examination, the point of interruption proves to be only the most immediately obvious characteristic of a basic Stravinskyan technique comprising three phases, which I call stratification, interlock, and synthesis. By stratification I mean the separation in musical space of ideas—or better, of musical areas—juxtaposed in time; the interruption is the mark of this separation. The resultant layers of sound may be differentiated by glaring contrast, as at rehearsal numbers 1 and 2 of the *Symphonies,* where changes of instrumentation, register, harmony, and rhythm, reinforce one another. The effect may be much more subtle, as at number 6, where instrumentation overlaps and there is no change of register. (All references, in this as in other works, are to the revised scores because of their more general availability.) In almost every case, however, there is at least one element of connection between successive levels. In the first example cited the interval of the fourth, F-B♭, is the foundation common to the two areas despite their striking difference in sound.

Since the musical ideas thus presented are usually incomplete and often apparently fragmentary, stratification sets up a tension between successive time segments. When the action in one area is suspended, the listener looks forward to its eventual resumption and completion; meanwhile action in another has begun, which in turn will demand fulfillment after its own suspension. The delayed satisfaction of these expectations occasions the second phase of the technique: the interlock. To take the simplest possible case, consider two ideas presented in alternation: A-1, B-1, A-2, B-2, A-3, B-3. Now one musical line will run through A-1, A-2, A-3; another will correspondingly unite the appearances of B. Although heard in alternation, each line continues to exert its influence even when silent. As a result, the effect is analogous to that of polyphonic strands of melody: the successive time segments are, as it were, counterpointed one against the other. The alternation of the first two contrasting areas of the *Symphonies* is an elementary example of this kind, but much more complicated alternations of three or more layers are common. (See exx. 1–3 on the foldout found at the end of this volume.) (The device is not without precedent, as a glance at the successive partial statements of the ritornello in the first movement of the Fifth Brandenburg Concerto will show. In this connection Stravinsky's own predilection for the Baroque concerto style is illuminating.)

The most interesting phase of the process, the synthesis, is the one most likely to be overlooked. Some sort of unification is the necessary goal toward which the entire composition points, for without it there is no cogency in the association of the component areas. But it is seldom as explicit as the original stratification, and it almost invariably involves the reduction and transformation of one or more components, and often the assimilation by one of all the others. The diverse elements are brought into closer and closer relation with one another, all ideally being accounted for in the final resolution. But the process is by no means confined to the end of a movement; sometimes it is at work from the beginning. It can take many forms: rhythmic, contrapuntal, harmonic. A small-scale example referring to a limited section begins at number 46 of the *Symphonies*. The material, first presented on levels separated by register and instrumentation, moves gradually into a *tutti* in which all strata are simultaneously stated.

A description of the technique would be incomplete without mention of two devices the composer uses for mitigating the starkness of the opposition between strata. One is the use of a bridge, such as the two measures just before number 6 of the *Symphonies*. This motif, linking the preceding statement at number 3 with the new area of number 6, effects the gentler stratification previously noted. It is not a transition in the conventional sense, but an area with a life of its own, as its future development shows. Although acting as a bridge in the immediate context, it reaches forward to its next appearance in the interlocking pattern.

The other means at Stravinsky's disposal is what I call divergence: the division of an original single layer into two or more. When the chorale, so long suspended through the course of the *Symphonies,* succeeds in achieving its full expanse, it engenders a divergence (initiated by the horns after number 66, carried on later at number 68 by the oboes). A more subtle example is the one introduced by the oboes at number 3. Here it sounds like a continuation of the first motif, but it proves to be the source of the entire large area beginning at number 46.

All the examples so far have been taken from the *Symphonies,* the most thoroughgoing of Stravinsky's works in the employment of the technique. Its entire form depends thereon, as I hope the following analysis will make clear. During the years that followed its composition, however, Stravinsky refined his method, as I shall try to show in analyses of the first movements of the Serenade in A and the *Symphony of Psalms*. Finally, a few references to more recent works will attest its continuing importance.

II

The sketch of the *Symphonies of Wind Instruments* is not meant to serve as a complete linear and harmonic analysis but is rather intended to make clear to the eye the way in which the strata are separated, interlocked, and eventually unified. The thematic material represented by the capital letters is easily identifiable through the corresponding rehearsal numbers in the score; my own notation presents the minimum necessary for following the important lines of connection. These should be read first of all straight across—from the first appearance of *A* to the second, thence to the third, and so on. If this is done, the continuity of each layer should become immediately clear. When the voice leading is unusual, or when it has been abbreviated in the sketch, paths are made by unbroken lines, as in the bass of the first appearance of *B*. Broken lines are used to show connections and transitions between areas, divergences, and elements of unification. The fourth underlying both *A* and *B*, for example, is indicated at the outset as a common factor. The transition from *A* to *C* at number 6 is similarly shown, as well as the double connection from *C* to the following statements of *A* and *B*.

One thing the sketch does not show is the contribution of the meter to the differentiation of strata. Taking ♩ = 72 as the common measure, we find the following relationship:

B:	♩	= 72
A:	♫	= 72
C, D, E:	♫♩	= 72 (actually notated: ♫ = 108)
F:	♫♫	= 72 (actually notated: ♫ = 144)

These relationships also contribute to unification. In the first important step toward synthesis, at number 11, the area referred to as *D* brings *A* and *C* together at a common tonal level against contrapuntal interjections by *B*. *A* is assimilated into the faster tempo of *C* as well, a movement at first resisted but eventually joined by a *B* transformed for the occasion. Out of this synthesis appears *E* as a long divergence that shows its close connection by retaining the same tempo. *E* in turn suffers frequent contrapuntal interjections by *D*, and after several more serious interruptions it returns to its parent, never to reappear.

The latter half of the piece is largely concerned with the development of the new area *F*. It has already been suggested that *F* contains several levels that are unified in the climactic *tutti* at number 54. The result is an unmistakable emphasis on the fifth A-E as a neighbor to the G-D of the beginning and end. At the same time, another line initiated by the original G-D fifth has descended through F♯-C♯ (number 9) to E-B (number 15, and especially after number 26), and its gradual return to the original level is completed in the final synthesis.

It is thus the role of the late flowering of area B to resolve both of these motions, a role beautifully fulfilled by the last chord. The linear aspects of this synthesis are indicated in the sketch, but even more impressive is the masterly way in which the harmonic progression toward the tonic C is handled. Foreshadowed by the premonitory chords at numbers 42 and 56, delayed by the long development of section F, clearly approached at number 65, momentarily circumvented by the divergence within section B, it arrives with inevitability and finality. And although its root is C, the chord is broad enough to contain within itself the triads of G major from the opening and E minor from the long central passage.

This connection of G to E is important for another reason: it demonstrates the influence of the opening motif on the entire course of the piece. Area A is concerned with the contrast of two fifths (or a fifth and a fourth) at the distance of a minor third: G-D and B♭-F. The expression of the same relationship horizontally in the upper voices gives rise to the basic opposition between areas A and B. The progression from G to E and back, again expressed in terms of their fifths, reflects the minor third in the opposite direction. The third thus operates within a single area, by contrast between areas, and through the movement of the whole.

Two recurring transitional passages should be noted: the ones marked X and Y. The former is first used between areas A and C; but later it occurs cadentially attached to A, B, and E—a significant unifying element. Y always functions as a preparation for a longer section: it is used to herald E, F, and the final B.

The most interesting detail of all, however, is the little passage at number 3. Interpolated as a conclusion to A, it looks forward, both metrically and motivically, to the future F. At the same time it summarizes the two important movements of fifths mentioned above: the neighboring motion from G-D to A-E and back, and the descent from G-D through F♯-C♯ to E-B. And the English horn, its lowest voice, forecasts clearly the tonality of C toward which the entire composition is to move.

III

The first movement of the Serenade in A is both a simpler and a subtler example of the same techniques—simpler because it is based on only one predominant stratification, and subtler because the two areas develop the same material and are consequently always in close touch with each

other. The initial statement of the two strata sets up the immediate contrast: A is *forte*, relatively high in tessitura, and based on a Phrygian
mode. B is *piano*, lower in tessitura, and more chromatic, moving from
the Phrygian to the major. The "Hymne" records the progress of the
gradual assimilation of these levels to each other. The first step on the
way, the sudden harmonic shift in m. 22, exemplifies Stravinsky's more
flexible approach to his own method, for this passage functions as both
a divergence and a unification. From the point of view of B, it is a divergence toward the more diatonic realm of A, a divergence that returns to
its origin only at m. 42. But in a larger context this area represents a
convergence of A and B, the first of a series leading to the synthesis of
the final measures. The sketch tries to make clear both relationships.

Stratum A makes an important step toward unification at m. 52, where
for the first time its *forte* interruption is continued *piano*, a dynamic level
heretofore associated exclusively with B. In mm. 63–65, a divergence
occurs that, like the one noted previously, is at the same time a step
toward synthesis. Here A enters the lower tessitura and outspoken chromaticism of B, and even when it returns to its own melodic level in m.
68, the harmony is still colored by the association.

The synthesis of the last few measures is within the range of B, it is
true, but it specifically resolves both levels as the sketch indicates. The
concluding open octave sounds appropriately neutral.

The opposition set up in the first few measures thus not only explains
the immediate interruptions so characteristic of this movement, but also
underlies the divergences within the larger sections. As in the *Symphonies*, an initial detail controls the course of the form. It can hardly be an
accident that if one adds all the sections labeled A and those labeled B,
the results are equal in length almost to the eighth note.

IV

The refinement already noted in the Serenade is carried still further in
the first movement of the *Symphony of Psalms*. Here the areas I have designated as B and C represent successive expansions of, and divergences
from, the original area A, which is the pure E-minor chord. (Pure but
not simple: its unique orchestration and doubling already suggest the
important role of G as a future dominant.) B, always easily distinguish-
able by the predominance of the piano, permits diatonic motion within
the static E minor; but C, the vehicle of the vocal lines, contains in its
instrumental parts chromatic neighbors that are continually pushing the
voices toward C minor or Eb major. Why?

The answer takes us beyond the confines of this movement. The last
appearance of C ends squarely on the dominant of C minor, the key of

the second movement. E♭, on which this movement in turn ends, is also prominent in the finale, which resolves its constant struggle between that key and C major in favor of the latter. This completes the circle, so to speak, by its close relation to the opening chord. The following diagram, linking by means of a double line those chords in which the root of one is the third of the other, indicates the progression of the whole symphony:

This progression is forecast in the stratum labeled X, which, unlike the others, does not relate directly to the opening chord. It begins by alternating the dominants of C and E♭ and moves now toward the one key, now toward the other. It is also an important element of unification. Its sixteenth-note motion constantly underlies B; its harmonies are constantly suggested in C, the accompaniment of which is appropriately based on an augmentation of X. But the true resolution of X comes only with the statement of the fugue subject of the second movement.

Here, then, is the same technique, but used in a highly complex way. B, although divergent from A in rhythm, develops its harmony; although in instrumental and harmonic contrast to X, it utilizes its rhythm. (At one point—during the transition to the first appearance of C—B even embraces the harmony of X.) C, in turn easily distinguished from its neighbors by its orchestration, nevertheless includes and synthesizes the harmony of them all; and the climax at number 12 combines C with B, and by implication with A. Interesting overlaps occur, as when the piano twice anticipates the entrance of B (once before number 2 and again before number 9), or when voices—the property of C—reinforce B's tonic pedal (number 9). Stratification in one dimension thus proceeds simultaneously with unification in another, and the process embraces not this movement alone but the symphony as a whole.

V

It was suggested at the outset that Stravinsky has never relinquished the method of composition outlined here. A cursory glance at almost any typical piece written before his present twelve-tone period will bear that out. An analysis of the first movement of the *Symphony in Three Movements,* for example, becomes much easier if the principle of stratification is applied. The introduction not only furnishes the basic material of succesive divergences forming the important areas of the movement, but also returns at the end to complete its own line and to synthesize the whole. The chief strata of the body of the movement, those beginning at number 7 and at number 38, are presented in interlocking pattern; and much that goes on internally within each can be explained by substratifications—such as the contrasting *concertante* areas that comprise the central section.

What is more surprising is to find the same principles at work in the twelve-tone pieces. There is no clearer example of the interlock, for instance, than the recurrent Hebrew letters in contrast to the Latin texts of the "Querimonia" and "Solacium" sections of *Threni.* Each stratum here forms a line unified by melody, harmonic progression, instrumentation, and choice of voices. A more primitive example of the same kind is to be found in the recurring orchestral refrains throughout the *Canticum sacrum.*

It could be argued that these are special cases analogous to stage works, and that only their textual and liturgical demands have elicited a technique characteristic of Stravinsky's earlier period. Yet I believe that a closely related method underlies *Movements* for piano and orchestra. Here, in a style characterized by wide-ranging, pointillistic melodies, a complete harmonic exploitation of the chromatic scale, and a flexible rhythm free from obvious ostinato patterns, instrumental differentiation becomes the chief source of stratification. This practice is especially obvious in the third and fourth of the *Movements.* In the former, one level is initiated by the piano, one by the oboe and English horn, and one by the harp and trumpets. Only the piano remains unchanged throughout. In the second level, the English horn is replaced first by the clarinet, then by the flutes. In the third, the trumpets are joined by the bass clarinet and are eventually replaced by a clarinet tremolo. This element serves as a unifying pedal in a final synthesis of all three layers.

The fourth movement presents one level always opened by flutes and sustained by chords in string harmonics. Each statement of this area is answered by one of the piano, but each phrase of the piano is in turn introduced and interrupted by an orchestral interjection. The interrupting area is always the same: solo cellos or basses. The introductory area constantly changes: from cello harmonics (m. 98) to clarinets (m. 111) to trombones and bass clarinet (m. 125).

These two movements are the most thoroughgoing in their use of the orchestra in this way, but all the sections are influenced by the same approach. It is symbolized by the peculiar layout of the full score—a notational scheme that in fact suggested the one I have used in my own analyses. What is more, the entire work shows evidence of a single plan of orchestral stratification, working its way through all the movements. This can be seen in characteristic idioms of certain instruments: the trumpets, whether playing intervals or lines, constantly emphasize the fifth; until the last movement the trombones are heard only as a group; the clarinet tremolo is carried over from the third to the fifth movement. The succession of the interludes emphasizes first the individual sound of each group in turn—woodwinds, strings, and brass—and then the unification of the three. Prepared as it is by the exceptionally clear differentiation of instrumental areas of No. , this interlude comes as a climactic synthesis—the only *tutti* in the entire work. It is typical of Stravinsky's current phase that this is followed by a movement of relative attenuation, decomposing the orchestra once more into stratified layers. It is symptomatic that even the harp tone is here divided, as it were, in two—into a harp and a celesta component (mm. 183ff.).

Many listeners have noted that *Movements,* for all its references to post-Webern serialism, still sounds unmistakably like Stravinsky. The foregoing account of an enduring feature of his style may suggest one reason why.[1]

[1962]

1. Since writing the foregoing, my attention has been called to Nicholas Nabokoff's "Christmas with Stravinsky" in Edwin Corle's *Stravinsky* (New York, 1949, pp. 123–68), in which Stravinsky describes his composition of the fugue in *Orpheus* in terms remarkably close to my own: "'Here, you see, I cut off the fugue with a pair of scissors. . . . I introduced this short harp phrase, like two bars of an accompaniment. Then the horns go on with their fugue as if nothing had happened. I repeat it at regular intervals, here and here again. . . . You can eliminate these harp-solo interruptions, paste the parts of the fugue together and it will be one whole piece.'" (p. 146). I could not ask for a more authoritative confirmation of my theory.

In Defense of Song:
The Contribution of
Roger Sessions

Those familiar with the critical writings of Roger Sessions will recognize the origin of the above title: it is derived from that of an essay of 1935, "Heinrich Schenker's Contribution."[1] I could, to be sure, have parodied a number of others used by the composer, all with some degree of appropriateness: "The Musical Experience of Roger Sessions," "Roger Sessions and His Message," "Observations on the Music Life of Roger Sessions," and even, though in the friendliest spirit, "Questions about the Music of Roger Sessions." Of all these, the closest runner-up to the winner would have been "Roger Sessions and His Message." But to some that phrase might imply a specifically verbal type of communication; and although Sessions has never hesitated to use words in explanation and support of his artistic positions, he has always correctly insisted on the nonverbal character of musical expression. Indeed, it is the chief burden of the essay just alluded to, "The Composer and His Message," that music is concerned with the ineffable realm of psychic energy: with "all, in fact, of the fine shades of variation of our inner life. It reproduces these far more directly and more specifically than is possible through any other medium of human communication."[2] Music not only *can* do this, it *must;* for, as Sessions writes in another context, "this is the *nature of the medium* itself, not the consciously formulated purpose of the composer."[3]

1. "Heinrich Schenker's Contribution," *Modern Music* 12 (1935): reprinted in *Roger Sessions on Music,* ed. Edward T. Cone (Princeton, 1979), 231–40. This and all subsequent footnotes refer to articles or books by Roger Sessions, except as specifically noted otherwise.
2. "The Composer and His Message," in *The Intent of the Artist,* ed. Augusto Centeno (Princeton, 1941), 124; *Roger Sessions on Music,* 19.
3. *Questions about Music* (Cambridge, Mass., 1970), 45.

To young musicians who may be infected by the notion, popularized by Stravinsky, that "expression" in music is impossible or at most irrelevant, Sessions expands on this point:

> If music is to consist of organized material, the choice of musical elements and the nature of their organization are already "expression," and will inevitably bear the imprint of the individual who chooses or organizes them . . . The materials of music . . . must include movement as such, and movement is, for good or ill, one of the stimuli to which our response is most instinctive, most immediate and most powerful . . . In perceiving it we already invest it with character, and cannot possibly avoid doing so.[4]

Once when I was an undergraduate I chanced to hear a classmate play the opening of Sessions's First Piano Sonata (ex. 1). "Don't you think

Example 1

4. "Song and Pattern in Music Today," *The Score* 17 (September 1956): 79; *Roger Sessions on Music*, 63–64.

that is a beautiful melody?" I asked him. "Yes," he replied, "but I find that it has no message." Behind my disgust at his pretentiousness, I had to admit to myself a feeling of vexation at my own inability to challenge him; for what, indeed, *was* the message of the music? Sessions would have pointed out that it was conveyed through the movement of the melody itself—in its rises and falls, its tensions and releases—through the gently rocking accompaniment and the harmonic pattern it revealed, and of course through the effect of each on the other. On this level the music could not fail to communicate. To suggest, as the pianist did, that a beautiful melody might have no message was to imply a contradiction in terms; but for me to feel frustrated because I could not find a verbal analogue for the message was equally misguided.

It should be clear, then, that I shall not talk about Roger Sessions's contribution in terms of what his music expresses. For the *fact* that his music is expressive, the composer can take no credit: that belongs to the medium itself. For the *nature* of that expression he is fully responsible— but the only way to appreciate that nature is to hear the music. Without attempting to adduce imperfect verbal substitutes for a perfectly clear musical message, however, I can try to indicate some of the reasons why Sessions has become such a commanding figure on the American and international musical scene: why his music has been important and his teaching seminal to a generation of younger composers.

To couple doctrine and composition in this way is to underline the fact that Sessions the man and Sessions the musician are indistinguishable. No composer of our day has stressed more cogently or exemplified more conscientiously the responsibilities that composers share with all other artists: "responsibilities of craftsmanship, of singlemindedness, . . . of vision and imagination."[5] At the same time, the artist must be a complete human being: "Other responsibilities they share with the rest of mankind, and obviously the specifically artistic responsibilities must be considered an integral part of these . . . What the human responsibility of the artist means is above all awareness of the human condition, a common involvement and a common stake in it."[6] In the case of Roger Sessions, those who know him recognize in his music the same qualities of conviction, of independence, of integrity that they have come to admire in the man.

To these must be added an exceptional clarity of vision that has enabled him to discern more clearly than most the signs of the times. Of all his contemporaries, only Arnold Schoenberg has approached his almost unique comprehension of the aesthetic problems confronting musicians

5. *Questions about Music*, 166.
6. Ibid.

in this century and of the historical conditions that gave rise to them. And Sessions's fine sense of fairness has enabled him to avoid the unfortunate polemical attitudes that often vitiate Schoenberg's otherwise keen perceptions. Sessions has put a broad and profound knowledge of musical literature at the service of an informed sense of history (again: both musical and human) in order to determine his own role—that is, to clarify his conception of the kind of music he must write; and in order to write it he has coupled discriminating taste with technical mastery. Or as Sessions would prefer to call it, craftsmanship: "the ability to cope, successfully and with assurance, with any problem with which a composer may be confronted."[7] And here we return to the point that, for Sessions, teaching and composing are really one. The ideal of craftsmanship is eminently embodied in his music; the achievement of craftsmanship on the part of his pupils is the goal of his instruction. Craft, not theory, is what a composer can and must impart to his students; for "an art is, first of all, and to an overwhelming degree, a craft."[8]

The historical and technical approaches to Sessions's music can be combined in a play on words: his compositions, which have often been praised for their "long line," take their place in what he calls the "great line of western tradition."[9]

It has always been his contention—supported by persuasive arguments and convincing examples—that the best contemporary music is the heir to this tradition. During the twenties, for example, the unfamiliar idioms and techniques adopted by the most advanced composers often lent their music the appearance of radical novelty; yet these same composers "felt very clearly that the freedom of resource they had acquired had been yielded ultimately by the classic tradition; that it had developed out of that tradition, which through its own inherent drive had led beyond itself."[10] But such traditionalism is not to be confused with historicism—with neoclassicism, say, of either a doctrinaire or a manneristic variety. The polyphonists of the sixteenth century were musical giants; so was Monteverdi; so were Bach and Mozart and Beethoven. Yet, as Sessions has always realized, the composer of the twentieth century cannot in any vital sense "go back" to Palestrina, or to Bach, or to anyone else: the "great line" leads through Palestrina to Bach, and through Bach to Mozart, and on to Beethoven, and the Romantics, and the early moderns. It is not a question of evolutionary progress but of continuity: just as the line itself makes no leaps, so we cannot leap out of it. One must recognize one's position in the "great line" in a double sense: as a measure of

7. "To the Editor," *Perspectives of New Music* 5 (1967): 81–82; *Roger Sessions on Music*, 205.
8. Ibid., 82.
9. *Reflections on the Music Life in the United States* (New York [1956]), 178.
10. *The Musical Experience of Composer, Performer, Listener* (Princeton, 1950), 121.

one's debt to that tradition, and as a realization of the responsibility of making one's own contribution. Thus the progressive composers of the twenties could not respond to the public's demands for easily comprehensible music in comfortably familiar styles; yet at the same time many of them, at least, could insist that their art was firmly grounded in the classics. "It was not a question of repudiating this tradition but of organizing the sequel to it."[11]

It was in this context that I once referred to Sessions as a "radical traditionalist: one who has recognized the continuing significance of the basic problems faced by the composers of the past, who has appreciated the validity of their solutions without considering these in any way binding upon the present, and who has consequently made a persistent and strenuous search for solutions in contemporary terms."[12] And certainly such an attitude toward the past is the safest guide for the serious artist who wishes to avoid a narrow conservatism on the one side and a shallow avant-gardism on the other.

In this connection, Sessions has always rightly insisted that the American past is the European past and that the foundation provided by the great line is basic to the development of music in the United States as well as in Europe. The search for a national style by an appeal to a self-conscious Americanism has all too often ignored our deep roots in Western culture. Despite the undeniable success of which each category can boast, Sessions cautions against reliance on folklorism, on evocative tone painting, on primitivism.[13] No doubt, in so doing he is justifying his own artistic direction; yet he maintains the general validity of his convictions:

> The American composer must learn to renounce the facile exploitation of specifically and all too definably "American" traits in his work. This certainly does not mean, for him, the equally facile adherence to this or that "school" of contemporary music, or the equally suspect eclecticism of a so-called "modern" or self-consciously universal style.
>
> His task . . . is that of discovering his genuine musical impulses and following them assiduously into whatever paths they may lead him.[14]

And into what paths did Sessions's musical impulses lead him? Here is where we may profitably return to our pun: to the connection between

11. Ibid.
12. Edward T. Cone, "Radical Traditionalism," *The Listener* 86, no. 2229 (1971): 849.
13. See *Reflections*, 140–53.
14. "America Moves to the Avant-Scene," *American Musicological Society Papers* (1937): 119; *Roger Sessions on Music*, 135.

the "great line" and the "long line." For as Sessions saw the task of his generation, it was to restore to its preeminent position the kind of musical line that had governed the compositions of Bach, of Mozart, of Beethoven, but had been obscured during the late nineteenth and early twentieth centuries by a profusion of coloristic detail. The "long line" in this sense is not to be taken as referring to melody alone: it encompasses every aspect of musical progression, of forward impulsion, of comprehensive formal organization. Sessions saw the nineteenth century as a period when

> synthesis, the real essence of musical form, became in increasing measure a merely passive element—a necessary evil as it were, instead of the essence of the music itself . . . [In the music of the late nineteenth and early twentieth centuries] dissonances are rather individual features than organic portions of a musical line . . . The musical coherence is there, to be sure—but in a passive sense; the detail is more significant than the line, and the "theme" more important than its development.[15]

When I was an undergraduate at Princeton (ca. 1936), the composer, who was teaching there, gave a memorable lecture in which he contrasted the way dissonances take their places in the harmonic span of a Bach prelude, each contributing to the constant flow (ex. 2), with the immediate and separable effect of a leitmotif from *Götterdämmerung,* an arresting moment in both the literal and the figurative senses (ex. 3). One could, as he demonstrated, easily pick out such a detail from the Bach passage. By isolating it and dwelling on it one could turn it into a serviceable leitmotif (ex. 4), but only through a total misconception resulting in a distortion of its function—by hearing it as a highly charged moment of great portent rather than as a passing phase of the complete progression.

The "apotheosis of detail"[16] reached its climax during our own century, with the masterpieces of Debussy, the late works of Scriabin, and the Russian ballets of Stravinsky, where harmony became increasingly coloristic and consequently almost static. Inevitably, music arrived at what could only be viewed as an impasse, due to "the constantly increasing refinement of detail, the increasingly static quality of musical language and perhaps above all the inevitable sacrifice of profundity and significance in musical expression to sharpness of sensation.[17]

This, then, was the situation which the composers of Sessions's generation faced. Sessions eloquently stated the problem in words; but his

---

15. "The New Musical Horizon," *Modern Music* 14 (1937): 60–61; *Roger Sessions on Music,* 47.

16. "New Musical Horizon," 61; *Roger Sessions on Music,* 47.

17. "New Musical Horizon," 62; *Roger Sessions on Music,* 48.

Example 2

Example 3

Example 4

Example 5

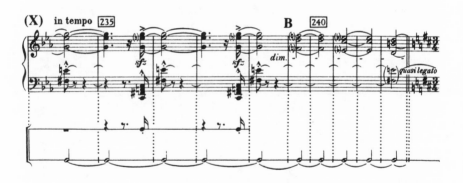

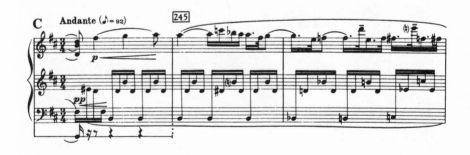

solution was framed, characteristically, in purely musical terms—in a style that attested its reliance on tradition at the same time that it made a bold step forward. And although I shall have to rely to a great extent on words in order to present an interpretation of that solution, a few specific examples will let the music speak so far as possible for itself.

Sessions has made that easy in the first instance, drawn from his early Piano Sonata of 1930 (his first), for he has given us a lucid account of its composition.[18] One germ of the sonata was a dissonant chord (ex. 5X), a motif as compressed as any of Wagner's, that, as he tells us, "rang through my ear almost obsessively one day as I was walking in Pisa, Italy."[19] When, shortly thereafter, he wrote the opening of the C-minor Allegro movement, he realized that it was derived from a simpler version of the chord, transformed into a rhythmically vigorous line (ex. 6). So it

Example 6

was natural that the movement should eventually lead to the original startling sonority as a climax (ex. 5A). The B-minor melody with which the sonata begins (ex. 1) and which serves as an introduction to the Allegro was actually conceived later. Had it any connection with the germ motif? The passage immediately following the climax shows that it had a very close connection indeed: it generates a natural transition (ex. 5B) that leads from the key of the Allegro back to that of the opening (ex. 5C). During this brief but crucial passage the right-hand component of the chord (G-E♭-G), consisting of elements of the tonic chord of the preceding C minor, moves gradually to a pivotal sonority (D-B-D) that can be related to a returning B minor; at this point the left-hand seventh (F♯-E), which sounded so strikingly dissonant in its original context,

18. *The Musical Experience*, 50–53.
19. Ibid., 52.

gently resolves as a dominant of the same B minor. Thus "the germ of the key relationship on which the first two movements of the sonata were based [was] already implicit in the chordal idea with which the musical train of thought . . . had started." [20]

What is remarkable about this story is that a composer should so unmistakably have found his way so soon in his career. For the prime characteristic of Sessions's style, from that early sonata to the Eighth Symphony and beyond, is its restoration of the long musical line without sacrifice of the expressive harmonic moment. The detail remains as striking as ever, but it is made to take its place in the line by the exploitation of its dynamic possibilities. The flow of that line, its sense of progression, the design it creates: these are the controlling elements of the form even when, as in the above example, all are ultimately derived from a single chord. It is typical of Sessions's appreciation of the demands of his own style that the chord which obsessed him during his walks in Tuscany should be limited to one telling appearance in the sonata which it helped to shape.

Such moments of harmonic saliency subjected to the utmost restraint can be found in the compositions of every period of Sessions's activity. Let me cite a few more of the most obvious from the piano literature. In the first piece of the set *From My Diary,* of 1937–39, an extended cadence on a characteristic chord produces a moment of harmonic stasis during the course of the opening theme (ex. 7). Again the propulsive power of the line defeats the temptation to overemphasize the detail, which recurs only once, as a final reminiscence.

Example 7

20. Ibid., 53.

N. B.

The Second Sonata of 1946 affords many instances. Probably the most striking occurs at the central climax of the Finale, when a steadily expanding chordal sequence (first three chords, then four, then five) collides with the reiterative sixteenths of the opening motif to produce a relentless hammering on a single complex chord. This sonority is itself subjected to another steady expansion, now purely metrical (from three to seven sixteenths), until the resultant tension reaches the breaking point, and the musical flow can be resumed (ex. 8).

In the Sonata No. 3 of 1965, the culmination of the last movement may have some programmatic significance, as indicated by its dedication, "In memoriam: Nov. 22, 1963." Be that as it may, the harrowing climax

Example 8

is a broad plateau rather than a peak. It is built on a succession of chords each of which is presented with sufficient emphasis—by repetition or by isolation—to allow it to make its own point tellingly. At the same time, each is bound to its neighbors by a progression that is made to seem all the more relentless by the consistent development of an easily discernible three-note motif that permeates the texture (ex. 9).

The preceding passages are of the kind that the runner can read. But they write out in big letters a lesson to be learned from every level of Sessions's music. Whether one looks at harmony, melody, or orchestration; whether one takes as unit the phrase, the period, the section, or the entire movement—in every case one finds that the detail vitalizes the progression, the progression imparts significance to the detail.

An appreciation of this mutual support in the music he most admires has always informed Sessions's approach to analysis. He therefore found much to admire in the theories of Heinrich Schenker, and much to emulate in Schenker's analytical methods, insofar as both supported his own intuitive realization of the interpenetration of detail and line, of harmonic and polyphonic progression. He could even assent, with reservations, to Schenker's controversial principle that a simple melodic-harmonic background controls and unifies each tonal composition: "Every composer is aware through his own experience of the reality of a 'background' in his musical construction that goes beyond the individual traits of melody and harmony which constitute the most immediately perceptible features of his work."[21] But at the same time he cautioned against the temptations of oversimplification—against the danger, inherent especially in Schenker's later works, of trying to locate musical value not in the texture of

21. "Heinrich Schenker's Contribution," 117; *Roger Sessions on Music*, 237.

Example 9

the composition itself but in the relation of that texture to the abstract *Urlinie* of its background: "But the composer . . . will recognize the fact that the musical line is, in its full significance, an extremely complicated affair . . . Most intelligent musicians, moreover, will realize that a musical impression is an integral thing, and that the various terms in which it is described and analyzed are, however useful and necessary, abstractions of a decidedly approximative nature."[22] For Sessions, an analysis must do justice to the detailed effects of the musical surface as well as to the integrative function of its deep structure. Thus he preferred Schenker's earlier expansive essays to his later reductive outlines, and in his own lectures on analysis he gave practical demonstration of what he meant when he told his students that they should "try to explain every note."

The distrust of abstraction becomes an increasingly developed leitmotif in the writing of Sessions's later years. If his earlier task, as composer and teacher, was the restoration of line without the forfeiture of detail, his later mission might be described as the maintenance of that line against the demands of abstract pattern-making. Sessions has never been interested in design for its own sake; for him structure is the concrete embodiment of the composer's expressive aim. "Musical form," he insists, "is something to be felt and perceived, and recognized, first of all as *sensation*."[23] For this reason he looks equally askance on the rigidity of total serialism and on the abdication of the composer's responsibility in aleatory and improvisational devices. He views them askance, that is to say, as principles, for there is always the possibility that genuine music may result from even the most unpromising hypotheses. Sessions's point of view, in this case as elsewhere, is characteristically pragmatic. As he puts it: "One cannot insist too strongly or too frequently that, in the arts generally and in music in particular, it is only productions that really count, and that only in these—music, written or performed—are to be found the criteria by which ideas about music, as well as music itself, must finally stand or fall: not the converse."[24]

In a single richly suggestive word, "song," Sessions sums up all the factors—melodic, harmonic, rhythmic, textural, dynamic, articulative—that contribute to what I have called musical line: "Each one of these various aspects derives its function from the total and indivisible musical flow—the *song* . . . Music can be genuinely organized only on this integral basis, and . . . an attempt to organize its so-called elements

22. Ibid.
23. *Questions about Music*, 103.
24. "Problems and Issues Facing the Composer Today," in *Problems of Modern Music*, ed. Paul Henry Lang (New York, 1960), 24; *Roger Sessions on Music*, 75.

as separate factors is, at the very best, to pursue abstraction, and, at the worst, to confuse genuine order with something which is essentially chaotic."[25] Analysis, whose functions as a valuable tool for the training of composer and performer Sessions has so well explicated and demonstrated, is now all too often called on to justify and to further this essentially unmusical, or at best nonmusical, pursuit of abstraction. Herein lies the explanation for the increasing doubt of the general usefulness of the discipline that Sessions has lately evidenced.[26] For the creation and analysis of art are two distinct activities, confused at the artist's peril: "Analysis cannot reveal anything whatever except the structural aspects of a completed work . . . Discoveries after the fact are necessarily verbalized in terms of preexistent contexts. In composition, the composer's ear creates the contexts; it *hears forward,* as it were, in terms of the contexts."[27]

In a word—Sessions's word—the composer must *sing.* And as a composer Sessions has always sung. Let me suggest a second series of examples, again from the piano works, to show how the composer's conviction that music is essentially song has informed his work during all periods of his activity. In Sessions's usage, the meaning of the word is broad enough to cover the entire range of musical expression; nevertheless I have intentionally chosen lyrical—that is, broadly melodic—sections, in order to demonstrate as cogently as possible the essence of this songlike quality: namely, the conception of musical form as phrase building, or the precise articulation of controlled movement in time, rather than as a kind of pattern-making necessarily based on a doubtful spatial analogy.

The opening of the First Sonata (ex. 1) applies this principle within a relatively conventional context: an obvious tonality, a uniform meter, a regular harmonic rhythm, a conjunct melodic line. By contrast, the second piece in *From My Diary* sets off a far wider ranging, disjunct melody against a similar but much freer accompaniment articulating a more complex harmonic background (ex. 10). What is unconventional and typical of the composer in both, however, is the motivic treatment: the prolongation of a melody through the free and continuous development of figures that are not only characteristic in themselves but also functional in their contribution to the propulsion of the line as a whole.

In the Lento of the Second Sonata, the second theme displays a complicated interpenetration of motif and phrase, producing a melody that

25. "Song and Pattern," 77–78; *Roger Sessions on Music,* 60–61.
26. See, e.g., "Song and Pattern," 78, and "To the Editor," 92–93; *Roger Sessions on Music,* 61–62, 220–221.
27. *Questions about Music,* 109–10.

Example 10

Tranquillo ed espressivo

finds its way with a subtle combination of hesitancy and confidence. Here the accompanying figure, as always in Sessions's music rich with polyphonic implications, is allowed on occasions to flower into full-fledged counterpoint (ex. 11). In somewhat the same mood is the contrasting *più tranquillo* of the Molto Allegro from the Sonata No. 3; now, however, not only is the accompaniment more independently conceived throughout but it develops the same material as the melody, although in individual fashion (ex. 12).

Despite the increasing textural complication of the examples in this series, despite their movement away from tonally oriented harmony, despite the ever-freer rhythmic and motivic construction of their melodies—they remain just that: melodies. They are not linear patterns, or temporal events, or combinations of parameters, or whatever the cur-

Example 11

rently fashionable description may be. And that they are, first and last, melodies, is, I take it, one important manifestation of Sessions's musical ideal of song.

Those familiar with the evolution of Sessions's style will have noticed that neither of the discussions of passages from the Sonata No. 3 mentioned the twelve-tone method exemplified by that work. The omission

Example 12

was deliberate, since I wished thereby to illustrate and emphasize Sessions's point of view about the technique and his own use of it. A composer who has always insisted on the importance of results rather than of systems must obviously approach the twelve-tone method in a practical, undogmatic way. In Sessions's view, "it was designed in order to provide composers with a basis through which they could find answers in principle to certain compositional problems; and the fact that it has done so in a fairly considerable and distinguished number of cases is not only ample justification for its existence, but in reality the *only possible* justification for any such principle."[28]

Sessions's own adoption of the technique during the 1950s was the result of a long and gradual development, the natural goal of the harmonic direction in which he had been moving for a long time. Some twenty-five years ago he described three directions that were open to the composers of his generation.[29] Although Sessions did not use the terms, the first two can be roughly summarized as neoacademicism and neoclassicism. The third, to which he himself would have claimed to belong,

28. Ibid., 117.
29. *The Musical Experience*, 121–24.

is harder to define, just as it is more difficult for a composer to pursue: "Its essential element is that it accepts all of the implications of what we may call the tonal revolution and seeks to organize them on a basis that is really inherent in their nature, and in a way that involves no contradiction or distortion of the past . . . I am not speaking of a specific technique . . . but of an attitude."[30] One of the specific techniques is, of course, the "much misunderstood twelve-tone technique, or twelve-tone system . . . I have not in fact ever adopted it myself in any thoroughgoing manner, though I shall do so without hesitation if I ever feel that it provides the answer to my particular problems."[31]

That Sessions should include the twelve-tone technique as one among other possibilities open to a composer of a certain type; that he could contemplate the eventuality of his own adoption of the technique; that he actually has, in recent years, found it valuable or necessary; together, these comprise a vivid illustration of his pragmatic approach to composition. Here, too, is an exemplification of his ideal of craftsmanship, which you will remember he defined as "the ability to cope, successfully and with assurance, with any problem with which a composer may be confronted." For Sessions, the adoption of the twelve-tone method is not a question of dogma but of utility: it presents the best way of solving certain problems that have arisen in the course of his evolution as a composer. It is, to be sure, a matter of principle, but the principle is concerned less with the method chosen than with the composer's crucial capacity for finding the means he needs.

Developing the theme of craftsmanship, Sessions explains that, like all other artists—and artisans as well—a composer must "acquire precision, fluency, and resourcefulness in the highest degree. Only on that basis can he move with assurance in any direction he may choose, and recognize—through experience—the technical problems he will have to face, and discover the means of solving them."[32] Precision, fluency, resourcefulness: Sessions certainly had no intention of suggesting himself as the model craftsman exhibiting in preeminent degree these artistic virtues. Yet I can think of no composer living who surpasses his ability to produce precise effects, fluently executed through a variety of methods.

At the outset I warned that I should have nothing to say about the "content" of Sessions's music. Yet I cannot forbear to try to give some indication of the expressive tasks for which his formidable technique is summoned. Again the composer has suggested an attack on the problem. He once dared—I think the word is appropriate—to offer a list of criteria

30. Ibid., 124.
31. Ibid., 124–25.
32. "To the Editor," 82; *Roger Sessions on Music,* 205.

of musical judgment: characteristics the informed listener, capable of forming a "disinterested" though not "objective" opinion, would look for in the best music. In addition to craft, which must be taken for granted, such a hearer would hope to find individuality, boldness, substantiality, consistency, and inevitability.[33] These attributes, I grant, tell us little or nothing about the subjects or objects of musical expression, but they have everything to do with the quality of that expression. Music that is widely and deeply informed by them is bound to be music of high seriousness and great intensity. Such is the music of Roger Sessions: its expressiveness is serious but not solemn, intense but not frenetic. But what is being expressed only the music itself can tell us.

[1975]

33. *Questions about Music*, 138–48. In the interest of concision I have slightly altered Sessions's terminology.

Music examples:
Sessions, Roger. First Piano Sonata. © 1931 by B. Schotts Söhne, Mainz. All rights reserved. Reprinted with permission.
———. *From My Diary.* © 1947 by Edward B. Marks Music Corporation. All rights reserved. Used by permission
———. Second Sonata. © 1948 by Edward B. Marks Music Corporation. All rights reserved. Used by permission.
———. Sonata No. 3. © 1969 by Edwards B. Marks Music Corporation. All rights reserved. Used by permission.

Edward T. Cone:
A Chronological Bibliography

Books

Musical Form and Musical Performance. New York, 1968.
The Composer's Voice. Berkeley, 1974.

As editor:

Perspectives on Schoenberg and Stravinsky, with Benjamin Boretz. Princeton, 1968. Revised second edition, New York, 1972.
Berlioz. Fantastic Symphony. New York, 1971. Includes three original articles: "The Composer and the Symphony," 3–17; "The Symphony and the Program," 18–25; "Schumann Amplified: An Analysis," 249–77.
Perspectives on American Composers, with Benjamin Boretz. New York, 1971.
Perspectives on Contemporary Music Theory, with Benjamin Boretz. New York, 1972.
Perspectives on Notation and Performance, with Benjamin Boretz. New York, 1976.
Roger Sessions on Music. Collected Essays. Princeton, 1979.
The Legacy of Richard Blackmur, with Joseph Frank and Edmund Keeley. New York, 1987.

Articles

"Roger Sessions' String Quartet." *Modern Music* 18, no. 3 (1941): 159–63.
"The Creative Artist in the University." *The American Scholar* 16, no. 2 (1947): 192–200.
"The Old Man's Toys: Verdi's Last Operas." *Perspectives USA* 6 (1954): 114–33.
"Musical Theory as a Humanistic Discipline." *Juilliard Review* 5, no. 2 (1957–58): 3–12.

"Words into Music: The Composer's Approach to the Text." In *Sound and Poetry,* edited by Northrop Frye, 3–15. English Institute Essays 1956. New York, 1957.

"Analysis Today." *The Musical Quarterly* 46, no. 2 (1960): 172–88. Reprinted in *Problems of Modern Music,* edited by Paul Henry Lang, 34–50. New York, 1960.

"Music: A View from Delft." *The Musical Quarterly* 47, no. 4 (1961): 439–53. Reprinted in *Perspectives on Contemporary Music Theory,* edited by Benjamin Boretz and Edward T. Cone, 57–71. New York, 1972.

"The Not-So-Happy Medium." *The American Scholar* 30, no. 2 (1961): 254–67. Reprinted in *Essays Today,* vol. 5, edited by Richard Ludwig, 87–96. New York, 1962.

"Stravinsky: The Progress of a Method." *Perspectives of New Music* 1, no. 1 (1962): 18–26. Reprinted in *Perspectives on Schoenberg and Stravinsky,* edited by Benjamin Boretz and Edward T. Cone, 155–64. New York, 1972.

"The Uses of Convention: Stravinsky and His Models." *The Musical Quarterly* 48, no. 3 (1962): 287–99. Reprinted in *Stravinsky: A New Appraisal of His Work,* edited by Paul Henry Lang, 21–33. New York, 1963.

"From Sensuous Image to Musical Form." *The American Scholar* 33, no. 3 (1964): 448–62.

"A Budding Grove." *Perspectives of New Music* 3, no. 2 (1965): 38–46.

"On the Structure of *Ich folge dir.*" *College Music Symposium* 5 (1965): 77–85.

"Toward the Understanding of Musical Literature." *Perspectives of New Music* 4, no. 1 (1965): 141–51.

"Conversation with Roger Sessions." *Perspectives of New Music* 4, no. 2 (1966): 29–46. Reprinted in *Perspectives on American Composers,* edited by Benjamin Boretz and Edward T. Cone, 90–107. New York, 1971.

"The Power of *The Power of Sound.*" Introductory essay in Edmund Gurney, *The Power of Sound,* i–xvi. New York, 1966.

"Beyond Analysis." *Perspectives of New Music* 6, no. 1 (1967): 33–51. Reprinted in *Perspectives on Contemporary Music Theory,* edited by Benjamin Boretz and Edward T. Cone, 72–90. New York, 1972.

"Webern's Apprenticeship." *The Musical Quarterly* 53, no. 1 (1967), 39–52.

"What is a Composition?" *Current Musicology* 5 (1967): 101–7.

"Conversation with Aaron Copland." *Perspectives of New Music* 6, no. 2 (1968): 57–72. Reprinted in *Perspectives on American Composers,* edited by Benjamin Boretz and Edward T. Cone, 131–46. New York, 1971.

"Beethoven New-Born." *The American Scholar* 38, no. 3 (1969): 389–400.

"Schubert's Beethoven." *The Musical Quarterly,* 56, no. 4 (1970): 779–93.

"Inside the Saint's Head: The Music of Berlioz." *The Musical Newsletter* 1, no. 3 (July 1971): 3–12; 1, no. 4 (October 1971): 16–20; 2, no. 1 (January 1972): 19–22.

"Radical Traditionalism." *The Listener* 2229 (1971): 849.

"Editorial Responsibility and Schoenberg's Troublesome 'Misprints.'" *Perspectives of New Music* 11, no. 1 (1972): 65–75.

"In Honor of Roger Sessions." *Perspectives of New Music* 10, no. 2 (1972): 130–41.

"The Miss Etta Cones, the Steins, and M'sieu Matisse." *The American Scholar* 42, no. 3 (1973): 441–60.

"Bach's Unfinished Fugue in C minor." In *Studies in Renaissance and Baroque Music in Honor of Arthur Mendel,* edited by Robert L. Marshall, 149–55. London, 1974.

"Sound and Syntax: An Introduction to Schoenberg's Harmony." *Perspectives of New Music* 13, no. 1 (1974): 21–40.

"In Defense of Song: The Contribution of Roger Sessions." *Critical Inquiry* 2, no. 1 (1975): 93–112.

"Session's Concertino." *Tempo* 115 (1975): 2–10.

"Yet Once More, O Ye Laurels." *Perspectives of New Music* 14, no. 2; 15, no. 1 (1976): 294–306.

"Béatrice et Bénédict." Boston Symphony *Program* (October 1977): 9–15.

"Beethoven's Experiments in Composition: The Late Bagatelles." In *Beethoven Studies,* vol. 2, edited by Alan Tyson, 84–105. London, 1977.

"One Hundred Metronomes." *The American Scholar* 46, no. 4 (1977): 443–59.

"Three Ways of Reading a Detective Story—Or a Brahms Intermezzo." *The Georgia Review* 31, no. 3 (1977): 554–74.

"Aunt Claribel's 'Blue Nude' wasn't easy to like." *Art News* 79, no. 7 (1980): 162–63.

"Berlioz's Divine Comedy: The *Grande messe des morts.*" *19th-Century Music* 4, no. 1 (1980): 3–16.

"The Authority of Music Criticism." *Journal of the American Musicological Society* 34, no. 1 (1981): 1–18.

"On the Road to *Otello:* Tonality and Structure in *Simon Boccanegra,*" *Studi Verdiani* 1 (1982): 72–98.

"Roger Sessions: Symphony No. 6." San Francisco Symphony *Stagebill* (May 1982): v–ix.

"Schubert's Promissory Note: An Exercise in Musical Hermeneutics." *19th-Century Music* 5, no. 3 (1982): 233–41. Revised version reprinted in *Schubert. Critical and Analytical Studies,* edited by Walter Frisch, 13–30. Lincoln, 1986.

"The Years at Princeton." *The Piano Quarterly* 119 (Robert Casadesus issue) (1982): 27–29.

"A Cadenza for Op. 15." *Beethoven Essays. Studies in Honor of Elliot Forbes,* edited by Lewis Lockwood and Phyllis Benjamin, 99–107. Cambridge, 1984.

"Schubert's Unfinished Business." *19th-Century Music* 7, no. 3 (1984): 222–32.

"*Musical Form and Musical Performance* Reconsidered." *Music Theory Spectrum* 7 (1985): 149–58.

"A Tribute to Roger Sessions." *Kent Quarterly* 5, no. 2 (1986): 29–31.

"Twelfth Night." *Musiktheorie* 1 (1986): 41–59. Original English version in *Journal of Musicological Research* 7, nos. 2–3 (1987): 131–56.

"Brahms: Songs with Words and Songs without Words." *Intégral* 1 (1987): 31–56.

"Dashes of Insight: Blackmur as Music Critic." In *The Legacy of R. P. Blackmur,* edited by Edward T. Cone, Jospeh Frank, and Edmund Keeley, 10–12. New York, 1987.

"Music and Form." In *What is Music?: An Introduction to the Philosophy of Music,* edited by Philip Alperson, 131–46. New York, 1987.
"On Derivation: Syntax and Rhetoric." *Music Analysis* 6, no. 3 (1987): 237–56.

Poems

"Hills of Judea." *The Palestine Tribune* 2, no. 9 (1946): 10.
"You Two." *Perspectives of New Music* 9, no. 2; 10, no. 1 (1971): 58.
"In Memoriam R. H. S." *Perspectives of New Music* 23, no. 2 (1985): 123.

Acknowledgments

327

Index

Analysis. *See* Criticism and analysis

Babbitt, Milton: essay, "Twelve-Tone Rhythmic Structure and the Electronic Medium," 58

Bartók, Béla: Fifth String Quartet, 51

Beethoven, Ludwig van
—— Bagatelles: Op. 33 No. 1, 180–81; Op. 119 No. 1, two-measure motifs of, 189; Op. 119 No. 7, ambiguity of *aba* form in, 190–92; Op. 119 Nos. 8 and 11, experiments in reprise and recapitulation in, 182–87; Op. 119 No. 9, relation with No. 10, 182; Op. 119 No. 10, succinctness of form in, 181–82; Op. 126 No. 1, phrase division in, 189; Op. 126 No. 2, experiment in form in, 197–200; Op. 126 No. 4, rhythmic ambiguity and experimental coda of, 192–93; Op. 126 No. 5, repetition and closing of, 187–88; Op. 126 No. 6, ambiguous cadences in, 189–90; experiments in metrical changes in, 194–97
—— First Symphony, 87
—— Ninth Symphony, 86
—— Piano Sonata Op. 106, 35
—— Piano Sonata Op. 109, 7, 53
—— String Quartet Op. 131, 35

Berg, Alban: simultaneity of tonality and atonality, 24; rhythm and serial rows, 25

Berlioz, Hector
—— comments about his own compositions: "inner intensity," 219; letter of May 25, 1858 ("Postscript," *Memoirs*), 217–18, 233–34; monumental forms, 241; musical content and external subject, 218–19; orchestration, 246–47; rhythm and expectation, 219–20; "surprise," 226
—— dramatic methods in, 242, 243–44; in *The Damnation of Faust*, 244–45; in *The Trojans*, 245–46
—— form, use of: large forms in the *Messe des morts*, 234–36; phrasing and musical line, 223; spatial effects used to clarify form in the Te Deum, 238–39; "standard" allegros and "free" adagios, 223–26
—— harmonic processes: ambiguity in function of chords, 230; chromatic contexts and reversed resolutions, 229; chromatization in melodies, 229–30; clichés in, 228; inner intensity of, 226; unexpected chordal progressions in, 226
—— melodic style: 232–33
—— and Mozart, 242–43

329